# THE BOTTOMLESS BAG

**BAG OF TRICKS**

Adventure Notes from
karl Rohnke

**KENDALL/HUNT PUBLISHING COMPANY**
2460 Kerper Boulevard  P.O. Box 539  Dubuque, Iowa 52004-0539

**Cover:** Lineart illustration by Plynn Williams

*First printing, 1988*

Page that indicates
who this book wouldn't have been finished without.

Hereby awarded many

## "Nice-going"s,
## Nods of approval,
## "Couldn't-have-done-it-without-you"s
## and
## Sincere thanks.

From the Author for:

Typing,
Collating,
Computing,
Experiencing Severe Eye Strain,
Expurgating,
Commenting,
Laughing at Appropriate Moments,
Searching,
Editing,
Proof reading,
Tolerating Electronic Frustration,
Accepting Divers and Sundry Deadlines with a Knowing Smile,

to

# Bonnie Hannable

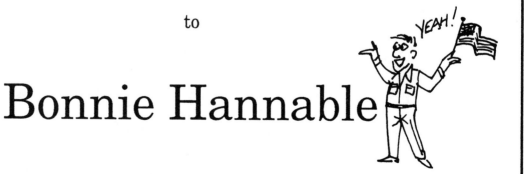

# DISCLAIMER

*It is important to remember that:*

- The opinions and ideas expressed in this book are the property and responsibility of the author alone and should not be attributed to any other individual or organization.

- Adventure curricula or activities should not be undertaken without the supervision of leaders who have successfully completed qualified professional instruction in the use of the skills necessary to implement adventure curricula or activities.

- Instruction and suggestions in this book for the construction and implementation of ropes course elements are subject to varying interpretations and the construction process is an inexact science.

- Before any attempt is made to use any ropes course elements whose construction has incorporated any of the materials contained in this book, a qualified professional should determine that safe techniques have been employed in their construction thereafter. Inspections by a qualified professional no less frequently than annually should be made to protect users against accident or injury that can result from the deterioration of materials caused by the use, abuse or the elements.

- The reader assumes all risk and liability for any loss or damage which may result from the use of the materials contained in this book. Liability for any claim, whether based upon errors or omissions in this book or defects in any ropes course the construction of which has incorporated any of the materials contained in this book shall be limited in amount to the purchase price of this book.

# *Introduction - Preface - Forward*

## *Let's get these three over with all at once...*

I started writing **Bag of Tricks** in December 1979 because: (1) I like to write, (2) I had beaucoup ideas and no systematic way to pass them along, except in training workshops for Project Adventure, (3) I had recently completed the book, **Cows' Tails and Cobras**, and needed another writing project, (4) It was wintertime (not my favorite season), and I needed something to do besides pull-ups, (5) There was more than one person who didn't think I could make a go of it.

So now, I'm coming up on ten years of writing and producing this unlikely quarterly. Ten years was the goal that I gave myself about 3-4 years ago when people asked how much longer I was going to continue **BOT's**. But now...I don't know. I've gotten so used to the routine of "getting out the copy" each three months that I'd probably miss the hassle and certainly the writing.

Things have changed a bit since that first December issue (other than the price). For the first two copies, I did the typing on an old Olympia portable and the copying on an older ultra-messy spirit duplicator. I even used bulk mailing the first couple years. Then Bonnie Hannable agreed to do the typing, I found a company to do the photocopying, and my young sons folded, stapled, and licked stamps for an in-house fee.

I've resisted the computer route because I like to write with pen and paper. Everyone tells me that if I try a Mac word processor that I'll be a computer convert. Maybe so, but for the time being, I'll stick with the ole ball point pen and yellow legal pad.

I don't think the number of subscribers during the last ten years has ever gone over 300, but then it's never gone below 200. Obviously not a big money maker, but it serves the intrinsic purposes mentioned above. I haven't checked, but I'd be surprised if anyone has subscribed for the entire ten years, however, some have been faithful readers, and I appreciated that support, particularly those of you who included a regular "howdy" with your renewals.

This book represents what I think is the best writing and most useable copy from the last 38 issues. I've cut and pasted, re-written, deleted, re-illustrated, made a few additions, and ended up with what you have here — almost ten years of tricks.

I suspect I'm on my way to another ten years. There're lots of ideas out there. Care to join me?

*Bag of Tricks* is a curriculum quarterly that provides a vehicle for sharing of ideas in the field of adventure and experiential education.

The publishing format is simple: six photocopied sheets (both sides, single-spaced) of adventure information, mailed every three months: December, March, June and September. Quarterly features include: offbeat games and initiative problems that work; variations of the "golden oldies"; ropes course elements that exhibit pizzaz and can be put together without an engineering degree or access to big bucks; innovative ropes course construction techniques; safety considerations; idea-sharing; smatterings of a "calculated abandon" philosophy; and a few tongue-in-cheek zingers to keep things from getting too serious.

If you are interested in a year's subscription, please write to the following address for current prices, and available back issues (beyond #38) information:

**Karl Rohnke**
**Bag of Tricks**
**P.O. Box 77**
**Hamilton, MA 01936**

# Table of Contents

For easy referencing, I've divided the book into the following chapters. Every activity is also listed alphabetically in the index. (I hated doing it, so you better appreciate it!)

Contents in the following chapters are not sequenced, except for a couple of items that resulted from a rare, compulsively organized evening. Refer to the index for specific named events.

# Chapter 1
# *Warm-Ups/Exercises*

Getting a student warmed up at the beginning of the period seems necessary (hours of academia on your backside is enough to make anyone's circulatory system sluggish), and generally proves troublesome: not many students want to be warmed up. So, your initial cardiovascular sequence should be active and unique. Being active is no problem. The take-a-lap-and-come-back-here-for-roll approach has been used and misused for years. But, providing initial and satisfying variety of movement requires thought, inventiveness, commitment and compassion.

Here are a few warm-up ideas that we have used randomly (not repetitively) which have been well received by most students.

## *Tag Games*

You played some kind of tag games when you were a kid, right? You had to! It was a prerequisite to growing up; a physical and social necessity. Take those "ancient" good fun games, change the rules and lingo a bit to fit the group and occasion, and see how useable they become as unique warm-ups.

### Hop-On Tag

The IT person must attempt to tag another student (one hand below the waist, two hands below the neck, three hands below the ears, whatever), at which juncture that tagged student becomes IT (complicated, eh?). The fun comes from trying not to be caught, coupled with the titillating fear of the chase, or more devastatingly of not being chased. The only safe area is inside the boundaries (you have to have boundaries or the game quickly dissolves into a one-on-one cross country chase) is on someone's back or body. This piggyback position grants a five second immunity to the pair, at the end of which time they must separate and run to find another partner to hop on or be hopped on. You may not hop on the same individual twice in succession. If the group is larger than fifteen individuals or so, designate two people as being IT to speed things up. With two people being simultaneously IT, they must do something to identify themselves, such as making a continuous sound or running with one hand over their head, etc.

### Dizzy Izzy Tag

Same basic tag rules as above, but after being tagged, the new IT must spin around three times before chasing another person. This vertigo pause prevents "tag backs," a heavy rule refinement in serious tag games.

### Sore Spot Tag/Hospital Tag

Same rules as above, except the tagged person must hold the spot where she was tagged (with one hand) until she tags someone else. The game is made considerably more difficult by requiring the tagged person to hold the spot with both hands, leaving only the tongue to tag with. If you took that last rule seriously, you're being too serious: relax. The handicap and good humored embarrassment of a tag varies considerably as to where the tag is affixed. It's hard to keep from laughing if the tag was on your posterior, and trying to run with a tag on your foot is a frustrating task.

*Sore Spot Tag* can also be played like *Everybody's It*. Hold the first spot tagged with either hand. Hold the next spot tagged with your only free hand. (Tag inventively.) Having no hands left, you may tag now only with your hip — an obvious disadvantage unless it's you against another hip tagger. After the third tag, you are mercifully OUT OF THE GAME.

### Foetal Tag

This tag game allows some practice with the moving front shoulder roll and thus should be played only after a how-to-fall session has been presented and practiced.

Same rules as other tag games, except the tag must be above the waist. It's too easy to grab a foot while a shoulder roll is being done, possibly causing an injury. The immune position (5 seconds) is the foetal position, which must be preceded by a shoulder roll. Because of the frequent self-initiated falls, this game should be played on grass, not a hard gym floor.

This tag game is best presented during the fall and roll instruction sequence because of the expertise needed to safely perform a series of shoulder rolls from a run.

### Grip Tag

A foreshortened game of Add-On Tag. Same rules as in the previous tag games, except the ITS and fleers form pairs by gripping their partner's hand tightly. The IT pair tries to catch another pair, etc., etc. There is no catch if the pursuing pair breaks their grip. A pair is automatically caught if their grip breaks.

## Everybody's IT

Sometimes referred to as the world's fastest tag game. When the GO signal is given, everyone is IT and must try to touch someone else. If you are touched, you must stand still with hands-on-head. If two people tag each other simultaneously, both are caught. Continue until only two players are left, which pair represents members of an endangered species and must remain uncaught. These two swift-of-foot survivors walk hand-in-hand toward the setting sun.

Restrict the playing area for more action.

Head tags do not count.


## Pairs Tag

Find someone you want to choose and/or be chosen by. Don't worry, there's no holding hands in this game. Deciding who is initially IT, that person tries to tag *only* their chosen partner, who, of course, attempts to keep from being tagged. If a tag is made, the IT designation switches over and the choosee becomes the chooser. Taken as is, this could be a very boring game. The interesting element is that a lot of other pairs are playing the same game in a restricted area; the smaller the group, the smaller the game area. Only fast walking is allowed and three seconds must elapse between tags. Watch for picks.


## Elbow Tag

Another aerobic warm-up tag game that provides enough variety to keep interest high.

Ask the group to pair up and lock elbows with their partner. The outside arm should also be held akimbo by placing a hand on the hip.

One or two people are designated as IT. Appoint only one IT at the beginning, until some strategies are developed. The IT must try to catch the only unpaired player within the boundaries (keep the boundary lines close for more action). The fleeing player must link elbows with one of the members of a pair to be safe. The other member of that pair must immediately take off, to prevent being caught, and look for an available elbow to link with.

If the playing area is kept small, a good player can go from one elbow to another without much movement. If too much running becomes a problem (a good runner controlling the game), include the 7 step rule. The person being chased can take no more than 7 steps before linking elbows. If 8 steps are taken, that person is automatically caught.

Make sure to play this game long enough so that players develop a feel for strategy and are not just running about willy-nilly.

**Flip Me the Bird**

Use as a warm-up activity — no more than 3-5 minutes.

Tie knots in towels to equal half the number of people in the group. These knotted towels are called birds. If your budget and sense of humor allows, buy rubber chickens to equal half the number of people...etc.

Assign 2-3 people to be IT. To be immune from a tag, a player must be grasping a bird. Since there are only 8 birds to 17 pursuees, there is much flipping of the bird. There can only be one bird in the hand. In keeping with the name of the game, the bird must be thrown, not passed from person to person.

**Needle & Thread** — *A Strategy Tag Game*

Ask your group to form a circle so that each person can, with arms partially extended, grab the hand of the person next to him/her. The IT person begins within the circle, while the person to catch locates her/himself outside the circle.

Every time the person being chased runs between a pair in the circle, the pair grasps hands, effectively "sewing up" that previously open space. The object of this one-on-one tag game is for the chaser to catch (tag) the chasee before that person sews up the entire circle with extended arms and clasped hands. There is more to this tag game than being simply fleet of foot.

**Team Tag Tag**

This tag game is more team-oriented than *Everybody's IT*, and tamer (though no less exciting) than gang warfare. Divide any group larger than six into two equal teams and distinguish them somehow (shirtsleeves rolled up or down, armbands, etc.). Identify boundaries for the playing area that will allow some moderate running. (You'll probably find that this tag game will be pretty aerobic even in a small area. If the area is too big, you may find that the game's aerobic value will out-distance its play value.)

Players can locate anywhere in the tag area before the signal to start is given. Once the signal is given, the object for all players is to tag their tagging counterparts before they are so tagged. Players who are tagged are "frozen" (if two players dispute who tagged whom first, then they're both frozen, as in Everybody's IT). Players can be unfrozen when a member of their own team squirms, squiggles, or crawls through their legs. The game ends when all the members of one team are frozen (or after an agreed upon time limit).

Having everyone yell, "Tag!" or "Tagged!" upon tagging or being tagged will add a nice verbal dimension to "Team Tag Tag."

**Triangle Tag**

A hand-held triangular game for four people. Use this as a quickie warm-up activity.

and the other two hand-holders act as blockers or protectors. The fourth person is IT, and must try to tag the designated odd person in the triangle, but cannot purposefully try to break a grip. The triangle personnel dance and jump about in semi-coordinated moves to keep the IT at bay. Change roles clockwise every 60 seconds or when a catch is made. Or, never change positions and play the same rules every day for two weeks to measure your class' potential for civic disobedience.

## Cooperative Competition

Try this slo-mo sequence as a cooperative/strength exercise for two participants. With a partner (same size or sex isn't necessary), stand toe-to-toe and palm-to-palm. Each participant tries to maneuver his/her partner off balance (moving either foot) by pushing on each others' palms in *slow motion* only. No fast moves are allowed, even to gain an advantage or win. This contest obviously requires a determined effort to cooperate, coupled with the desire to prevail. Most contests end with both folks simultaneously losing their balance, and that's obviously a tie. Well and honestly performed, this event is a vigorous and cooperative blend that combines the aesthetic flow of dance and the starkness of one-on-one confrontation. You better have some breath mints ready for this one, coach!

### Bottoms Up

A one-on-one warm-up stunt that combines strength, balance, and a very odd position.

Sit facing one another and place the bottom of your feet against the bottom of your partner's feet. Legs should be bent and posteriors skooched fairly close to one another, then attempt to push against your partner's feet (while putting all your weight on your arms) until both of your derrieres come off the ground. You will notice a tightening of the tricep muscles and considerable laughter. Hold for 5 seconds.

### Stork Stretch

Do a few warm-up activities or individual limberness exercises before trying this triad stretch.

Split up into groups of three. Stand facing each other in a triangular configuration. One person raises his right leg and places the right foot on the right thigh of the person to his right, as that person continues the identical action to his right. Right! So, it's everyone's right leg as parallel to the ground as possible, as their right leg is supported on their right-hand partner's thigh. The left legs (3 of them in most groups) support the trio. After achieving this unique balanced position, each member tries to lean over and place their head on their right knee, or, depending upon the triangular rapport, on their partner's knee. As you attempt this movement, a certain tightening of the hamstrings will occur, accompanied by various deep-throated guttural sounds.

triangular rapport, on their partner's knee. As you attempt this movement, a certain tightening of the hamstrings will occur, accompanied by various deep-throated gutteral sounds.

This "stretcher" is not designed for everyone's body, but the cooperative results are worth an attempt.

## Heads and Tails Tag

Another quick warm-up game. Split the group in half and designate half as HEADS and half as TAILS. Flip the coin and let it land on the ground. If it comes up heads, then the HEADS are IT, and must chase all the TAILS until they are all caught. Time how long this takes and flip the coin again.

*Considerations:*

- Do not call out how the coin lands; let one of the players do that.
- No one decides if they are to be a HEAD or TAIL until the coin is in the air.
- Restrict the playing area so that each session doesn't take more than 45 seconds.
- Designate the teams so that they are easily identifiable. *Heads* put a hand on their heads; *Tails* put a hand on their bottom.

## Sun Salute

In past *PA* workshops, we have asked teachers to show us (the workshop leaders) some of their favorite warm-up and/or stretching exercises. The Sun Salute has been mentioned more than once. Here is a sketch outline of the Sun Salute, a contiguous series of body stretch positions. One leads fluidly to two, and flows to three, etc. The positions depicted are ideal examples, but often difficult to achieve (ex. #3). Do the best you can at your own rate, and remember that speed is not a criteria for successful completion.

## Invisible Jump Rope

There *is* a reason why boxers jump rope: it is a fine (although somewhat boring) cardiovascular exercise. Jumping rope is not, as I was led to believe as an adolescent, just an innocuous pastime for sweet-young-things. If you continue to think that a twirling rope is a bit on the distaff side, try hopping into a staccato, hot pepper, double dutch set-up for a bit of humble pie. Most students (male and female) respond well to rope jumping in its many forms, if presented as a means of achieving fitness and coordination.

As you watch an adept jumper windmill his/her way through a complex routine of cross-overs, jig-like steps and double jumps, the uncomfortable knowledge that tripping over your own feet is easy enough, suggests that you don't need a rope to complicate things. In other words, you need a warm-up routine that will allow you to emulate the good guys without having to look bad. (The only time it's OK to look bad is when everyone is looking bad and even then, it's a strain on chronically pumped-up egos.)

So, just pretend. Measure the length of your pretend rope by standing on the rope and bringing the ends up under your armpits. You can't expect to do all the following tricks if your pretend rope is too short!

Begin slowly, jumping and casually turning the rope in sequence with your hops. See how easy it is to coordinate the hand and foot movements.

Try a trick! Cross your hands (and your arms up to your elbows) vigorously in front of you each time you jump. This crossover move isn't that difficult and will definitely impress your friends. Try a double crossover. Nicely done, and not a miss yet.

You, of course, recognize by now that almost anything is possible within this format, so use your imagination — here are a few starters for this anything-goes workout.

1. Try a double jump, a triple...then six turns with one jump. If you make it, you have just broken the world's record. (Five turns in one jump is the record — no kidding.)

2. Try some fancy footwork, any ole dance step that you can think of will do; a jig, a fling, an *entre chat*, etc.

3. Entice someone near you to jump at your pace and initiate a "follow the leader" sequence. At the end of a few wildly impossible moves, hop away from one another and at a wink, both throw your ropes high in the air toward your partner, grasp the falling, flailing rope, and continue jumping without missing a beat. Fantastic!

4. Hop toward someone and jump as a pair, intertwining each other's rope so that your feat is as impossible as it is delightful.

5. End with some kind of Brogdingagian group jump — and not one person has missed a turn. Hot pepper!

**Toss-a-Name Game**

If you have trouble remembering a bunch of new names in a just-met group situation and you dislike name tags (Hello, my name is BLANK...) as much as I do, this game provides an action-packed sequence that makes forgetting harder than remembering.

Break up into groups of about 8-10 people, and stand in an informal circle (no holding hands or dress-right-dress is necessary). A leader says his *first* name and tosses a tennis ball (or whatever) to his/her right or left. Continuing in one direction, each person says their first name and continues tossing the ball in sequence until the leader again has the ball. The leader calls out someone's name in the circle (you *do* have to remember at least one person's name!) and lofts the ball to her/him, and that person calls another individual's name, etc., etc. Notice that I used the word LOFT, not ZING.

After the ball has been flying about for a few minutes, or more usefully, after you begin to get a feel for all the names in the group, start up another ball, increasing the frequency of names being called and the action. Add a third and fourth ball toward the end of the game just for fun, because at this point, the law of diminishing returns creeps in; names and balls are flying about so rapidly that it's hard to pinpoint who's who, as balls careen off your head and body.

If there are other groups playing the same game, stop occasionally and ask a third of a group (3 groups) to transfer to another group and begin the action again. After a while, announce to the three groups that anyone can change groups whenever they want to, insuring that everyone gets to hear each person's name.

As a finale, have all the individuals mingle about, with the number of balls in play equal to 1/3 the number of people. Hectic certainly, but it provides a humorous ending to a functional game.

**Peek-a-Who**

Whatever name-game you have been using (Toss-A-Name-Game, Wampum), this bit of whimsical latter-day Peek-A-Boo will further cement faces with names. Peek-A-Who is a learning reinforcer and a grand excuse for copious laughter.

Obtain a blanket or bedspread for the game; a sheet will do, but it doesn't have the heft or opacity of a good ole USN battleship gray, surplus, keep-the-grass-stains-off-your-knees blanket.

Ask two players (substitute freely) to hold the blanket between them with arms extended upward so that the blanket provides a vertical shield that can be lowered and lifted easily. Two chosen volunteers sit on either side of the blanket. When the blanket is dropped, they must verbally identify one another by name. Second place moves over to the winner's side, and this corporeal action continues until one team has eliminated the other team or competitive ennui sets in.

Ask two players to sit back-to-back (blanket between) and attempt to identify the other player by listening to how their teammates describe the other person. Spelling out names is not allowed.

## Waumpum

This appropriately designated name-game involves a sure-fire attention-getter — being smacked with a foam sword.

Place yourself in the center of a people circle (8-15) so that the peripheral folks (they are all peripheral in a circle) are within foam sword length of your reach. Everyone is seated (except you), with legs extended forward. Extended legs are mandatory to prevent getting whacked on the head. Foot hits are de rigueur, head hits aren't.

Someone in the circle says the name of someone else in the circle. You try to whack that named person before he/she names someone else in the circle, and so on. When you finally end up waumping someone before they can verbalize a name, that person replaces you in the center of the circle. After you hand the sword to the next IT person, you have 5 seconds to say someone's name, or a sword strike ensues.

This game almost demands that an individual learn names quickly. You won't have to worry about lack of attention as the waumping action develops.

*Waumpum* was passed on to me by an old outdoor adventure associate, Dr. Lee Gillis, now at Georgia College in Milledgeville.

If you don't have access to a foam sword, either (1) write to Project Adventure for the price of an ethafoam plank (the makings for ten foam swords), or (2) loosely roll up a newspaper and tape the roll to produce a temporary but useable sword.

9

## Chapter 2
# *Trust Activities*

### A Variation on Stress

Blindfold students on belayed ropes course or high gymnasium elements. Removal of sight and therefore visual reference points makes balance events very difficult to navigate and commitment elements poignantly felt.

Two cautions:

1. Allow the student to feel comfortable with an event before introducing the blindfolds.
2. Request **volunteers only** for this high commitment activity.

Isn't everything on a volunteer basis? Certainly, but there is a fine line between a conscientious attempt (the expectation) and a volunteer effort that seems beyond expectation.

Having students talk one another up a climbing wall (leader sighted, belayed climber blindfolded) is another fine exercise in trust and communication.

### Human Ladder

*Purpose:*    To develop trust, to be responsible for each other's safety, to engage in physical contact with members of your group.

*Materials:*    Several smooth dowel rods, about 3 feet long, and 1-1/4 to 1-1/2 inches diameter.

*Directions:*    Students are paired and given one "rung" of the ladder. Several pairs, standing close together shoulder-to-shoulder, form the ladder. A climber starts at one end of the ladder and proceeds to move from one rung to another, each rung being held jointly by one pair of students. As the climber passes by, the students holding that ladder rung may leave their position and proceed to the end of the ladder line, adding their rung to what becomes an infinitely long ladder.

*Note:*      The direction of the ladder may change at any time, and the height of the rungs being held may also vary.

*Considerations:*

- Pairs should be made up of participants who have about the same body size.
- Do not allow the students to hold the rung in such a position (above the shoulders) which makes maintaining the rung orientation difficult.
- Allow the "rung walker" to use people's heads for balance.

*Discussion:*  How did you feel when you were climbing, when you were holding the rung? Did your feelings change after the first climber went? Did trusting some people make your climb easier?


**I Trust You, But...**

Here's a neat action-oriented way to develop trust within a group. Blindfolds will be necessary for most folks.

Ask an individual to stand at one end of a basketball court, back to the wall. Have them assume the hands-up/palms-out (bumpers up), protect-yourself position. In this position, they are either blindfolded or have committed to keep their eyes closed. Ask the participant to *jog* toward the far wall at a steady, unchanging pace.

The remainder of the group will be spread out with their backs to the far wall that the blindfolded jogger is approaching. Their job is to stop the jogger before s/he encounters, vis-a-vis, the wall. Hand-to-hand braking is compassionate and functional.

The results are impressive and the student choice is generally to try it more than once. This activity makes a nice preliminary to the trust fall.

Don't allow *any* fooling around by the spotters. Ask the spotters to be as quiet as possible in order to increase the commitment of the jogger.


**Sherpa Walk**

This follow-the-leader, action-oriented walk is probably the longest duration trust activity (other than marriage) that I've taken part in. It is also a fine activity for developing communication, no matter how outlandish the message means become.

You will need a blindfold for each participant.

1. Cut the blindfolds long enough so that tying them around the head doesn't become an initiative problem.
2. Offer *clean* blindfolds for hygienic and humanitarian reasons.

3. Use cloth that does not admit light or that can be doubled.

4. Have more on hand than you anticipate needing.

Ask the entire group (8 - no more than 15) to tie on a blindfold. If you have not previously mentioned the trust aspects of participating in a blindfolded activity, those comments would be appropriate at this juncture. To wit, the instructor will not make fun of or make anyone appear to be foolish because of being blindfolded. Such shenanigans are usually not funny and even so, the loss of confidence is hardly worth the bit of low humor.

You need a story line to relate that gives this upcoming sightless bash some reason for being. Use the following slice of fantasy as an outline to develop your own patter.

"Your travellers' group has adventurously elected to tour an exotic and politically forbidden area of the Asian continent. The charter flight, aboard Xanth Airlines, was difficult to obtain (visa problems) and prohibitively expensive. However, because of personal wealth and governmental leniency, the plane and your group has arrived in the country of Ultimo Sotto Voce to the strains of their national anthem; a 12-note dirge in 4/4 time repeated in endless succession. The reason for this metronome-like anthem is that all the people in USV are deaf (very small and insular country — inbreeding and all that), and wouldn't appreciate a longer or more varied melody: they like the beat. Considering their removed location on the continent (with resultant limited exposure to other people), it would come as no surprise that their meager language (actually, almost a complete lack of verbal communication: 2 vowels, 5 consonants) is incomprehensible to your group.

Sadly, about a decade ago, the populace became endemically afflicted with leprosy as the result of the unlikely situation of a Polynesian immigrant's having brought the disease via an aborted airline hi-jack and resultant emergency parachute attempt (refer to page 1 story in Leahali Gazette, November 14, 1969 — 'Leaping Leper Leaves Legacy')" etc., etc., etc.

*The Problem*

After having lightheartedly presented the background information, tell your blindfolded travellers that two Sotto Voce citizens will lead them blindfolded through a sacred area to where the tour bus will pick them up.

Tap two members of the group on the head (SV tour guides) and tell them to come with you so that you can point out the route through the sacred ground. Explain to the remainder of the group that you will return within five minutes and that they should take this time to arrange themselves in some way for sightless travelling.

Take your two chosen leaders (blindfolds now off) and point out a preselected route that you want them to lead the group through. Spend some time, prior to the group's initial meeting, to establish a challenging and enjoyable route. Include: bashing through some bushes, having to crawl under and over something, walking next to water (which you can splash threateningly), passing over and down a 6-8 ft. drop-off, etc.

Explain to the leaders (and eventually the group) that they are not allowed to say anything (language, inflections) that the group will understand, but can make whatever sounds they like; whistles, clucking, clapping, etc. Guides are not allowed to touch any members of the group (leprosy — remember?). So, obviously, a means of communication must be established in a minimum amount of time. Give the leaders a couple minutes to discuss communication strategies while you walk back and explain the situation to the now highly-organized (?) travellers.

Assure the group that you and one other proctor will be silently attending this walk to provide spotting in case of any potentially risky moves. As you see the leaders eventually approach, say, "The next semi-human sounds you hear will come from your Sotto Voce leaders."

As you walk along with (what becomes) a very verbal group of travellers, watch for potential danger and put yourself in a good spotting position, if necessary. Point out the route to the leaders if they seem lost. Watch and listen for situations that will be valuable to relate during the post-trip discussion.

Try to end up the walk in an area that allows the group to be physically close together. After you announce that they have arrived at the "bus terminal" (blindfolds can be removed), and the initial exclamations of "Where are we?", etc., have been made, ask the leaders to walk the group back through the route to satisfy their curiosity and allow spontaneous sharing of reactions and sensations. Finish up with a sit-down debrief session.

## Human Camera

Here's a useful trick for outdoor education teachers or interested educators that I saw used at an O.E.A. conference at Bradford Woods in Indiana.

The teaching theme is to demonstrate how you can use a partner as a camera. After having made appropriate comments about how a camera is like a human eye, ask your partner to close their (plural used to avoid repetitious her/his, him/her) eyes, and then lead them to a spot where there is an interesting object that you would like to record on their retinal film. Using the human camera's body as an infinitely mobile tripod, set up your partner's head (the camera) in such a way that their closed eyes are directly in front of the chosen subject. Gently pull their ear lobe (or push on the acromion process) to activate the shutter. At this encouragement, the "camera" opens and closes their eye lids (shutter) *very quickly* in order to record the scene. Lead your partner to a few more photographic possibilities and then talk about what you two have jointly recorded.

Vary the scenes from close-ups to distant landscapes. Switch roles after you have talked about the experience with your partner or as a group. I think you can easily recognize that this is not only a shared experience of high quality, but also a trust sequence that leads to good feelings and a useful pairs rapport.

**People Pass Steeplechase**

*People Passing* is a useful activity for building trust that requires no props, but some preparation time. The object of this group activity is to pass a member of the group the distance required to complete a steeplechase course.

*Rules and Procedures*

The steeplechase course must be planned before the group arrives. In setting up the obstacles, be creative, spontaneous, and compassionate. Don't expect more from a group than they can deliver — respect the fine line between challenge and unreasonable risk.

1. Some useable and acceptable obstacles include: through shrub growth (not somebody's garden), over shallow water (lots of splashing), down or up stairs, over and down a low wall (maximum of 6'), through the front seat of a car or van.

2. The passers may not move their feet when operating as the vehicle for passing. As soon as a passer has lost physical contact with a rider, s/he can run to the front of the passing line and continue the rider's progress.

3. Riders may not touch the ground (any solid obstacle included).  Make up your own penalties for an infraction...maybe increasing the weight of the rider, or more creatively, switching after each infraction to the next heavier member of the group.

4. Let the group choose the initial rider.

5. The distance covered obviously varies as per the challenge level and the types of obstacles.  Try to make the steeplechase course long enough so that the group has to work together for at least 15 minutes.

6. Everyone must be involved in the passing procedures, but it becomes obvious, because of physical limitations and individual prowess, that some people will do more lifting and others more planning.  That might be worth talking about.

7. This event can be timed in order to establish a touchstone for future efforts, but if this approach is chosen, the obstacles must be minified for safety reasons.

**Footsie**

In sequencing your program activities, this one doesn't come first — or second, or third.  Let the students experience a couple weeks of atypical programming before you ask them to start feeling each others' feet.  Actually, their feet have little to do with this move-beyond-the-expected experience, because everyone should have their shoes on.

On a rainy day (you're inside today), with everyone sitting on the gym floor, and wearing a blindfold, ask the participants to move slowly around the floor like a crab and without saying a word until you tell them to stop.  After everyone has moved around sufficiently to change their starting positions (and whom they were near), indicate they are to make contact with another person (first contact) and for these various pairs to explore each others' shoes in some detail.  (Allow about one minute for this footwear check-out.)  Absolutely no talking or making sounds is allowed during this time.

Say, "Now, move," and all the pairs must crab-crawl away from one another.  Allow random crawling until the pairs are well separated.  Then, announce a stop and allow all to take off their blindfolds.  See if the various pairs can reunite by rediscovering each others' Nikes, Pumas, NB's, Reeboks, etc.

Try this activity more than once, hopefully allowing the group to get over any nervous or self-conscious reactions.  If the group responds well to foot feeling, try the same activity using each others' hands as the objects of discovery.  "Hands-on" may be too intimidating for a young co-ed group, so stick to the clod-hoppers.

If feet and hands are both met with hoots and hollers and never-the-twain-shall-meet comments, break out the ponchos and head outside for a little wet character-building (and lesson plan rewriting).

## Boundary Breaking

This excellent exercise was sent to me by Paul Bernard of South Portland, Maine. I have slightly changed the directions and added parenthetical choices to a few of the questions in order to make the exercise more applicable to all ages.

*Procedure*

A.  Seat the group in a close circle on a padded floor (or provide pillows, etc.).

B.  Each person must answer every question, with the proviso that he/she may pass in order to think. If a person passes twice, do not pressure him/her for an answer.

C.  Group members should not repeat the answer of someone else, if at all possible.

D.  Explanation of answers is not necessary and is, in fact, counter-productive to the flow and mood that you are trying to establish.

E.  Limit the size of the group or the number of questions so that the exercise does not become tedious.

*Directions to Participants — Read the following to your group.*

I'd like you to respond to a series of questions. Every answer you give is the correct one; no one will question your response or react to your answer in any way.

Please do not "cop out" by stealing someone else's answer. We will proceed around the circle, starting with a different person for each new question. If you can't think of an answer, you may PASS, and I'll come back to you.

Speak loudly so that everyone can hear. Be as honest as you can. Remember that we are interested in discovering good things about each other.

We are here as a group only to listen to each person's response. This is *not* a debate. We are not here to disagree, only to seek the person that is in each of us.

As each person answers, begin developing an idea of each person in the group and perhaps a few of the invisible boundaries, held up by ignorance of one another, will begin to tumble.

### *Boundary-Breaking Questions.*

1. What is the best movie you have ever seen?
2. What is the most beautiful thing about people?
3. What is the ugliest thing you know?
4. What do you like to do most with a free afternoon?
5. On what basis do you select your acquaintances?
6. What is the greatest problem in the United States?
7. If you could smash one thing...what would you smash?
8. If you had one talent to choose, what would that one talent be?
9. What is the greatest value that guides your life?
10. What quality do you look for in a really good (friend) teacher?
11. Other than a relative, what one person has greatly influenced your life?
12. What gives you the most security?
13. What is the biggest waste you know of?
14. What is your greatest fear?
15. Select a word that you feel describes kids (people) of your age?
16. If you could give your principal (employer) one piece of advice...what would you tell her/him?
17. Name the most unreasonable thing that you know.
18. If you could choose to be a book...what book would you choose to be?
19. If you were to paint a picture...what would you paint a picture of?
20. What do people like best about you?
21. What do you consider to be your biggest fault?
22. When do you feel most lonely?
23. What TV commercial bothers you the most?
24. What one thing would you change in your (life) school?
25. Describe your feelings about (fast food) hamburgers.
26. Choose one word to describe old (young) people.
27. What future discovery are you looking forward to the most?
28. What subject is the most frequent topic of discussion among your peers?
29. If you could be a song, what song would you choose to be?

30. What is the very last thing that you will be willing to give up?

31. What is the best advice you have ever gotten?

32. When you are depressed, what cheers you up the most?

33. If you were tape recording the sound of violence...what sound would you use?

34. Who is your favorite rock or new wave or country music star?

35. What is your least favorite food?

36. Describe the ideal family.

37. What is your favorite holiday?

38. If you could have any car in the world...what kind of car would you choose?

39. What cartoon character do you identify with?

40. What scares you the most about next year?

## Coming & Going of the Rain

This "hands-on" group activity is an old outdoor education standby that can be used effectively in an adventure program. It can be presented in two ways, depending on how "together" your group is.

Ostensibly, the object is for the group to audibly experience the sounds of a summer rain approaching and leaving a geographic area. If the group cooperates and performs their individual roles well, there is the distinctly rewarding experience of hearing the increasing wind, the pitter-patter and eventual drumming of a brief rainstorm. But I feel the greatest benefit comes from achieving the cooperation and trust level that is necessary for the elements to be realistically heard and felt.

Ask your group (any number up to 50) to make a circle and then turn to their right (or left, it doesn't matter). Have them close up the circle by side-stepping toward the center of the circle until they can easily touch the person's back in front of them. Explain that the group is going to try and experience the rain shower mentioned above, and that their utmost cooperation is needed for this to happen.

With the person in front of you (you are standing as part of the circle), demonstrate the movements necessary to achieve the sounds desired, as follows:

1. With your palms flat on the person's back (shoulders) in front of you, rotate your hands to achieve a swishing sound (the increase of wind preceding a shower).

2. Change to a drumming motion with your fingers on your partner's back (beginning rain drops).

3. Change to a heavier slapping action (harder raindrops).

4. Return to the motions of #2.

5. Return to the motions of #1.

6. **STOP**, and wait for all sounds to cease. When you begin #1, at the beginning of this exercise, your partner passes along the motion to the person in front of them and so on, until the motion is returned to you; i.e., feeling the hand rotation on your back, at which point you begin #2, and so on until the end.

This exercise is much more effective if the group decides to keep their eyes closed for the duration of the "coming and going of the rain."

Pick your geographical location for this group exercise wisely. Do not ask a group of students to try this with "strangers" wandering by, and try to pick a spot that is as quiet as possible — no lawnmowers or chainsaws to interrupt the emotionally fragile sound sequence that you are trying to build.

If your group can't handle the touch that is required in this method, place yourself in the center of the circle and have everyone face toward you. Ask the group to follow your lead and you change the sounds when it seems appropriate. Unfortunately in this case, the sounds do not meld into one another, but it's still an effective experience.

The sounds are made by:

1. Rubbing your palms together.
2. Snapping your fingers alternately.
3. Snapping multi fingers.
4. Slapping your thighs.
5. Pounding your chest and reverse the order.

# Chapter 3
# *Stunts*

## Dog Shake

If the group has been working with you for a couple days (or weeks, if the meetings are less frequent or shortened), and they obviously need or are in the mood for a bit of shared nonsense, tell them (at the beginning of your session) that you have an exercise designed to physically loosen up a group.

*Don't* present this exercise until the group has had a chance to figure you out. You may want to practice the following routine a couple times before demonstrating it. Pick your practice site wisely.

The Dog Shake takes its name directly from the way a dripping wet dog shakes himself (right next to you), kinetically demonstrating a biologically ideal way to initiate the drying process. You will never be able to duplicate the unhinged, explosive wiggling movements that a dog achieves, but in relative slow motion, the human miming attempts are fun and uninhibiting.

To convince an understandably dubious group to join you in a Dog Shake is largely dependent upon the instructor's charisma and/or acting ability, for s/he must initially demonstrate the moves (and countermoves) including a running and sometimes garbled commentary which goes something like this: "A dog's shake always begins at the tip of the nose." (Begin wiggling nose.) "It's hard to wiggle the nose without including the cheeks and mouth." (Exaggerate mouth and cheek movements.) "Let's include the ears now (if you can) and the hair" (if you can, I'd like to see it, but it's good for a laugh). "If you are worried about what other people are thinking of you, relax, because here go the eyes." (Roll your eyes randomly in their sockets.) Now, move smoothly (?) and consistently down from one body part to another.) "The whole head begins to bounce around, which starts the shoulders to moving and then the arms can't help bobbing about." "Don't forget the head and eyes." "The chest is part of the shoulder movement, which goes right on down to the waist and hips." (If you have never done the hula, here's your chance: much exaggerated hip gyrations.)

"Are you into it?" "Can you feel the water flying off your body?" "The thighs are next, which start the knees." (Move those knees, while keeping everything else going, of course. By this time, you are nearly 100% convulsive.) "And then finish it off to the toes." "We made it — now, don't stop." "Do it — do it — do it." Continue a complete shaking for about five seconds or so.

People are usually laughing and obviously enjoying your antics at this point. Don't give them time to lose the laughter; ask them to join you in a Dog Shake sequence and begin as above. Talk them through and join them in the Shake. The whole sequence should take no more than 60 seconds.

After you have finished (everyone usually applauds themselves — a nice gesture, really, there should be more of it; i.e., more opportunities which allow that type of relaxed freedom and spontaneous self-approval), demonstrate a complete Dog Shake. Start your nose twitching and let the movement transfer immediately and directly to your hips — kind of an impulse, manifested in a torso twitch and subtle hip shake. It's hard to verbalize, but try, and if it feels good, it's probably right.

Ask the group to do it with you a couple times and applaud their actions (no matter what spasmodic efforts are forthcoming). Move on to the next exercise amidst a nice feeling of shared spontaneity.

### Toothpicks

I don't like toothpick or match problems, but I like this one.

Move only 2 toothpicks (matches) to exclude the cherry from the cocktail-like enclosure.

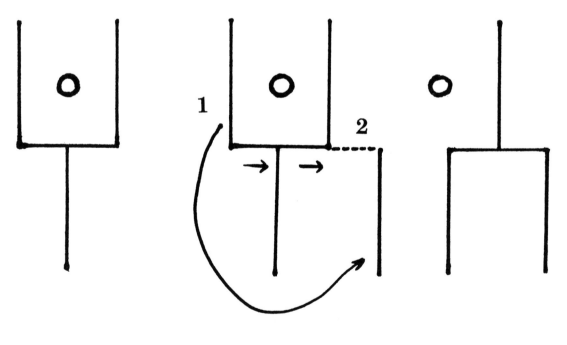

## THE CHERRY PICKER

## Stunts - Optical Tricks to Play on Yourself

Roll up a piece of paper (the paper you're reading right now is a good size) so that the core (I.D.) measures about one inch. Hold up the formed tube so that you are looking through it like a telescope (right eye) and hold the tube next to (touching) the knife edge of your left hand — palm facing you. See illustration.

Keep *both* eyes open and let it happen. No hole?

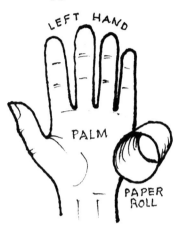

How about trying to see a finger-link sausage instead? OK, get rid of the tube and hold both of your hands about 10-12" in front of your eyes with the index finger of each hand just touching the tip of the other index finger (no illustration). Do you see the sausage? The sausage has fingernails!

No link sausage? I give up — you're hopeless.

## Texas Big Foot

Need a simplistic task that can't be done (almost can't be done)? *Texas Big Foot* takes little time to explain or attempt and provides a humorous low-key task that is bound to fail. If personal expectations aren't paramount and image isn't on self-destruct, it's sometimes fun to fail — particularly as a group.

Ask the group to form a circle (with you included) so that everyone is holding onto their juxtaposed partners; arms around shoulders. Then announce that this activity is extremely hard to accomplish and that morphological cooperation is essential to success and injury avoidance. Indicate that all the group has to do (in their present arm-over-shoulder configuration) is take three giant steps toward the center of the circle. To be successful, the final step must end with the group still intact, and standing.

Count off the first step, then stop. Give encouragement and praise. Count the second step — no comments are necessary or useful at this point because of the laughter and convolution of the one-time circle. The final giant step invariably results in falling down by some participants or complete disfiguration of the circle; i.e., failure to achieve the announced goal.

Admittedly a "lightweight" activity, but a nice tone-setter toward sharing laughter and unselfconscious touching.

### Tickle-a-Pickle

This quick-laughter-producer is a natural follow-up to *Texas Big Foot*.

As the group collapses at the end of the third step, ask them to pack closely together and pretend briefly that they are pickles in a small jar. There is only one thing to do in that type of situation — the instructor initiates a quick tickle move on someone, saying loudly, "Tickle-a-pickle." The tickling sweeps through the group as laughter and a diffusion of the cluster takes place.

### Stunt-Pole (Sapling) Vaulting

Simple field vaulting is a spontaneous, just-fooling-around activity that involves a good upper body workout and a sense of risk-taking that encourages continued efforts. Additionally, vaulting is fun and doing it is much more exciting than watching. I didn't write that last sentence as a "don't be vicarious" platitude; there really is a sense of weightlessness and swift movement that can be achieved with a simple (sturdy, please — no mop handles or skinny bamboo poles) vaulting pole.

Provide a number of hardwood sapling sections (about 8') that will support *your* weight (i.e., try them out), to big or little folks in a grassy area and ask them to vault from place to place; done simply by jogging forward, placing the pole in the turf (a la TV's Wide World of Sports) and vaulting. I'm not going to burden you with a detailed or anytailed explanation of the kinesiology of vaulting, and you shouldn't have to explain, either. If the pole is planted solidly and a person thrusts forward from that juncture, forward progress (hopefully, free of the ground) will occur. If not, there's plenty of time, grass, iced tea, and tries left.

If the vaulting pole continues to end up between a person's legs, you might want to assist with some basic technique suggestions, like: "Don't let the pole go between your legs."

If rapidly gained expertise indicates a desire for self-testing, set up a vault for distance over grass, sand, or even a small gully. If the situation presents itself, don't ignore a wet or muddy area as a consequence for a grand challenge.

### Sacky Hack

Undoubtedly one of the most frustrating and infectiously popular and portable pastimes to come from California in a long time is the frenetic, small circle, down-time beater called *Hacky Sack*. Essentially, the Hacky Sack is a small (about testicle size) stitched leather bag filled with cherry pits. I'm not kidding about the pits. I've never cut one open to check (and considering the price, I doubt if I ever will), but I have been assured by native Californians that there are indeed cherry pits inside...there must be something exotic in there to justify the price tag. Maybe it's the stitching.

The game idea is to kick this small sac or strike it with some part of your body (as in soccer, contact with hands, arms, and shoulders is verboten), so that someone else can also experience the personal embarrassment of completely missing or misdirecting this miniscule ersatz soccer sac. I will admit that trying to keep the sac aloft for an established number of hits, kicks, etc., is a just-one-more-try affliction that is not only individually insidious but wildly contagious.

You might assume from my irreverent tongue-in-cheek comments about various players' abilities, that use of a Hacky Sack is an elitist activity. Not so! Everyone has the same opportunity to look inept and descended from Son of Maladroit. Skill level obviously increases with practice, but not everyone has 10 hours a day to kick around a pit sack, so here's a suggestion or two for those of you who are employed.

I have invented the Sacky Hack, for us hackers who want almost instant gratification from our physical endeavors. Simply do this. Blow up a balloon that has a couple ounces of water in it and kick away. The sloshing water provides erratic flight characteristics (the challenge), but the size of the balloon allows a better-than-average chance of making contact (the satisfaction). If even this slowed-down version gives you trouble, fill the balloon with helium, and after the first kick it will disappear, providing the opportunity to seek other diversions that require less practice time...like windsurfing.

**Funny Face**

After having experienced the *Mirror* and *Anti-Mirror* activities, *Funny Face* is a natural and often hilarious follow-up sequence that produces some of the most distorted facial expressions seen since the third grade.

Announce to the entire group that the purpose of this encounter is to try and make everyone else smile. And, although smiles are ordinarily well received, in this case, even the slightest upward tilt of your mouth is cause for elimination from the circle and the game. If you generally have trouble not smiling and can't suppress a giggle, you're meat for this zany activity.

Split your large group into smaller encounter circles, say 5-7 per silly set. The rules, recently established and constantly being amended, state that after the GO signal, everyone in the circle tries to make the other members smile. If you slip and show the slightest smile, you are eliminated, and can then step back and watch the experts do their thing. A participant is not allowed to touch another player and all eyes must stay open — otherwise, anything goes. The facial and anatomical gymnastics that result are indescribable.

When the group is reduced to the last two or three, stop the action and announce that these stone-faced competitors are the regional champs and will go against the other regional champions (whoever is left from one of the other smaller encounter circles) in a face-off. This final face-off can result in some classic moves and reactions.

Don't approach this activity seriously. (Can it be done?) The value of *Funny Face* lies in the spontaneous reactions of the players and the unselfconscious participation that generally results. People, particularly adults, like to have an excuse to be silly occasionally.

## Prone Mortars

I'll present the essence, you provide the rules. Get some (a dozen) used bicycle inner tubes from a bike shop (it's good PR for them, 'cause they just throw the tubes away). Also, get some (or make) large (5" x 5") bean bags. Don't use ball bearings as bag fillers.

In a large room (gym, field house) or outside, lie on your back with half a dozen bean bags within reach. Put your feet (the legs follow, if you noticed) inside an inner tube and spread your legs to tighten the tube. The double section of tube in front of you is the propulsive element of a leg-supported slingshot. Put a bean bag onto the double rubber and fold it around the rubber so that when you pull it back (toward your head), the bag can be released and propelled forward. With your feet held at about a 45° angle to the floor, the flight of your bean bag (considering the "quick twitch" characteristic of the rubber) will arc satisfyingly toward whatever target you have in mind. These projectiles are fairly innocuous (if the arc is high enough), so even some person-to-person catapulting shouldn't be dismissed.

*Try:*

1. Accuracy contexts (use hula hoops as targets).
2. Knocking over objects (plastic pins).
3. Distance contests (everyone else uses the same bean bag and rubber?).
4. Sliding shots on a slippery gym floor (lower the angle of incidence) to score points; a la shuffleboard.
5. Shooting at people who are walking perpendicular to your flight path — like an arcade game. Provide whatever protective gear seems necessary as to the speed and weight of the bean bag.
6. Just shoot for the fun of it — try vertical shots straight up; that's a lot of fun...

## Fast Draw

Since you already have a number of small pocket mirrors around for use in the game *Mirrors & Mortars*, try this fast-action, one-on-one confrontation.

Hold the mirror on your hip, as if you were reaching for a six-gun. In a paired-off situation, with the potential Wyatt Earp's standing about 10 yds. apart, you are ready for a showdown. The first fast-draw artist to hit an opponent's retinal area with a flash is the winner. Play again, or challenge the champion. Note the opportunity for inventive role-playing.

When two people face off, the sun must be situated so that each player has approximately the same light angle to use, otherwise one player has a distinct advantage. Skewing the angle might not be a bad idea to develop parity amongst combatants.

Have the pairs stand farther apart to offer a more difficult target. There should be no doubt in the players' minds (via the optic nerve) when they have been flashed.

If the thought of "gunfighting" does not appeal, have the two flashers face up-sun toward a shaded wall. Using an agreed-upon target on the all, the fast-draw contests can be considerably less sanguinary.

Think of team contests, although team affiliation isn't the appropriate word in this case — think...family (the Earps, Dalton Brothers); or game (Jessie James, Hole-in-the-Wall Gang, etc.). Picture groups of mirror wielders trying to "wipe out" the opposing flashers. Such a contest could begin in an open field and spill over to a wooded or building area. Have you ever been flashed from behind a Shag Bark Hickory?

## Solar Shoot Out

During a recent workshop, some of us were fooling around with mirrors, flashing reflected sunlight onto a shaded wall and watching the dancing spots of light form a random "atomic movement" display. None of us were in a hurry to do anything meaningful or competitive with the mirrors, being content with watching the crazy scooting of light circles on the bricks. Inevitably, someone shined a blast of reflected solar light into another participant's eyes — the retinal response was predictable and immediate — YEOW — combined with a reflexive head jerk. Shades of *Fast Draw*, leading to talk about other fast-draw games with mirrors and resulting in this new histrionic variation of earlier flasher games.

In the past, fast-draw aficionados would either face one another in a reflected ray shootout (the first person receiving a retinal hit was the loser) or more sanguinely, all arriving at a specific mark on the wall with the winner designated as the first light spot arriving at that mark.

Shouts of "I'm first!" followed by unbelieving and good-humored expletives indicate the difficulty of maneuvering and identifying your own light spot. To alleviate this confusion and give more people a chance to join the fun, ask a group of people (determinators) that equal the number of mirror-wielders to line up against the wall facing the ersatz Jedi warriors. Each light shooter should be paired with a determinator, whose back is against the wall. When the signal is given to "draw" (after each shooter has properly "holstered their weapon"), the shooter tries to hit his/her partner's retina with a solar blast. When this happens (and believe me, there is no doubt when the brain receives such a massive light overload), the receiver loudly shouts to indicate a hit and falls to the ground, if that seems appropriate. Such a display indicates without question or argument who is the fastest mirror in the west — or east, or wherever you happen to be standing.

**Macro Cat's Cradle**

I have to admit that I (at some juncture) thought of trying this next activity, but didn't because I suspected it wouldn't work. I'm pleased to find out that the George School folks were creative and stubborn enough to make it work. It is Cat's Cradle, and the following instructions were written by Bill Hallowell.

"Here's one that I wouldn't believe until I saw it...and darn, if it doesn't work! It is called Life-Sized Cat's Cradle, and we used it during our Outdoor Challenge Orientation Day for new students. It is a take-off on the old child's pastime, but this macro variation requires cooperation and patience.

*Materials*

- One length of rope about 60 feet long...tie the ends together to make one big loop. Do not use rope that will splinter...the smooth nylon stuff is best. The rope's diameter is not important, but 1/2" worked well for us.
- 10 people
- One regular sized Cat's Cradle rope for reference (optional).

Below is the standard starting position:

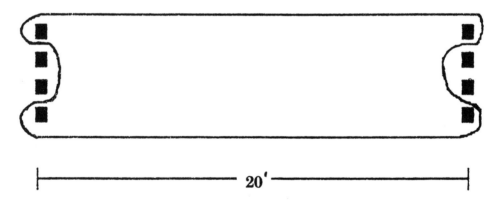

Notice that eight folks are the "fingers." That leaves two who are busy directing and figuring out what to do next. This activity is great for finding the leaders and followers in a group. It brings out all that good group dynamic stuff that experiential educators thrive on.

From here, the leaders and "fingers" pull, push, loop, fold, and thread the rope in the basic Cat's Cradle moves. The moves are far too messy to describe on paper...you will have to rely on childhood memories...or, better yet, ask a school child.

There are no losers or high stress, cut-throat competition. The only hazard is rope burn. Participants should be cautioned to move slowly and not let the rope rub hard against their skin. Chances are that it will take several attempts before a group achieves the ultimate goal: Cat's Cradle.

## A Rope Trick

This trick is a solo take-off of the *Almost Infinite Circle* stunt, as defined in *Cows' Tails & Cobras*, pg. 69. The object is to form an overhand knot in a rope that is tied to an individual's wrists; i.e., both wrists, without taking off the rope, untying the wrist knots or cutting the rope.

*Solution:*

1. Take a bight in the center of the rope.
2. Pass this bight under either one of your wrist loops.
3. Pull the bight through with your other hand and open it to a size that will accommodate your hand.
4. Pass the bight over your hand and pull the bight down and through the wrist loop.
5. An overhand knot should form before your wondering eyes.

If you include a metal ring as part of the bight, it will become part of the formed knot — complemental legerdemain at no extra cost.

## Dollar Jump

This idea provides a fun filler at the end of a class period when you have a few minutes before the bell or as a surefire series of $ contributions at a cocktail party.

If you have all your debts paid and you have a spare dollar, place a dollar bill on the ground and tell the students that anyone who can jump over the bill lengthwise earns the dollar.

The catch is...they must grab their toes (or both feet) reaching over the front of their feet and not let go while they jump.

Additional stipulations —

1. You must jump forward over the bill.
2. You may not fall backward (long jump rules are in effect).
3. You start with your toes as close to the bill as possible and your heels must clear the vertical plane of the end of the bill after you jump, in order to be successful.

If you are strapped for funds, you can use a piece of paper the same size as a dollar with an **IOU** written on it.

Be sure to try this tricky and difficult event yourself before you start handing out cash — you may even want to put two bills end-to-end because of the shrinking dollar...

## 10 Person Pyramid Redux

While watching the *Guiness Book of World Records* TV show, I saw a group of talented young girls (and one boy) build a 10 person pyramid and travel (crawl) 25' in 32.8 seconds: a new world's record (the old record was 35+ seconds).

The 10 person pyramid is a great way to show a group that there is "more than one way to skin a cat." To further the fun, use the record established above as a functional touchstone for your group's attempt.

People love to break (or attempt to break) records. An unknown group (they or them) is the best kind of group to want to topple. Pitting yourself against a distant and unknown opponent precludes the negative vis-a-vis consequences of the Redbirds vs. the Bluebirds. When it's all over, not many really care if a record was set; being involved more with the enjoyment of the attempt(s).

## Beerhunter

This game (stunt) is not for everyone, but the name and resulting nonsense appeal to a baser sense.

The name is based on the movie "Deerhunter," in which there is apparently (I haven't seen the flick) a Russian Roulette sequence that is quite dramatic. To duplicate the same scenario with a loaded pistol would certainly be in poor taste, but substituting a six pack of beer for a revolver has a certain primitive panache to it.

If your imagination has not already grasped the crux of this foamy gambit, let me elucidate.

Take one (1) of the cans and shake it with gusto. Place the shaken can next to the other five cans and (with everyone's eyes closed) mix up the cans. Place all the cans back into the cardboard six-pack holder.

The six players then choose a can and hold it in front of their faces. With everyone's thumb inserted in their respective pull-tabs (triggers), the stage is set for drama, suspense and a face full of foam.

Hey...I said the game wasn't for everyone. I do like the name, 'tho — sounds better than Dr. Pepperhunter.

## Flubber Ball

Take the ball and run with it — if you can catch it. Take your favorite inflatable sport ball and inject it with a heady dose of helium. Your ball won't float away, but the results are noticeable, particularly with *Moonball*. If the ball is made of lightweight material or is thin-walled, the ball will react more dramatically to the helium — the ultimate thin wall/lightweight ball being, of course, a balloon.

I suspect helium help is against somebody's U.I.A.A. formal rules, so beware using your flubber ball in sanctioned games.

I wonder how a cage ball would handle if filled with helium?

**Rodeo Throw**

It appears that not many folks use "hula hoops" for hip spinning now-a-days, although keeping that infernal circle above my hips is still a task that befuddles my ability to hula. Curious storekeepers now ask, "What are you going to use them for?", as scientists, educators, mathematicians, and recreation specialists find an increasing number of uses for these simple but intriguing plastic hoops.

Try the following activity on a wooden gym floor (a rubberized gym floor provides too much friction). Throw a hoop away from you with an underhand motion and in the same motion, impart a backward spin to the hoop. The hoop will travel, spinning and gently bouncing, away from the thrower until the backward spinning motion overcomes forward momentum, causing the hoop to spin in place for a couple seconds and eventually return in the general direction of the thrower.

Practicing this type of throw is preliminary training for the next event; the *Rodeo Throw*. Try to have lots of hoops on hand to include as many people as possible.

Two participants stand next to one another at one end of a gym; one as the runner and the other as thrower. The thrower spins the hoop on the floor (as above) and the runner attempts to sprint out and dive through the vertically spinning hoop without knocking it over. Timing is important, as the best chance to scamper through the hoop is when it briefly spins in place. Two trips through the hoop is possible, but requires a good throw, quick feet, and/or a small bod.

Variations quickly present themselves from this simple beginning, as people align themselves differently (opposite ends of the gym for simultaneous throws and dives), or try increasingly difficult tricks (feet first through the spinning hoop).

**Squirm**

Place a slightly deflated beachball (Moonball) between the foreheads of two participants. The object is to maneuver the ball from forehead to knees and back up again, without touching the ball with your hands (elbows, arms, etc.). Mucho balls; mucho action.

**Balance Practice**

Remember how, at the circus, the clowns would balance plates or a chair at the end of a long pole that was planted on the chin or forehead of the performer? That type of balance skill takes a lot of practice, and more time (or patience) than you have available in a 50 minute class.

Try some small-scale balancing "tricks" using a 1" x 3' wooden dowel. Almost everyone can gain some immediate success and satisfaction from balancing such a rod in a vertical position on the palm of their hand. It will, predictably, require some hand, arm, and body movement and, in some cases, jogging this way and that to keep the rod from falling, but that's fun and given to repetition.

As skill or luck increases, try balancing the rod on your chin, forehead or even your nose.  Contests for maximum vertical time aloft or distance covered while balancing are natural incentives.  Also try tossing the dowel in a balanced position from person to person.  Try a 180° toss from hand to hand.  Try not whacking yourself (or your partner) in the head.

## Rug Remnants

I'm sure you have seen or perhaps used these small, four-wheeled scooters designed for free-wheel movement on gym floors.  They seem like a lot of fun, but cost prevents their widespread use.

Some frugal and inventive teachers have substituted sections of rug remnants for scooters for use on smooth-surfaced floors (wood, not Tartan). You put a small section of rug on the deck (fiber twist to the floor), sit on it, and get pushed around by your DP (designated pusher).

Here's the next step — cut some sections of rug (this is where that old saying, "cut-a-rug" came from —— no, really!) somewhat larger than 12" long and glue (sew) velcro strips onto the back side so that two pieces can be used as "rug skates" for whatever slip-and-slide game you have in mind. The velcro strips aren't really necessary, but they look snazzy.

Olympic speed-skating records (around the gym) are a natural and are sure to be broken repeatedly.  I timed one "skater" for the length of a gym at just over 6 seconds!

## Spinner

Place the parachute (P) on the gym floor in its spread-out circular pattern and ask two people to sit back-to-back, directly in the center of the chute (do not allow locked elbows).  Ask the remainder of the group to firmly grasp the edges of the P and begin rotating either to the left or right.  Try to rotate, holding the P somewhat loosely, so that the two seated people do not spin. The P will wind about their bodies, beginning low and moving up toward their heads; however, attempt to keep the winding P below their arms for safety reasons.

After the P is wound to its maximum, ask the group to pull the grasped edges firmly and quickly away from the two seated people; alerting the seated pair that this is about to be done.  The two will spin rapidly for about 2-3 turns.  Temper the muscle with concern until you see what speed of rotation results from the group's pull — the spin rate can be dramatically fast.

## Seat Spin

If your group is into spinning, ask each person to try this simple maneuver.

Sit on the gym floor (the slipperier, the better), and throw or thrust your extended legs to the right or left in order to initiate a spin on your buttocks. As soon as the spin has started, tuck your knees and arms up to your chest to feel the immediate acceleration and rapid spin rate; a la figure skaters. If you can hold two revolutions before tipping over, you are doing well.

This simplistic spin-a-roo stunt does not work well on asphalt (hot top).

The world's record for glute spinning is held by Tillie Haversac, who in 1957 spun around 14 times before losing her all-American lunch (hot dog, large Coke, and a Twinkie). Awesome!

### Another Nonsense Knot

Here's a nifty sequence to establish a quick solution to an impossible problem. Ask if anyone can tie an overhand knot in a short piece of rope (3'-4') if both ends are being held by the person attempting to tie the knot.

The following illustration provides the simple solution. "Now, why didn't I think of that?"

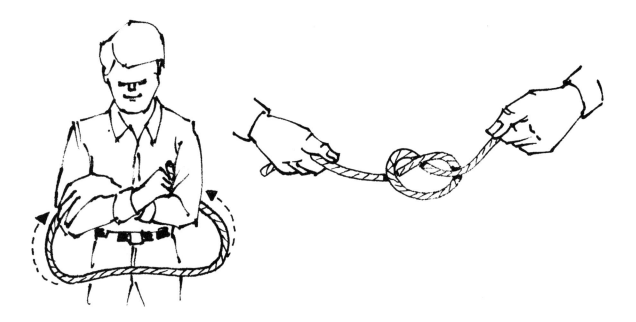

### Scooter Swing

This swing-on-wheels idea came from Dave Villandry of the UMPA (Urban Modification of Project Adventure) program in Cambridge, Massachusetts.

I have observed other people trying this swinging idea in past workshops, but I recently tried it myself and can now attest to what I was observing; people having fun and being challenged.

For this activity, you will need a floor scooter (essentially a 12" x 12" section of 3/4" plywood that has four ball-bearing casters attached on the bottom of the plywood in each corner), and a dangling rope somewhere near the center of the gym. Use of the 20' gymnastic climbing ropes that many schools still have, will work fine. You will also need a person with a helmet on, and lots of other folks to stand in a circle around that person. (Brief reference to the helmet situation, because I'm sure it caught your attention. In some instances of adventure programming, you are safer with a helmet on, and this is one of those times. The Scooter Swing activity is not dangerous, but an unplanned fall to the floor is possible. If you are on a belayed ropes course activity 50' in the air, a helmet is superfluous and probably uncomfortable, considering sizing problems and chin strap hassles.)

Ask the group to make a large people-circle around the rope to be used. The chosen participant stands on top of the scooter and grips the rope. Someone walks in from the circle and gives the center person a shove, which scoots the rider toward the far circumference of the circle where they are pushed back toward the other side of the circle. This compassionate pushing and scooting continues in a random fashion until the person tires of the ride or falls off the scooter. As long as the rider holds onto the rope, a fall is simply slipping off the scooter and sliding to a stop. Do not allow riders to use black-soled shoes, or the gym floor will suffer and so will your relations with the custodians.

As the rider becomes more adept, the circumference of the circle can be expanded considerably.

This is fun, folks — give it a try. It's a natural for making up games. Two games to try:

1. After each successful push across the circle, expand the circle's circumference by half a step until the rider eventually slips off the scooter.

2. Place a ten pin (or empty tennis ball can) in the center of the circle. The rider starts on the scooter at the edge of the circle somewhere. The group attempts to knock over the ten pin using the rider as the "bowling ball." The rider tries to miss the ten pin by foot movements and body English. Count the number of shoves necessary to knock over the pin. The circle's circumference remains the same throughout each attempt. The larger the circle is, the more chance the rider has of missing the pin.

## Snowflake

"The simplest are the funnest."

Obtain a mess of loose styrofoam packing material; say a small box full. These ultra lightweight objects are your "snowflakes." Did you know that no two pieces of styrofoam are ever exactly alike? No, really...that's true; I read it somewhere.

Climb to the top of something (staging, tree, ladder, astrodome) and launch a snowflake or two. Watch their slow and erratic descent. I'll bet it would be tough for a person down below to catch one on his/her tongue.

Note from the U.S.D.A. — Dispose of all tongued styrofoam pieces because of inevitable hygienic concerns. If your floor area is "clean enough to eat off of," recycle the missed "snowflakes." If the floor's cleanliness is suspect, you can play "Squash the Grub," a quaint foot-stomping survival activity indigenous to the African pygmy.

## Snowflakes — of Descending Velocity and Permutations

Yesterday, I was absently rifling my hand through a box of "snowflakes," when I noticed that there were three different basic shapes represented; the cup, the peanut, and the figure 8 types. Since no one was watching (you have to be somewhat reserved, as President of the Corporation), I tossed a representative sampling into the air and noticed that their flight (descent) characteristics varied considerably — thus, the crux of this in-depth inquiry. (I had approached *Scientific American* magazine with the results, but snowflakes in June were of "topical interest only," so...)

The cup shape was definitely the most predictable and the slowest descender. I'd suggest its use with special needs groups or those needing a higher success ratio: not much challenge, but definitely a floater worth watching.

The peanut configuration varies considerably because of an apparent inconsistency in the manufacturing process. A "good" peanut shape falls fairly predictably, providing a catch ratio consistently higher than 50%. The mutant peanuts, however, are devils to predict and establish — in my mind, the most difficult and frustrating objects to tongue successfully. Be prepared to grade your "snowflakes" for descent consistency, if success is the criterion. Some groups could care less, so you know what do do in that case.

Finally, the figure 8, a beautiful piece of aerodynamic foam that is both predictable and frustratingly difficult to catch — a sportsperson's paradox that is akin to the skill of nabbing catfish by hand. The whirling *and* spiral descent of this snowflake will test the mettle and oral dexterity of your most adept student: quick twitch muscles are key for these video game-like descents.

So, there you have it; as definitive a treatise on styrofoam bit descent as you will probably ever read — and, once again, BOT's was there first.

## The Rope Push

Halve your group and ask each half to stand on either side of a marker line (chalk line or rope). Hand them a 60-80' length of rope (any diameter or material) so that each side has an equal amount on their side of the marker line. Mark the center of the rope with a piece of tape. At this juncture, they are probably ready for a good old Tug-O-War, BUT the object this time is, at the end of a one minute time limit, to have more of your rope on their side than they have of their rope on your side! WHAT? Right, fox, this is a rope push, not pull. Here are a couple rules to ease the transition from tradition to chaos.

No one on either team is allowed to cross over and touch the other team's turf or person (no intentional contact). Tugging on the rope is tabu — only push. Throwing the rope *is* allowed.

Judging this event is well-nigh impossible, but who cares? And, a tie is usually well received by all, except the most die-hard competitors. This confused bash may be worth trying again, so suggest taking a minute or two to develop team strategies and subterfuges, or sneaky initiative ideas.

## Double Dutch

Using the same section of rope that you used for the Turnstile or Tigger's Toy, double it so that each section is about 20" long, and with one piece in each turner's hands, have them turn a "Double Dutch" tattoo on the floor or street. If you don't know what Double Dutch is, ask any street-wise student, because verbalizing the sequence is harder than doing it. This is the stuff of pure nostalgia for some, an aesthetic and physical awakening to others, and flagellating frustration for most. I have seen young women perform feats of endurance and skill among, on top of, and underneath those spinning double ropes that would make a *Sports Illustrated* photographer's index finger itch. Try stepping into those whirling ropes for a little "hot pepper"; it's a humbler!

## Orange Teeth

Try this simple stunt and listen to the "Hey,-how-do-you-do-that?" comments. It's a useful lunch time diversion.

Cut an orange (the tough, thick-skinned oranges work best) into quarters and eat the edible part down to the whitish rind. Take a knife and cut the peel as indicated in the crude drawing below (all my drawings are crude), to form teeth.

Put the rind in your mouth so that the exterior of the peel faces in (white out) and fit the edges of the rind between your lips and gums. Tasty, eh?

Your reversed ascorbic false teeth are now in place. Stick your tongue through the "teeth" slots for a touch of bizarre realism.

The idea is straight from the 4th grade via my son, Matthew. From the mouths of babes...

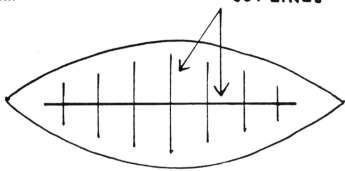

CUT LINES

## Scooter Spin

The set-up for Scooter Spin is simple, and it goes like this...Place a four-wheel gym scooter in the center of a basketball court or other large smooth floor area. Sit a volunteer pilot on top of the scooter. If the rider is large, use two scooters; one for the feet and one for the bum. Offer the rider a knotted end of a 20' rope; any substantial rope that's easy to grip. Begin to slowly rotate the rider on a foreshortened section of rope — this allows you (the spinner) to establish yourself as the central power source for the accelerating rider. As the centrifugal force builds, slowly let out the remainder of the rope, while maintaining the rider's speed (which to a first-time, wide-eyed pilot will seem in excess of Mach 1. I'd estimate the rider's actual maximum speed at between 15-20 m.p.h.

### A Caveat

According to the immutable laws of physics, if either you or the rider lets go during the spin sequence, both will travel apart from one another with equal velocity. Practically speaking, you will end up meeting the floor with surprising abruptness and the solo pilot will continue (at speed) toward the first solid object encountered beyond the boundary of the smooth surface. The resulting impact is impressive; don't let it happen!

Tie a slip knot in the rider's end of the rope and place it over his/her hand. Tie an overhand knot about 12 inches above the slip knot so that the rider can hold onto the rope without experiencing constricting pressure from the slip knot. Also put a loop (bowline) in the spinner's end of the rope to maintain a tight grip.

If the set-up allows (field house, parking lot, Logan Airport), release the rider at top speed and see what kind of maximum distance can be achieved.

There must be a formula that can be experimented with that relates centrifugal rotation to distance.

A more rider-controlled spin is possible if the rider lies ventral (belly) down on the scooter. In this position, the rider can drag his/her feet if speed seems excessive. In addition, the lower center of gravity that this position produces builds confidence for novice pilots.

Helmets should be worn by all riders, and you might even want to put one on. Goggles and silk scarf are optional.

## Scooter Slalom

Use the same type of scooter explained previously in the Scooter Swing. You will need a minimum of two scooters, but having a few more keeps things moving; i.e., less standing around and waiting.

This aerobic activity requires that the students work in pairs. They will be "scooting" through a slalom course set up on the gym floor in an attempt to establish a time. Each additional attempt offers a chance to better their record. Emphasize pair self-satisfaction, because time comparisons with other pairs is inevitable.

The rider sits on a scooter and puts his/her feet on top of a second scooter. The second member of the pair stands behind the rider and provides the GO, by pushing. The slalom course, a sample of which is outlined in the illustration, should include a few right angle turns, a couple "hairpins" and a straightaway — be inventive (tough, but realistic).

A couple people in the group with digital watches can be timers until their turn comes up. As the pair attempts to make their fastest trip through the slalom markers (cones), it become obvious that the pair which works together (the rider uses his/her hands as outriggers to aid balance and turning), shows the most improvement. There is an infectious quality to this activity, because each pair is sure they can "do it faster next time."

*Rules*

1. One pair on the course at a time.
2. For each pylon or cone touched, a second is added to the total time. If a marker is knocked over, add two seconds.
3. If the rider's feet come off the front scooter and touch the floor, the ride may continue. If the rider's posterior hits the floor, the ride is over.
4. Slingshotting the rider is not allowed.
5. Rider and pusher must maintain physical contact throughout the run...particularly over the finish line.
6. Riders should wear a helmet.

Try to set up the slalom cones (using the entire gym floor) so that the start and finish is at the same end of the gym.

As this activity uses up a lot of energy, a pair should be encouraged to switch roles as rider and pusher. This suggestion is usually well received by the pusher.

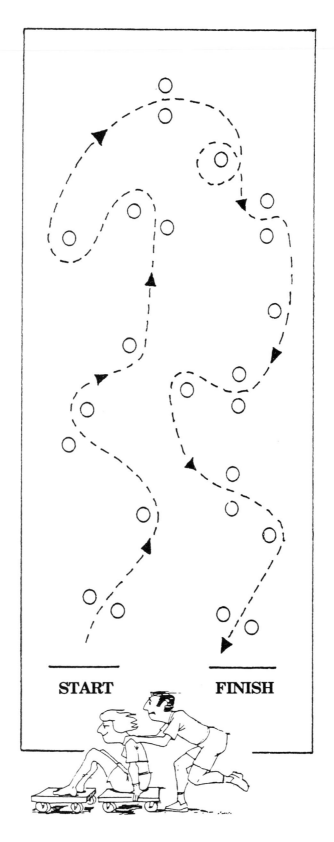

START          FINISH

## Chapter 4
# *Just Plain Games (Cognitive)*

### Calculator Hop

Looking for that ideal cognitive/psychomotor combination that encourages learning through activity? Here 'tis, and just a hop or two away.

Using inexpensive masking tape, reproduce the grid, numerals, and arithmetic symbols of a pocket calculator on a gym floor — not within the basketball key area, because of the 3 second rule. Make the grid so that each square is 12" on a side. The final "calculator grid" will contain 15 square feet and should look something like this: (Note: Multiplication and division signs are not part of this illustration.)

This grid set-up is going to take some time to fabricate, so pick a spot on the gym floor that is out of the way and will allow semi-permanence (at least a week).

The procedure is to present a simple math problem to a student and expect them to hop through a correct answer. Just getting the answer right or just hopping through the grid doesn't meet the criteria for completion. For example, 4 X 9 = 36. The student must hop (one foot) to the 4 from outside the grid, then hop to the X sign, then to the numeral 9, on to the ='s sign, and finally to the 3 and 6; landing on these final two digits with both feet simultaneously. (This double foot landing and stretch may be impossible for younger, smaller students if the answer is 70 or 90, etc.) You can either end the problem with this double-footed landing, or require that the student jump free of the grid as a final move.

If a grid line is hopped on, the problem ends and if an incorrect numeral or symbol is used, the problem also ends.

*Considerations:*

- No pencil or paper allowed — except for long division or decimal problems.
- Encourage operating as a team, with each member being responsible for hopping through the sequence. (Rote memory ploy.)
- Present the math problems in sequence and see how many correct answers can be hopped through in a one minute time span: two minutes for the varsity players.
- Fractions can be used (if the group can handle it), if you insert the minus sign between numerals (numerator and denominator) in the problem. For example, one-fifth is represented by hopping to the numeral 1, then to the minus sign, then to the 5. The problem must be announced as a fraction problem to avoid the confusion of considering the numerals to be part of a subtraction equation.

## Farkel

I'm writing up this sit-down game because (1) It's brand new (to me), (2) It's highly portable, (3) I like it, (4) and because Jim Johnson said I'd have trouble "putting this one on paper."

Jim (Australian contributor) had discovered this dandy game from friends who knew the originators, and as far as they knew, the game is original.

Their name for the game is FARKEL (my spelling), with the accent on the FAR. The name is important because it is used often during the game, and so spoken becomes a pejorative exclamation.

You need 3 pair of dice (6 di's) and a pencil and paper. One person of the 2-4 people playing can be scorekeeper. On the paper, list each player's name and make 12 pencil marks below each name — your choice of how fancy you want the pencil marks to be. The following works pretty well. 2 or 3 line space filled by 12 marks ///////////. These are called Farkel marks. Ten thousand points wins the game; i.e., the first player to gain 10,000 big ones — wins. Five thousand points can be used for the short game version.

OK, no more fooling around — here's the game. (Let me know if you have trouble with the rules, Jim — I'll send you the video!)

Roll in rotation, choosing who goes first however you want to.

First person rolls all 6 dice. If a 1 is included in the roll, it counts 100 points. Remove that di. If a 5 is included in that roll, it counts 50 points and can also be removed if you choose. If in that roll, two 1's and a 5 were included, you could score 250 points, but you have the choice to roll again, so it might make sense to not remove the 5 and include it in the next roll in order to perhaps score higher; perhaps another 1 (100 points).

So you remove both 1's and roll the remaining 4 dice. Only 1's and 5's can be scored, so if your roll does not include any 1's or 5's, you FARKEL (lose all accumulated points for that turn and cross off one FARKEL mark under your name). At any time during the game, if you roll and no 1's or 5's come up, you FARKEL. This *can* occur on the first roll and regularly does. A no-score first roll is called a **Fanny Farkel** and the penalty is losing *two* Farkel marks.

On to the next roller. (You Farkeled and got no points.) This time, three 1's come up, and scores 1,000 points (big time — be careful now). Remove the three 1 di's. You can stop now and take the 1,000, or try to get more points by rolling the remaining three dice, but if a 1 or 5 doesn't come up — you FARKEL, losing the 1,000 points and a Farkel mark. Let's say that you sensibly decide to keep the 1,000. Record that 1,000 under your name. The next roller has the choice of rolling all six dice and scoring in a regular fashion, or of taking the remaining three dice that you didn't use, and gambling that a 1 or 5 will come up, in which case they get 1,000 (not your 1,000 — you keep that), plus any other points they may accumulate. In order to pay for this chance of earning a quick 1,000 points, the gambling roller must pay one Farkel mark per di to be thrown; in this case 3 — cross off 3 Farkel marks. I'd better tell you now, before you FARKEL-OUT, that once you use up all twelve Farkel-marks, YOU'RE OUT OF THE GAME! For example, say they luckily throw two 5's and a 1. PLUS (big plus) you have used up all the dice and get to start over with all 6. If you choose to continue, throw all 6 dice and record no 1's or 5's, you FARKEL (Fanny Farkel, actually), losing the 1,000 points and two Farkel marks.

If you score say 250 points on the turn, add those points to your 1,000+ points and the roll goes to the next person, who may gamble like you did for the now higher points (1,250+), or simply start over with all six dice. Don't forget to pay one Farkel-mark for each di thrown when you make the gamble on the previous thrower's points.

These are the basic rules, but there are obviously subtleties that will emerge as you become more skilled at the game.

Here are a couple points to remember that I didn't emphasize. Every time you throw the dice, a 1 or 5 has to be removed. Say you throw all six dice and only one 5 shows (no 1's). You *have* to take that 50 points and remove the 5 di in order to continue and throw the remaining five dice.

If, during a turn, three of any denomination shows (a triplet), you can take those dice as ten times the denomination. For example, three 4's show, and that scores four hundred points; three 6's is six hundred points.

I've played this game with my sons, ages 12 and 15, and they like it. I think the name adds a lot to the game — particularly for that age group.

There you go, Jim — *Farkel* in a nutshell.

## A What's-the-Key? Game

As I've mentioned in previous game write-ups of this genre, the play rationale (other than fun, which is a taken-for-granted ingredient, or I wouldn't be writing about it) is twofold: (1) The puzzle encourages players to "see" solution possibilities other than just the obvious answer; i.e., emphasizing lateral rather than vertical thinking — "taking the blinders off," so to speak. (2) Allowing participants to experience the frustration, discomfort and anger of what it's like being on the outside of a group.

Players sit in a circle and the leader says, "I'm going on a trip to Boston (or wherever) and I'll take anyone along who wears the *proper* clothing — we are going to *Boston*, after all!" The leader then describes his own sartorial set-up and asks if anyone would like to join the trip — that person who's dressed appropriately, of course.

The correct attire (top half) is whatever the person immediately to your right is wearing and the de rigueur bottom half attire is what the person to your left is sporting.

Skip a person to the right or left if you think the answer is too obvious.

## The Point of the Game

I think this is what you would call a "party" game, but it has the ingredients — with slight modifications — of a useful group game that emphasizes cooperation, being comfortable as the center of attention, thinking on your feet, good-natured humor and incisive thinking.

The object is to have one or two people (volunteers) leave the room and upon returning, to try and determine what "the point of the game" is that the group has decided to play. (If two people leave the room, upon returning, they operate as one person; i.e., a team of two.)

The out-of-room volunteers begin the action by asking questions of the large group. Any number of questions can be asked, but a time limit for questioning is set. Before a deadline is reached, the person asking the questions must correctly determine *the point of the game*.

For example, the group decides that all answers to the questions must be responded to sequentially in a pre-determined order by members of the group; i.e., 1-15, or however many people are in the group. If the person asking the questions determines that the group is indeed answering the questions in that manner and makes the discovery within the time limit, then he/she "wins," and receives a standing ovation or whatever.

Sequential answering is a fairly easy game to discover, but if you add an alphabetical twist to the answering, the "point" is not so sharp. For example, each person answering in sequence must also use sequential alphabet lettering in order to begin the first word of their answer. *Example:*

Question #1 - Is what you're thinking of in this room? Answer #1 - Always keep your questions to the point. (Emphasize A in *always* as the first letter of the alphabet.) Question #2 - Was my last question too nebulous? Answer #2 - Bob is a better judge of that. Question #3 - Which Bob do you mean? Answer #3 - Can't you be more specific? This ploy obviously makes discovering the point of the game more difficult and immensely humorous to the "in" crowd.

Also try: (1) Alternating male and female players as those answering each question. Obviously, the answers need have no relevance to the questions, as only the alternating of sex is significant. (2) Each answer must include the name of a prominent article in the room.

Use shoe size, height, or age for other sequential ploys.

*Point of the Game* is a rainy day gem that may well last the entire period.

## Help Me Rhonda

This is a minimum prop, small group word game that is usually well received by older students (folks who can spell). Divide a larger group into triads or troikas. Each group of three must have a piece of paper and pencil (pen).

The leader (not necessarily you) calls out the name of a person (three to six letters in the name) with no repeating letters — try RHONDA. The designated recording secretary of each group spells the name at the top of a sheet of paper, like so:

R          H          O          N          D          A

The leader then calls out the name of a category, say "animals." The troika must then list as many animals as possible underneath the letters of the name RHONDA, so that each animal's name must start with R-H-O-N-D or A. E.g., Owl under O, Dog under D, Aardvark under A, etc.

The teams score one point for each acceptable answer, and two points for each animal name that no other team thought of. Choose other categories for additional contests, and let the players choose the categories. Try - "flowers," "cities," "trees," "brand names of foods," "sports," etc. If the students in the group are math, English, science or whatever majors, specialize the categories: "protozoans," "circulatory system," "bones of the body," etc.

## Bang, You're Dead (Around-the-Ole Campfire Game)

This game and many like it are of the I-know-there's-a-clue-but-I-can't-figure-it-out collection.

The object is for a group to figure out why whatever you're saying is true or why their reply is wrong.

In this particular game, for example, you say, "Bang. You're Dead!", point to anyone, and then wait for a response from someone in the group indicating whom they think you shot. The guesses begin slowly and the frustration level grows apace as you indicate, apparently without reason, who has been shot. Then you begin again with another, "Bang. You're Dead!" exclamation.

The key clue in this particular game is, whoever makes the first verbal response to your statement "Bang..." is the victim. Too easy? Try the game and see how long it takes for the group to figure it out. Remember, "Truth is obvious, after its discovery."

Other clues could be body or limb positions. If the group becomes adept at spotting clues, try using "eraser clues;" i.e., body movements or positions that indicate just the opposite for a clue. Example: If your legs are crossed, then an uncrossed leg position is the key.

Be aware that there has been some negative feedback received as to the "*Bang, You're Dead*" title of the game — too violent. Try changing the game and name (*Troika* - a team of three) with this presentation: "A connection has been formed between the following three people (name any three people). Who caused this bonding? The answer is the same as in the *Bang, You're Dead* approach.

## Your Add

This simple, no-prop game has so many good things going for it that you should try it right now. Grab a partner — husband, roommate, wife, sibling, anyone with a few fingers (10 digits are not necessary; in fact, amputees have an advantage).

Tell them to put their hands behind their backs (command is SET!), and on the word SHOW! both players, standing vis-a-vis, thrust their hands forward with from 0-10 fingers extended. The first player to come up with a calculated total for all fingers is champion. Example — 1st player shows 8 fingers, 2nd player shows 2 fists; total is 8. Also try subtracting and multiplying, using a third player's one hand finger total as the subtractor or multiplier.

If your group is involved in an extended workshop or retreat (more than one day), this game can emphasize spontaneous interaction between people. Whenever two people approach one another, one can say SET!, which is all that's needed to initiate a quick *Your Add* contest, leading to further conversation, maybe friendship, further involvement — perhaps even marriage, financial commitments, pets, two cars, wall-to-wall carpeting, kids — what more can you ask of a simple game?

## Four-Letter Word

A thinking, fast-action game for large groups; 30-50+.

This catchy title, approached by the timid teacher with a veiled shudder, has nothing to do with THE four-letter words, but the anticipation and harmless titillation is worth a soupcon of unease.

As an interesting aside, I have, on occasion, accused workshop participants of trying to get me to say the F word as the result of their weak participation efforts (or complete lack thereof). Incensed, they say, "What do you mean?" My reply includes references to their proclivity for non-success; i.e., the four-letter F word — FAIL. It's a sometime tool for the right group, and it's yours to use appropriately and humorously.

Back to the game — which I've said nothing about so far via asides and beating about the bush — also a four-letter word. Note how many four-letter words there are just in these two sentences. Quick, guess how many. Did you guess 12? You're wrong.

Before introducing *Four-Letter Word*, obtain a pack of 4" x 6" blank file cards. Using a felt-tipped pen, print the alphabet — one letter per card — on the cards. Then print additional cards for those letters used most often in word makeup. If you have a Scrabble game at home, you will get an indication of which letters are used most often by their assigned point value. AEIOU should have at least 3 cards per letter; X and Z, only one.

Ask each person in the group to take a card. If the group is small (25-30), have each person take two cards.

Announce that it is the task for each lettered person to get together with other people in the group (on a signal) and form a proper four-letter word within 45 seconds. If card-carrying players are still fumbling at the end of that time or are simply without letter partners, they and the other fumblers are eliminated.

Continue until only the last *Four-Letter Word* participants remain — the champs.

Alternate 3, 5, and 6 letter word requirements occasionally to add variety. The rules are up to you, but using Scrabble guidelines for allowable words is acceptable to most players. Real, you-know-what-I-mean, four-letter words are obviously not allowed.

Add a couple underlined J cards which act as Jokers; i.e., wild cards. Jokers can be used as any letter except the vowels.

## Big Word

Steve Butler developed this game as a variation of *Four-Letter Word*, but I think it deserves its own name. It's a fine game to promote cooperation and brainstorming.

Buy a couple packs of 4" x 6" blank cards. Using the letters of the following listed words, duplicate them on the cards (one letter per card) using a felt-tipped pen. Make sure there is one pile of cards more than the number of groups to maintain the flow. Use a rubber band to keep the card piles (words) distinct. When the cards get mixed up (and you know they will), put them together by words and run a different colored felt-tipped marker over the card edges. Just trying to make the tedious part of you job easier.

Ask your group to split up into smaller groups (2-5) and to go from room to room where they will find in each room a pile of these shuffled letter cards. They must then try to make the longest possible word they can from the letters on the cards. One point is awarded for each letter used in a word, and if all the letters are used, a five point bonus is granted. After five minutes, each small group rotates into another room (area) to another set of cards. This continues until all the sets have been encountered. Scores can be compared or not, depending upon the group and the situation. CONGRATULATIONS • COOPERATION • INTERDEPENDENCE • COMPASSION • TOGETHERNESS • CAMARADERIE • TEAMWORK • MISUNDERSTANDING

Make up your own set of words to fit whatever student population you work with. Try to make all the words fit a theme.

## Four-Letter Word Again...

Since having presented the game *Four-Letter Word* in an earlier BOT's, people have asked, "How many letter cards do you use and how many of each letter?" I guess my reference to Scrabble scoring wasn't specific enough. OK, here's the exact breakdown of letters I use.

A-3, B-1, C-1, D-2, E-3, F-1, G-1, H-1, I-3, J-1, K-1, L-2, M-2, N-2, O-3, P-2, Q-1, R-2, S-2, T-2, U-2, V-1, W-1, XYZ-1.

This comes out to a total of 42 cards (4" x 6" unlined). Remember to add a couple JOKER cards, if a wild card approach is appealing.

## Which Way? Softball

Trying to referee this game can be as confusing as trying to follow the rules. Where a player runs after hitting the ball, in ordinary softball, is predictable, but by radically changing the base-running rules, a ho-hum game becomes a physical *and* intellectual challenge.

| | |
|---|---|
| 1st inning | Run the bases in reverse. |
| 2nd inning | 2nd base becomes 1st base. |

3rd becomes 2nd.

1st becomes 3rd.

3rd inning     When the ball is hit to the right side of the field (or infield),   the player runs to 3rd base first and proceeds around the bases in reverse.  If the next batter hits the ball to the left side of the field, then the player runs to 1st base.

If the players are on base, they must determine which is the correct direction to run, based on where the ball is hit.

## Another Name Game

After the group has played some other game to learn the various names (Toss-A-Name Game), this quickie can serve as a review.  It's a quick-thinking, speedy-action, couple-laugh, name tune-up.

Everyone stands in a circle with you in the center.  You point to someone and say, "right" — then say the complete name of your school.  For example, "Right, Lakeview Elementary School."  The person that you pointed to must say the name of the person to their *right* before you finish saying, "Lakeview Elementary School."  If they flub the name or don't say anything, then that person takes your place in the center of the circle.  If you say, "Left"...

To make the game more difficult, say, "Three Right," or "Two Left," indicating the person 3 or 2 spaces to the right or left.

If the group is large (20 or more), put more than one person in the center. This game is somewhat like *Speed Rabbit*, but more goal-oriented.

## Paper Golf

Chasing a golf ball around the links is a comparatively unphysical means of spending exercise time, from a cardio-vascular standpoint.  I'd like to further reduce your oxygen uptake by introducing you to *Paper Golf,* a fiendishly clever, intriguing, and fascinating paper and pencil game of golf.

You will need 18 sheets of unlined paper to duplicate an 18 hole course.  The size of the paper is up to you, but generally the larger the paper, the more demanding (not physically) the game becomes.

The following illustration depicts a typical Paper Golf hole set-up.  Your imagination and golf experience will allow you to make up the other 17 holes on separate sheets.

The game is best played by a foursome (that's golf talk for 4 players playing a round — 9 or 18 holes — together), but can be played by any number; i.e., until the pen or pencil lines become confusingly intertwined.

*To Play*

Player number one places the point of his/her pencil or pen directly on the paper anywhere between the two markers designating the tee. (It quickly becomes obvious that this paper game of golf uses the same vocabulary and rules of regulation golf, and as such, provides an enjoyable method of teaching the basics of the game without suffering the frustrations of "keeping your head down," "maintaining a straight left arm," "controlling the back swing," etc.)

The player eyeballs the distance from tee to green, recognizing the obstacles that will increase the score and planning a first move (drive) that will place the ball (tip of the pen) in a safe area for the next stroke.

After the player has planned her drive, she must *close her eyes* and keep them closed for 5 seconds before moving the pen. Only one continuous move (straight or curving) may be executed. If the pen tip *ends up* in a bunker or hazard, strokes are added to the score.

The player must then plan the next stroke (with eyes open) and execute the stroke (eyes closed) toward the pin (hole). To finish the hole, the pen tip must end up directly in the open area of the hole.

As you develop each hole on the separate pieces of paper, use your imagination to vary the obstacles and distance and thus the par value for each hole.

## How're Ya Doin'? Just Fine, Thanks

Ask a group of 10-15 students to put on blindfolds, and then arrange themselves facing you (make some noise; continue talking); shoulder-to-shoulder. Then, starting from the right or left of the line, have them count off, and remind them to remember *their* number.

Depending upon whether this is your first blindfolded initiative problem, you should mention the trust aspect of no-see situations. Assure the group that you will not do anything to jeopardize their safety or embarrass them. Considering that trust is such a fragile and sometimes hard-won group feeling — value and nurture it as your most valuable teaching tool in adventure education.

Lined up, numbered and waiting, ask each participant to ask the person to their immediate right or left this question, "How're ya doin'?" Each person asked will answer, "Just fine, thanks!" Continue this verbal flood of questions and answers so that all the participants hear the repetitive Q&A's at least 3 or 4 times.

Now, have the participants mill around (still blindfolded) in the hands-up-palms-forward-protect yourself position until their sequential number positions have been entirely scrambled.

Ask them to stop and return, shoulder-to-shoulder, to their initial numbered position. They are allowed to talk, but the only thing they are allowed to say is, "How're ya doing'?" "Just fine, thanks!"

In order to further involve the first and last person in line, have the group initially line up in a circle. Line up in a circle? Hoo haw! Is that great, or what?

## Balloon Frantic

The rules to this slow-motion photogenic game nearly duplicate those of tennis ball *Frantic*. Since I reported on those basic rules so long ago, here's a quick repeat so that *Balloon Frantic* will be understandable.

## Expurgated Frantic Rules (c. 1979)

If thirty players are on the gym floor, thirty tennis balls are thrown, rolled or bounced simultaneously onto the floor by one of the three refs. It is the group's task to try and keep all the team's balls moving by kicking them.

There are three referees; one at each end of the court and one off to the side at mid-court. It is the duty of the two refs on the floor to try and spot balls that have rolled to a stop, and to record that as a penalty. The group has five seconds to start the ball rolling again, or another penalty is assigned. The group is allowed six penalties. When the last penalty is assigned, time is stopped and recorded so that the group can try to better their own effort with another attempt.

Every fifteen seconds after the start, the sideline ref puts an additional ball into play and continues this sequence until six penalties have been received...Now with balloons - *Frantic* with balloons is best played indoors in a high ceiling gym or outdoors only on a windless day.

Ask each participant to blow up a 12" balloon. (Don't use the so-called "penny balloons." They are too small and don't provide enough action.) Inflate at least 6-8 extras to serve as throw-ins for the 15 second rule, or as replacements for the inevitable broken balloons (boomers).

The rules for both games are identical except for the start. Ask each player to throw their balloon into the air, rather than having the ref start things with a kick.

Be sure to have a camera or video camcorder on hand, because the technicolor action of BF is color poster material. Need I say that Picasso would not play mono-color *Balloon Frantic*? You shouldn't, either.

**Pick and Choose**

Ask the group to split up into teams of 10, and give each group 50 old tennis balls. Place a paper core or waste basket approximately 20 feet perpendicular from a throw line marker and place another one on the same perpendicular 30 feet from the marker, so that it looks like this:

Using a two minute time limit, ask the group to see how high a score they can achieve by throwing the balls into the cores. The closest core scores 1 point, and the farthest core scores 3 points. The group of 10 can separate themselves as they choose, to be either a thrower or a retriever. The throwers must remain behind the throwing line. The retrievers may stand any place they wish, but may not "help" the balls into the cores. Their job is simply to retrieve missed shots and get the balls back to the throwers as fast as possible. Once the clock starts, the throwers and retrievers may not exchange positions.

This is a decision-making game. Resist the temptation to make suggestions and let the action flow. The game is obviously designed to play more than once. Add another core 5' further out, that scores five points to stimulate interest and increase the difficulty of the decision-making process. Also try *Pick and Choose* as one large group (no team) so that all the participants are competing against their own previously set score. I like the big group game best.

## A Game Called Blockhead

Steve Butler of *Playworks, Inc.* (Chairman of the Board, President, Grand Master and Playful Plenipotentiary) brings by games and toys from time to time and this particular store-bought item has potential. The commercial name of this bought-in-a-box game is *Blockhead*. The game paraphernalia (those things that come tumbling out of the box) are brightly colored wooden blocks of varied shapes. The blocks are about one to three inches in length or width, and are not easy to describe because of their polygonal makeup — lots of square corners, not many round.

With a playing partner(s), the game object is to construct a balanced stack with the blocks. Each player(s) chooses a block, as their rotating turn comes up, and adds it to the precarious spire. If the stack falls as the result of their misplaced block, they are designated "acting blockhead" until the next tower topples.

It's easy to recognize how this type of game fits well into an adventure curriculum.

1. A sense of risk-taking and uncertain outcome is constant.
2. Conversation and decision-making are ongoing.
3. The blocks can be home-made by the students. Make macro blocks for maximum action.
4. Instructions and proctoring are minimized, while action, anticipation and creativity are undeniable.
5. Occasional and expected failure is an accepted part of the game.

*Caveat:* Don't use cinder blocks.

## Mine Field

Scatter your collection of rabid nuggets (tennis balls) onto a floor area and arrange them so that they are randomly but equally distributed within and about the available area of play. About 300 balls are required for a typical mine field arrangement.

The object of this polka-dot problem is to verbally guide a blindfolded partner through the mine field to the far safe side. Verbal directions must come from the sidelines; i.e., the verbal leader is not allowed to stand next to his/her partner within the mine field.

The soft-footed jaunt from boundary to boundary is timed. For each nugget touched, there is a 30 second time penalty added to the final time. Have each pair trade positions after an initial attempt.

For intense alternative action, try the pursuit variable of releasing a heat-seeking missile (HSM).

In this game action, the blindfolded player (as above) is called the Sidewinder, a highly accurate and devastatingly destructive missile. The Sidewinder (SW) is aimed at a target on the far side of the room (chair, table, etc.) and is set in motion by the person giving step-by-step instructions. If the SW touches a tennis ball, he/she must swing both arms in a full circle 15 times, counting aloud each revolution.

Sixty seconds after the SW is launched, an anti-missile missile is also launched. The second blindfolded player represents a heat-seeking missile and is trying to destroy (tag) the SW before the target is reached. If the HSM touches a nugget, he/she must bend over and touch their toes (ankles, knees, whatever) 10 times, counting each repetition aloud.

Filling the floor with SW and HSM's provides a military melee of more than modest proportions. Great fun for all, warhead affiliation notwithstanding.

## Medley Relay

This is a relay where the group competes against itself or, more specifically, against a time or distance that they have previously established. In this case, total distance achieved by the group is the criterion.

Each member of the relay team must perform his/her best effort toward increasing the team's distance from a starting line. The performances are done in sequence; i.e., one after another, with each attempt being carefully marked.

The events to choose from are as follows, but the sequence is up to you. I have found that finishing with the handstand walk provides an exciting finale. All of these events are measured from an initial starting line.

Medley Relay Events - (1) Standing broad (long) jump; (2) Standing backward jump; (3) Running long jump; (4) Cartwheel; (5) Dive and Roll; (6) One-legged hop (right and left leg); (7) Front forward flip from a stand; (8) Handstand walk. Add whatever type of forward movement that seems to make sense, or more appropriately, that is well received by the group. This is an activity that becomes more enjoyable through repetition.

**Warp Speed**

This neatly-wrapped initiative problem involves getting to the solution by operating at warp speed. The problem itself is a variation and extension of *Group Juggling.*

Choose one soft, grabbable throwing object (fleece balls are good — Lacrosse balls are bad) for the fast-paced action. Ask the group to form a circle (about arm's width between people). Include yourself in the circle and make sure either you or someone has a digital stopwatch. (Remember, this is warp speed, so the timing mechanism has to be accurate to the nearest 100th of a second.)

Ask everyone to raise one hand and to keep it raised until they have received the thrown object, at which point they can put their hand down. This, I think, simple bit of instructions has caused more confusion than a judo teacher in the karate studio. Tell a group to raise both hands and catch the ball with their teeth — no problem, but ask them to raise only one hand and the questions flow non-stop. Also ask everyone to *remember who they throw to and who they receive from*: emphasize this.

You (instructor) start the action by throwing the ball to someone on the far side of the circle. Do not time the first two attempts; the group is simply establishing a pattern. That receiver throws to anyone across the circle, etc., etc., until you receive the ball last. Go through the pattern one more time to cement the sequence and to build confidence.

Now ask the watch holder (not you or the person you throw to) to time a sequenced throw/catch attempt by starting the clock when you say GO and stopping when you say STOP. Whatever time you achieve is your current WORLD RECORD. Ask the group how many seconds faster they think the sequence can be done. If the first time for 20 people is 16 seconds, maybe 12 seconds as a final time would be a prudent guess — certainly not in the warp speed category, but an acceptable beginning.

More attempts and misses are made until the next level of time is achieved amidst considerable conversation and some trial and error. Ask for a lower time commitment, which will probably be met with hoots of disbelief amidst some cries of *"Let's go for it!"*

As each level is achieved, ask for a lower time, allowing changing of position in the circle and whatever else their imaginations come up with. Don't be strict with the rules, because remember, there aren't any.

When someone finally suggests sweeping the ball past everyone's sequentially outstretched hands, your time should come in below one second — a substantial accomplishment for a team that first guessed 12 seconds as their ultimate goal. Strange things happen at warp speed. "Beam me up, Scotty, there's no intelligent life down here."

**I'm Speechless**

Distribute balloons to equal half the group and using a magic marker, number the inflated balloons sequentially.

Have the group pair up and offer a blindfold to one member of each diad. The sightless member is handed any balloon and on a signal, each balloon is released into the air. The task is for each pair, which has been assigned a number, to find the balloon with their number on it and then, holding the balloon, to line up shoulder-to-shoulder with the other blindfolded participants so that the line extends from 1 to whatever; i.e., 1, 2, 3, etc.

*Rules:*

1. The sighted member may touch their partner, but may not physically direct their movements.
2. (a) The blindfolded member is mute and may not make any sounds.

   (b) The blindfolded member and their partner cannot converse (or with anyone else), but may use sounds as long as the sounds are initially unintelligible; i.e., yes and no grunts are disallowed.
3. The sighted partner is allowed to talk and give directions.

The various attempts are timed. In doing so, you are encouraging group cooperation in working toward the goal (a number sequence line). By cooperating and sharing ideas, the second and third attempts are invariably accomplished more efficiently and thus faster.

Tell the blindfolded players to constantly protect their heads and faces, particularly when they are bending over to pick up a balloon.

Use rule 2(b) to increase the difficulty of the basic problem.

**Happy Landings**

*Purpose:*

To develop cooperation, trust and imagination through physical and verbal group activity.

To develop group support and awareness of the problems of the physically disabled.

To develop the capacity for taking responsibility in guiding others and in following directions.

Explain to the class that this is a group activity designed to test their concentration and ability to give and take directions. Tell them you will need two volunteers — one a rower and the other a dock worker. The rower will be trying to maneuver his boat through a rock-strewn channel and land at the dock. Explain that the rower is the lone survivor from a ship that exploded. He was blinded in the explosion but escaped in a small rowboat.

The dock worker who saw the explosion is now trying to guide the blind rower to safety. The other students are to be the rocks and channel sides. Some of them should stand in two lines along the channel (boundaries), while the others (rocks) may stand, kneel or sit at random in the channel area. When the rower docks successfully, or bumps into a rock or channel boundary, both he and the dock worker lose their turn and must choose replacements. While the new rower is putting on his blindfold, the "rocks" should change positions in the channel.

The game continues until everyone has had a turn at being rower or dock worker.

*Procedure:*

Set up the boundaries for the channel — sides and length. Have the rower stand at one end wearing a blindfold and standing with his back to the dock worker who will be at the other end of the channel. The other students should place themselves at random in the channel area to be the rocks and channel sides.

## Happy Landing Variations

- Try offering a touch of acoustic realism to this trust/communication problem by adding some "authentic" ocean noises. Begin to create the sound of wind and rain (vocally and with whatever props are immediately available). As you might expect, the dock worker soon has to yell to the rower above the crashing waves and howling wind. The rower, in turn, has to struggle to understand the wind-tossed directions.

  While these actions somewhat alter the tone of the exercise, the bond between the dock worker and the rower is enhanced as both jointly struggle to work together under adverse conditions.

- Allow more than one rower to attempt simultaneous passage through and among the "rocks, buoys and reefs." The dock workers shout their directions from the sidelines in a cacaphonous chorus reminiscent of the game *Hog Call*. Blindfolded rowers must return to the start if they are unfortunate enough to make contact with an obstacle.

## Moonball

*Moonball* is an excellent one-prop-game that develops coordination and fast reactions. Play becomes intensely competitive, as a group competes against its last best effort.

Scatter your group (any size, but use two or more balls as the group size demands) on a basketball court or a field. Use a well-inflated beach ball as the object of play. The group's objective is to hit the ball aloft as many times as possible before the ball strikes the ground. Depending upon the group, set a goal of 50, 75, 100 hits to add incentive.

*Rules:*

1. A player cannot hit the ball twice in succession.
2. Count one point for each hit.
3. Two points are allowed for a kick.

Not too complicated, eh?

The tension and expectation builds as each "world record" is approached. Moonball is popular with all ages, because it's simple to understand, requires little skill, and involves (like it or not) everyone. This is a particularly useful activity to initiate when a new group is just getting together, especially if you want early arrivals to become involved and not just self-consciously stand around.

## Moonball Variation

I'll tell you something honestly. *Moonball* has programmatically saved my bacon on a couple occasions when I needed a quickly explained, moderately active game for people standing around at the beginning of a session wondering why they were there. (That last sentence seems a bit run-on, but I'm talking now, not writing, and you know what I'm saying.)

After you have messed around with Moonball, here's a variation, and Lord knows this isn't the only one. Beachballs (aka Moonballs) give vent to flights of curricular imagination, because what else are you going to do with a gaily colored, balloon-like ball that doesn't pass or bounce worth beans, or kick with any predictability?

Ask the group, after playing basic hit-the-ball-37 times, to see how many times the group (6-60+) can hit the ball in sequence through all the players without, (1) letting the ball hit the ground, or (2) missing a sequenced player. Alternately, see how fast the ball can travel from player to player in sequence; i.e., through the whole group. If the ball touches the ground, assign a time penalty — say 5 seconds. The ball must be hit, not simply passed.

Set up a regular Moonball game and record the most number of ball strikes (hands only) during a two minute time limit. Only count those hits that are not preceded by a ground bounce. The ball must touch each player sequentially. Allow the group to arrange themselves in whatever position they decide is best to achieve the greatest number of hits.

When the ball begins to leak air (it's bound to happen eventually — these things only cost $1.27), try a quick round of *Five-a-Side Flatball.*

## Moonball - Big Leak Variation

When your beach ball finally splits (literally), extend that split to a size that allows you to put a pair of shoes inside the ball. As you travel, the ex-Moonball provides a colorful way to transport your muddy field shoes without getting your clothes dirty. I'm not kidding — this works. Colorful conservation at its finest.

## Unholy Alliance

This is an advertisement of sorts, but for you do-it-yourselfers, it's an introduction to a surprisingly complex decision-making tug-o-war.

Project Adventure, Inc., sells this 4-way tug rope, and I'll quote directly from the description in the Ropes Course Source catalog.

## Four-Way Tug-O-War Ropes

Use of these 1" diameter multiline ropes gets away from the pull-your-arms-off contests so characteristic of single rope tug-o-war. With 4 teams of up to 15 participants each, players are able to develop strategies and temporary affiliations that bring people back for "just one more try."

These soft-to-the-touch ropes have an impressive tensile strength of 17,000 lbs. That multi-ton strength, in conjunction with the 4 - 30' spliced lengths, precludes any danger of rope breakage under strain.

The 4 lengths of rope are eye-spliced in the center (4 galvanized thimbles around a 5/8" diameter galvanized drop forged steel ring. Each rope end is back-spliced.

*How to Use the Alliance Tug Rope*

Procure a 100' length of 1/4" polypropalene (or some such cord) and tie the ends together (splicing looks better) to form a rope circle as it lies on the ground. Marking every 25' of this rope length, change the circle to a square. This rope square designates the boundary marker. Stake out the square using tent stakes or 3/8" staples.

Since each of the 4 pulling ropes is only 30' long, it doesn't make much sense to put more than 15 pullers on a length — there just isn't room for more to pull efficiently. Nonetheless, split your group into 4 equal smaller groups and ask them to assume the pull position (whatever that means). Do not allow the last person to tie into the rope. As a matter of further safety, don't allow any knots to be tied in any of the ropes.

As the Pull Master (PM), take the 4 pulling ropes and set the center ring into the center of the boundary square so that the 4 ropes perpendicular the 4 sides of the boundary rope.

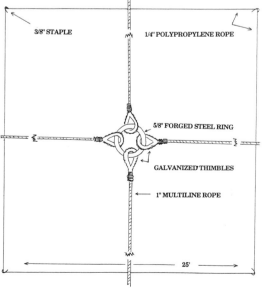

3/8" STAPLE      1/4" POLYPROPYLENE ROPE

5/8" FORGED STEEL RING

GALVANIZED THIMBLES

1" MULTILINE ROPE

25'

**UNHOLY ALLIANCE**

The PM advises, "Take up the strain," at which time all pullers slowly begin to put pressure on the ropes. After a couple seconds of holding the ring on center, as the pressure increases, the PM shouts PULL and steps quickly and nimbly back.

The action has obviously begun, but the deception and strategy during the first pull-off usually gives way to pure physicalness. It takes a couple pull-offs for the teams to discover how brief alliances with the pulling teams to their right and left can sometimes produce victory for their team. This very physical game is an announced *antitrust* activity.

A win is achieved when a team pulls the center ring over the section of boundary rope that marks their part of the square. If the ring goes directly over any of the 4 right angles, it is a NO PULL, and the teams begin again from a starting position.

Make sure you let the teams try this activity often enough so that team strategies can develop.

If you are the *Pull Master*, watch out when you yell "PULL" at the start, as rapid movement of the rings can result in a horizontal PM.

If you plan to put together your own 4-way pull ropes, please be sure to choose rope that is advertised as stronger than the estimated combined pulling power of the participants. I'd also suggest using metal thimbles for the splices and a 7/8" diameter drop-forged ring in the center. Do not allow anyone to grab the ring or spliced thimbles during a contest, or broken fingers could result.

This activity can be exhausting — so don't count on a full period's participation.

## Shark

Objective: The object of *Shark* is to gain the most points during the activity through group cooperation and fast action!

*Materials:*

Large field

1/2" plywood circles 3 or 4 feet in diameter for each group to use as a "ship"

*Procedure:*

1. Divide students into two groups with 8 to 10 members per group.
2. Give each group a "ship" and instruct all members to hold onto its sides.
3. Groups are to run with their "ship" until a staff member yells "Shark!" Then all members jump on board the "ship." The first group on board with *all feet* gains a point. Repeat

this procedure several times. The first group to reach the finish line gains 5 points.

4. Add up points to decide the winner.
5. Debrief with specific suggestions on how to improve next time.
6. Repeat the activity.

**Help Me — or Else**

This ball-in-a-bucket game demands cooperation. As represented in the following highly-detailed illustration, place a trash can or paper core in the center of a people circle. Each player is given six rabid nuggets (tennis balls) and stands four full backward steps from the target can. At GO, each person attempts to throw a nugget (one at a time) into the can. If successful, the thrower takes one full step backward and tries to repeat the first shot. This pattern is continued until all six balls have been "sunk" at six different (one step) distances.

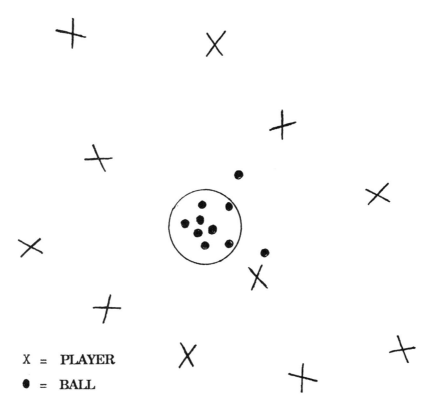

X = PLAYER

● = BALL

If a miss occurs, the throw must be repeated FROM THE SAME SPOT until the shot is made — *you are not allowed to move.* A thrower who has missed must depend upon the compassion and generosity of some other player to retrieve the errant ball. Be aware, however, that no one can move UNLESS a player decides to selflessly retrieve a ball for a teammate and incur the consequence of STARTING OVER.

Since the whole shoot-hit-miss sequence is being timed, the emphasis is obviously on cooperation. The watch doesn't stop until each shooter in the circle has "sunk" all their nuggets.  An adult group will probably see through this mandatory cooperation ploy, but a younger set may end up being pleased with themselves as the result of such spontaneous team cooperation toward achieving a goal.

As a variation, suggest that the shots must be taken on a one-bounce basis; i.e., ball contact with the floor before the goal is made.  Errant rabid nuggets provide the justification for much programmed cooperation.

## To Tell the Truth

A party game?  I suppose, but also a useful and entertaining get-to-know-you-better tool for a group that has already spent some time together.

Arrange chairs in a circle so that there is one chair per participant, including yourself.

*Procedure:*

Participants in the seated circle ask a question aloud that can be answered either yes or no.  Each person silently answers the question by remaining seated (a *no* response), or moving one seat to the right (answers *yes*).  No conversation is necessary, but repartee is expected, contagious and encouraged.

If someone answers a question "no" (example — Did you brush your teeth this morning?) and the person seated to their left thinks "yes," then a lap sitting situation develops.  With ensuing positive and negative responses, multi-lap people piles invariably develop.

Make sure your chairs are substantially constructed.  Ostensibly, the idea is to develop lap stacks by question responses and then try to move everyone back to a single seat status by asking "moving" questions.

*Rules:*

1. Questions must be oriented to yes/no responses only.
2. Answers to questions must not be self-apparent.  Examples — Do you have on long pants?  Are your eyes blue?
3. Questions begin in sequence around the circle until everyone has asked a question (or passed, if that is their choice), and then the questioning continues spontaneously.

*Concerns:*

Limit the type of questioning, if necessary, or as you perceive your group.  Sexually-oriented queries or those that pertain to bodily functions are best avoided.

The end of the game occurs when:

1. Everyone returns to and occupies a single chair (improbable).
2. Everyone tires of increasingly continued and often trite questioning and quits. Be there to justify terminating the game before it becomes boring or offensive.
3. You like the lap that you are sitting on and decide to continue the questioning, interfacing as a diad.

*Variation*

Whenever a chair is left empty, remove it from the circle and see what develops: a quadriceps delight.

## Chapter 4
# *Just Plain Games (Psychomotor)*

Dan Hussong from West Windsor-Plainsboro High School in Princeton Junction, New Jersey, sent in the following explanation of what appears to be a good, fun game. Here's a variation outline of the game taken directly from Dan's letter. Thanks for taking the time to share your creativity.

### Jugball

"About the game itself, *Jugball* is played on a field hockey field (can also be played indoors), using a 'beat up' tennis ball. The 'Jug' is made by cutting off the bottom of a 1 gallon plastic jug of milk or water. (I recommend a piece of tape be placed around the cut edge, as it reduces the chance of being cut and also preserves the jugs.) Players hold their jugs by the handle. I had all the students who planned to sign up for this activity bring their own jugs. One student who lives on a dairy farm volunteered an unlimited supply, so we were all set to go. I cut the jugs as uniformly as I could, but found that many students wanted to "customize" their own jug and I encouraged this. 'Jaws,' 'Super Scooper,' etc., were born. (Ed. note: The 'jugs' can also be used for the initiative problem *Save the City,* which appeared in an earlier BOT's.

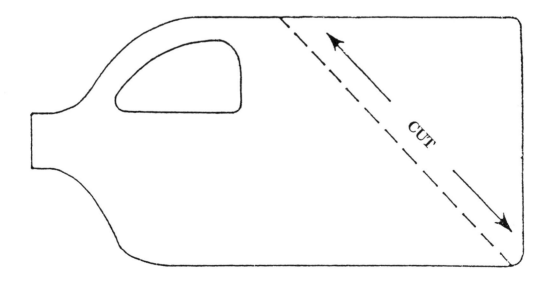

The object of the game is to advance the ball up field by throwing and catching the ball with your jug, and eventually hurling the ball into the opponent's goal.

Some worthwhile restrictions to place on energetic high school students are:

1. No physical contact.
2. No running forward with the ball, only lateral or backward movement allowed.
3. No close-range shooting (the arc on a field hockey field serves as a good boundary line).
4. To alleviate 'scrums' with an entire class trying to pick up a ground ball with their jugs, allow players to pick up a 'dead' ball with a bare hand and throw it high overhead.

Pre-class warm-up exercises are sometimes more fun than the game itself. I like to bring out a bag of tennis balls and have the class start out playing catch and then do a little group initiative. An example would be forming two lines facing each other and establishing the goal to be moving a ball through every jug as quickly as possible. This gets them in the mood, and they work hard together to beat the clock instead of each other.

Jugball has been well received by most groups and we haven't introduced it to the Freshman class yet; Freshman love to do anything new, exciting, and physical!

We are adapting it to an indoor setting in the second term as an elective choice. Our auxiliary gymnasium is perfect for it, as we let the ball play off the walls just like in Raquetball or Jai-Lai. After two days of witnessing this mania, we are convinced that Jugball is here to stay..."

## Uno-Dos-Tres (Anerobic Tag)

This is a multi-national game, assigned a Spanish flavor in this case by using the first three numerals in Espanol for the title, but it could just as well have been French (Un, Deux, Trois), Japanese (Ich, Nee, San...), etc.

The activity idea comes from a game book called *Keywords*, given to me by a participant (Ian Hoey) in a games workshop at the University of Ulster in Coleraine, Northern Ireland.

Divide your group in half and ask the players to visually distinguish themselves somehow — rolled up pant leg, hats/no hats, shorts/no shorts (better interpret that last one correctly, coach).

Throw a fleece ball or rubber ring into the dispersed group. Whoever catches it may run until tagged or has thrown the ball to another member of his/her team. The object is to pass the ball 15 times amongst the members of the group before the ball touches the ground or is intercepted by the other team.

*Rules:*

- Throws may be made to any team member, but not to the same person twice in a row.

- If a person is tagged (two hands below the clavicle) that person MUST pass the ball to a teammate immediately (2 seconds or less).

- When a team reaches 15, they score a point. The ball then goes immediately to the other team so that the restart isn't a time-wasting hassle.

- Another way to keep things moving. When a team reaches 15 consecutive throws, they start again immediately from zero to try and score another point. The onus continues to be on the other team to tag a runner and intercept the ball.

- If the use of numbers by both teams is confusing, assign letters to one of the teams. When the letter team completes sequential throws from A to O, a point is scored.

- If you want the game to last a bit longer (like six hours), ask the teams to number themselves sequentially and pass the ball in sequence from player to player in order to score a point: a game to last the semester for sure.

I have taken certain liberties in presenting and changing the rules of this game (as always) — I expect you to do the same.

## Shoot Out

This game can have either a lot of rules or very few, depending upon how it's presented and "where the players are at."

If the group is into fantasy and fun, the extra rules and ritual are usually well received. If the group is young and active, they will want action and less explanation.

Give the groups what they want — it's a good work-out either way.

*General Rules* (add or subtract appropriately)

The playing area can be inside a gym (field house) or on a marked field (football, etc.). There is a certain intimacy gained inside a gym that seems to add to this running, throwing melee.

You need two teams of about 5-15 people. The old "skins and shirts" bit works well for this game; i.e., male versus female.

Separate the two teams (however you decide to split the groups) and give each member a frisbee (plastic flying saucer), making sure that each member of a team has the same color saucer.

At this juncture, explain to the teams that they must develop a verbal insult to hurl at the other group. The insult may include no obscene words or ethnic slurs and may be delivered in unison or by the chosen DI (designated insulter).

After some in-depth insult discussion, the groups line up facing each other about 30 yards apart. All *Shoot Out* participants must, at this point, holster their frisbees. This is done by sticking the saucer into the waist belt of their shorts, pants, etc., in such a way that a quick draw can be accomplished. (Gentlemen should be aware that shoving the frisbee too far down into their "holster" might result in a pre-game injury that could remove them from the competition. Substitutions are not allowed, so be careful).

As both groups ritualistically glare at one another, the signal to begin is given. All members, of opposite groups, stalk slowly toward one another (VERY purposefully — you know, like in *High Noon*, *Gunfight at the OK Corral*, etc.), until they reach a line that separates the groups by about 10 yards. When both groups are aligned, the DI says, "When you were a baby, you were so ugly that your mother fed you with a slingshot!" or some such invective. The responding group, shocked and infuriated by such an incisive remark, says in unison, "Oh Yeah?!" This traditional response is the signal for everyone to go for their frisbee, which weapon *must* be thrown within 2 seconds after the first frisbee is released.

If a thrown saucer hits a player *below the waist*, they must die a dramatic, histrionic and noisy death (like in *Rio Lobo*, or *The Magnificent Seven*), and lie on the floor or field until that segment of the game is concluded.

After a saucer is released, that color only may be picked up by a team member as the participants dash about trying to find and pick up a frisbee and, at the same time, trying to protect themselves. Players may knock a thrown saucer aside, but may not catch a saucer that has been thrown at them.

Play continues until all members of one group have been properly "drilled," "plugged," i.e., eliminated. The groups then realign themselves at opposite ends of the field to discuss strategy and prepare to give or receive the next insult.

There is obviously a lot of tradition and ritual that must be enjoyed (relived) to make the above "work." If the group is young and more into activity than tradition — line them up as before (10 yards), and let them blast away at a given signal. Use a throwable object softer than a frisbee with younger groups (any group that can't control the urge to "head-hunt").

This game can also be played "one-on-one." In such a confrontation, the two players make their own rules. For example, each player carries 2 saucers; a hit must be below the knee; start as in a duel; i.e., back-to-back, etc.

### Follow Me!

An indoor (not necessarily), fast-moving, perceptual game that allows total participation without intimidation.

A player volunteers to briefly leave the room, and a leader is appointed among the remaining people in the group: 30 people per group is better than 10. You explain that when the IT person returns, the leader will initiate a movement (clapping, finger-snapping, head-rubbing, anything visual). Whenever the leader changes a movement, the group must immediately follow his/her lead. The IT tries, amidst this movement melee, to identify who the leader is.

Indicate that the group should not all look at the leader — it's a give-a-way. When the leader is finally caught, he/she can be the next IT or anyone who wants to volunteer.

The game action is fast-paced and fun. Try adding music from a BOOM BOX to establish the game pace. Debussey's *Afternoon of a Faun* is probably not a good choice. Hava Na Gila (forgive the phonetic spelling) would produce spectacular allegro results.

## Suck and Blow

This is a very intense game. Actually, the game name should be *More Suck Than Blow*, but why split hairs about something so meaningful?

Before I offer the very minimum game rules, you need to practice a bit to be ready for the aerobic challenge in store for you. Go get a 4" x 6" card. Hold the card up to your pursed lips and suck hard (not suck actually, just draw in air forcefully enough to keep the card positioned on your lips). A good suck will keep it there for maybe 3-4 seconds. Try it a couple times. Have contests with your friends to see who can keep a card juxtaposed to lips the longest. Tilting your head back is obviously cheating, so don't do it.

OK, here's the game. The object is to try and pass the card around a circle of consenting people as rapidly as possible using the above suction technique and without having the card fall to the ground.

You will find that as you transfer the card from person to person (or attempt to), it is important for the sucking person to choose that proper moment to blow (small puff, actually) when the potential sucking person has built up sufficient vacuum potential to allow the transfer to take place.

I hope you recognize my compassionate choice of card size; I could have suggested a 3" x 5".

Definitely a game for all seasons and no reason.

## Cage Ball Bombardment

This fire-at-will throwing activity humanely replaces corporal bombardment; you remember — highly inflated red rubber playground balls ricochetting off your head and "thwocking" solidly into the crotch area, as compassion, cooperation and empathy were put aside in place of nearly pure aggression. An S/M outlet for sure, but with disagreeable side effects (pain ranks right up there). Except for the rare psychopath, *Cage*

*Ball Bombardment* provides an acceptable outlet for whatever you need to let out and is surprisingly fun.

Try to follow and enforce the following rules, or the activity can quickly degenerate into Team Bombardment — a cooperative step above solo head-hunting.

Place a partially inflated cage ball (partial inflation makes the activity last longer) in the center of whatever area you have delineated for play, so that there are two parallel end lines about 20 ft. apart. See the illustration below.

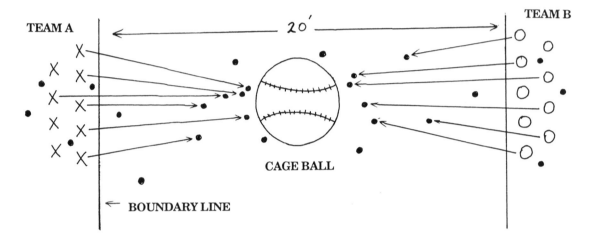

Each player is provided with a sponge (fleece) ball (must have some substance — not as light as a Nerf ball, but not as hard as a tennis ball), and on a signal, they must try to strike the cage ball with a thrown ball to forward the larger ball over the other team's end line, resulting in a score. If any "head hunting" begins, stop the game and threaten a permanent end to play. The kids like this activity and will usually police themselves adequately.

After the game begins, provide each team with more (equal quantities) balls. Players are allowed to cross the boundary line to retrieve a ball, but most cross back over in order to throw.

*Do not* use tennis balls for this game.

## Catch 10

Here's a fast-paced, blatantly competitive game for 3-6 people, that I remember developing with a group of friends on the beaches of southern California many years ago. At that time, we used a football and that's still a good idea, but you may have more luck with a diverse group, using a frisbee (the 97 gm. model, of course).

The playing area can be any field area that doesn't have obstacles to run into or trip over. There are no boundaries. Grass, as in most active outdoor games, is the best playing surface, unless a beach is handy, and that is absolutely the ultimate barefoot surface for jump-around, feel-good, land-on-your-head games.

The object is to try and make the person you are throwing to, miss the frisbee, for which slip of the fingers a point is disawarded. When a player accrues 10 points, she/he is out of the game and the remainder of the players continue until only one remains.

The throws are made in keeping with a pre-game determined sequence (Pete, to Jill, to Rod, to Liz), and continues this way unless a player, who has just missed a frisbee, thinks he/she has been taken advantage of for one reason or another and shouts, "STOP" (or whatever invective comes to mind). The offended player gets to make a standing throw with the frisbee at the person who made them miss, from a measured distance of 10 yards. In the event of either a miss or catch, the frisbee continues in the new throw/catch sequence direction — opposite to the way it was going.

Gentlemen's rules are in effect throughout; i.e., when a throw is made, the catcher *must* exert a 100% effort to snatch the frisbee, but if the disc drifts beyond catchability, the point is added to the thrower's total; if the catcher obviously dogs it or short-arms an attempt, the point is his.

Catch 10 strategy — Running toward the person you are throwing to is OK and is actually a good offensive move, but a player must throw the frisbee from a distance of at least 10 yards away from the catcher. Trying to keep the sun at your back is another bit of gamesmanship that works. Try to make it as much a running/catching game as possible by lofting high throws well beyond where the catcher waits or by running to place yourself as a potential catcher near to the person you will be throwing to. Think up strategies, add rules, change rules — make the game yours.

### Nerf Ball Knockaround

This game works as well on a field as in a gym. The use of a Nerf soccer ball allows those youngsters who are afraid of the speed and momentum of a regulation ball to participate without worrying about getting bopped on the nose. The rules are simple and hooray for that.

Set out two street hockey nets a distance apart that makes sense for your available area. Divide your group into two teams without employing the sociogram technique of choosing up sides. Then differentiate the teams with pinneys, rolled-up pants, hats/no hats, blue pants/other color pants — not male/female, please! Throw out two Nerf soccer balls and play regular soccer rules. When a goal is scored, you record the goal and throw the ball back in play near the center of the field. In this way, there is no need to stop the action. If you are part of the action, so much the better.

**En Garde or Else**

This idea was going to make me a million dollars (...couple hundred bucks, anyway), but I never got around to the implementation stage. So, you try it and tell me how things work — and if you go public on stock options, give me first shot.

Dueling with foam swords (referred to in many past BOT's and used in such games as *Samurai, Boffer Bonkers, Balance Broom, Swat Tag, Foes & Questors*), is great fun and from a "who cares?" standpoint of winning a duel, foam swords are tops because it's hard to tell who got whom. BUT, if someone's honor has been besmirched, a more definite means of win/lose must be achieved. To wit, the idea.

Some pre-duel material and fabrication is necessary. You need (1) one-half inch velcro strips, (2) cloth glue or a sewing machine, (3) one inch diameter styrofoam balls (like the ones you buy at Christmas to make tree ornaments that look lousy, but are dripping with sentiment). Affix a chosen T-shirt with 3 half-inch sections of the velcro — one on each arm (ventral deltoid), one at the sternum (ladies optional), and one on the back for people that try to run away (just kidding — that makes 4, anyway). Each of the three balls also has a section of velcro glued on.

When ready, attach the balls (via velcro) to the shirt and begin the duel. Make up your own rules, but when a ball is knocked off the shirt by a sword, there should be no doubt as to a fair hit, precluding the inevitable and often tedious, "Yes-I-did, no-you-didn't" badinage that goes on.

If you want a particular match to last longer, velcro more balls to the shirt. Place a ball in the axillary area if you want the duel to last beyond interest and tolerance. Use a permanent magic marker to make the white or gray T-shirt look like chain mail — it shouldn't take more than 4-5 hours.

**Frantic**

A good game has an easily identifiable aura of tradition; e.g., *Kick the Can, Stick Ball, Tip Cat,* etc. For a good game that just hasn't had enough time to be established, the most expeditious route to traditionalist acceptance is to develop and establish a vocabulary surrounding the game and its play. Remember: "knucks down," "ring-ring-a-levio," "alle-alle-in-free," "one patata-two patata..." etc., all important spoken parts of the games, essential to proper play, fun to mouth, and incrementally traditional. *No one* escaped from JAIL without having two feet inside the jail and shouting ALLE-ALLE-IN-FREE.

Here is a unique game that requires little skill, includes any amount of people and is 100% active. I don't think there is another game like it. The name of the game is *Frantic* and the object of play is for a group of any size to keep an equal number of assigned tennis balls moving about a gymnasium floor until six penalties have been indicated by the referee.

The vocabulary, which remember is the key to contemporary tradition, goes like this:

***Rabid Nugget*** — A moving tennis ball.

***Hectic*** — A stationary tennis ball.

***Berserk*** — A referee's scream, designating a penalty.

***Frenzy*** — An elapsed time period measuring six Berserks.

***Logic*** — A tennis ball that becomes lodged unintentionally on or behind something.

***Illogic*** — A tennis ball that is craftily stuck on or behind something.

***Paranoia*** — A player's feeling that the refs are picking on him/her.

*Rules and Use of Terminology:*

If thirty players are on the gym floor, thirty *Rabid Nuggets* are thrown, rolled or bounced simultaneously onto the floor by one of the refs. There are three refs; one at each end of the court and one off to the side at midcourt. It is the duty of the two refs on the floor to try and spot *Hectics* and to generate a hysterical scream (a *Berserk*) so that all will recognize a penalty. The group has five seconds to start a *Hectic* moving again or another full throated *Berserk* is issued. The *Berserking* ref must point condemningly at the *Hectic* until it is again provided impetus.

Every fifteen seconds after a start, the sideline ref puts an additional *Rabid Nugget* into play until the final *Berserk* has been recorded. The team is allowed six *Berserks*, at which juncture the ref on the sideline, who is responsible for timing this melee, jumps up and down waving his arms and yelling, "*STOP-STOP-STOP.*"

The team intent is to keep the *Rabid Nuggets* moving as long as possible before six *Berserks* have been recorded. This time span is called a *Frenzy*. After a *Frenzy*, ask the group to talk about and develop a strategy in order to keep the *Rabid Nuggets* moving for a longer span of time; i.e., increasing the duration of the *Frenzy*.

*Rule Refinements for Frantic Freaks:*

A rabid nugget must be kicked (only kicked) randomly or to another player. It may not be held underfoot and simply moved back and forth. This rule was recently included to counter the basically sneaky player who's always looking for a way around the rules in the guise of initiative.

If a rabid nugget becomes a logic or illogic, the ref must get the nugget back into motion. An illogic receives an immediate *Berserk*.

Official optic yellow USLTA tennis balls are not essential to active and satisfying play. You could probably have a bonzer game if everyone brought their own piece of Silly Putty.

There are no official time-outs except for double loss of contact lenses or sun stroke. Frostbite was considered, but it is possible to kick a nugget with numb toes, so continue play.

**Variations of the Game Frantic, Etc.**

In *BOT's* No. 1, I introduced a game called *Frantic* that involved keeping a bunch of old tennis balls (rabid nuggets) moving non-stop on a gym floor. Variations of the game are possible using other implements of play.

Try spinning hula hoops instead of keeping the nuggets moving. When a hoop stops spinning and comes to rest (like a spinning quarter on a desk top), that earns a BERSERK.

Use balloons for the game, one per student. A BERSERK results from letting a balloon touch the floor. (See *Balloon Frantic.*)

Speaking (I mean writing) of balloons, after a group is finished using a quantity of balloons, the best way to dispose of them (storing balloons doesn't work very well) is to put one between two people and have those two folks attempt to break it by squeezing their bods together. Or, for more fun and efficiency, put 2 or 3 balloons between a cluster of squeezers and listen for the muffled booms.

**Valloon**

Here's a game to follow up *Balloon Frantic*, particularly since there are so many balloons bouncing around, and it's too early (or inappropriate) to play *Fire in the Hole.*

Stretch a length of nylon cord (#4 cord is good because it's strong and stretches — also called parachute cord) across the gym at a height of about 7 feet — 5 feet for younger, smaller players.

Halve the group quickly (number and size of players shouldn't matter much), and ask them to stand on either side of the "net." Start with one inflated balloon per player.

*Object*

For a team to cause any five balloons to hit the floor on the opposite side of the string (net).

To start the game, ask each player to hit their balloon as high as possible over the net. As the game continues, add a new inflated balloon to the action at 30 second intervals.

*Rules:*

The rules are up to you and the players. Come on, I just made this up — now, it's your turn.

**Comet Balls**

Old socks, weighted with sand or rocks, have been thrown around by kids for years and years; I can even remember doing it. The New Games Foundation popularized this spontaneous fun by replacing the sand (which doubled as a weapon) with a Nerf ball and calling the centrifugal device a something-or-other — it's a whimsical name that I can't recall. (Did the old spinning sock have a name when you were a kid? I can't seem to remember ever calling it anything but a "rock sock"; a sobriquet that mothers and homeowners near my turf learned to hate.)

Recently, as part of a game Steve Butler and I have been working on called *Foes & Questors*, we "re-invented" the rock-sock as a sand-sock and called it the Mage's Mortar, a sand-filled sock thrown with a mortar's flight producing a devastating penalty if you are unfortunate enough to be within 10 feet of the point of impact. Admittedly, I'm getting off the original subject (I think), but the point is that these weighted socks are multi-use items that are great fun to experiment with, particularly in open areas.

Try playing catch with a weighted sock. Keep moving apart as you become more adept at throwing and catching. See which pair of throwers on a football field can move the farthest apart and still make a catch.

If you don't have any sand around for filling the sock, try slicing open a tennis ball (2" slit), then insert 2 ounces of heavy material (lead sinkers, nuts, smooth rocks). Then place the ball into a pantyhose leg (drawn and quartered). Pantyhose "rock socks" have greater aerodynamic qualities than regular athletic-type socks.

Don't catch the weighted end, but try and snatch the flapping tail; much more aesthetic and not nearly as painful. The first few tries at throwing for distance are usually wildly inaccurate, and dangerous if you are standing too near the thrower. A discus-like spin produces the farthest and most errant throws; some tosses heading straight up!

## Comet Ball Horseshoes

Use two hula hoops or inflated bicycle innertubes as targets and place them approximately 25 yards apart. Play regulation horseshoe rules using this suggested scoring system.

10 pts. — sock completely inside the tube or hoop

5 pts. — sock touching the tube or hoop

2 pts. — 6" away

1 pt. — sock hits or rolls through the hoop

6" or more away — Forget it!

## Ultimate Comet Ball

"Yep, you guessed it — right from the world of Wham-O." Rules duplicate those of Ultimate Frisbee. The behind-the-back shot is an absolute classic move with a weighted sock.

Before leaving the world of used socks and pantyhose, a couple suggestions: (1) If possible, use long socks (much better flight characteristics and centrifugal leverage. (2) Make sure the socks are one of a kind or well used, to maintain marital Wa. (3) Fill the socks with flour and have bludgeon-each-other contests (no head shots, please).

## Comet Ball Horseshoes Redux

Having played Comet Ball Horseshoes (*Silver Bullets,* pg. 25) a few times lately, I'd like to pass along a couple suggestions:

1. Have a Comet Ball (Rock Sock) for each player on one side so that there can be a team throw; i.e., all the players on one side throw simultaneously. This picks up the action of an otherwise ultra-laid-back game.

2. Change the scoring:

   10 pts. — sock completely within the circle

   5 pts. — sock touching the circle

   3 pts. — sock within 5 ft. of the circle

   2 pts. — sock hits within circle (first contact) and bounces out. This might combine with the 3 pt. score above, resulting in a 5 pt. throw.

3. Use pantyhose instead of socks — much better flight characteristics and less expensive. Colored (red, purple, green) knee-high's cost about $.80 the pair. Packages of 6 black mid-calf length hose cost just over a dollar — lots of action for a buck.

4. Slice open (2" slit) a tennis ball and insert some small, heavy objects (rocks, lead slugs) so that the total weight is about 2 ozs. Use this weighted ball inside the pantyhose as the object du aire.

5. Watch your head — and shoulders, neck, groin, etc.

## Comet Ball Miscellaneous

Three hundred foot throws are possible, as your technique improves.

- Don't bother tying a knot in the open end of the "sock" — it's not necessary, and the knot increases the air drag.
- Pantyhose material does not take well to asphalt landings, so try to keep your games on the grass.
- Flesh-colored pantyhose are not well received by your basic male adolescent. Buy a couple packages of the brightly colored knee high variety.

## Sardines

I was introduced to this hide-and-go-seek game by the participants in an adventure workshop in North Carolina. The game works best in an area that has lots of nooks and crannies (of ample size) to jam lots of bodies into. A gymnasium is not a good choice.

*The Game*

To maintain tradition, the person designated as IT in a hide-and-go-seek game should count to 100 with their eyes closed, while everyone runs to hide. In this Sardine variation, the IT person runs to hide and everyone else must try and find that person...97,98,99,100...anybody around my base is IT.

As the seeking folks wander about, poking into closets or behind trees, they should be aware that if they spot the IT person, they must join the IT in hiding by sharing the hiding place (thus the name Sardines).

The game continues until everyone has found everyone and the seekers become one group with IT.

This is *NOT* a game to build trust, as you must be fairly sneaky to join the IT without being seen by the other seekers. For example, "Sue, you go over behind the barn and I'll go this way" — knowing full well that "this way" is to join the hiding IT, while Sue seeks the wild goose.

I was recently perusing a book called *The Fun Encyclopedia* (copyright 1940), and noticed SARDINES listed in the index — same name, same rules. Sometimes I think that there aren't any new new games, just new old games.

## Off the Wall (Indoor Frisbee Game)

This atypical frisbee game (is there such a thing?) is an elitist variation of the old *GUTS* model. This is not a game for everyone, because considerable skill in throwing and catching a frisbee is required. But wait — let me offer the rules with dispatch before you skip this game and miss out on some off-the-wall-fun.

Arrange and disperse 6-8 people to each end of a vacant gym. As in the game *GUTS*, a frisbee is thrown back and forth with the attempt to make the other team miss (drop the frisbee). The major rule change here is that the frisbee may hit the back or side walls (or any other obstacle that can be aimed at; a backboard, for example).

*Further Rules:*

1. Ceiling shots result in a "no throw" — neither team adds or subtracts a point.
2. Short throws also result in a "no throw" situation.
3. The frisbee must approach the defenders between a 45 degree and horizontal level, or a "no throw" results.
4. Impossible-to-reach shots are judged individually and result in some memorable arguments.
5. Skip shots are allowed if the frisbee reaches the defenders at a minimum of knee height to the catchers.

6. Only one hand catches are allowed unless the decision of both teams is to make the game easier, and then two-hand catches are OK.

7. Tip or rebound catches (from player to player) are OK, and in a heated contest can be spectacular.

8. No "flying missile," knock-your-fingernails-off shots are allowed. Direct shots are acceptable, however; i.e., not off-the-wall.

9. A two-three or possibly four-point throw can be made, by hitting 2,3,4 (or more?) objects before the frisbee is dropped to the floor.

*Off The Wall* is a fine game for the talented frisbee thrower, but its drawbacks include:

1. At least a moderate skill level is required to enjoy the game.

2. Only a comparatively small number can play.

3. An entire gym is needed to play.

## Frisbee Shuffleboard

Since you have taken over the gym for a game of *Off The Wall*, try this subtle variation of shuffleboard.

As in shuffleboard or horseshoes, two players compete against two other players. The object is to throw your team's frisbees (3-5) into the key (circular) area at one end of the gym from the far end of the gym. Throwers stand just beyond the out-of-bounds line under the basketball backboard.

The basketball key area is divided into three smaller areas. The closest (and smaller) area is worth 3 points. The next area scores 2 points and the far area 1 point. If the frisbee is touching any line, no points are scored.

Smooth, low, gliding (on the floor) throws work best. With additional practice, it's possible to knock an opponent's frisbee out of a scoring area, or into one. Each team must use a different color frisbee to avoid confusion and wrestling matches. Try using "softies" (foldable frisbees) for this game.

## Balloons

Balloons are fun and cheap. Get some and try these games.

*Braaaaack-Whffff*

Everyone gets one balloon (I'll be writing the word balloon a lot, so let's have capital B stand for balloon). The B's should be purchased in as many different colors as possible; ecru, vermillion, puce, etc. Also, buy decent sized B's; the small penny B's don't remain aloft long enough or provide enough action for these games.

Ask everyone to stand inside the "key" at the end of a basketball court (or fabricate your own round boundary area), and blow up their B's just short of popping. (Have some spare B's available.) Don't tie off the B's neck, just hold on and get together with other folks who have the same color B as yours.

*The Contest*

One person representing each color lets go of their B, allowing it to jet willy-nilly about. Wherever it comes to rest, another team member of the same color advances to that point with their B filled and cocked and releases their rubber missile in an attempt to further their team's distance from the circle's perimeter.

This pattern continues until all the B's have been released. The team color champion is, of course, that final B which is the furthest from the circle. (Have a 50' tape measure on hand for disputed distances.)

There is practically no skill involved in this game, so no one seems to care who wins. The fun is in the doing.

## Booop

Blow up *one* of the balloons and tie off the neck. Ask your group of 3-4 people to join hands in a circle and try to keep the B aloft (off the floor) by batting the B with announced parts of their body, including hands, which must remain clasped. If the B touches the floor, the group loses use of their hands. As the B continues to eventually fall to the floor, keep removing parts of the anatomy that are allowed to strike the B; for example, elbows, shoulders, head, thigh, etc. The group that eventually loses use of their feet is out and can then recycle to any point of the game they choose. Watch for high kicks in a small circle!

## Fire in the Hole

It's time to put the B's away — permanently. You're going to like this! Divide into groups of 3-5 with your B's.

Place 3-5 B's between your 3-5 person group. Position the B's carefully at about mid-torso level. As in dealing with dynamite charges, it's the placement that counts. Then, put your arms about your partners' bodies and prepare to squeeze, BUT...before initiating any psycho-motor synapses, the group shouts together, "Fire in the hole" — that's to warm bystanders of the impending explosion(s). You don't need any further instructions after the squeeze starts. Try standing in a circle so that each person is facing the person's back in front of them. Have each person place an inflated B between her/him and that person — initiate a group squeeze.

If a particular B is giving your small group a problem, ask for help and other squeezers, I'm sure, will hurry over to add their contractions and emotion toward a final solution.

**Basic Killer**

*Object* — For an unknown killer to "kill" all the people involved in the game, before they discover who s/he is.

*Set-Up* — There are many ways to pick a killer, but the easiest and fastest is for the leader to ask everyone to close their eyes, and then walk briskly and obviously around and among the players, touching one of them on top of the head to indicate their sanguine role.

*Rules:*

To "kill," the killer must wink at a player. If the wink (not a blink) is recognized as the gift of eternal sleep, that player is dead and must histrionically die, ending up flailing about or shuddering on the floor/ground while emitting outrageous sounds of agony, outrage and defeat: This is not meant to be a subtle role. DO NOT die immediately after being killed. Give the killer a chance to move away by waiting 15-30 seconds until your terminal sequence begins.

As the group mills about the playing area, eyeing each other carefully (you must keep your eyes open), and when someone thinks they know who the killer is, they shout "J' accuse!" — or more domestically, "I accuse!" The accuser must be seconded by another player within ten seconds or the initial accuser is eliminated (bumped off) by the referee's (you) pearl-handled revolver.

However, if there is a second, you (the referee) say, "On the count of three, I want you both to point accusingly at the killer." If both players point at the same person and it is, indeed, the mass murderer — the game is over. If the accusers point at different people, you quickly reach for your revolver and polish off the two maladroits who have so crassly offended the group's sensibilities. The game continues until the killer is caught or until all the players have been killed; a feat worthy of applause and a couple rousing "good shows!"

*Variations*

1. Allow the killer to pass on the death knell by shaking hands and pressing the victim's wrist with an extended index finger. It is obviously not necessary to kill every time a hand is shaken. So then, here we go about the room enthusiastically shaking hands with everyone and looking frantically for the deadly digit. All the above rules for basic killer apply here also.

2. If the vibrations of all this noise and cascading bodies is distressing, try the following "nice" variation. Everyone in the group must go around the room whispering something nice to each player they encounter, except, of course, the killer, who will whisper something having to do with your demise. For example, "I sure like your knees," or "That blouse is outstanding," or "Your crew cut is _____."

The killer might say, "Here comes the kiss of death," or "Tomorrow you die," etc.

3. If the games are dragging a bit and you want to speed things up, introduce the plague variation.

Whenever a player is killed, s/he can (after waiting a few seconds to let the killer move on), take others players down with them by touching (the plague) someone as they fall to the floor. That infected player can then pass it on to another poor soul if they are slow enough to be caught. The dying person cannot run around the room tagging a series of people, nor can the initial person with the plague fall on the killer. If the killer carelessly gets caught in a plague sequence, then it's either fast-talking time or just keeping a low profile.

It always seems that everyone gets in on the fun of these games except you — so here's a way to pick the killer and join in the game yourself.

Everyone joins together in a cluster and puts one fist into the group center with a thumb sticking up. You announce (with everyone's eyes closed, including yours) that you are going to squeeze a person's thumb once. That person will then reach around all the extended thumbs (all eyes still closed) and squeeze someone else's thumb twice. The person with the double squeezed digit is the killer. Neat, huh?

Play *Killer* more than once to discover some of the subtleties and stratagems that make this game so popular.

## Miniature Monuments

The object is to build the smallest possible monument. The group that accomplishes this task within a reasonable time limit gets to knock down everyone else's cairn with a feather amidst shouts of huzzah and gnashing of teeth.

*Rules:*

1. Each team of three is offered a pair of tweezers and a magnifying glass to help with their engineering efforts.

2. Only three stones are allowed to be used in building the monument.

3. The monument can be built upon a piece of rock or wood only.

4. The decision of the judge(s) is final, unless the other teams complain a lot, in which case victory usually goes to the loudest and most obnoxious threesome.

5. The only penalty is for inadvertent blowing over of the monuments (or parts thereof) by sniffing or sneezing. The penalty is adding one stone to the total.

Official Miniature Monument T-shirts and matching shorts are de rigueur for regional meets and are well received by knowledgeable spectators.

**Trash Ball**

Divide your group into half and situate them on opposite sides of a volleyball net (fortunately, the playing dimensions of a volleyball court exactly duplicate the NCAA Trash Ball specs.). Offer each group an equal amount of *dry* trash. (There is a wet trash variation of this game called *Garbage Ball*, but permission slips from parents and custodians are required.) An example of dry trash is — wastepaper, cardboard boxes, light plastic, etc.

Make sure there is an ample amount of trash: trash equals action.

On the GO signal, each team tries to put their trash over the net. Do not set a time limit for the game, rather indicate that you will signal when the game is over. This unexpected signal prevents a team from collecting all the trash and throwing it all over seconds before the time limit.

The winner is, justly, that team with the least amount of trash within bounds on their side of the net. So that the teams won't suspect favoritism by the referee, the ref must write down on a sheet of paper the proposed time limit for each game.

This melee of random physical movements and laughter is a philosophical breakthrough in experiential education, ranking right up there with Mud Wrestling.

## *Parachute Possibilities*

**Shark**

There are innumerable games to try, using a cordless parachute and many of them are so simplistic as to be a bit tedious, but this one plucked my sense of humor and fantasy. It is of the touch-me/don't-touch-me, or humor/horror genre.

As a group, stand in a circle, holding the edges of the parachute (is there any other way?) and sit down on the gym floor, pulling the edges of the chute up to your waist with your legs underneath.

Appoint a person to act as the SHARK. This nefarious individual scoots under the chute and begins patrolling the confines of the chute's perimeter (the SHARK pool). When the shark spies a pair of feet that look delectable, s/he *grabs* those appendages and while alternately squeezing and relaxing their grip (chewing motion), they pull their victim under the chute to join them as a zombie shark. All this is accomplished amidst much screaming and thrashing about by the victim. These *two* sharks continue patrolling the pool, looking for more wiggling meat. Continue play until the last victim becomes the next shark.

Seeing a "shark" slowly approach your feet produces a surprisingly tense feeling. Being grabbed, finally, gives you a chance to release your anxiety by acting like a victim.

Indicate to your sharks that subtly cruising the pool adds considerably to the activity; i.e., don't grab every leg you pass by.

People with an uncontrollable foot fetish are subtly encouraged to play with themselves until this particular game is over.

### Parachute Tug-o-War

A parachute quickie that doesn't work if your chute has holes in it — the holes get bigger, fast...

If your chute is divided into colors, setting up the contest is easy. Reds against whites, or reds against yellows against whites, etc.

Whatever — simply have your group securely grasp the edge of the chute and pull with their "team" until one group pulls another group steadily in one direction. Watching the amount of tension applied to the rip-stop nylon and the stitches, gives an idea of how well made a parachute must be.

### Cat and Mouse

*Position* — Group kneels around the perimeter of a P and grasps the edge.

*Object* — For a mouse to stay hidden (uncaught) under the P, while a cat, crawling on top of the P, tries to pounce on the mouse. The group tries to help the mouse by rapidly shaking the folds of the P up and down. Such irregular wave-like motion gives the mouse some hiding space and is confusing for the cat. If your gym floor is dusty or dirty, this active sequence will fill every orifice and crevice you have with fine dust. Contact lens wearers beware!

### Where-Am-I?

*Position* - As in *Cat and Mouse*, except standing.

*Object* - For a blindfolded person, standing on top of and in the center of the P, to try and find the only path out of the P. The path is designated by one or two people holding their piece of the P's arc to the floor, while the other standing folks moderately flap their sections up and down.

Verbal sound effects of a violent storm add to the realism and make the task more challenging and fun.

### Boffer Bonkers

This simplistic, blatantly competitive game is one of the most aerobic and least serious one-on-one confrontations I know of. Bonkers can be played as teams, but the pure form is one balloon, two players. Action on a gym floor is most convenient because of the permanent boundary lines. Use the center line of a basketball court to place your well-inflated balloon (12" balloon works best — penny balloons don't provide enough action). Both players, armed with a boffer, back off to the next parallel line — I'm sure this line has a name, but you'll recognize it because it looks very much like the one that you put the balloon on. The playing area is designated by the distance from one back line to another.

Play begins with each player, kneeling on their back line, facing each other and ritualistically slamming their boffer against the floor three times in rhythm with the other player's similar efforts. On the third hit, both players rush forward and try to hit the balloon past their opponent's back line *so that the balloon hits the floor* beyond the line. An offensive player is not allowed to physically cross over their opponent's back line.

A point is scored when the balloon touches the floor.

Best two out of three is guaranteed to bring your heart rate up to 120 BPM, unless you have chosen a real maladroit as an opponent (or vice versa), in which case you must go best 7 out of 10.

*Aggression Bonkers* allows a player to cross over his/her opponent's back line. A point is then scored by either hitting the balloon to the floor (as before) or bouncing the balloon off the back wall. If you are playing on an outdoor basketball court, the back wall rule is waived — a winning shot in this case puts the balloon off the court; i.e., out of bounds.

If you wish to play Team Bonkers, simply supply more people with Boffers. Do not substitute 2' x 4's for regulation Boffers, because splinters may cause the balloons to burst. Am I kidding? Right!

Boffers can be purchased from most athletic supply catalogs. Save some $ and make your own from pieces of old gymnastic mat material called ETHAFOAM. Use 2" thick sections and cut the swords to any size that appeals. Don't substitute styrofoam for ethafoam — the former breaks easily and hurts when hit. Project Adventure sells ethafoam.

## Full House

This mini-bombardment game has been played during a number of adventure workshops with enthusiastic results. A large house or gymnasium is best suited for the fast-paced action, but a heavily wooded area has appeal, and in a pinch, I suspect an open field would be suitable, too.

You need a few articles of play — weapons, actually. For this, tinted (two colors) marshmallows work as a safe and tasty throwing implement for freezing (cryogenic suspension) your opponent.

Two equally numbered teams separate and go to opposite ends of a house, gym, field, etc. Each member is given 3 marshmallows of a particular color (red team - blue team) and instructed to try and get to the opposite side of the house, gym, field, to a designated SAFE area until their entire team is assembled there. The first team to get all their players into the SAFE area gets to eat their weapons (yuck!) or receive trophies. As the players are passing by each other, they can freeze an opposing team member by hitting them with a thrown marshmallow (anywhere below the neck). A suspended player must remain immobile for 30 seconds after being hit. Players may only collect and throw marshmallows of their team's color.

You can probably imagine the potential for fun as players run upstairs, through doors and zip down hallways, hotly pursuing one another with their gaily tinted *objects du guerre*.

Use blindfolds as headbands to differentiate team members. Remember, that's blindfolds as headbands, not vice-versa.

## Samurai & a Kamikaze Variation

The game, *Samurai*, is explained and pictured in the *More New Games* book, from the New Games Foundation, of California. The book may be purchased from Project Adventure.

The reason I mention the above is because Samurai has become a workshop favorite. In addition, a recent Project Adventure workshop group developed an embellishment to the game that is worth passing along.

There are a number of game success ingredients included in Samurai that almost guarantee acceptance and active participation by almost any group.

1. Rules can be quickly explained and easily understood.
2. Participants can unobtrusively remove themselves from the game, if they so desire.
3. Role-playing is encouraged and applauded.
4. Simple physical skills are used.
5. Satisfaction results from both participation and observing.

A bare-bones description of the basic game follows: (refer to the *More New Games* book for additional details)

Ask your group to form a circle around you — about 4' - 6' between people. Armed with a boffer (ideally) or any easily manipulated and innocuous sword-like weapon, the person in the center attempts to symbolically eliminate everyone in the circle with high or low slashes of their ersatz sword. These slashes are token strokes only; actual contact must be avoided or the players in the circle will either lose trust and disperse, or lose trust and retaliate.

If the Samurai (person with the sword) slashes high, each participant included within the arc of the stroke must duck or lose his/her head and be eliminated (falling to the ground). If the sweep of the sword is low, a hop must be made, or their legs are removed, as is the player. Mid-torso, belly button shots are not acceptable, as any certified Samurai knows. All of this martial manipulation is accompanied by inscrutable yells of the Samurai and groans of dismay and simulated agony of the players — a cacophony of oral action and reaction.

The last person to remain standing is the next Samurai.

After the basic game has been played a couple times, try the following variation.

As the game begins, place a second similar sword in the center of the circle. As the Samurai begins his/her circular sanguinary forays, anyone in the circle can try to grab the second sword (boffer) without being hit (actually hit) by the Samurai. Then, mouthing whatever challenge or oriental invective comes to mind, the two adversaries have at one another in a duel to the finish.

*Rules for the Duel:*

1. No slashing strokes allowed — only thrusts to the torso.
   This is a safety rule to protect a player's eyes.

2. A Win is achieved by touching your opponent, with the tip of the boffer, on the torso only — head and appendages do not count as a touche.

3. Do not use a rigid pretend sword (modified 2' x 4') for this duel.

If the Samurai wins, the challenger joins the other downed player and places his/her sword back in the center.

If the sword-snatcher wins, all the previously vanquished players stand up and return to the game and the new Samurai takes over against a full circle of players.

## Mirrors & Mortars

I think this game is unique. I have only tried pieces of it as parts of another game, but its potential is worth developing — the action and reactions are fast and well received. Here are the objects of play and an outline of game possibilities.

## Mirrors

These surrogate laser reflectors can vary in size from the small purse type, to as large as you can afford or attempt to carry. The mirror serves as a weapon. If reflected sunlight is seen by an opposing player, that player is frozen temporarily (movement from the immediate area is restricted for 2 minutes). A small mirror is easy to carry, but is hard to aim accurately. A larger mirror, say 10" x 12", reflects considerably more light and is easier to aim because of the more visible light beam. There is no doubt whether you have been zapped by a mirror; the reflected glint of the sun sets off a retinal alarm that's hard to ignore.

A pre-game joint decision that adds to the game's enjoyment is the agreement that all players hit by a light flash must punctuate their retinal trauma by falling down and simultaneously yelling, thus indicating to the light wielder that s/he has scored. Picking off a player from 200-300 yards is undeniably fun and strategically useful.

Various ploys can be used to counteract the flash. (1) Don't look at a person who is trying to flash you. (2) Wear a set of goggles (we call this prop, the *Goggles of RA*), that are somehow woven into the game to provide immunity from the mirror's devastation. (3) Try reflecting the sun back at the person initiating the flash: called the Quid Pro Quo Flash or QPQF (pronounced simply, Cue Pee), to knowledgeable players. (4) Try to maintain as much of a "downsun" position as possible. Be careful though, a large mirror is capable of reflecting *360 degrees*, depending upon the sun's position in the sky.

## Mortars (Second Weapon)

A mortar is represented by a long sock partially filled with sand or flour or a combination of the two (for weight and visual effect). Pour in about 2-3 oz. of fine, dry sand and tie off the top with an overhand knot to prevent spillage.

The sock mortar is used as a weapon by lofting it (like a mortar is projected) in a long parabolic ar. The rules concerning such a throw are: (a) The mortar, to be effective, must land within 10 feet of the opposing player. (b) The mortar must achieve at least a 10 ft. apogee (height) to be armed. (c) All players (including the thrower) within the 10 ft. diameter devastation zone are "frozen" for two minutes.

If the mortar's *tail* is caught during its descent by the proposed victim, the thrower and anyone within 10 ft. of him/her are frozen for **three** minutes.

Long-arcing throws (50 yds. or more) are possible by twirling (discus fashion) the sock before letting go.

Ultimately, there should be some definable reason for all this flashing and twirling; perhaps a team competition of sorts? Pattern it after the game, *Capture the Flag*, where each team seeks a particular object and must take the retrieved talisman to a winning area. To extend the length of the game, use two retrievable objects.

The obvious limitation to this game is the need for sunshine. A perfectly clear day is not necessary, however, because intermittent clouds add a different twist to the game; reducing the power of the light wielders. If it's an absolutely gray day — stay home; who needs it?

Admittedly, the above rules are not in logical order and the context is a bit shaky, but here's your chance to make up your own rules. We have used the socks and mirrors successfully as part of the game, *Foes & Questors*, so I know they work as "weapons": fun to use and fun to avoid.

## Tree Soccer

During an adventure curriculum workshop, a group of us got together before dinner to play a bit of soccer. Teams were quickly arranged, but no one could agree on how large the goals should be, or where they should be located. A suggestion was made to use two large trees as the goals. The trees were about 40 yds. apart on an otherwise open field. The object (scoring a goal) was simply to hit the tree trunk with the soccer ball; all other rules remained the same, with the following two exceptions. (1) There are no out-of-bounds. (2) After a score, the opposite team is allowed to make first contact with the ball from wherever it caroms after hitting the tree. Considering the above, it's apparent that there are no timeouts or stoppage of play — a very aerobic game.

## Forlies & Fodder

Forlies & Fodder is a physical bash meant to be played on a field covered with a minimum of 6" snow, or within the shallow water zone of a beach. The rules are few and studiously different. The game format faintly resembles rugby; the play resembles something else.

The object is to punch, strike or kick a ball through the opponent's goal (2 shirts on the ground, soccer net, football goal posts, 2 frisbees).

To begin, divide the group into two teams and request that each team choose a Forlie. Each team has one player, a Forlie, who acts as a combination forward and goalie. At the start, Forlies from opposing teams stand between the goal markers of their respective teams. Each Forlie holds a game ball (any acceptable object of play) and waits for the signal to begin.

The remainder of the group (both teams) line up along an imaginary marker that extends across the field of play. If you are playing on a football field, for example, use the 50 yard line. An unlimited number of people (Fodder) may play on each side, co-ed or otherwise. There are no boundaries and, therefore, play does not stop except for arguments, getting a drink, tying shoes, cooling off, warming up, and various pinney adjustments. Be strict about limiting timeouts.

Forlies stand ready and the Fodder is ready to go! Action begins as the Forlies sprint downfield, trying to score a goal by running the ball through the goal markers, while the remainder of the players either try to help or hinder their player.

*Rules:*

1. The Forlie is the only player who may pick up the ball and throw or run with it. A Forlie who chooses to run may be tackled (see #3 below). When tackled (no forward momentum or "in the grasp"), s/he must throw or release the ball without hesitation. A Forlie may play anywhere on the field and is the only player who wears a pinney (or some type of identifying marker).

2. The other players (Fodder) may forward the ball by kicking or striking it with any part of their body. Fodder may not pick up, catch, or throw the ball.

3. *Any* team member, at *any* time, may grab (and guide to the ground) *any* opposing player in order to impede their progress (a tackle). All tackles must be above the waist. The tackler is not allowed to hold onto or sit on the person tackled.

4. Points are scored as follows:
    a.  A Forlie runs the ball over the goal line. — 3 pts.
    b.  A Forlie passes the ball to a teammate over the goal
        line (which is the only time that a team player can
        catch the ball). — 2 pts.
    c.  Any player kicks or strikes the ball over the goal line.
        — 1 pt. The ball must pass through the field side of
        the goal.
5. After each goal (remember, there are 2 balls in play), the
    referee shouts out the point total and throws the ball
    immediately back onto the field (no timeout).

As soon as the ball is again in play, the teams switch goals; i.e., try to score
through what was previously their opponent's goal markers. At this juncture, a
Forlie may give up his/her pinney to another player on their team. This can be
done on either or both teams, and only after a goal has been scored.

Play continues uninterruptedly until the end of your time block or until the
players decide to collapse. Played with gusto, there will be no complaints about
being chilly or having to run in the cold snow.

*Considerations:*

Forlies & Fodder is not meant to be an everyday game and should be used only
when the snow or water conditions allow safe tackling. Played on a grass field
without protective gear, an unacceptable number of injuries will occur.

An alternate rule that results in higher scoring allows 2 Forlies per team. Forlies
may not pass to one another in order to score a goal, but may do so at any other
time. While running with the ball, Forlies may not fend off a tackler; i.e., no
straight arms.


**Off the Wall Team Ball**

This "full court" gymnasium game is a team variation of "Off The Wall,"
played with a frisbee.

The object of play can either be a 4" playground ball that is well-inflated, or
for more action off the walls, use a *large* "Super Ball." I prefer the 3" *Super
Ball* because of the crazy bounces and unpredictable spins that result from
a hard throw.

Divide your group in half (good games result from a one-on-one, oxygen-
debt confrontation, to about 10 on a side), and then blow your whistle and
clear the gym of any remaining round-ball riff-raff — you need the whole
floor and room space for this throw-bounce-catch game.

The team that's "up" stands at the end of the gym that provides the best far
wall to throw against; i.e., far wall and side wall that have the least objects
to break or deface. Standing behind one of those numerous and inscrutable
lines on a basketball floor (you choose whichever line you like, there's lots of
them and different colors, too), each member of the team individually takes

his/her turn of trying to throw the ball off the wall in order to score the most points. Awarded points are added after each throw, until all team members have had a turn, and a team point total is achieved. Then the teams switch ends and the catching team becomes the throwing team.

*How to Score:*

There have been many fascinating books written on this subject, so I'll just stick with the basics of how to record points.

The scoring object is for the thrower to ricochet the ball off as many surfaces (walls, backboards, moulding) as possible before the ball hits the floor. Ceiling shots are generally not allowed because of the delicate nature of drop ceilings or sound-proofing material. A point is scored for each surface hit IF the catching team fails to catch the ball before it hits the floor. Points are also added for each bounce on the floor before being caught. A good throw and poor catch might result in as many as 6 or more points. If the ball is caught directly off the wall (no floor contact), no points are scored for that throw, no matter how many surfaces were hit. For a lower scoring game, allow one floor bounce before the catch must be made.

Don't move floor mats or gymnastic apparatus, etc., from the field of play, as such obstacles lend themselves to innovative shot-taking, and a level of unpredictability that prevents skilled players from "playing the angles."

A word about play in gyms that have lots of windows — don't.

## Asteroids

An active offering of benign mayhem and a useful lead-up to the game *Ankle-Biters*.

Provide each player with a throwable object that they wouldn't mind being hit with: nerf balls or objects of that genre. I would not want to be hit with a tennis ball, red playground ball, soccer ball, or shot put.

Ask the group (from 10 to 100) to spread themselves out within a definable playing area — this game works best in a gymnasium, because of the built-in boundaries. At a signal, all players loft their "throwable" object in the air. Each person must then, with great dispatch, grab a thrown object (after it hits the floor and being sure that it is not their own), and using this as a weapon, try to hit someone — speed is essential, because everyone is trying to do the same thing.

If you are hit, sit down — you're out. Continue playing until only one player is left, and then start another round before the champion has a chance to gain a breath — usually ensuring that a champion does not repeat or get a chance to repeat.

*Considerations:*

- A player may gather as many throwable objects as he/she wishes, but must drop them immediately when hit.

- Large balls may be hand-held by a player to serve as a deflector of other thrown objects.
- Balls may not be caught.
- This is a self-elimination game; i.e., if a player feels threatened by the game or just doesn't want to play, he/she can simply sit down and remove themselves unselfconsciously from the action.

If you would like the action to continue longer, refer to *Ankle-Biters*, or require multiple hits for elimination.

## Ankle-Biters

The above title is a change from the original name, *Gremlins*, that I received initially from the folks at the Renbrook School in West Hartford, Connecticut. As with all games, change the name(s) if it doesn't suit you. Historically, there has been a noticeable lack of creativity in naming our most popular (national) games — baseball, basketball, football; descriptive, but...How about Batsball, Stick-Whacker, Pitch Stick, Hoop-Stuffer, Peachy Dribble, Dance Hall Ball, Smooch Ball, Bust Ass Bash?...Back to biting ankles.

Each player (warrior) is issued a foam sword and three lives. The object of the game action is to become the last player remaining as a warrior.

Each player tries to eliminate the other players by hitting them (no head shots) with a foam sword: each hit subtracts a life. After being hit three times (being whacked three times in succession by the same adversary is unchivalrous and illegal), the afflicted warrior immediately loses his/her sword and metamorphoses into an Ankle-Biter. In this new role, the downed player loses use of his/her legs and must assume a kneeling-on-the-turf position. An Ankle-Biter may pivot from this position off either foot, but such restricted mobility is the limit of lateral movement allowed.

From this demoted status and position, the angry, alienated Ankle-Biters may fight back against the warriors by attempting to grab their ankles if a sword-wielder is unwise enough to step within the pivotal area of one or more Ankle-Biters. Having an Ankle-Biter or two tightly gripping a leg causes a noticeable restriction of mobility with resultant decrease in sword-fighting efficiency.

Play continues until all the warriors, save one, have metamorphosed into Ankle-Biters. Restrict the play area for more action. A wrestling room presents an ideal "field du combat." A grassy field is also well received, except by the person responsible for getting out Ankle-Biter grass stains.

If your budget cannot handle supplying that many swords (hey, everybody can't play polo...), give each player a softie (flexible frisbee) or a nerf ball to use as a "soft-war" weapon: 2' x 4' s are not suitable surrogate swords. These items must be thrown to effect a hit (head shots are still illegal), therefore, each item is commonly owned ordnance and can be used by any still active warrior. Ankle-Biters, as self-professed pacifists, shun weapons of any kind and would not tolerate their use within the ranks. Although Ankle-Biters share a common physiological affliction, they are extremely territorial and ethnically chauvinistic; truly a formidable character. The ankle grip of a mature male Ankle-Biter has been compared to the leverage torque developed by the Jaws-of-Life (an auto extrication tool) — awesome!

The game plan above was written over two years ago and since that time, Ankle-Biters has changed a bit. It has become the most well received active game used in a workshop setting. The rules are basically the same, but the nerf (fleece) ball has replaced the sword. Some new rules:

- When hit by a fleece ball, you must drop to one knee and randomly throw however many balls you have in your possession. The thrown balls must travel beyond your pivotal reach.
- At this juncture, you can either (1) become an ankle-biter, or (2) wait for a ball to roll within reach and get back into the action.

There is literally no end to this game and I sense that this fact, plus the rapidly changing player roles is what makes *Ankle-Biters* such a popular activity.

### Aerobic Tag Revisited — Results in Hooper

Aerobic Tag provides a non-pareil, cold morning warm-up activity. In order to explain a new variation of Aerobic Tag called *Hooper*, I'm including a brief recounting of the rules from an earlier BOT's issue.

### Aerobic Tag

1. Teams of equal number (also try for skill, size, sex split...good luck) are needed and players must be easily distinguished by the timekeeper — use pinneys; light shirts/dark shirts; pants rolled up or down, etc.

2. The object is to maintain team possession of a play object (frisbee, softie, nerf ball) for 30 seconds (depending upon the interest and physical level of the players).

3. Players may run with the object, but if tagged by a player on the opposite team, they must release the object within one second or risk losing a point to the other team.

4. A point is scored if a team keeps possession of the play object for 30-60 seconds. If the play object is on the ground, it is still in possession of the last team that touched it.

5. Play begins again, after the score, when the timekeeper throws the play object straight up.

As a result of having played this game over the years and having recently discovered that using rubber deck tennis hoops as the play object on windy days is best (frisbees always end up blowing out of bounds), the game *Hooper* evolved, and it's a winner.

## Hooper

You need a rubber deck tennis ring and four hula hoops as props for this game. Rules of play for Hooper are identical to Aerobic Tag with these exceptions and additions:

1. The four hula hoops are placed on the field of play to form the corners of an imaginary square. They should be at least 20 yards away from one another.

2. A team has to keep possession of a rubber ring for 15 seconds, at which juncture the timekeeper yells, "HOOP."

3. To score a point, a player whose team has maintained possession for 15 seconds and hears HOOP, must place him/herself inside one of the hula hoops and catch the rubber ring by having it actually "ring" his/her hand. This catch is most easily accomplished by bringing all the fingers of the hand together and overlapped (not the thumb) to form a "spear."

4. Both feet must be inside the hoop for the point to count.

5. If two players both grab the rubber ring during play, the timekeeper yells, "RELEASE," and one of the players immediately throw the ring as high as possible overhead.

6. Some boundaries are necessary to prevent cross-country runners from dominating play, but keep the lines far enough apart to allow unrestricted running.

*Hooper* combines the aerobic value of a tag game with the skill and strategy necessary to play position and make a difficult catch. This is a three-star game — take the time to wade through the words and give it a try. Refer to the game *Uno-Dos-Tres* for another aerobic tag variation.

## All Catch

Group stands in jump circle in center of gym. Group numbers about 25 and holds 10 balls. When instructor calls, "Throw," all release the balls (volleyball type) up to a height of at least 10 feet. If you throw a ball, you cannot catch a ball. Throws are made only on command. Only catchers have to be in the circle. If a ball touches the floor, it is out of play. When three balls are left, the game is over. Count the number of catches made to establish a score.

## Add-on-Tag

The object of this duo running game is for one IT pair to catch another pair and become a catching quartet (hands joined to form a line) and catch another pair to become a sextet, etc. Only the two people at the end of the line are allowed to tag a fleeing pair (one hand anywhere...well, almost anywhere). If the line breaks at any point, a catch is disallowed. This catching sequence continues until only one fleeing pair is left and, as undisputed champions of speed and chicanery, become exempt from further chase and harassment.

To prevent injury, do not allow pairs to run through or under the catching line. Restrict the playing area so that the game is active, but not so small that the catching line becomes an unbeatable seine. In the past, I have set up three fixed boundary lines and left the fourth boundary to be an imaginary line marked by my extended arm presence. This allows a comparatively small play area to begin with (when it's hard for a single pair to catch another pair), and an incrementally growing area, as I occasionally and unobtrusively shuffle a few feet back. The students are so much into the game that no one notices my gradual extension of the boundaries. I haven't been caught yet!

## Hoo Sow

I am reminded again by this action classic that there is a wealth of games and stunts still used (and unrecorded) by young people who don't know how innovative they are or how much fun they are having (or care; fun being an end in itself).

This type of spontaneous tradition reminds me of a two year growing up stint I spent in the hot-top/vacant lot environment of Staten Island, New York — a veritable testing ground for how-do-we-entertain-ourselves-now? ideas. City streets and vacant lots provide the blank canvas for spontaneous and creative action artistry that should be prerequisite training for all those who aspire to teach in the fields of physical education and recreation.

Back in the BD (before drugs) and PTV (pre-TV) days, Saturday and Sunday entertainment (free time), other than imaginative forays into radio, were spent playing traditional low cost games (stick ball, SPUD, King Rock), and making up equally low cost games that were constantly being amended and added to until a general acceptance of play was reached.

These "street" games were generally disliked by adults and so much the better; a condescending and organizational parent (usually male) was a sure-fire game snuffer, as their interests were overly oriented to skills and scores and how well **their** kid was doing.

Hoo Sow was reported to me by Tom Ness of Blue Diamond Camp in Pennsylvania. His enthusiasm in recounting the game strategy made up for my initial confusion with the rules. Tom also, being convinced of Hoo Sow's potential for fun, encouraged us (workshop group) to try a round and even supplied the basic props. You will need: 6-12 wooden dowels (broom handles to branches), depending on the number of players and a non-aluminum tin can (a condensed milk can works well) — aluminum cans are too easily dented (remember when it used to be a sign of strength to bend a beer can in half or even more impressively, *with one hand*?) I'm really into nostalgia with this piece.

The contesting area can be either dirt or hot-top (hot-top is the New England name for asphalt or tarmac). Dirt is the more traditional play area and lends itself more to enjoyment by dirt-bound youngsters. "In a cloud of dirt" is a descriptive phrase for Hoo Sow game action. If asphalt is chosen or is used of necessity, chalk is needed to outline play parameters.

*Setting Up the Play Area* - Lightly mark out a circle (diameter varies as to the number of players, but should be large enough to allow 5-6 feet between players distributed around the circumference). Dig a shallow hole in the dirt so that there is one hole per player (less one) and equally distributed around the circle's circumference. This hole is by no means neatly dug or of any required depth or diameter — just slam your heel into the ground a few times. An additional and larger hole (wider and deeper) is dug directly in the center of the circle.

Each player in the circle, holding onto one end of their 5' stick or dowel, places the other end in a hole; one player per hole, except for the IT. The IT player also has a stick and control (fleeting as it may be ) of the can. The ongoing object is for the IT to try and get his/her stick end into one of the other player's dug holes (recognizing that two sticks cannot occupy the same hole and proprietary ownership is absolute for that person whose stick end is there first). The ability to stick-the-hole is gamely called stickmanship or stickwomanship, depending upon the sticker.

Knowing that if you remove your stick from the hole, someone may "stick-your-hole," why move? Because the IT person tries to maneuver the can (via the stick only) into the center hole, and if successful, yells with gusto, "HOO SOW!" Everyone is then obligated, by game tenets so ancient that to question them is tantamount to admitting your age, to move their stick from one hole to another. During this obligatory change, the IT is, of course, looking for an empty hole. If he/she sticks-a-hole, the odd person then becomes IT.

Although what I have already related results in considerable action, the real melee begins as players try to whack the IT's tin can as far from the circle as possible. To do this, a player must temporarily abandon their hole — the results are vacantly obvious.

*Considerations:*

Active play can result in skinned knuckles and battered shins. To dedicated Hoo Sowers, such superficial slow-downs are of minor import; to parents and suit-conscious teachers, the use of alternate playing implements might be of interest. Use foam swords as sticks and rubber deck tennis rings as holes. Since the rings will have a tendency to move, include a rule that requires only having the rings inside the circle and not strictly on the circumference.

*Only if you're interested* - The name Hoo Sow comes from the esoteric art of pig-calling; accenting the word Hoo and extending the O sound. This game was originally played by boys and girls whose fathers had taken them to market to sell the family pigs at auction. Finding the economics of pig sales less than engrossing, gaming began and a name was chosen that copied an often-heard, adult-used, and fun-to-duplicate sound.

## Night Exercises

If students are spending the night away from home at an outdoor education center or retreat and the evening hours are warm enough to support some nocturnal activity at your site, try these four feel-comfortable-with-the-dark games. Don't limit these activities to just elementary-aged folks — I've experienced excellent results (positive feedback: "Hey, that was fun..." comments) from adults in adventure curriculum workshops.

## Commandant

The object of the first game is for one person (The Commandant) to keep all the rest of the players from making it back to home base in the dark. You will need one powerful flashlight and a portable home base. The portable home base isn't necessary, but it allows some flexibility in choosing game sites. An automobile makes a good home base. The field area that you choose for play should be free of rocks and stakes and whatever else could put holes and dents in people.

The Commandant stands at home base and counts to 50 slowly, while the rest of the players scatter to begin their nocturnal scamper back to home base, hopefully unseen. Each player must physically touch two large announced objects (trees, cabin) out in the field of play before they are allowed to try and get back to home base. These two objects must be in the Commandant's field of vision and at opposite ends of the field (at least 90 degrees apart).

The Commandant may either stay near the base or roam far afield in order to try to catch someone. A catch is made if the Commandant spots someone and can call their name. At the initial stages of the game, a name must be used. Toward the end of the game, as people are dashing toward home base, simply hitting a player with the light is enough for a "catch." A successful player, upon touching the home base, yells, "FREE." A caught player walks back to home base, and shares humorous insights about nocturnal bushwhacking with the previously-caught players already there.

The first person to make it back FREE is the next Commandant, if the game is to be played again.

*Considerations:*

Certain chances are being taken by playing this fast-moving game in the dark. Players move quickly, with severely reduced vision, and although a certain amount of retinal adaptation takes place (night vision: a good teaching topic for an outdoor education center), there is still the chance that someone can trip and fall over or onto things that shouldn't be there, or run into unseen branches, etc. If you know the area (to be played in) well, the chances for injury are probably minimal, otherwise I'd have to recommend against this game.

The chance-taking on your part, as sponsor, group leader, etc., is the responsibility that you have as the decision-maker. Can this game be played safely within the parameters of the players' maturity level, the physical geography of the area, and whatever Murphy-like laws control each 24 hours?

## Whooo?

Another nighttime acclimatization game which allows a player to travel and/or hide alone in the dark without having to be very far from other players or home base...

Ask for six volunteers to be hiders (ersatz owls, if you will). The number of hiders will vary as to the size of your group. Six hiders is sufficient for about 15 seekers. These folks hide in whatever wooded area avails itself in your camp area, recreation center, etc. The hiders try to pick a spot that allows their clothing to blend into the dark and shades of gray.

Each hider takes about a dozen identically numbered pieces of small paper with them, and heads for their chosen hiding spot. Giving the hiders a few minutes to situate themselves, the seekers begin their individual search.

Each hider has the option to make a characteristic sound occasionally in order to help the searchers, particularly if no one is even getting warm (cold, warm, warmer, etc. — you know!). This compassionate rule is included to not only help the seekers, but gives the hider a role other than just hiding.

When a seeker actually makes contact with a hider, the found body soundlessly hands a numbered piece of paper to the discoverer. When a seeker has collected a predetermined number of slips or a particular numbered sequence, he/she can retire from the game and either watch the proceedings or try to confuse things with animal calls of their own.

The game helps younger players get used to the dark, and affords an engrossing evening activity that appeals to all ages.

No flashlights allowed. Make sure the hiders are well dressed if the temperature is cool. Sitting motionless in one place for a period of time is a good reminder (or lesson) of how physical activity helps to maintain body warmth.

## Izzat You?

A nocturnal hunt that sometimes shows things and people as they aren't. In an outdoor setting, split your group in half. Ask which group would like to be the outdoor hiders first. Take that chosen or volunteer half outside to a well-known or established trail, not far from the main cabin or building. The area along the trail should be partly cleared; i.e., not dense undergrowth. Visibility should be such that no street lamps or building lights can be seen.

Talk to the hiding group about how motionless objects (people) in the dark can take on other forms that appear to be rocks, stumps, logs. Indicate that as hiders they will want to cover all parts of their body that stand out (white skin or clothing), and camouflage body parts so that they blend into the surroundings. Then begin hiding members of the group along the trail, following these rules and guidelines.

Hide people individually unless there is reluctance to stay alone, and then, allow a pair to hide together.

A hider must be in a partially exposed position. Completely concealing a person behind something is not allowed. Try to blend the hider with the natural surroundings; a rock, tree stump, etc. A hider must be no more than 20 feet away from the trail.

The seekers wait patiently in the building until the leader of the hiding group comes back and announces that all is ready. Guidelines for seekers are as follows:

1. The object of the game is to find as many of the hiders as possible.
2. Point scores are kept for each team.
3. The seekers are taken to the trail head and told that from here on, they can expect to find hidden people on each side of the trail.
4. *The seekers may not leave the trail.*
5. When someone thinks they have spotted a hider, they call others over to have a look. If the consensus (vote?) is that there is actually someone there, the attending instructor shines his/her flashlight *directly* at the spot indicated by the seekers. If a hider is revealed, the seekers get a point. If there is no one there, the hiders get a point.
6. If all the seekers pass a hider on the trail, the instructor will call the group back and point out the hider with a flashlight. The hiders then get a point, and that particular hider can join the group and silently cheer on his/her group.

This procedure continues down the trail until the last hider has been found or is revealed. Points are added up to establish a nocturnal champion. The teams then reverse roles and the game is played again.

The reason that the seekers remain indoors until the hiders are set, is to show what a difference retinal adaptation (night vision) makes toward safe walking in the dark. In an outdoor education setting, this exercise is a natural lead into a discussion about the adaptations that nocturnal animals make toward existence in a reduced light environment: Mention bats, owls, cats.

I have personally led this game many times and can attest to its popularity. There is something exciting about being hidden only a few feet away from many probing eyes and remaining uncaught. Many of the hiders report that they heard strange noises as they waited silently for the seekers to reach their hopefully hidden area.

Do not allow any flashlights to be carried, except those held by an instructor.

## Mission Impossible

Finding a nighttime game that is fun, non-threatening, and safe is not an easy task. This active game (capture-the-flag genre) was suggested recently as a fun-for-all-ages, after-hours contest.

*Object* - For a team to find hidden papers (secret documents that outline plans which are of global significance) and return them to a home base without being caught.

*Game Set-Up*

Divide the playing area into three or four distinct sections. These sections should be well defined by a fence, hedge, road, etc. An instructor hides the documents (make up a manila folder that looks official) in some outdoor portion of one sector, making sure that some part of the folder can be easily seen.

Each player is told to bring a flashlight or is supplied with one. Without fail, everyone at summer camp has at least one flashlight. (Have you noticed the recent American fascination with expensive flashlights that's evidenced by exotic catalog ads that claim wondrous and amazing things for devices that supply portable light? Miniaturization; lithium batteries, high-tech bulbs, waterproof to 600', case and compass included. I even read about one recently that fires tear gas toward the area it illuminates — what every camper needs, at only $37.95.)

The two teams must establish their own home base from which to operate, and as a goal area. A home base can be located in any of the sectors. The situation that makes this game different from other similar games is that no one knows in which sector the papers are hidden, so that offense and defense from both teams must infiltrate all areas to look for the papers and prevent them (once found) from being brought back to a safe haven; i.e., home base — game's over!

The flashlight is each player's weapon. If a player is hit by a light flash, she/he must return to home base before starting their quest again. Considering this "flash" ability and the necessary wide dispersal of players, the chance for an exciting finale is evident.

As a safety consideration, don't include any playing area that has picket-like stakes protruding from the ground or neck-level rope or cable hazards.

Thanks to Donna Bayliff, a teacher at the Fox Lane Middle School in Bedford, New York, for this nocturnal game idea.

**Frog Wars**

For this game(s), you need:

1. Spot markers - 9" diameter rubber or plastic gym markers. Enough for 1/2 of the players.
2. Fleece balls (tennis size) for at least 1/2 of the players, plus a few extra.

These items (and many other game goodies) can be obtained from Project Adventure, Inc., P.O. Box 100, Hamilton, MA 01936 (508) 468-7204. A free catalog is available.

Want to know how to play the game(s) before reducing your equipment budget? Good idea.

Hand out spot markers (henceforth referred to as lily pads, which is obviously what they were meant to be), to half the group. This lily pad group designates a team, and the players are called "Rana Pipiens" (RP's) — a rather common greenish amphibian with great jumping ability.

The other team is assigned as many fleece balls as you have to hand out. DO NOT substitute tennis balls for fleece balls: they hurt. The members of this fleece ball armed team represent Rana Pipien's greatest predator, the pre-pubescent male (PPM).

*Object* - For the frogs (RP's) to move their entire herd the length of a basketball court (timed effort) while the pre-pubescent males (PPM's) attempt to prevent this movement. Teams change roles after an attempt and then compare times.

*Procedures & Rules*

1. RP's move by flipping their lily pad forward onto the gym floor and double foot hop onto the pad. The lily pad throw must be at least 3' minimum. Any length throw beyond the minimum is accepted, but increases the frog's vulnerability.
2. A player is safe from being hit while standing on a pad, or with a pad in hand.
3. A player can be hit by a thrown fleece ball while hopping, in which case they must return 1/2 the distance to the starting point and begin hopping along again.
4. When a player reaches his/her goal (far end of the gym), they achieve *super frog* status and may return to the lily pond (double-footed hops continue to be de rigueur) to aid their frantically hopping cousins. Super frogs are immune to fleece ball strikes, so they may try to shield their more vulnerable green friends in transit until all RP's have completed their journey — stop the clock.

5. PPM's must throw from behind the black out-of-bound lines that parallel the basketball court, in fact, which delineate the court itself.

6. Fleece balls may be retrieved by any PPM from any place on the court, then refer to #5.

7. Optional - If a super RP catches a fleece ball, that ball is removed from the game.

*Game #2*

Same basic rules as above, except whenever an RP is hit, the PPM thrower takes the frog's place on the lily pad and reverses hopping direction; i.e., moves to the opposite end of the gym.

The starting position for this game is mid-court.

If you need an active game that rarely ends, this variation of Frog Wars is just the thing. Lots of throwing, nebulous and transitory team affiliation, a modicum of confusion, and loads of random action.

**Lily Pad Soccer**

Remember the lily pads (rubber gym spots) that you used in *Frog Wars*? Get 'em out again for a fast pinball-like game of indoor soccer. If you want a fast game with NO body contact, here it is:

Two teams — two balls. If possible, use the new fuzzy indoor soccer balls or even an appropriate sized NERF soccer ball. Or, use a red play ball or beach ball or Earth Ball, or whatever you want.

Each person gets a lily pad and can pick whatever location on the gym floor that suits them, but once situated, they cannot move except to pivot on the foot that is planted on the lily pad.

Two balls (no team/ball affiliation) are constantly in play, so even if a goal is scored, action continues. The goal ball is simply thrown back onto the gym floor. If a ball comes to a stop between players, give it a lateral (not toward a goal) kick.

Soccer rules are somewhat followed; if you want to.

**Count Down**

This simple activity combines action, anxiety, team effort and humor with a minimum of explanation and props.

Ask a group of 10-30 to form a circle so that everyone is eventually facing front-to-back, as if you were going to do a Lap Sit. Give a fully inflated balloon to a designated captain and explain that the balloon is to pass through everyone's legs (front to back or back to front, their choice) until the circle is completed. Each person is allowed one-half second for the passage between their legs. If there are 20 people in the group, to be successful the group must complete the circle in 10 seconds (in this case). Blow an airhorn or sound some other raucous noise-maker to indicate that the group has been engulfed in asbestos-impregnated Fluff or whatever inventive disaster comes to mind. If a balloon breaks, the full disaster is immediately experienced.

If you have just finished playing *Balloon Frantic* so that there are enough balloons for each person, try the same through-the-legs game with this variation. Each person starts with a balloon marked with their initials (felt-tipped marker). The game ends (same timing system) when each player gets their own balloon back. Try a double rotation or clockwise one way and counter the other.

Since everyone now has a personalized balloon, ask them to take care of that balloon over the next few hours (or days) to see whose air container has the most staying power. Use 4" diameter of remaining balloon to establish a terminal criteria.

Such a long-term inoffensive imposition can result in helping to maintain contact between group members beyond their initial get-to-know-you activities. Especially effective in a camp or retreat setting when a group will be together for an extended period.

Make a big deal about daily balloon checks, making humorous inferences about sizes, hot air, wrinkles, staying power, etc.


**Predator & Prey**

A field game for the younger student (grades 4-7) that requires no props, and which is particularly useful in an outdoor education setting.

*Object*

For a chosen student (predator) to visually "kill" all the rest of the players (prey) by calling out their names and where they are hidden. The killed prey then joins the predator and attempts to capture still hidden prey. Captured prey may not call out names until the word FLUSH has been called. (See FLUSH rule.)

*Rules & Procedures:*

The initial predator is a volunteer or is chosen in whatever way you think is appropriate.

The predator stands on an elevated area — small hill, back of a pick-up truck, etc.

The predator is not allowed to leave the assigned area.

The prey is given one minute to hide in a place that allows them to see the predator; i.e., not 100% concealed.

The predator may, at any time, say FLUSH, at which time all the remaining prey *must* leaving their hiding places, advance a brief distance toward the predator, and rehide. After saying "FLUSH," the prey has 20 seconds to rehide. All predators must close their eyes or put on blindfolds during this 20 seconds.

The game continues until all the players have become predators except one, who is designated an endangered species and becomes the initial predator for the next game.

Be sure to play the game in an area that allows many and varied hiding places.

## Italian Golf

I've had a lot of fun with this throw and catch game, punctuated as it is with upward cultural thrusts of manual emotion. If that verbal mishmash doesn't make any sense, refer to the expressive catching position (soon to be detailed), and its reference to an emotional Italian hand and arm gesture.

The hidden agenda of Italian Golf is to offer a game that teaches by example the rules, vocabulary and etiquette of actual golf combined with a format that is low key and enjoyable enough to encourage 100% participation.

You will need about a dozen rubber deck tennis rings. These soft rings are obtainable from various physical education equipment catalog suppliers and from Project Adventure, Inc. As far as I know, deck tennis rings are used on the deck of a ship to play a game that resembles tennis, when hitting tennis balls off the court (into the ocean) doesn't make economical sense. The rings are soft, but substantial enough to allow a good long throw. People seem to like holding and throwing the rings, just for the sake of doing it — I suspect dogs would like them, too.

### The Game

Break up into small groups of 2, 3, or 4. Four players together designates the classic golf FOURSOME. As you stand where you are, look around and try to envision a playable GOLF HOLE — something in the 100-300 yd. category with perhaps a DOG LEG and a couple obstacles (tree, pond, car). Declare "This HOLE looks like a PAR 8," or however many throws you think it will take your team to HOLE OUT. The first person in your group to DRIVE (throw a ring) gets set on the established TEE and throws to another person in the foursome that has assumed a catching position some distance toward the HOLE (final destination).

To legally catch the rubber ring, the catcher must extend a hand (palm toward face) upward with fingers and thumb held together so that the incoming ring will encircle the hand and pass over the wrist to the forearm. Anything less is a miss, and the STROKE (throw) must be taken again. Once the catcher establishes a position, that person must return to his initial position, at which point the next thrower in the foursome sequence takes over at the point of the last miss, and play continues. Each throw is counted as a STROKE.

The foursome continues throwing and catching in sequence until the "HOLE" is reached. The SCORE is recorded on the SCORE CARD, then the next hole is conceptualized and attempted.

Spend some time letting the players throw and catch before the game is explained. The throw/catch is an enjoyable preliminary to the game and gives the players a better idea of how far they can throw accurately and also how well they can't catch.

Be inventive in establishing holes, taking advantage of natural WATER HAZARDS, and other OUT OF BOUNDS obstacles. Particularly intense HOLES include brief sojourns into and out of buildings.

Keep score over a series of HOLES so that FOURSOMES can compete against one another. If two foursomes are playing a hole one after another, golf vocabulary that fits the occasion includes: PLAY THROUGH: LET OUT SOME SHAFT: NEVER UP, NEVER IN: BIRDIE-EAGLE (or more likely DOUBLE BOGEY): NICE HIT: HOW MANY DO YOU LIE?

Have you figured out the Italian connection? Hold up your hand, palm facing you, in the approved finger together catching position. Shake your hand and arm up and down vertically in this position 3 or 4 times to alert your thrower that you are ready. Get it? Maybe you have to be there.

## Butt Off (or, THE Wave)

Everybody needs a chair. Flimsy chairs do not work well for this highly active game that involves moving your posterior rapidly from one chair to another.

Sit in a circle with the chairs fairly close together. Designate (ask for a volunteer— maybe you) a person to leave his/her chair empty and stand within the circle of seated bodies. As soon as the IT person moves toward an empty chair, it must be filled by the person sitting next to the chair that will result in a clockwise movement of people. As one person moves, the next person must be in motion, etc., etc., in order to fill the rapidly vacating seat sequence. When this game gets moving, the rapid seat changing results in a flow of people that looks impossibly choreographed.

When the IT person finally gets his/her posterior into the appearing/disappearing empty chair, the inevitable displaced person must immediately look for and pursue the elusive empty chair: there are no timeouts.

Change directions (from clockwise to counterclockwise) occasionally in order to confuse and confound a floundering IT — you'll know when. Play until quivering quadriceps plead for relief (or you run out of replacement chairs). This is one of those games that has to be played to appreciate the potential for (1) fast, physical action (2) unself-conscious touch (3) copious laughter and a sense of posterior abandon that borders on chaos. Get into it.

## Foes & Questors

F&Q — the game has been around for years, ever since Steve Butler and I first introduced players into the otherworld of Ords, Bolds, Mages, and Omnis. F&Q has since then been played in and on beaches, woods, gymnasiums, office buildings, and even open fields by enthusiastic semi-adults (not meant as a slight), who find that an occasional quest beyond their day-to-day persona is exhilarating, revealing, cathartic and even fun.

I have never attempted to include the rules to F&Q in this quarterly for a couple of reasons. (1) The rules are too numerous and somewhat convoluted, resulting in the potential use of many pages for explicit explanation. If you like the game, that's great, but I don't feel justified inundating some readers with fantasy overflow. Pat, pat, pat — what a sensitive guy. (2) F&Q is a wondrously unique game and is apt not to be soon duplicated in its inventiveness, enjoyable complexity, range of characters, and player compatibility. Further, it is wholly the product of Steve's and my imagination, and I feel it's unethical to detail a jointly owned game in a publication that belongs to only one of the originators.

F&Q is played regularly at various sites in Massachusetts by fantasy-oriented folks looking for a weekend workout. Write to Box 77, Hamilton, MA 01936, for the next game date and location. Participation is free. Bring your camera, because what you see and do is almost unexplainable.

## Striker

Remember when you were first learning to play soccer? "No hands, use your feet...phweeet...penalty — hand ball. Come on, kid, use your feet."

Are you kidding? I've spent every adolescent waking physical hour (except in glandular timeouts) learning how to throw, catch and smack balls of various types, and now my hands are appendages-non-grata.

Here's a game that offers relief from the foot fetish aficionados, called *Striker*, and you are *not allowed* to kick the ball. Score one for the prehensile let's-play-catch fans.

Obtain a 16" beach ball ($1.27 at Zayre's) and inflate it roundly. Halve your group on a playing field and ask the two teams to separate by about 10 yards. The team with the oldest player can elect to either receive or smack the ball. The team that initially delivers the ball (smack-off) begins by having one player loft the ball and having another player hand-strike the ball so that it sails toward the other team. Or, as an alternate START, have the two shortest players pair off for a jump ball. Play has begun, so here are a couple rules.

1. The ball cannot be hit with any part of the body except the hands and arms. (It's my game and my rules, so I'm getting even for all those years of hearing "...keep your hands down!"

2. No purposeful body contact is allowed.

3. There are no timeouts, penalties (self-enforced rules; usually by the biggest, strongest player), or whistles. Play is continuous. After a goal is scored, a member of the defending team is allowed to pick up the ball and gets a free hit toward the far wall.

4. Strike only with an open hand.

A score is achieved by hitting the ball over the end line or hitting the wall at the end of the gym. If more than 20 people are on the court, put another beach ball into play.

## Five-a-Side Flatball

This is one of those "spontaneous generation" games that occurs full-blown as the result of some serendipity and more than a dollop of PGE (playful group energy). Five-a-side also plays better than it reads, so give it try when group energy is high — after a heady game of Striker, perhaps.

Deflate a Moonball (aka beach ball) to about 66-2/3 maximum to provide the object of play.

Ten players make up the official roster for this fast-moving game with five players arranging themselves on each side as opposing teams. Use the basketball lines near the end of the court that are parallel to one another and about 6' apart to act as boundary designators. The two teams line up facing one another. Team players should be a little more than arm's length away from one another and facing the members of the opposite team. The suggested lateral boundary line is just beyond the last player in line.

*Object* — To smack the flattish ball over and past the opponent's line using only the front or back of an *open* hand.

*Rules:*

1. Players must stand with their toes on the line while waiting for a playable hit.

2. When the ball approaches, a player may make one pivot step forward to smack the ball, but may not make purposeful physical contact with an opposing player.

3. A point is scored if the ball crosses the opposing player's line. If the ball sails *over* that player's waist height, no point is scored.

4. Play begins with a back-handed hit of the ball (called a backy).

5. The ball may not be picked up, held or carried.

6. Five consecutive hits of the ball per side are maximum before the ball must be touched by someone on the other team.

7. Kneeling is not allowed.

8. Penalties are judged and assessed by the players.

If the ball splits a seam as the result of all this whacking about, insert a balloon into the hole and inflate it until the beach ball assumes its 2/3 flat appearance.  Ah...don't forget to tie off the balloon before resuming play.

## Onion Jousting

Here's *OJ* in a nutshell.

Outline a circular area bout 5-6' in diameter using an old section of webbing or sling rope.  Two people stand in this circled area, each armed with two teaspoons (tablespoons, for the less adept), and one small onion.  Considering that each contestant (this activity is wildly competitive) has a spoon in each hand, place the onion in the spoon of the non-dominant hand.  The contest is to try and dislodge the onion from the spoon of your opponent.

*Rules:* (without which, play becomes warfare; "moral equivalent of"...notwithstanding)

- A player must not step out of the circle.
- You *are* allowed to hit your opponent's onion or spoon with your free spoon.  Any other contact can result in forfeit.  If an onion is dropped, the player having dropped the onion loses.  If both onions are dropped simultaneously, the first onion to hit the ground loses.
- Combat begins by both players eyeballing each other, and ritualistically clicking the bowls of their free spoons against one another twice before any offensive action is allowed.
- You may substitute a mango for the onion, if both players agree to the change.
- Raw eggs, of course, replace onions for the ultimate macho contest:  mano-a-mano until huevos ranchero is achieved.

## Clothespin Tag

A pinchy good addition to your tag game collection.

Give each player four clothespins (the spring type that hold tightly, and which used to be made of wood and are now usually fabricated of plastic and don't look and feel as good as they used to).  If you want a faster game, offer less pins per player.  Also, remember that restricted boundaries mean more action and enjoyment.  Widely spread boundary markers favor good runners, and you are quickly back into the I-want-to-play/don't want-to-play schism that downgrades an otherwise good game.

*Game*

Each player tries to get rid of their pins by attaching them to other players' clothing (everybody wears shirts).  A player's 4 pins must end up on 4 separate runners.  The first player to successfully attach all four pins is the champion.  A pin must remain attached for 5 seconds to be valid.  A player cannot rub up against another player or the wall in order to dislodge a pin(s).  Redistribute the pins and begin again if interest remains high.

If the thought or possibility of pinched breasts and genitals (sounds funny, but it isn't) is a concern, allow only dorsal attachment of the pins. Dorsal pinning adds considerably to the skill level of the game. Players look like swirling matadors as they attempt to set their spring-loaded banderillas.

## Freezebee Tag

My BOT's filing system isn't all it could be. Three years ago (the date's right on the paper) this game was sent to me by Sally Wallace and Tom Steele from SUNY Cortland. One of their students, Cheryl Mason, originated the game. I filed (stuck) the letter in a drawer and it curled up behind the drawer — out of sight, out of mind, until someone sat on my desk recently and broke the drawer runner. You know what I found when I pulled the broken pieces out. What a surprise!

Here it is, as penned in October of 1984. Belated thanks, you all.

*Object of Game:* For all of the players to be frozen by the "tagger."

*Materials Needed:* One frisbee for each player.

*Description of Game:* One person is selected to be IT. This person does *not* have a frisbee — all the other players do. The person who is IT runs around and tags (freezes) the players by touching them. Once a person is tagged, he/she must stay in place until "unfrozen" by any of the other players. In order to be "unfrozen," another player must be standing at least five feet away and toss the frisbee at his/her feet or legs. The game continues until everyone has been "frozen."

*Variations*

Rather than being unfrozen by having a frisbee tossed at the leg, there are three game variations.

- Frisbee must be caught by a frozen person.
- Frisbee must go through the person's spread legs.
- Frisbee must go through the person's connected arms.

Also, if the number of players is small, the playing area can be limited, or two people can be selected taggers. Ed. note: Substitute any soft, throwable object for frisbee.

## Speed Rabbit

You may recognize this stand-in-a-circle activity as an old beer-drinking game, because that's exactly what it is, but I've changed the rules slightly so that rule infractions result in people switching, rather than mandatory beer-quaffing. The fast and ludicrous action, however, remains the same, so chug away for nostalgia's sake (better use soft drinks for a student group — I have a feeling that parents may complain, otherwise).

Ask the game initiator to stand in the center of the circle. Her/his job is to point to a person in the circle and say either (1) elephant (2) rabbit or (3) cow. The signified individual and the two people to her immediate right and left must perform a ritualized and symbolic pantomime sequence before the center person can count to 10. If the sequence is not done correctly or in time, then the offending person must take the place of the initiator. If the sequence is performed correctly, then the initiator points to another person until someone eventually makes a mistake or doesn't complete the sequence within the allotted time.

The animal sequences are as follows and, of course, can be (should be) amended or added to as play continues. Noah was pretty good at this game.

### Elephant

The person pointed to: (1) Extends their right arm forward, palm down, hand lightly cupped. (2) Brings the left hand under the arm and up to pinch the nose. (3) Flaps the right arm up and down, as in flapping their trunk. The two players to the right and left of the flapping trunk must flap their "ears" by waving their hands next to their ears.

All this happens simultaneously before 1, 2, 3...10 is reached.

### Rabbit

1. Center person hops up and down.
2. Person to the right stomps his/her right foot. Person to the left stomps his/her left foot.

### Cow

1. Center person interlaces fingers of both hands and presses both palms out away from her/his body, resulting in both thumbs point to the ground.
2. Side people must grab a thumb and mime a milking motion.

Make up your own series of sounds and motions for a chicken, horse, porpoise, skunk, dog, etc. To increase the action and eventually end the game, begin to put more and more people into the center.

### Hoop Relay

Halve the group and have each half form a queue facing you. The folks in this file should be holding hands front-to-back. This relay requires two starters, each holding 3-4 hoops. Each starter, on a signal, begins the action by placing a hoop over the head of the first person in line and as soon as that hoop moves to the 3rd person in line, the 2nd hoop is started, etc. If the starters want to become part of the action, they simply start the last hoop and become the first person in line. When the first hoop reaches the last person in line, that individual runs to the front of the line with the hoop, grabs the hand of the now 2nd person and starts the hoop moving toward the end of the line. Continue until the original front line person returns to that position.

The game can be made somewhat more difficult by requiring that each person reach between his/her legs before grasping the hand of the person in front or in back of them.

## Hand Grenade Relay

If you have trouble with the Ramboesque title, try *Lob It*, or *Hook Shot Relay*.

This game is designed to move a group from one activity to another without having to say, "Let's all walk (or jog) over to the next event." Or, it can be used simply as a low-key competitive activity that is different enough to spark some interest and let's-do-it action.

Divide your group quickly into smaller groups of three or four players. Give each group a 4" diameter playground ball that is not fully inflated — this less-than-round fabrication cuts down on the rolling action.

Indicate that each member of each group will, in on-going sequence, lob (straight arm, overhead style, like lobbing a hand grenade), the ball toward a goal. The "goal" is moving the ball through, over and around a series of natural obstacles in order to deposit the ball at a distinct final destination. Obstacles can include: through a swing set, dog leg around a tree, over a backstop, through a swinging tire, through the front seat of my car (doors open), up and down stairs, and many etc.'s. Design the course with imagination, eschewing predictability for unsuspected challenge.

Continually emphasize that the throwing motion must be "hand grenade" or basketball hook shot style. This limited orbital lob will handicap the best throwers in the group (a leveling ploy) and keep the teams closer together.

*Rules:*

1. Each person and team keeps track of their own score as they alternate throws toward achieving the final goal (perhaps a lob into a 55 gallon drum from a minimum peripheral distance of 30 ft.).

2. Each throw must come to a stop before the next team member can pick up the ball.

3. The next lobber must have one of their feet on the spot where they picked up the ball.

4. Any ball thrown rather than lobbed is a no-throw, and must be repeated with the other arm.

5. The initial person-to-person sequence must be maintained.

6. Teams do not have to wait for one another, and so, can sequence their lobs as rapidly as they like, although there is no reward for finishing first.

7. Teams may not interfere with one another or touch each others' balls.

**Hooper Relay**

Using the same format as played in *Hand Grenade Relay,* throw a rubber hoop (deck tennis ring) as the object of play.

*Rule changes include:*

1. The hoop can be thrown using any hands-only propulsion; i.e., no Jai-Alai type implements allowed.

2. The thrown hoop must be caught to be counted. A missed hoop results in another recorded throw from the same starting point. The catcher may change position, however.

3. To make the catch more difficult, require that the hoop be "ringed" over an extended hand in order to count (as in the game *Hooper*).

Because of the high incidence of missing the hoop in long throws, some interesting decision-making situations develop as to throwing distance and catching ability.

See *Italian Golf.*

## Chapter 5
# *Initiative Problems — No Props*

**The Reversing Pyramid**

Divide your class into groups of 10 and ask those 10 people to arrange themselves into a 4-3-2-1 standing pyramid, like this —

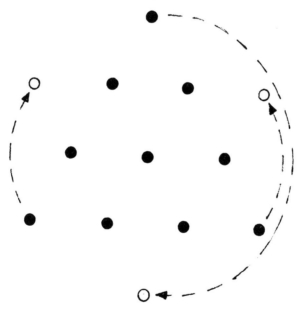

Once pyramidally arranged, ask that symmetrical group of 10 to reverse the apex and base of the pyramid (triangle) by moving only three people. Simple? How come you looked at the answer?

**Count Off**

This activity is so simplistic that you may initially ignore its possibilities. Try it with a group during some down time, or if there are a few minutes before the change of class bell.

Ask a group of ten people (the numbers may vary, but try to have one person per number) to count to ten without pre-planning who is going to say which number, and try to do this without having two (or more) people saying the same number simultaneously. It seems easy — it isn't.

For example, anyone can begin by saying, "one," then someone else tries to sneak in a "two," and then a quick "three," "four," and then "fi.." "five," and back to zero to begin again. How come? Two people tried to say five at the same time. Get it? Got it! Good.

## Impulse

This lightning-fast, hand-holding game is suitable for practically any age level, and particularly for a group that likes to compete against itself.

Ask your group to form a hand-in-hand circle around you. A larger group, in this case, will observe more taking place as the impulse travels the circle and will usually have more fun than a smaller group — say 30 versus 10.

Using a stopwatch (can you believe those electronic LCD watches? — flashing rapid-fire numbers from who knows where and accurate to 1/100 of a second. Functional and oozing mystique — what a deal!), time how long it takes to send a hand squeeze impulse around the circle. Ask an individual in the circle to start the impulse and to simultaneously say *"GO"* and, eventually, *"STOP"* when the impulse returns.

Repeat the attempt a number of times to see how much the group can improve their speed (cooperation, physical reaction, anticipation, efficiency). Vary the activity by trying the same thing with everyone's eyes closed and compare times. Additionally, ask the initiator to start the impulse going in both directions at once by squeezing his right and left hands simultaneously. See if the impulses can pass through one another, or if they get lost at the juncture.

Circle-centered impulses can be passed in a variety of other ways. Slaps, bumps, smacks, whistles — this can be a very intense experience. Experiment! Try lying down in a circle — foot-to-hand!

## Gimme a Leg to Stand On

This is a variation of an old initiative problem (*The Four Pointer* or *Monster, Cows' Tails and Cobras*, page 86), but this time the task is to see how many anatomical contact points are necessary to support a group of 10-12 people off the floor. A balanced, ambulatory pose must be held for 7 seconds for the attempt to be valid. Ideally, the minimum contact points necessary is one (1), but your pocket calculator will quickly reveal a very large number indicating how much a group of 12 weighs. Trial and error amongst the group (no digital decision necessary) will also rule out one (1).

Not a bad little problem, from a cooperation-decision-making standpoint, and you know there's bound to be lots of unselfconscious touching going on — perhaps even a bit of conscious touching. Let's hear it for conscious touching!

*Caveat* — Look out for and control unthinking enthusiasm.

## Everybody Up

Using this cooperative exercise is a useful way to introduce the concept of cooperation and initiative problems.

Ask two people of approximately the same size to sit on the ground (gym floor) facing one another so that the bottoms of their feet are opposed, knees bent, and grasping each other's hands. From this stylized sitting position, ask the duo to try and pull themselves into an upright standing position. If the pair is successful (most are), ask them to seek another partner and try three people, then four, etc., until the entire group makes an attempt. Criteria for a successful attempt are: (1) Hands grasped so that an electrical current could pass through the group. (2) Foot contact with the same electrical set-up. (3) All derrieres off the ground at about the same time.

Something that begins as a simple cooperative stunt soon becomes an initiative problem that includes the entire group.

An expanding group will functionally find that the seemingly logical circular configuration of bodies cannot be continued beyond 8 or so. A change of thinking (initiative) must be employed to come up with a solution that allows large numbers (50 people) to complete the problem.

If an adrenaline-pumped group of 8 or 10 jogs over to you, after having stumbled and jerked to a tenuous standing position, and breathlessly asks, "Did we do it right?" — need I say what your answer should be? Are they high? Yes. Do they feel good about their effort and themselves? Yes. Did they do it right?

An alternate or additional way to present this problem is to ask the participants to sit back-to-back and try to stand as a pair, a trio, etc. Do not allow interlocked arms for safety reasons (shoulder dislocation possibilities).

## Popsicle Push-Up

This cooperative activity can be used as a simple-four person stunt, or you can continue to add people, ending up with a useful large group initiative problem.

To set up the initial four-person attempt, ask for four volunteers that can do at least one push-up. Ask one person to lie face down on the ground, as if preparing to do a push-up. The second person lies face down, perpendicular to the first person, so that the tops of his/her feet are on top of the first person's lower back. The third person repeats the procedure, using the second person as their foot rest. The fourth person fits in this weave so as to connect everyone in a square configuration. Everyone should be face down with their feet (instep) on someone's back.

On a signal, everyone does a push-up and, if done together, there will be four raised bodies, with only eight hands touching the ground: simple, but impressive.

If one of the participants has trouble getting up (foot pressure on their back might cause a problem), tell them that you will count to three to say GO, and that the "permanently prone" individual should attempt a push-up on the count of two, offering just a bit of a head start.

After your groups of four have had some fun with this quartet push-up (including a 360° rotation attempt while in the up position — doomed for failure, but worth a laugh or two), ask the group to continue to add people to one of the quads in an attempt to include the whole group (4 to infinity) in a mass popsicle push-up. There is more than one solution.

This problem is time-consuming, not from the standpoint of discovering a workable solution, but because of how long it takes a group to decide on a technique and implement it. The attempt needs a leader.

People who cannot do a push-up or have back problems can still include themselves in the group solution by lying face down on a strong person's back and, using their arms, try to assist their partner during the push-up attempt — a sharing of strength.

### Popsicle Push-Up Variation

I've seen a couple innovative variations recently of this highly useable initiative problem. The variations were the result of my presenting the problem in a simpler, more direct way. In the past, I have always demonstrated the tic-tac-toe grid solution and so all the attempts to add extra people were variations of that theme. Now, I simply say (with no demo), "...try to get your entire group supported off the ground with only the participant's hands touching the ground — hands only."

Try this approach and I'll bet you will see solutions you never knew existed. After the problem has been solved appropriately, you can show them what a "proper" Popsicle Push-Up looks like, because it's fun, too, and worthwhile doing together.

### Line Up

Sitting here at 29,000 ft. (so announced by the Eastern Airlines captain, not by a sherpa's instinct or altimeter), on the way to Puerto Rico for some monkey business, I was trying to think of a topic, game or event not yet detailed in past BOT's, and this old workshop standby (*Line Up*) came to mind. Flashed-to-mind is more like it, because by some memory malfunction, I had left this excellent initiative problem out of the collection in *Silver Bullets*. I don't want to be overly effusive, but this simple exercise in communication and trust is one of the finest. It "works" best with a mature group of participants: K-6 teachers either adapt or move on.

Group size can vary from 8-15. If participants number from 20-30, ask half the group to try the problem while the others observe. Tell the observers that their solution should occur in less time because of what they perceive and communicate to one another — don't count on this actually happening, though. Observed experience does not effective participants make.

Ask the group (when assembled in front of you) to close their eyes and keep them shut for the remainder of the problem. Even some adults have trouble with this request, so offer blindfolds in this case and require their use with younger groups.

Using the "bumpers up" position (both hands in front of the face, palms facing away) for protection, ask all the folks to mingle about slowly without talking. This is done to change everyone's position so no one knows who is where. After about 10-15 seconds of this giggling, shuffling affair, ask them to stop, keep their eyes closed, put down their hands, and listen to the pre-problem instructions. At this juncture, tell them this is an exercise in communication and trust; communication that they develop among themselves and trust that they are not going to be made fun of, or purposefully made to appear ridiculous.

Indicate that you are going to assign a number to each participant and that you will do this by walking among them and tapping each person on the shoulder, saying a number at the same time. To facilitate your job (because I always forget), ask everyone to raise a hand and to lower that hand when they receive a number from you. Dig?

Supposing that there were 12 people in the group, you now have 12 sightless, numbered, disoriented folks who have no idea what to anticipate next. This approach is purposeful and not unkind, because you now say, "I want you to line yourselves up, shoulder-to-shoulder (or back-to-front, or hand-in-hand — doesn't matter) by number from 1 to 12 without saying a single word; i.e., no talking."

If blindfolded people can look dumbfounded, they will — you just hit them with a blockbuster request. There will be some utterances or halting questions. Re-state the problem, underlining that talking is not allowed.

After some stumbling about (physically and conceptually), ideas begin to actualize and progress is made, albeit slowly. Make specific observations about what's happening, so that you can facilitate a discussion afterwards, or simply to relate a humorous vignette that they *can't see*.

Clapping, tapping, stomping, skin-writing, whistling all have their place in this primitive evolution of communication. Having two or three of the above techniques attempted (at or on you) simultaneously can be somewhat confusing and uproariously funny to observe. The value of video-taping this activity goes without saying.

Offer encouragement at times in order to assuage growing frustration.

Allow 10-15 minutes for a solution. If the group is still largely disoriented after 10 minutes, ask them to stop, keep their eyes closed, and wait for you to touch their shoulder, at which time they loudly announce their number. Then let things continue apace.

When it's obvious that the sequenced solution has been achieved, ask them to open their eyes and count off. Allow a couple of minutes for the explosion of conversational sharing that predictably occurs as the result of pent-up, who-did-this and you-did-thats.

As facilitator, mention or ask about: frustration, fears, trust, applicability, leaders, followers, and don't worry about humor, there's plenty at the tip of every rested tongue.

## Baker's Dozen Variation

If a group has had fun with this problem and you think is mature enough for a no-trust variation, then for sure try this:

Number all participants as above, but designate one player as the "fooler." Do this by tapping a person on the shoulder without assigning a number. That person then opens his/her eyes (or removes a blindfold), and begins operating as the dastardly and doggedly dishonest fooler.

As the group attempts to correctly align themselves, the fooler tries to mess up their attempts by giving (non-verbally) wrong information. Each person, to combat the fooler, has one hypodermic needle (a finger) filled with sodium pentathol (truth serum). If a player thinks they are being fooled with, they point their finger at the supposed miscreant and if their finger is still pointed at the fooler when they say, "Squirt," the fooler is obliged to moan, "You got me," or some such verification. Upon hearing that exclamation, the group is awarded one minute of pure honesty; i.e., the fooler backs off and is not allowed to play his/her dirty tricks for one minute. If a player uses their "needle" and misses the fooler, all their serum is lost for the remainder of the game — just one "squirt" per player is allowed.

If the fooler can keep the experienced group from lining up in less than 10 minutes, s/he wins and is allowed to stick her/his tongue out and make faces at the blindfolded crew. If the group wins, they get to blindfold the fooler and do the same — a form of benign harassment. There are also sartorial consequences associated with debriefing the fooler, but details are too risque for mention in this family publication.

# Chapter 5
# *Initiative Problems - Minimum Props*

**Paul's Balls Variation**

Refer to page 21 in *Silver Bullets* for a write-up on the group initiative, Paul's Balls. If you are having trouble finding the discarded paper cores needed to make the problem function — try this.

Suspend a box (plastic or cardboard) at about the same height as 8-9 of the paper cores can be stacked (16-18'). Use a four-corner suspension system so that the box hangs true and doesn't tip easily. Arrange the cord rigging so that the box can be lowered easily in order to remove balls.

Use the suspended box as the target for all your super shooters (as in Paul's Balls). Not a bad variation for not much $.

**The Porcupine Progression**

During a recent workshop, a participant offered this problem to our group. This is a particularly appealing and useful initiative problem because: (1) The solution is neat and attractive (a why-didn't-I-think-of-that type). (2) Small, inexpensive and easily obtainable props are required. (3) Initially, there appears to be no solution so that when the visually appealing answer is achieved, the word "impossible" becomes less of an obstacle the next time.

Offer the following props to an individual or a small group. Thirteen 40 penny common nails (that's lumberyard talk for 5-1/2" long nails with a big round head), one of which should be started vertically in a small piece of wood. The problem is to balance the remaining 12 nails on the head of the vertical nail.

It doesn't take long to figure out that a solution beyond a stack-'em-up attempt is necessary. I don't mind admitting that the final answer to this "impossible" problem slipped by my steel-trap cognitive capabilities. An

M.I.T. freshman workshop participant conjugated the right stuff in about five minutes. Obviously, I could have come up with the same simple answer, but I wanted the group to feel that it was their solution. The following illustration attempts to show the nail arrangement.

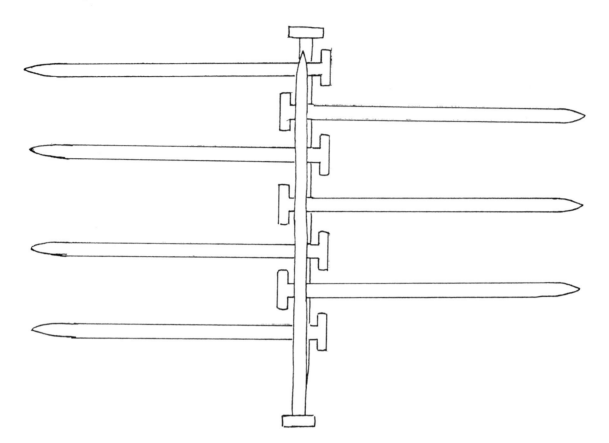

**PORCUPINE PROGRESSION**

Lay the bottom nail on a hard surface, then alternate the next 10 nails on top of this first nail. Lie the top nail on so that its head is opposite to the bottom nail's head. Grip this symmetrical nail arrangement at both ends and place it on the head of the vertical nail. This may require some fiddling about, but this low center of gravity arrangement balances surprisingly well. Eureka! Voila! Neat-o!

*Porcupine Considerations*

- The nails do not have to be any particular length, but I have found that the longer and larger common nail type are the easiest to work with and are more visual.
- The current "world's" record is 84 nails on the head of one nail — I have a photo to prove it.
- To make this problem more portable, pre-drill the block with a drill bit the same size as the diameter of the nails

being used. In this way, the vertical nail can be easily set and also removed.

- Have two or three Porcupine Progression sets available for use if the group numbers over 10 participants: More props = more action.

### The H Problem

This is a nine-person initiative problem that has a simple solution — but aren't most solutions simple when you know the answer?

Arrange 7 people in the following H-shape: solid lines and solid circles. Circles represent people. If you draw a line through each 3 people, you end up with 5 lines. The problem involves adding 2 more people (dotted circles) to the H figure to achieve 10 lines through groups of 3.

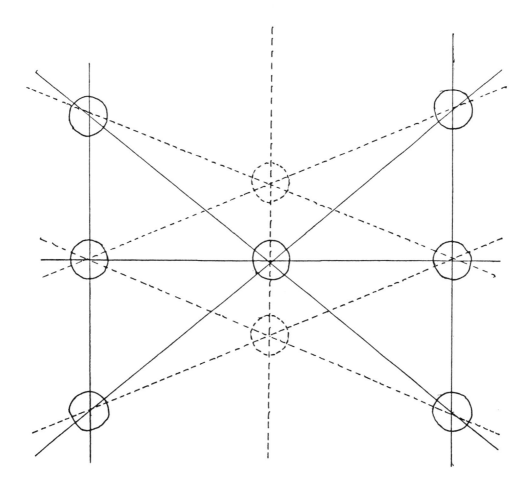

The additional five lines are dotted.

*The H Problem Again*

In a past BOT's, I suggested a people poser (*The H Problem*), and it was indeed that. The solution needs a person overhead to act as a choreographer.  Try this addition to make the solution more visible and doable.

When you draw the "imaginary line" between three people, use a sling rope or webbing (usually 26') to represent that line.  Have the three included folks lay the rope at their feet.

You need a total of 10 ropes and it helps if five are one color and the other five are another color.

## Polar Bears Around the Ice Holes (Petals Around the Rose)

This odd game has been around for decades.  See if your mom and dad remember it.

You need three or four dice (I'll bet that's wrong — it's probably three or four di, or more appropriately, two sets of dice — but you know what I mean), and a couple 1" x 1" squares of styrofoam.  The one inch measurement isn't critical — anything that looks like an ice cube is OK.  I recently found some plastic ice cubes in a novelty store that make great props for this game.

These squares represent the 6 faces on a di.  If you throw out a 1, 4, and 5, you will have 2 ice holes and 4 polar bears.  Look at this di illustration for the reason.

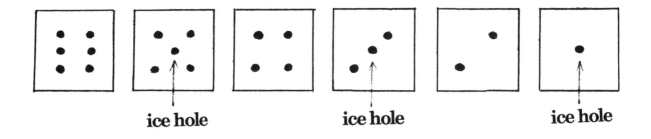

Any center hole in a di is an "ice hole," so dice 1, 3, and 5 have ice holes; 2, 4, and 6 do not.  "Polar bears" are the di holes around the center hole, so di 3 has 2 polar bears around an ice hole.

If the following combination shows up, what do you say?

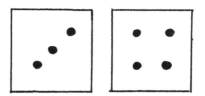

"I see 1 ice hole and 6 polar bears, but only 2 bears are around one ice hole."

What do the plastic ice cubes have to do with the sequencing? Nothing; they are window dressing only.

Is this game confusing for students? You bet — I love it.

## Save the City

The object of this compassion-based initiative problem is to transport a radioactive isotope (tennis ball) from beginning to destination without letting the isotope touch the floor (reverses the ionization of the sub-floor re-bars, resulting in a decomposition of structural integrity and collapse of the horizontal supporting mechanism (floor), or touch any body part (I won't go into detail about the anatomical consequences — too brutal).

It's your group's civic and humanitarian responsibility to use the available customized lead shield transporters (milk carton with the bottom cut off) to transport the isotope up, over and across a few well-chosen obstacles.

*Rules:*

- Isotope (ball) must touch only the transporters (jugs).
- Isotope must make contact with the interior of each transporter; i.e., the ball must be transported from jug to jug.

*Considerations:*

- Establish a deadline for completion. This is a timed event.
- As a variation, require that everyone choose a place to stand and then have to stay there — pivot action on one foot allowed.
- Each student must supply their own isotope transporter (to keep you from having to slice up beaucoup milk cartons).

## Mirage

This simple set-up could become a classic in communication confusion. The object of the exercise is to see if a group member can communicate to the remainder of the group (pencil and paper in hand) the geometrical abstraction (see illustrations) that has been given to him/her.

Four separate pictorial attempts are made with four separate abstractions, following these guidelines:

1. The presenter vocalizes the abstract illustration with his/her back to the group.
2. Again, verbalizing a different abstract figure, but this time facing the audience. Gestures are allowed by the communicator, but no questions may be asked or answered.

3. Now, face the audience and use gestures only: no talking or making any sounds (except laughter, which is hard to stifle at this point).

4. And, finally, facing the audience, gesticulating to your heart's content and responding to the group's question.

After each attempt, allow the group to compare their separate drawings with one another and with the master abstraction. Note which attempt produces the most accurate representation and discuss why you think this is so.

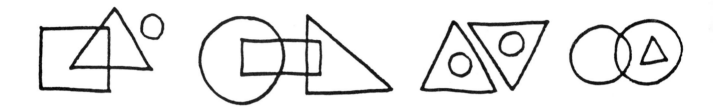

These illustrated abstractions are examples that have been used successfully in the past, but they do not represent any holistic, spiritual, religious or secular anything. Make up your own and I suspect you will get the same humorously insightful results.

## Tangrams

You have probably tried to solve puzzles like these (illustrations) at one time or another, but on a smaller physical scale. A group solution of the puzzle necessitates some sense of spatial relationship and an appreciation of leader/follower rules to efficiently discover the figure forming positions for the jigsaw-like pieces.

Cut the puzzle pieces from 1/2" fiber board (an inexpensive and fairly tough plywood substitute) or whatever durable material you have available. The sections are cut much larger than the commercially packaged pieces, in order to facilitate group interaction.

Hand out the unassembled pieces to the first problem (use small groups of 3-5 people), and ask the enigma experts to form a Greek Cross (Red Cross symbol). After they have accomplished this task, ask them to form a square using the same pieces.

The other three puzzles should be self-explanatory as to what shapes or configurations form the solutions.

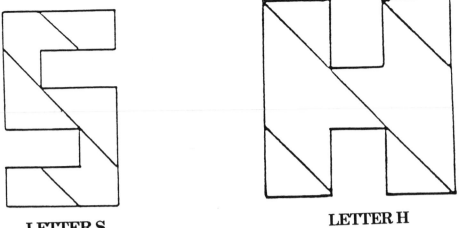

**LETTER S**  **LETTER H**

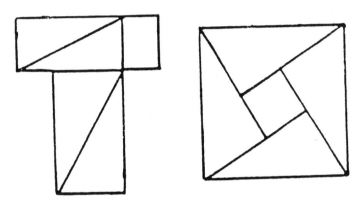

**LETTER AND SQUARE**

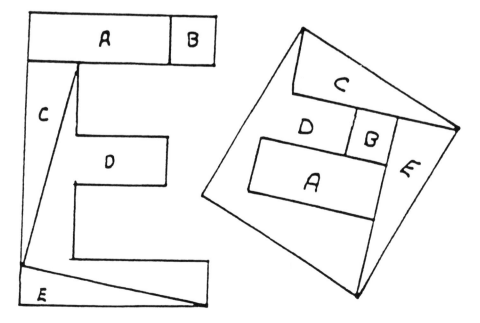

**LETTER E AND SQUARE**

121

Use the measured distances as proportion guides only. If you want the figures bigger or smaller, keep the proportions the same and cut away.

After the group has solved the problems, or occasionally not come up with a solution, ask a question or two about how the group interacted (or ignored one another) to stimulate conversation about something other than rock 'n roll, the Celtics, or blemishes. Here's an effective way to allow a person to express him/herself about something that's not a news item or a self-centered topic.

An interesting exercise in communication skills results from asking two people to sit back-to-back on the floor, supplying one of the individuals with an assembled puzzle and the other participant with the jumbled pieces of an identical puzzle. The person with the assembled puzzle attempts to verbally explain to her partner how to put the pieces together to achieve congruent solutions.

The procedure can be hilariously turtle-like or impressively swift. A joint working knowledge of geometric vocabulary makes the task much easier.

## Stepping Stones

Divide your group into smaller groups of five. Each group is given 4 rubber (plastic) gym markers and asked to physically cross the width of a basketball court as quickly (timed) as possible. Allow 2-3 minutes of planning time before the start.

*Rules:*

- Only the markers can be stepped on.
- No one may touch the gym spots with their heels — ball of the foot only.
- If someone inadvertently touches the floor, he/she must return to the start, and anyone touching them must also return.

*Considerations:*

- Try to emphasize efficiency and group cooperation in your debriefing.
- Try different combinations of gym spots and group sizes.

## Hands Down

People generally see what they want to see or perceive only what is being shown to them.

This simple problem (demonstration, actually) is designed to point out that the obvious facts are not necessarily the combination needed for a solution.

Obtain five lengths (about 6") of any type of matching material; e.g., pencils, dowels, sticks. Kneel down on the floor, pavement, ground, etc., and place

the five pencils on the flat area in front of you so that a pattern is formed —
any pattern will do.

*For example:*

Indicates the Number 3          Indicates the Number 1

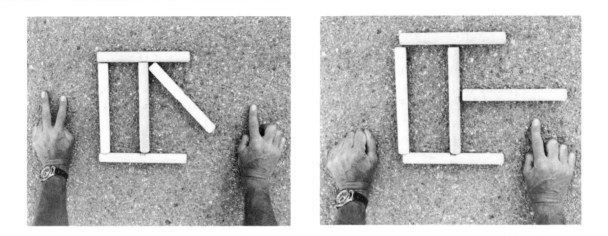

— or whatever your imagination produces.

Ask the group surrounding you to indicate the number from one to ten that
this arrangement of sticks demonstrates.  Set up two or three different
patterns so that the group gets to see and guess additional numbers that
you are depicting.

*The Gimmick* — As soon as you set down whatever fanciful combination of
sticks your imagination conjures up, place your hands on the floor next to
the sticks with the number of fingers exposed indicating the number you
have in mind.  (See photos above.)  The sticks do not indicate anything.
Change the pattern of sticks and change the number of figures you leave
out (two fists on the ground is zero; two hands palms down is ten).

Someone will eventually figure out what you are doing.  Use that person to
maintain group interest by asking them to name the number indicated by
each new pattern.  If no one catches on, place your hands closer to the
sticks or try throwing the sticks over your shoulder and ostentatiously
slapping your palms on the area in front of you.

Be sure to finish up this exercise with a brief statement of what you were
trying to accomplish, and what the gimmick was, because there will
inevitably be a couple folks still baffled by your overt/covert display of digits.

### Passing Crossed or Uncrossed

This around-the-campfire game is historically played with a pair of
scissors, but can be as effectively played with two pencils, two sticks, etc.

A leader initiates the activity by passing two pencils to the person sitting to their left or right in the circle. The leader says one of two things, "I am passing these pencils to you crossed," or "I am passing these pencils to you uncrossed." The leader indicates to the group that each person is to individually receive the pencils and then pass them on crossed or uncrossed, also verbally stating both how they were received and how they are being passed; i.e., crossed or uncrossed.

Confusion begins when a player receives the pencils parallel to one another and the passer says, "I am passing these pencils to you crossed." The group looks to you for confirmation that this person is bewildered. Your confirmation of the passer's correct assessment and action increases the confusion. Why are obviously uncrossed pencils being passed "crossed"? As in all these where-is-the-key problems, the obvious pencils have nothing to do with the crossed or uncrossed situation.

The "key" is the legs position of the person doing the passing and the legs position of that person to whom they are being passed. For example, the person receiving the pencils says, "I am receiving these pencils crossed." (Are the passer's legs *crossed* or uncrossed?) And, "I am passing them uncrossed." (Are the receiver's legs crossed or uncrossed?)

"I see, said the blind man, as he picked up his hammer and saw."

**I've Got the Beat**

Utilizing any object or even your own finger, establish a simple beat by striking that object on a table, floor, etc. There should be no more than 8-12 movements to the beat. Perform the movements of the beat a couple times in front of your group, so that they have a chance to understand what you are doing. After you have performed the sequence a couple times, tell them that, "I have the beat." Then offer them the object to tap with and ask if anyone else thinks they have the beat. If your beat sequence is simple enough, you will have a couple volunteers who think they can duplicate your actions.

As in all these do-as-I-do problems, the key is not the obvious movement, but is revealed as a pre- or post-movement, position, or sound. In this case, a *deep breath* or *clearing your throat* before starting the beat is the indication or key to a "successful" beat. The key can be any number of things, but the group must begin to realize that the answer to these types of problems (and many initiative type problems) is often not the visually obvious one.

Predictably, the people who think they know how to duplicate your beat are concentrating on exactly what your physical motions are with the beat object. If, after a few tries, no one has "The Beat," make the *deep breath* before starting more obvious. It is amazing how zeroed-in some people can become to extraneous actions that they think are essential movements. As obvious as you think your actions are in trying to expose the "key," there will still be some myopic individuals who say, "Do it one more time." I can commiserate, having been that short-sighted person more often than I'd like to admit.

## The Straw that Broke the Bottle's Back

*Problem* — To pick up a 12 oz. glass bottle (Samuel Smith's Nut Brown Ale is a good one) with a plastic straw.

*Rules:*

The bottle must remain off the floor, desk, etc., for five seconds. No other props (glue, rubber bands, etc.) are allowed: one bottle/one straw. No knots are allowed to be tied in the straw.

*Solution* — Bend the straw about two thirds of the way down, or one third of the way up. Stick the bent straw into the bottle orifice until the bent part flips partially open and seats itself against the interior shoulder of the bottle. Lift the straw and the bottle follows.

## The Great Egg Drop

Paul Radcliffe, Adventure-Based Counseling designer and resident verbalist, recently passed on this idea. Paul uses this gambit as a culminating activity during ABC clinics, and reports that the results are particularly useful in emphasizing what the group has learned about cooperation, followership, and resource utilization. The exercise is quoted verbatim. Contact Paul at (508) 468-7981, if your eggs keep breaking. (It may have something to do with excess dietary mercury contamination resulting in a reduced shell calcium level.)

"Your task is to design a delivery system that will protect a raw egg dropped from a height of approximately 8 feet.

Your challenge is to achieve this goal using the LEAST AMOUNT OF RESOURCES.

Your resources are limited to 20 straws and 30" of 1/2" masking tape. YOU MAY NOT USE ANY OTHER MATERIALS. Please keep an accounting of how many straws and how many inches of tape are used in developing your delivery system.

In addition to constructing your product(s), it must HAVE A NAME, and you will be expected to deliver a brief creative promotional pitch highlighting benefits and features of your design(s).

All groups have been given the exact same task and will meet together for presentations and product testing in 20 minutes.

Remember, finishing early and using less raw materials helps to make your product look better to the buyers, but the essential criterion is a whole egg after the drop.

Hint: Share your vision, work hard, but more importantly, work smart!"

## Eggsactly right!

## Chinese Checkers Pyramid

The Cracker Barrel restaurant off I-75, just outside Chattanooga, TN, serves a fine meal for a decent price, and you get grits whether you want 'em or not. As part of the down-home hospitality (it comes with the grits), you will find a multi-holed triangular time-spender included on the table among the sugar, salt, and just near the ketchup. I'd mention the fresh carnation flower arrangement (no plastic), but you wouldn't believe that.

A "time-spender" is something offered by the establishment to keep you from getting antsy or bored while waiting for the waitress. This particular gimmick is fairly common, but it's unique in that its solution is applicable to use as an initiative problem by substituting people for golf tees.

The problem is illustrated as follows:

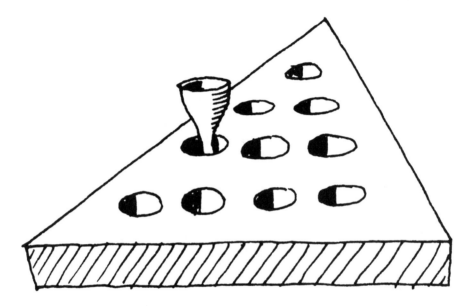

On this particular dining table, the pyramid holes were filled with upside-down golf tees. One hole is left empty (any one). The announced task is to begin jumping tees (any tee with any other adjacent tee), until any further jumping is impossible. If only one tee is left, you are congratulated highly, if two are left, you get a "nice going," and on down the scale until your family's genetic I.Q. is questioned.

For your purposes, simply substitute people for golf tees and use rubber gym spots (like in *Frog Wars*) as substitutes for the holes. Since everyone in the triangular arrangement is involved with the problem, there is usually keen enough interest to maintain attention to the task. Lots of discussion, trial and error, some frustration, and challenging enough to ensure another try. Thank you, Cracker Barrel Restaurant off I-75.

## 38 Special

Is a person who measures 5'6" tall the world's shortest giant or the world's tallest midget? It's all in your point of view.

Reproduce the illustrated multi-shaped polygon so that you have enough copies for each student in your class. Ask the participants to count the number of triangles within the hexagon. You will find that the numbers will vary considerably from the correct count (38 triangles) because it's all in your point of view. Use this simple exercise as a jumping-off point for a discussion of how people "see" solutions. Does the correct answer come from the individuals' working on their own, or from people who shared their results? This visual sit-down problem is a natural preliminary to more physically active initiative problems.

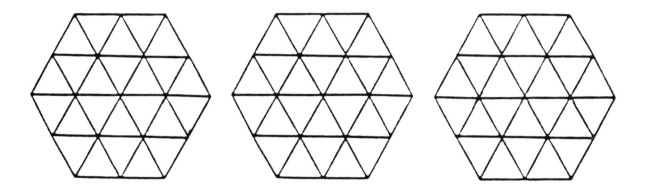

## A Lightweight Idea

Haul out your stash of balloons. Ask each member of the group to blow up and tie off a balloon. Use a "nickel" balloon (12") so that you can achieve an inflated size that is large enough for decent whack-it, smack-it action.

As the balloon-festooned group hangs on your every word, point out a steeplechase route that you had planned previously. In laying out the course, think OBSTACLES: trees, fences, indoor/outdoor, bleachers, ups and downs.

On a signal, have the players move to the first obstacle from a starting line, and continue through the course without ever gripping their balloon. The balloon must remain airborne at all times. If the balloon touches the ground, the player either loses 15 seconds, or must repeat the previous obstacle (their choice). If a balloon breaks, the player must reach into their pocket for the single spare held in reserve. Blow-up procedure follows and the steeplechase continues.

If the second balloon breaks, that player is disqualified for the time being. "Time being," according to the bureau of weights and measurements is 150 seconds (151 seconds during a leap year).

## Touch My Can

Object — For a group of about 15 students to make physical contact with an empty beer can without making physical contact with one another. Hair longer than 4" is not allowed as a portion of the body.

## Circle the Circle

Ask your group to form a hand-in-hand circle. Place two hula hoops together between two people (resting on their grasped hands). See how quickly the people in the circle can cause the hoops to travel around the circle in opposite directions, through each other (i.e., hoop through hoop), and back to the originating position.

## Three In a Row — or Tigger's Toy

Using a piece of retired goldline or kernmantle (a fifty foot section will do nicely) as a jump rope, ask a group to see how many people can make three consecutive jumps together without anyone missing. Twenty people is challenging, but certainly not impossible. There must be a world's record for this bouncy event.

Change "turners" occasionally to combat arm fatigue and to keep a consistent turn and arc. To be an effective and constant turner is a valued street skill.

## The Turnstile

Using the same section of rope as above, begin turning at a slow rate and ask the group to see if they can *all* get through the spinning rope from one side to another by: (1) Going through one at a time. (2) Making one jump while in the air. (3) Not missing a beat of the rope between people. Not a hard assignment for one person or two or three, but a cooperative and often frustrating group challenge.

## #10 Tin Can Foot Pass

Try to pass a #10 can (empty) from foot-to-foot (shoes on) around a seated people circle. That's it. GO! Time this event.

*Variations:*

- Shoes off
- Let the can touch the ground twixt feet.
- Use two cans and start them in opposite directions.

## Chapter 6
# *Sit-Down, No-Sweat Activities*

### Silence Reigns

A quiet game. A leader sits in the center of a people circle (standing, sitting, whatever...). Distance from leader to players should be a minimum of 10 feet. The leader announces him/herself as the Emperor of The Sounds of Silence (as per those guidelines established by Simon & Garfunkel), and invites those qualified to become part of the royal court. Obviously, only *very* quiet people may join him/her.

The emperor beckons grandiosely and silently to a specific candidate in the circle, whose response is to try and move toward and touch Le Gran Mogul without making a sound. Any squeak, rustle or softly lambent sound made by the approaching peasant (serf, lackey, etc.), and heard by the fox-eared chief is reason enough for a rapid seat return, followed by another kingly gesture as further invitation to another candidate for this silent challenge.

Whoever makes the trip without making a sound becomes KING or QUEEN immediately — no time for inaugural folderol — and the game continues.

### The Bow Knot - Everyone's Common Experience

Ask a few people to untie and retie their shoes (loafers and velcro users are excused), and note the different finger manipulations used to end up with what we accept as the common bow knot.

In these days of both parents' working and not as much classic parenting being done, many traditional learn-it-at-home skills have been shunted aside and either not learned or picked up, as we used to say in the Army, by OJT (on-the-job training, a common service acronym for whatever you learned by experience or military osmosis).

An exception to this pervasive learn-it-at-school attitude is the highly complex (if you make the mistake of trying to think about what your fingers are doing) knot arrangement that holds your shoes onto your feet — the bow. This kindergarten knot used to be invariably taught by family and is as sure an indication of your lineage as any other invalid ethnic or cultural touchstone.

Are the laces thrown across one another at the start? Definitely Germanic; or are the twin strands folded and placed just so? This purposeful start indicates French background and probably Freudian anal. If the laces are turned concurrently into two equal bights and tied directly together (the so-called Bunny Ears technique that's popular with harassed mommies that compassionately relate unsavory tasks and tastes to kitties, puppies, bunnies and iguanas), you might rightly suspect Italian or Scandinavian. Be aware, however, that there are some controversial theories extant concerning this ethnic grouping by digital dexterity. Academicians take note — here's a thesis topic that I'm sure no one has pursued and just in time for summer study: esoteric, dreary, and practically useless — perfect!

Come on, Karl, do I have to wade through all this folderol just to find out what the game is? Yes, and since you're this far, don't complain, 'cause here we are at the start.

As I've said in past workshops, I don't approve of speed contests for teaching knots. I think the emphasis on speed is counterproductive, resulting in anxiety (worry) and, more significantly, a finished knot that is often poorly tied. In fact, I can't think of a time when it's necessary to tie a knot fast. But, speed contests relating as to who can tie their shoes the fastest provide 10-15 minutes of good-humored, fast-paced competition, the results of which don't depend upon a well-tied safety knot.

Designate a common starting position (1) laces draped toward the floor on each side of the shoe (2) one lace in each hand (3) the first overhand knot already tied, etc. Also indicate if this is a one or two shoe contest — the double shoe situation demanding more skill and conditioning, and not so much dependence on a couple of lucky moves.

A digital watch makes the contest more exacting and intense, as contestants often finish hundredths of a second in front or behind other competitors.

I've had a lot of fun with this simple activity and utilizing a non-serious approach, I'm sure you will, too.

## Wordles

In recent workshops, I have been using these word puzzles more and more to avoid going outside during inclement weather, and somewhat more significantly to practice brainstorming techniques.

Make up a serious of 3" x 5" cards as outlined in *Silver Bullets* (pg. 102). Rather than offering the small number of cards as suggested, for variety and larger groups, make up about 30 wordle cards (one set for each group of 5-6), and offer the cards to the groups, announcing that they have 20 minutes to figure out as many as they are able. How they approach the actual problem is up to the group. When time is up, have all the groups get together and share their solutions. Be prepared to allow more than one answer per card, because some of the responses prove to be as ingenious as the puzzles. Spend some discussion time talking about what technique the group found to be the most efficient in figuring out the various letter and symbol combinations.

Will students really sit still long enough to work together on these word problems? Have them look out the window at the collecting snow, puddling rain, etc., then suggest a few outdoor activities...

Here are 90 wordles that I gleaned from various game books. I'd like to say that I made some of these up, but although I enjoy the ingenuity inherent in wordles, I don't have a bent for creating them. I *did* make one up, however — it's #51 in *Silver Bullets* and number 91 in this book. I apologize to anyone who made it up before I did — it's yours; no hassle — don't sue me!

1. GREENNV

2. <u>10 J Q K A</u>
   FACTS

3. ___ G O ____
   JAN 6 FEB 3

4. LOOK KOOL CROSSING

5. SIDK DKIS

6. HIS . TORY

7.        HE
   NOW   RE

8. <u>21 LB. 18 LB.</u>
   HAND   FOOT

9. <u>I</u>
   8

10. 1935 ALONG 1975 1983

11. PpOpD

         √ √   √
12. C O U N T E R

13. EILN PU

14. IT

15. SIGHT LOVE
    SIGHT
    SIGHT

| 16. | HO |
| | HO |
| + | <u>HO</u> |
| 17. | .THAT'S |
| 18. | TILL IME |
| 19. | H-O-P-E-S |
| 20. | OFTEN |
| | OFTEN NOT |
| | OFTEN NOT |
| 21. | VAD ERS |
| 22. | 1/4 1/4 1/4 1/4 1/4 |
| 23. | HAND |
| | HAND |
| | HAND |
| | DECK |
| 24. | F AR E FAR W |
| 25. | CY CY |
| 26. | SHRIF |
| 27. | T |
| | T |
| + | <u>T</u> |
| 28. | BUDGET |
| | ^^ |
| 29. | WIRE |
| | JUST |
| 30. | BALLO-T |
| 31. | COME CO |
| 32. | PERFORMANCE |
| | PERFORMANCE |
| 33. | COLOWME |
| 34. | CLOSE |
| | CLOSE |
| | CLOSE |
| | CLOSE |
| 35. | W.I. |
| 36. | WEEKKKK |
| 37. | XQQQME |
| 38. | YUO'ER |

39. NIRENDEVOUSGHT

40. COPI COPPY <u>COPY</u>

41. <u>LEAN</u>
    REVO

42. H/E/A/D

43. LET/GONES
    BE /GONES

44. LOI'MVE/YOU

45. SEA SON

46. $ $ IT

47. <u>HEAD</u>
    LHEOEVLSE

48. MOTH
    CRY
    CRY
    CRY

49. ME QUIT

50.    O
    M.D.
    Ph. D.
    L.L.D.

51. <u>ii</u> <u>ii</u>
    o  o

52. <u>STAND</u>
       I

53. DICE
    DICE

54. O! — 144

55. LOYOUOK

56. CYCLE
    CYCLE
    CYCLE

57. KNEE
    LIGHT

58.    GROUND
        FEET
        FEET
        FEET
        FEET
        FEET
        FEET

59.    HE'S/HIMSELF

60.    DOCTOR
        DOCTOR

61.     R
     ROAD
       A
       D

62.    SIDE SIDE

63.    YOU/JUST/ME

64.    BAN ANA

65.    <u>ONCE</u>
    A TIME

66.    NOON LAZY

67.    F             F
     R   STANDING   R
     I             I
     E     MISS    E
     N             N
     D             D
     S             S

68.    RRRRRRR
        RRRRRRR
        RRRRRRR
        RRRRRRR
        RRRRRRR
        RRRRRRR
        RRRRRRR

69.    <u>T I M E</u>
    ABDE

70. ED
+ <u>ED</u>

71. TIMING TIM ING

72. MCE

MCE

MCE

73. WHEATHER

74. ME NT

75. ALL world

76.          M

DISHOES

          M

77. ECNALG

78. 2UM
+ <u>2UM</u>

79. H O

80. HIJKLMNO

81. IECEXCEPT

82. BJAOCKX

83. PAS

84. YOUR PaAnNTsS

85. GESG

86. ONE

ONE

87. ISSUE   ISSUE

ISSUE   ISSUE

ISSUE   ISSUE

ISSUE   ISSUE

ISSUE   ISSUE

88. NA FISH

NA FISH

89. _____  IT

90. LAL

91. THHAENRGE

## Wordle Answers

1. Green with envy
2. Hand over the facts
3. Go on a double date
4. Look both ways before crossing
5. Mixed up kids
6. A period in history
7. He came out of nowhere
8. Wait on hand an foot
9. I over ate
10. Along in years
11. Two peas in a pod
12. Check out counter
13. Line up in alphabetical order
14. It remains to be seen
15. Love at first sight
16. Tally-Ho
17. That's beside the point
18. Till the end of time
19. Dashed hopes
20. More often than not
21. Space invaders
22. Close quarters
23. All hands on deck
24. Few & far between
25. Cyclone
26. Short shrift
27. Teetotal
28. Balanced budget
29. Just under the wire
30. Absentee ballot
31. There's more to come
32. Repeat performance
33. Low income
34. Foreclose
35. I'm upset
36. Long weekend

| 37. | Excuuuse me |
| 38. | You're confused |
| 39. | Midnight rendezvous |
| 40. | Copyright |
| 41. | Lean over backwards |
| 42. | Headquarters |
| 43. | Let bygones be bygones |
| 44. | I'm in love with you |
| 45. | Open season |
| 46. | Money market |
| 47. | Head over heels in love |
| 48. | Mothball |
| 49. | Quit following me |
| 50. | Three degrees below zero |
| 51. | Circles under the eyes |
| 52. | I understand |
| 53. | Paradise |
| 54. | Oh, gross! |
| 55. | Look around you |
| 56. | Tricycle |
| 57. | Moon light |
| 58. | Six feet under ground |
| 59. | He's beside himself |
| 60. | Paradox |
| 61. | Cross road |
| 62. | Side by side |
| 63. | Just between you and me |
| 64. | Banana split |
| 65. | Once upon a time |
| 66. | Lazy afternoon |
| 67. | Misunderstanding between friends |
| 68. | Forty-niners |
| 69. | Long time, no see |
| 70. | Added |
| 71. | Split second timing |
| 72. | Three blind mice |
| 73. | Bad spell of weather |
| 74. | Apartment |

75.   It's a small world after all
76.   Mom breaking dishes
77.   Backward glance
78.   Forum
79.   Half an hour
80.   Water
81.   i before e except after c
82.   Jack-in-the-box
83.   Incomplete pass
84.   Ants in your pants
85.   Scrambled eggs
86.   One on one
87.   Tennis shoe
88.   Tuna fish
89.   Blanket
90.   All mixed up
91.   Hang in there

## A Verbal Enigma

This is an unusual month — Santa, snow and so on. This is an unusual paragraph, too. How quickly can you find out *what is so uncommon about it?* It looks so ordinary that you may think nothing is odd about it until you match it with most paragraphs this long. If you put your mind to it and study it, you will find out, but nobody may assist you, or possibly may not want to. Go to work and try your skill at figuring it out. Par on this paragraph is about half an hour. Good luck — and don't blow your cool.

Answer — The letter <u>E</u> is not used anywhere in the paragraph.

## Gooney Likes

Add this tricky word game to your collection of no-prop, sit-down, where's-the-key? games.

Begin by saying, Gooney likes the MOON, but he doesn't like the SUN. The object of the game is for your audience to guess why Gooney likes some things but doesn't like others. Gooney likes BILL, but he doesn't like JOHN. Gooney likes FEET, but he doesn't like SHOES. Gooney likes the color YELLOW, but he doesn't like BLUE.

Can you guess what the key is? Don't feel badly, it took me 15 minutes and a couple generous hints before I discovered the gimmick.

Gooney likes TOOLS, but he doesn't like GEAR. Gooney's favorite word is BOOKKEEPING. He likes BEER, but not BREW.

Gooney likes any word with double adjacent letters...LETTER, BOOK, SHEET, SOOT, etc. Ooh! That's SOO easy...

## Rainy Day Code Quiz

On a day when you would just as soon not be outside, pass out this list of crazy codes and ask small groups (3-4) to see how fast and accurately they can come up with correct decoded answers. This activity is not a test of any kind and shouldn't be presented as such; it's simply a way to provide an interesting sit-down topic that will encourage discussion, ideas and cooperation.

1. 101D
2. .22 CR
3. 10Y in a D
4. 186.280 MPS is the SOL
5. 7th IS
6. 10 - 4 GB
7. 7 W or the W
8. 52 C in a D
9. 4x4 is 4WD
10. 60 S in a M
11. 12M in a Y
12. 31 F in B's
13. 26 F at HJ
14. 9 out of 10 D recommend C with F
15. RADD 3 men in a T
16. 4 Q in a $
17. 11 M on a FBT
18. 1 BW in a gigawatt
19. The SR of 4 is 2
20. 99 B of B on the W
21. 26 L in the A
22. .44M = MMD
23. R & F of the 3rd R
24. 88 K on a P
25. 4 Q in in a G

### Answers to Rainy Day Code Quiz

1. 101 dalmatians
2. .22 caliber rifle
3. 10 years in a decade

4.  186,280 miles per second is the speed of light
5.  7th inning stretch
6.  10-4 good buddy
7.  7 wonders of the world
8.  52 cards in a deck
9.  4x4 is 4 wheel drive
10. 60 seconds in a minute
11. 12 months in a year
12. 31 flavors at Brigham's
13. 26 flavors at Howard Johnson's
14. 9 out of 10 dentists recommend Crest with fluoride
15. Rub a dub dub, 3 men in a tub
16. 4 quarters in a dollar
17. 11 men on a football team
18. 1 billion watts in a gigawatt
19. The square root of 4 is 2
20. 99 bottles of beer on the wall
21. 26 letters in the alphabet
22. .44 magnum = make my day
23. Rise and fall of the Third Reich
24. 88 keys on a piano
25. 4 quarts in a gallon

## Patience Puzzles

I had included some of these word puzzles in an earlier BOT's. I listed them because they made you think (not *too* hard) and the solutions were satisfying. Recently, I came across this bunch, but with a difference — no solutions were offered.

Not only was my cerebellum, et al., being titillated, but I was subtly challenged. So, I'm passing the list and the challenge on to you. My first time through I came up with 6-7 answers. Presently, there are still 6 that still have me stumped — but I'll get 'em — just a matter of time.

If you have no idea how these acronym enigmas work, the answer to #3 is: 8 days minus 24 hours equals 1 week. Of course! "Truth is obvious after it's discovery." Have fun and don't tell me the answers.

1.  M. + M. + N.H. + V.+ C. + R.I. = N.E.
2.  "1B in the H. = 2 in the B."
3.  8D. - 24H. = 1 W.
4.  H.H. & M.H. at 12 = N. or M.
5.  3 P. = 6

6.  4J. + 4 Q + 4K = all the <u>F.C.</u>
7.  S. & M. & T. & W. & T. & F.& S. are <u>D. of W.</u>
8.  A. + N. + A.F. + M.C. + C.G. = <u>A.F.</u>
9.  T. = <u>L.S.</u> State
10. 23 Y. - 3 Y. = <u>2D.</u>
11. E. - 8 = <u>Z.</u>
12. 8 P. = 1 <u>G.</u>
13. C. + 6 D. = <u>N.Y.E.</u>
14. <u>S.R.</u> of N. = 3.
15. A. & E. wre in the <u>G. of E.</u>
16. My F.L. & South P. are both <u>M.C.</u>
17. "N.N. = <u>G.N.</u>"
18. N. + P. + S.M. = <u>S.of C.</u>.
19. 1 + 6 Z. = 1<u>M.</u>
20. B. or G. - F. -M. = 0
21. "R. + R. + <u>R.</u>"
22. A.L. & J.G. & W.M. & J.K. were all <u>A.</u>
23. N. + V. + P. + A. + A. + C. + P. + I. = <u>P. of S.</u>
24. S. + H. of R. = <u>U.S.C.</u>
25. P. & N. & D. & Q. & H.D. were all <u>C.</u>
26. Y. - S. - S. - A. = <u>W.</u>
27. Y. + 2 D. = <u>T.</u>

## Have You Ever...?

Suggestions for the use of these questions...

- As an icebreaker:  These simple answers/questions lead to shareable "war stories" that lead to other war stories, etc. Everyone seems to have an adventure vignette that serves as an invitation to further friendly and listenable can-you-top-this? stories.

- Use as a means to stimulate discussion or initiate creative writing attempts in an academic setting.  This can be achieved by handing out a list pertinent to your age or experience group or by asking students to verbally answer a series of have you ever? questions.

- Verbally ask the questions, then ask the participants to raise a hand if they answer yes to a question.  In this way, all the participants can see who has done what, and it also allows sharing of certain poignant experiences.

- In your instructions, don't forget to add that raising hands is voluntary from question to question, so that if a particular query is impositional, embarrassing or objectionable, no one need feel obliged to respond.

- Don't try to figure out a reason why or how these questions have been sequenced, because there is none. The questions are randomly listed with absolutely no psychological or psychiatric intent...just fun, mates.

- Make up your own list or series of questions to best fit your audience or demographic needs. There are approximately 520 questions in this list.

## Have You Ever...

◊ been in a parade?

◊ eaten two raw oysters?

◊ been bitten by a dog (broken skin)?

◊ watched 4 VCR video movies in a row?

◊ participated at a nude beach?

◊ seen a moon bow?

◊ broken an established school athletic record?

◊ helped an animal give birth (not your wife)?

◊ been to a professional world championship game?

◊ viewed an autopsy?

◊ given a shot?

◊ taken blood with a hypodermic needle?

◊ performed CPR in an attempted life-saving situation?

◊ actually used the Heimlich maneuver in a life-threatening situation?

◊ developed and printed your own B&W film?

◊ free dived below 30 feet (no scuba gear)?

◊ swum 50 yards non-stop underwater?

◊ flown in a glider?

◊ operated a bulldozer?

◊ eaten — tripe; cow's tongue, pig's knuckles, brain, mountain oysters?

◊ been within 25 feet of a bear in the wild?

◊ been to a high school reunion after 20 years?

◊ caught a wave with a surf ski?

◊ walked on stilts?

◊ written a "letter to the editor"?

◊ climbed a tree to rescue a cat?

◊ seen the rings of Saturn and/or the moons of Jupiter (not a photo)?

◊ seen a whale in the ocean?

◊ been within 25' of a shark in a natural setting (no boat or flotation device)?

◊ been towed aloft on a parasail?

◊ thrown a curling stone?

◊ been stopped for speeding?

◊ played catch with a raw egg until it broke?

◊ done push-ups in an airplane?

◊ traveled more than 1,000 miles continuously on a train?

◊ traveled more than 1,500 miles on a bus?

◊ stayed up all night studying?

◊ drank more than 10 cups of coffee in a 24 hour period?

◊ spun a hula hoop around your waist at least 20 times without stopping?

◊ snapped a leather bull whip?

◊ had an idea that was eventually used by thousands of people?

◊ written something that made you cry?

◊ shaved your legs?

◊ inadvertently flipped a canoe in 40° (plus or minus) water?

◊ done over 20 pull-ups (male), 10 pull-ups (female)?

◊ as an adult, gone to a costume party in a costume?

◊ slept in a water bed?

◊ made love in a water bed?

◊ kept a piece of chewed gum overnight and chewed it again?

◊ been submerged in a submarine? (not Disneyworld)

◊ fired a machine gun on full automatic?

◊ eaten fiddleheads?

◊ eaten dandelion greens?

◊ used a breath-activated animal call; e.g., crow call?

◊ purposefully aimed a loaded gun at someone?

◊ worn a hand-tied bow tie?

◊ shaved with a straight razor (entire face or legs)?

◊ had a manicure?

◊ had a paid-for massage?

◊ owned a watch that cost more than $500?

◊ owned a watch that worked for more than 10 years?

◊ slept more than 14 hours straight (no chemicals or pills)?

◊ ridden a "century" on a bicycle?

◊ owned a bicycle that cost more than $1,000?

◊ held your breath for more than two consecutive minutes?

◊ done an inadvertent 360° spin in a braking car situation?

◊ kept a diary as an adult (over 12 months)?

◊ stayed in a motel/hotel that cost more than $100/night?

◊ shared a meal (2 people) for more than $100?

◊ tried a recreational drug?

◊ had a wart removed?

◊ had one of the following as an adult (over 21); whooping cough, diphtheria, chicken pox, measles, mumps?

◊ worked a night shift?

◊ had a job on a boat or ship at sea?

◊ seen a polar bear in the wild?

◊ seen a koala bear in the wild?

◊ seen a panda bear in the wild?

◊ been tied up as a restraining move?

◊ tried on a straight jacket?

◊ been to a morgue?

◊ ridden a multi-speed, muscle-powered tricycle?

◊ shot a crow?

◊ listened to a heavy metal album from beginning to end, non-stop?

◊ laid down in a casket?

◊ held someone's corporeal ashes?

◊ had altitude sickness?

◊ given blood?

◊ carried a pack weighing more than 60 lbs. for more than 5 continuous miles?

◊ cried because of a movie scene? a song? an aroma?

◊ had a parasitic infection?

◊ seriously pondered what quasars are expanding into?

◊ read at least two of Carlos Castenada's books on Don Juan?

read the following children's books?

  ◊  *The Black Stallion*

  ◊  *Black Beauty*

  ◊  *The Phantom Toll Booth*

  ◊  *Lad, a Dog*

  ◊  *Whitefang*

◊    *Superfudge*

◊    *The Lion, the Witch and the Wardrobe*

◊  taken a picture of your anatomy on a copying machine?

◊  belonged to a national fraternity or sorority (Greek)?

◊  shot flies with a rubber band?

◊  had an IV administered?

◊  owned a BB gun?

◊  worked for less than $1.00 an hour (not babysitting)?

◊  read a complete book by kerosene or candle light?

◊  tithed?

◊  eaten frogs' legs?

◊  had a Mohawk haircut?

◊  colored your hair orange, green, purple, or blue?

◊  purposefully jumped off something more than 10' high? (not into water)

◊  killed a songbird?

◊  returned an entree at a restaurant?

◊  owned a CB radio?

◊  volunteered a day's work as a service (no pay)?

◊  been to a chiropractor for an adjustment?

◊  been Rolfed?

◊  been to an EST seminar?

◊  been a participant (student) on a ropes course (excluding the military)?

◊  thrown a live hand grenade (pin pulled)?

◊  owned more than 10 credit cards at one time?

◊  participated as part of a real search and rescue scenario?

◊  won a state championship (not necessarily athletic)?

◊  drunk 16 ozs. of beer in one quaff (without taking a breath)?

◊  ordered something "flambe" in a restaurant (not a pupu platter)?

◊  bought and drank a bottle of Ripple or Thunderbird wine?

◊  worn lace?

◊  written a letter of more than 10 pages?

◊  made a long distance call of more than 10,000 miles?

◊  suffered from Montezuma's revenge?

◊  had heat exhaustion?

◊  had frostbite that caused blisters?

◊  treated someone with hypothermia?

◊ urinated outdoors in less than minus 20°F?

◊ experienced an outdoor shade temperature of more than 110°F?

◊ experienced an outdoor temperature of under -35°F? (no wind chill)

◊ been in every state of the U.S. (all 50)?

◊ built a fire on a frozen lake?

◊ slept on a frozen lake?

◊ made butter?

◊ made ice cream by hand (no electricity)?

◊ written something with an ink pen (not felt or ball point)?

◊ sat at a desk at school as a student that had an ink well with ink in it?

◊ ridden in a Rolls Royce?

◊ been to a double feature movie?

◊ owned a pair of white bucks?

◊ been to an opera?

◊ seen a stage play in NYC?

◊ been to a pro game in at least three major sports?

◊ fallen more than 15 feet onto an unyielding surface?

◊ sanded an entire hardwood floor?

◊ been in a yurt?

◊ spun wool?

◊ been a bartender at a commercial bar?

◊ had your hair styled?

◊ refinished a piece of furniture?

◊ owned more than one cat at a time?

◊ tried a Nautilus workout?

◊ hitchhiked over 200 miles?

◊ jumped a train?

◊ totaled your car?

◊ had your car totaled?

◊ forgotten a good friend's name when introducing her/him?

◊ wallpapered a room?

◊ painted a house (exterior)?

◊ seen a living amoeba?

◊ thrown any object more than 300' (not downhill)?

◊ eaten an entire meal using chopsticks?

◊ swum a mile in ocean water?

◊ paddled a canoe at least one mile off shore (ocean)?

◊ drunk at least 25 different imported beers (not at once)?

◊ gotten intoxicated on grain alcohol (190 proof)?

◊ dug up a human skeleton?

◊ owned a Rolex watch?

◊ owned a pair of "penny" loafers and put a penny in them?

◊ carried more than $5,000 in cash?

◊ reduced your waistline by more than 6"?

◊ lost more than 50 lbs. of body weight?

◊ been stuck in an elevator for more than 8 minutes?

◊ walked to the top of the Washington Monument?

◊ worn braces on your teeth?

◊ had your initials entered on a commercial game computer as one of the best ten scores?

◊ spent more than $10.00 on computer games in one day?

◊ operated a motorcycle?

◊ driven a 16 wheeler?

◊ ridden a bicycle more than 750 miles on a trip?

◊ ridden a unicycle more than 100 yards without falling?

◊ heard the "buzzing of the bees" during an electrical storm?

◊ confronted a stranger because of something they were doing (breaking in line, hitting a child, etc.)?

◊ missed a plane?

◊ stayed out all night, as a minor?

◊ had the "whirley beds"?

◊ meditated regularly with results?

◊ spent over 24 hours without seeing or talking to another person?

◊ gone 24 hours without eating anything?

◊ bleached your hair (even partially)?

◊ swallowed a raw egg straight from the shell?

◊ done a one-arm chin-up?

◊ flown in a helicopter?

◊ been in a dance contest?

◊ ridden a bicycle up a hill longer than 5 miles, non-stop?

◊ ignored a ringing phone (no recorder screening allowed)?

◊ climbed a ladder more than 50' high?

◊ had to have a tetanus shot because you stepped on a rusty nail?

◊ hit a golf ball more than 300 yards?

◊ had 5 pieces of bubble gum in your mouth at one time?

◊ read a book of over 1,000 pages?

◊ been a Boy or Girl Scout?

◊ bought a copy of *The Joy of Sex*?

◊ had a subscription to Playboy or Playgirl magazine?

◊ typed over 60 w.p.m.?

◊ spoken a foreign language fluently?

◊ been involved in a menage-a-tois?

◊ wondered where the numerals and letters came from in a digital watch?

◊ shaved your head?

◊ had acne?

◊ ditched a blind date?

◊ had a tooth pulled?

◊ bush-whacked 5 miles (no trails)?

◊ walked in the woods nude?

◊ tried hang-gliding?

◊ flown in an ultra-light?

◊ received a belt other than white in Karate, or one of the other martial arts?

◊ run at least two continuous miles in soft sand?

◊ bench-pressed your own weight?

◊ tried roller skis?

◊ had poison ivy on your genitals?

◊ had a dog lift his leg on you?

◊ had a dog try to mate with your leg?

◊ been bitten by a human (broken skin)?

◊ been knocked out?

◊ cracked a windshield with your head?

◊ lost your driver's license?

◊ owned a car that cost more than $25,000?

◊ had a ride in a Model A or T Ford?

◊ spun a doughnut with a motorcycle?

◊ run a mile in less than 6 minutes?

◊ lost over $100 in cash?

◊ played a game that involved taking off your clothes?

◊ climbed a building facade (bottom to top)?

◊ owned a knife that cost more than $100?

◊ been more than 300' below the earth's surface?

◊ raised bees?

◊ stayed back a year at school?

◊ had a marriage proposal turned down?

◊ turned down a marriage proposal?

◊ eaten an entire apple — seeds, core, and all?

◊ owned a Cuisinart?

◊ purchased wall-to-wall carpeting?

◊ water skied on one ski?

◊ gone over a jump on water skis?

◊ dived using a helium mixture?

◊ had to make decompression stops on the way up from a deep dive?

◊ dived under ice with scuba gear?

◊ caught an octopus by hand?

◊ been stung by a Portuguese Man-o-War?

◊ spent the entire night in a (a) bus terminal (b) train station (c) airport?

◊ had part of your body tattooed?

◊ broken a window purposefully as a vandal?

◊ played stickball on a city street?

◊ ridden on the outside of a trolley?

◊ used skates that needed a key?

◊ been so nervous that you threw up?

◊ cut a lawn using a push lawn mower (no engine)?

◊ moved more than a yard of dirt by hand (shovel, only)?

◊ buried a treasure and made a map?

◊ been to an Outward Bound school as a student?

◊ been an OB instructor?

◊ eaten nothing for three days (72 hours)?

◊ climbed inside a commercial clothes dryer?

◊ slid down a laundry chute?

◊ driven a vehicle on a frozen lake?

◊ seen St. Elmo's Fire?

◊ seen the Aurora Borealis?

◊ seen foxfire?

◊ seen a true mirage?

◊ ridden on a steam-powered train?

◊ ridden on a camel?

◊ seen real quicksand?

◊ competed for prize money in a sport?

◊ seen lightning during a snow storm?

◊ been aboard a Navy warship (while commissioned)?

◊ watched the sunrise in a foreign country?

◊ travelled outside the U.S. to work?

◊ been refused entry to a foreign country?

◊ been in a crowd of more than 40,000 people?

◊ performed a magic trick before an audience (not family or friends)?

◊ owned a cowboy hat as an adult?

◊ made a piece of functional furniture?

◊ done a flip off a diving board?

◊ worn your hair to your shoulders (male)?

◊ gone six months without shaving (male); your legs (female)?

◊ been in a crevasse?

◊ used an ice axe for climbing ice or snow?

◊ placed a piton, bolt, friend, chock, nut for protection?

◊ counted to 1,000 just for the heck of it?

◊ written out a googol?

◊ played Monopoly where somebody won in less than 30 minutes?

◊ experienced tear gas?

◊ lived in a dorm?

◊ lived in a condemned building?

◊ swung on a rope from one point to another that covered more than 30' ?

◊ worn an article of clothing regularly for more than 20 years?

◊ had a tire blow out at over 55 mph?

◊ carried the same knife for over 10 years?

◊ said, "You can do it," to someone, knowing that they probably can't?

◊ put a bumper sticker on your car that has a heart on it?

◊ said, "Go for it" when you knew that you probably wouldn't?

◊ swung on a rope and let go into water?

◊ struck out in bowling?

◊ slept between satin sheets?

◊ gone to sleep during a college (university) class?

◊ been chased by an animal (not a human or dog)?

◊ been in a sanctioned bike race?

◊ competed in a national championship?

◊ competed in a world championship?

◊ strung barbed wire?

◊ been dumped on by a seagull or the like?

◊ observed a bird of prey in a stoop?

◊ owned a DeSoto, Packard, or Studebaker? An Edsel?

◊ surfed (board or body) in waves over 10'?

◊ undergone fraternity hazing; i.e., "hell week"?

◊ eaten a Twinkie? eaten two Twinkies?

◊ gone a week without using deodorant?

◊ been able to spell hors d'oeuvre or hemorrhage?

◊ been accused of having an accent?

◊ paid extra money for a vanity plate?

◊ sold a painting done by yourself (not to family)?

◊ been on a TV game show?

◊ seen the movie, Psycho?

◊ dived into a swimming pool and lost your shorts or top, as the case may be?

◊ soloed in an airplane?

◊ won an official eating or drinking contest?

◊ run a toll booth?

◊ crossed Route 128 (Boston) or a comparable highway at rush hour on foot?

◊ attended a parochial school?

◊ seen someone break a world's record (not on TV)?

◊ performed an athletic task at 30 years old plus, better than when you were 20?

◊ stayed up for 48 consecutive hours?

◊ gone to sleep at the wheel and ended up off the road?

◊ changed the oil and filter in your car?

◊ owned a comic book that cost 10 cents?

◊ purchased a mail box?

◊ hot-wired a vehicle?

◊ driven while so drunk that you don't know how you arrived at your destination?

◊ spilled a hot cup of coffee in your lap while driving?

◊ driven a vehicle over a mile in reverse? (not in a circle)

◊ owned a pair of sunglasses that cost more than $75 (non-prescription)?

◊ broken the posted speed limit by more than 40 m.p.h.?

◊ hit 15 consecutive free throws with a basketball (not necessarily in a game)?

◊ gone more than 100 miles out of your way because of a map reading or directional error?

◊ rolled an automobile over, or have been in one that has rolled over?

◊ been the first person to give aid at an auto accident?

◊ lighted a flatulation, or seen it done?

◊ tried to use a dowsing rod?

◊ bent metal via mind control — forks, spoons?

◊ bought a cup of coffee or Coke for a nickel (not a special)?

◊ bought a condom from a men's room?

◊ jumped off a bridge into water?

◊ used a glass-cutter?

◊ paid more than $8 for a six-pack of beer?

◊ won or lost more than $50 gambling?

◊ found more than $50?

◊ driven a car with opposite hand drive for more than 5 miles?

◊ written a poem? (not an assignment)

◊ had snowblindness to any degree?

◊ been in mud up to your waist?

◊ seen a flying squirrel "fly"?

◊ gone through a stop sign at over 30 m.p.h.?

◊ flown first class?

◊ set off a fire alarm on purpose (the kind that requires breaking glass)?

◊ eaten a meal and discovered that you had no money to pay for it?

◊ chewed on a piece of raw sugar cane?

◊ taken the husk off a coconut?

◊ pretended to be Superman (has to include the cape)?

  been on top of:

◊      Sears Tower?  (Chicago)

◊      Statue of Liberty?  (New York)

◊      Empire State Building?  (New York)

◊      Trade Center?  (New York)

◊      Prudential Building?   (Boston)

◊      St. Louis Arch?  (Missouri)

◊      Space Needle?  (Seattle)

◊      CN Tower?  (Toronto)

◊ started a fire without matches or a lighter (not just smoke)?

◊ speared a fish while under water?

◊ cut down a 12" minimum diameter tree with a chain saw?

◊ slept outdoors two weeks in a row?

◊ paddled a canoe in Class III water?

◊ been above the Arctic Circle or below the Antarctic Circle? (not in a plane)

◊ fired a .44 magnum pistol?

◊ butchered, cleaned and eaten a fowl?

◊ held a poisonous snake in your hands?

◊ had to personally kill a dog or cat for humane reasons?

◊ done needlepoint?

◊ climbed a mountain over 12,000 feet?

◊ streaked at a gathering?

◊ cross-country skied with a pack (tent, sleeping bag, etc.)?

◊ made love outdoors (no tent or tarp)?

◊ been 30' up in a tree?

◊ knitted a sweater?

◊ fallen through ice at least to your waist?

◊ parachuted from a plane?

◊ rolled a kayak?

◊ completed a marathon (26 miles)?

◊ successfully climbed a 5.6 (minimum) pitch?

◊ soloed in a wind surfer for over 1/2 mile?

◊ competed in an organized triathlon?

◊ seen an animal underwater bigger than yourself (not at Seaworld)?

◊ been mugged?

◊ fired a 12 gauge shotgun?

◊ seen a child being born (not a movie)?

◊ been in a coed nude sauna or hot tub?

◊ been across the International Date Line?

◊ crossed the equator?

◊ slept out overnight in less than 0° temperatures?

◊ had morphine administered for pain relief?

◊ broken a bone?

◊ won a medal or trophy in competition (20 years or older)?

◊ milked a cow or a goat?

◊ ridden a horse bareback?

◊ been near death?

◊ made an impulsive purchase for more than $1,000?

◊ cheated on your income tax return?

◊ made an obscene gesture at someone while driving your car?

◊ caught a fish that weighed more than 25 lbs.?

◊ written a fan letter?

◊ touched a live electric fence?

◊ driven at 100 m.p.h. or over?

◊ saved someone's life (other than drowning)?

◊ jumped into the water from over 35'?

◊ rappelled over 165'?

◊ driven a one-owner car over 150,000 miles?

◊ driven over 1,000 miles in one day (24 hours)?

◊ eaten 1/2 gallon of ice cream at one sitting?

◊ seen a human die violently (not on film)?

◊ seen an iceberg (at least automobile size)?

◊ taken an ocean dip in January-February on the New England coastline (complete immersion, no wet suit, etc.)?

◊ made up a game that you play regularly?

◊ gone ten years without seeing a son/daughter? mother/father?

◊ done silk screening?

◊ gone to bed before midnight on New Year's Eve (after your 21st birthday)?

◊ smashed an alarm clock?

◊ stolen a motel towel?

◊ told a smoker, face to face, that you *do* object to his/her smoking?

◊ built a doghouse?

◊ met a movie celebrity?

◊ driven at over 100 m.p.h. for over five minutes?

◊ hopped a freight?

◊ flattened a penny on a railroad track? flattened a penny and a nickel together?

◊ written some serious graffiti in a public place?

◊ had gum stuck in your hair?

◊ mooned someone? been mooned?

◊ had an out-of-body experience?

◊ taken a ride on/in a shopping cart as an adult (in store only)?

◊ tried a pinch of Skoal twixt your cheek and gum?

◊ been transported as a patient in an ambulance?

◊ run over a dog?

◊ eaten canned dog food? eaten canned cat food?

◊ removed a bottle cap with your teeth?

◊ shingled a roof?

◊ worn a gold chain (male)?

◊ been hit by a car as a pedestrian?

◊ written a letter on birch bark?

◊ cut down a 12" minimum diameter tree with an axe?

◊ taken a dip through lake or ocean ice?

◊ played Santa Claus for a group other than family?

◊ been to an auction and bid on something over $50?

◊ cut and split a cord of wood?

◊ hiked 20 miles in one day?

◊ been on a rollercoaster that turns upside-down?

◊ played a musical instrument in front of an audience (not family)?

◊ flown in an airplane for more than 8 hours non-stop?

◊ appeared on live network television (not tape)?

◊ had an acupuncture treatment?

◊ travelled in a communist country?

◊ had something you've written published?

◊ had a loaded gun pointed at you?

◊ had to stay in a hospital for longer than two consecutive weeks?

◊ ridden on a bicycle-built-for-two?

◊ been involved in a barroom altercation?

◊   spoken to a group of more than 200 people?

◊   driven a car across the United States more than once?

◊   scuba dived below 50'?

◊   seen a bat in a cave?

◊   had a blind date?

◊   passed out from excessive alcohol consumption?

◊   punched anyone in anger (adult)?

◊   had a root canal?

◊   showshoed?

◊   been to a black tie function?

◊   spent a night in jail?

◊   fired a compound bow?

◊   rafted Class 5 white water?

◊   been on a glacier?

◊   been to 7 different countries?

◊   seen an active volcano?

◊   coasted downhill on a bike at over 50 m.p.h.?

◊   discussed evolution with a fundamentalist?

◊   experienced a paranormal event?

## Caught Ya Peekin

This teensy game may warm the cockles of your heart. The cockles are anatomically located just proximal to the mitral valve, and are largely responsible for flutters (ref. ..."she caused my heart to flutter"). Cockles function better when warm.

Sit or stand in a circle so that everyone can see everyone. The object of the game is to catch someone with their eyes open. I'm not indicating that you should keep your eyes closed, just that if someone in the group sees you with your eyes open, they say, "Caught Ya Peekin." If this is an elimination game, you are then OUT, because you were caught with your eyes open. The game continues until only two or three people are left.

If you want to play the game so that no one is eliminated, just keep playing after you are caught, and continue the game until it's over; i.e., someone decides to change the game.

If, in a flash of intuitive insight, you determine that the best strategy in this game is to never close your eyes, you automatically win the "smarter-than-thou" award, and the silent condemnation of all those timid souls that play by the obvious rules. A Steve Butler game — which he plays very well.

## Chapter 7
# *No Competition Scenarios*

**Clap Trap**

Circle up, Podners!  I mean, line up in a circle, then start a clap wave. You clap, then the person next to you (right or left, doesn't matter), then the person next to the person next to you, etc., etc.  This sequenced clapping has to be done quickly, you know...like a wave.

Let the wave travel around the circle a few times in order to establish the rhythm.  Try reversing the wave in mid flow.  Try clap waving with everyone's eyes closed.

Now that you have the idea (the zen of undulation), try initiating the following sounds and movements.

- Two or three claps in sequence
- Stomping and clapping alternated
- Whistling
- Make up sounds and movements
- Send two different sounds in opposite directions

Why the name Clap Trap?  Why not?

**Handicapped Lunch — Idea from Loraine Baxter at Sarasota Palms Hospital, Florida.**

*First Task* — Pair-up before lunch.

Lunch should require some assembly, such as making sandwiches, ice cream sundaes, etc.  One member of each pair is blindfolded.  The other member cannot use his/her hands.

*Second Task* — To eat lunch.

The two handicapped team members must obviously help one another to locate the food, put it together, and eventually get it into their mouths.

Since this is a working lunch, allow enough time for sufficient preparation, civilized eating, and fun. To quote Loraine, "...not only is the attainment of the goal its own primary reinforcer, it's also a great spectator sport."

## You Take My Breath Away

The purpose of this sit-down stress situation is to give students the opportunity to function efficiently through short periods of discomfort and anxiety.

You will need a digital stop watch and a folded piece of paper (per student) with a short division problem on it ( 713÷8, for example), or substitute for the division problem with the word COOPERATION (see #2 below).

*The Scenario* — Divide the group into pairs. (This problem can be accomplished by a single person, but participation is more fun and functional with a partner.) Ask each student to hold his/her breath for as long as possible, as their partner times their attempt. Record the result and reverse the roles. At this point, do not tell the participants why they are holding their breath for time.

Ask the students to hold their breath again, but this time, when they are 15 seconds short of their personal pre-anoxia record, they are to either (1) open the folded paper and solve the division problem down to one decimal place (have a pencil available), or (2) write down seven acceptable words taken from the letters in the word COOPERATION, before a breath is taken. They are to fantasize that they are SCUBA diving and their life depends upon performing the task quickly and correctly.

Examples of words taken from COOPERATION — pat, pet, tar, not, rot, poor, rope, cat, note, pact, peat, pert, notice, and, I suspect, many, many more.

After the exercise is over, take some time to talk about the phisiology of oxygen debt and carbon dioxide build-up. Also offer the opportunity for comments about how they felt during and after the exercise. A low-key facilitation approach toward achieving verbal student input (beyond the yes/no dead end), is to ask a few obvious questions: "How did you feel when you opened the paper?", "Where was the physical discomfort centered — where did it hurt?", and then ask each student to say one word about their emotional reaction to the task. Such a minimum commitment response may open the (their) door to further discussion.

## Body English

A group tries to spell out the words to a well-known proverb by using their bodies as letters. (Forming letters with the fingers is not allowed — too easy.) Another group tries to decipher what the first group is trying to say.

The groups switch roles from time to time so that everyone gets the chance to be histrionic and contorted. *Body English* encourages discussion, decision-making, cooperation, and laughter.

## Categories

"Karl, I have a couple hundred people that I would like you to do something meaningful with — something...you know...meaningful!"

Thanks, but no thanks. We (Project Adventure) have been doing meaningful stuff with folks for years, but the usual group size numbers closer to 20 people; looking at 15 as ideal. Every now and then, it seems a situation arises where one of our staff gets stuck, agreeing to work with a group that is sized well above the advertised maximum. Here's a partial escape mechanism that works well with practically any size group over 30, and the more diverse, the better.

Ask the large group (if there are more than 200, you might have to use a loudspeaker), to separate quickly into the smaller groups that you are about to announce. Alternate A/B splits (only two groups) with multi-groups (many choices). Be upbeat and definite in your presentation, and keep the groups moving. As soon as the groups have established themselves, give the participants time enough to look at one another, say hi, and then announce the next split.

The following group splits have been used successfully and are presented in an approximate sequence. Don't hesitate to use your own "grouping" ideas.

1. Everyone fold your hands. If your right thumb is on top, get together with other right-thumbers. Left-thumbers do the same. (This is a hereditary trait, but you don't have to say that — and it's not in any way associated with baldness.

2. What month were you born in? Notice that we have gone from an A/B group to a multi-split situation. Give the participants time enough to see if anyone was born on their birthday. What a thrill to find someone born on the same year and day.

3. Fold your arms and separate as in #1; i.e., which arm is on top.

4. How many children in your family? From an only child to ?

5. Which leg do you put in your pants first? This may lead to three groups, because some people sit and put both legs in at the same time. Don't laugh, we're all weird in some way.

6. Are you left or right-handed? Ambidextrous?

7. What kind of bed do you sleep in? Spring mattress? Water bed? Fouton?

8. What state or country were you born in?

9. Do you put the toilet tissue roll on so that the paper comes over the top, or comes out underneath? This is a serious topic.

10. What astrologic sign are you?

11. When putting on a sweater, what goes first: head, left arm, right arm, or all three at once?

12. What make of watch do you wear? No watch?

13. What color are your eyes? Red doesn't count. Get verification from two people.

14. Do you wear glasses, contacts, or none?

15. If you sleep with someone, do you sleep on the right or left side? If you sleep alone, do you get in on the right or left side? Over the end? Come on!

There are also a number of, what is your favorite _____? type of questions that fit into this group-splitting format.

Examples: What is your favorite

- daily hot drink?
- color?
- movie?
- movie actor or actress?
- song?
- instrumentalist?
- sport (spectator or participant)?
- vocalist?
- state?
- pet?

The answers to these questions are not as definitive as the previous ones, so expect more laughter, and discussion (disagreement). If arguments result that threaten to upset the fun and flow, switch quickly to another game or topic. If you don't have another activity to retreat to, don't start the first one.

## Bombs Away

I hesitate reporting on this oral debacle because, despite the funny results, the activity itself is demeaning and, in fact, has been (probably still is) used as a fraternity hell-week harassment. But after receiving a letter from Bill Hallowell relating how much summer campers enjoyed his modified approach — well, here it is in its 1950's unexpurgated form and Bill's more acceptable fun format.

## Hell Week Variation

Inject (hypodermic needle) a raw egg with asfedida (spelling is probably wrong, as this is a phonetic attempt at a word I haven't used in 30 years). Asfedida has the salubrious effect of immediately rotting albumen and yolk, and producing an appropriate foul odor.

The trick (bad joke) is to drop (10-20 ft.) the liquid part of the altered egg into the oral cavity of a coerced kneeling person. This is *NOT* an activity to engender trust and compassion, but (and I hesitate to admit it), the results are very funny — if your oral cavity is the one not being used as a target.

The above scenario has been recorded only for its historical significance. The author suggests trying the following set-up in a camp situation for some obvious fun. As presented here, the activity is an end in itself, but could easily be included in a game or as a benign consequence for doing something wrong in the game.

## Jello Drop

"We do a Jello Drop at summer camp each year and it is very popular with the 8-13 year-old group. Although they may not readily admit to it, the counselors have a blast with it, too.

*Materials:*

1. A pan of Jello (any flavor) cut into cubic inch blocks.
2. Elevated platform (baseball backstop, step ladder, low roof).

Once set up, this is an easy, fun activity requiring cooperation, coordination, and a steady mouth. The dropper climbs up any elevated platform with the pan of Jello (pre-cut) in hand. S/he carefully drops one cube at a time into the wide open mouth below. A ten foot drop makes for a good splat when the catcher is off by an inch. A large group of spectators/participants makes it fun, because everyone ends up laughing at each other. Once I had half a cube dribble down the inside of my T-shirt. The other half was dangling between my teeth and lower lip.

Try it...you'll love it."

## Funnel Your Fun

While I was attending college in the late '50's, it was the rage to fire water balloons from one side of the football stadium to the other amid beery shouts and high-pitched distaff shrieks. Being more often a target than a perpetrator, I missed out on how a water balloon could be fired such a long distance. Rumors of rubber bands and angles of incidence were appealing, but so were the initiators of high-pitched shrieks, so my ballistic education remained unfulfilled.

My next exposure to ballistic ballooning was in Boston, as members of rival skulling crews fired balloons at one another across the Charles River — a formidable distance. I was once again at the receiving end (a spectator, actually).

During the first years with Project Adventure (early '70's), there was much physical and academic curriculum experimenting going on. One of the more interesting ideas was to make Physics 101 less text-oriented and more hands-on. Pupils would venture out to the ropes course and determine qualitative and quantitative values of such erudite items as height of elements, mass of logs, mechanical advantages of pulley systems, and levers, etc. As part of this in-depth academia, a potential Pulitzer Prize winner suggested firing water balloons for distance on the football field to determine how mass, parabolic arcs and inertia affected accuracy. (I'll admit the cognitive aspect was a bit shaky, but we're actively pursuing the fun/function formula here.) The results were entirely nonacademic and inconclusive, as students joyfully committed themselves as non-moving targets to prove their nebulous findings. Also, the use of football goalposts and bicycle tires as a slingshot combination did not provide the impressive distance results I had previously observed.

Finally, as the result of a recent *Foes & Questors* game, I have the formula for sure-fire, hyperthrust, long distance, slingshot water ballooning. Two game participants (Joan and Phil) brought a new weapon that they wanted to introduce and as the result of an impromptu, long-distance demo, the other players enthusiastically accepted what was soon called a "Funnelator." This slingshot device was capable of firing small water balloons over 100 yards. Impressed? Here's how.

You need two 10 ft. sections of 5/16" diameter surgical tubing (sells for about $.40/ft.), a large plastic auto oil funnel with a long neck, and many penny balloons.

Drill the upper lip of the funnel (5"-6" diameter top) with a 1/2" drill bit on both sides of the circumference so that the 5/16" tubing can be inserted and tied off with an overhand knot. Slip a 3/8" slug washer over the tubing end before inserting and tying this knot.

Have two people hold the separate surgical tube sections (the slingshot) over their heads and stand 6'-8' ft. apart. A third person (making up the Funnelator team) places a small, water-filled balloon into the funnel and gripping the long neck, pulls it back and down (down to gain a higher arc), and releases smoothly.

If the two rubber band holders are able to stand on benches, step ladders or a small hill, the balloon can be launched at a higher arc to achieve greater distance.

It's a good idea to fill the funnel hole with putty (or whatever) to prevent an occasional flashback of water as the balloon breaks because of too rapid acceleration.

If some of you extremists are not pleased with the 100 yard distance, purchase another set of tubing, drill another set of adjacent holes in the same funnel, and prepare for FAA regulations of your missile.

Contests from opposite ends of a football field, with more than two sets of Funnelator teams functioning, provide cooling competition on a hot day.

*Considerations:*

- Do not fire a Funnelator directly at another person; i.e., no arc. A ballistic water balloon packs a big punch.
- Tie a knot in the end of each section of tubing to provide a firm grip for the holder.
- Check the tubing for tears, particularly near the knot/funnel contact area.

***Funnelating*** is an end in itself — don't worry about reasons for doing it.

### Jack & Jill

My mother taught me this silly scenario years and years ago, and considering its entertainment potential for young children, I think it's worth learning. If you have children or work with children, they will like this — it plays better than it reads.

Take a small, ripped-off piece of tissue paper (toilet tissue or Kleenex-type, about the size of your fingernail), moisten it with some saliva, and stick it to the nail of your index finger. Do the same thing with your other index finger. Don't get bogged down by neatness — any ole torn piece will do.

Sit down and rest your hands (index fingers extended) on your knees. There is a little dialogue that accompanies the imminent action, and it goes like this:

"Two little blackbirds sitting on a fence; one named Jack (wiggle the right index finger) and one named Jill (wiggle the other index finger)." "Fly away, Jack!" (lift your right hand rapidly to a position behind your head and simultaneously exchange and extend your middle finger for the index finger. Then, as rapidly, bring your hand back down to your knee. All this is done in one smooth action. The middle finger is now extended with no tissue attached, and the index finger with tissue affixed is held tucked under the hand.

"Fly away, Jill!" (Perform the same procedure with the left hand.)

"Come back, Jack!" (Switch fingers of the right hand again by raising the hand as before and making the switch behind your head. Now the tissue is again apparent.)

"Come back, Jill!" (Same return sequence with the left hand.)

This covert digital display will amaze and mystify young boys and girls, and they'll want you to do it again and again before they figure out what the trick is. Older children (our age) may also be initially baffled, but usually won't admit it.

I just timed the whole Jack Magic sequence and it takes me about 15 seconds from start to end.

A nifty trick that I'm pleased to pass along. Thanks, Mom.

## Existential Volleyball

This funny title indicates nothing more than good ole *Moonball* with a goal orientation.

The group (any size) divides in half and faces one another over a line (rope on the ground, painted gym line, etc.). The announced object is to score points for your team by hitting the beach ball over the line and onto the opponent's turf, but the hidden scenario involves more magic motion than competition, as evidenced by the following lack of rules. (Paradoxically, it often takes more words to define less rules.)

1. Any hit over the line must pass the line on the level or while ascending; i.e., no downward hits (spiking).
2. The ball can be hit as many times on a side as deemed necessary by a team.
3. There are no side or end boundaries.
4. Anyone can serve from any position.
5. Rotating players is either allowed, not allowed, or partially allowed.
6. There is no such thing as "carrying the ball," except when you actually carry the ball.
7. Rules can be modified to include a one-bounce-on-the-floor variation.
8. Any part of the body can strike the ball. Foot serves are particularly impressive and non-effective.
9. If point-keeping seems more significant than pure excellence of play, bombastically announce a change of serve after every point. Lower your voice an octave and exclaim, "Side out!" while pointing toward one of the teams with one hand and holding the other hand overhead with three fingers extended. If anyone asks what you are doing, say, "Your ad, serving two" ...gets 'em every time.

*Final Point Clarification* — To win, a team must be ahead by two points when 53 points is reached. Keep things moving by alternating answers (yes or maybe) to all players' questions.

## Tattoo

It's hard to appreciate the use or enjoyment of this multi-ball activity unless you become involved, but the activity satisfies a need for movement, accomplishment, and personal satisfaction, in addition to being more totally kinetic and visual than any other group activity I can think of, besides rock 'n roll.

Give each participant (10-50 people) 3-4 rabid nuggets (tennis balls) and ask them to arrange themselves behind the mid-line of an indoor basketball court; facing toward one of the backboards. (For this throwing sequence to work, there must be a wall behind the backboard; i.e., no bleachers.)

Indicate that on GO, they are to aim and throw their hardest in order to hit the basketball backboard, and continue throwing, attempting to produce a drum-like "tattoo" sound on the backboard. After firing their initial nuggets, they must nab a rebounding ball or 2 or 3 and continue this fire-at-will melee.

All the nuggets will not rebound back to the throwers, so a couple volunteers must position themselves somewhere under the backboard to retrieve stray projectiles. Being a retriever is not as crazy as it sounds, since all the throwers are aiming well over the downcourt volunteers' heads. A ricochet might bound off your head or body, but the potential and minor consequences make the "under fire" position more attractive.

Let the action continue for a couple minutes. The sound and movement are rewards in themselves. In addition: (1) Those people who like to throw and throw well can "chuck" as many balls as hard as they want to and cheer their own efforts and accuracy (because no one else is paying attention or can tell who's throwing what where). (2) Those folks who can't throw well can either throw a few nuggets or none at all without fear of censure, because (as above) nobody's watching *their* efforts.

After things slow down a bit (2-3 minutes), ask each person to retrieve and hold a couple nuggets. Indicate that you want to start the same activity, but this time by throwing with the other arm (opposite their adept one). The results are humbling and laughable. Almost everyone does poorly, except the ambidextrous few, so reluctance to try is quickly put aside. After 30 seconds of high arced and poorly aimed throws (and much good-natured ribbing), let them finish up with a few *good ones* by letting them return to their natural throwing arm.

### Nugget Alternatives

1. Ask a nuggeted group, standing at one end of the basketball court (backs against the wall) if they can hit the far wall with a ball thrown by their "opposite" arm. After a few attempts (some success, some not), let them finish up with a couple throws with their "good" arm.

2. Request that everyone pair up for the next activity, the "Howitzer Throw." The object of this command/response bit of cooperation is to have one participant tell his/her blindfolded (eyes closed) partner where to throw a ball in order to hit a target (backboard, championship pennant, buzzer, etc.). The partners may not touch one another; only

words of direction are allowed. Six shots at one target are delivered and then another target is chosen. People should not become target material. Switch roles after a few attempts.

## Where the Balls Are

It becomes soon obvious that to properly offer the preceding tennis ball activities, you need "beaucoup" balls. From past experience, the following sources for used balls are worthwhile pursuing.

*Best* — Make a deal with a tennis club or tennis pro to barter or buy their used balls. Tennis facilities use an inordinate amount (hundreds) of balls, retiring them after only a few sets. Tell the owner (usually wealthy) that the balls are to be used in an educational program and are not to be recycled for proletarian court play.

*Not Bad, But Seasonal* — Check the rooftops of a school's gymnasium. Gym roofs are invariably flat (that's why they leak), and they eat tennis balls (and shoes, locks, golf balls, etc.).

*Poor, But Good for a Few* — Stand around a municipal tennis court and sneak off with out-of-bounds balls. Be fair, though — let the ball come to a stop.

## Longevity Line-Up

Line up by age to the nearest year, month, day. The advantages of using this method is that it allows the participants to say something about themselves that is normally a withheld fact and only spoken of jokingly. This rookie-to-venerable line works particularly well with an adult group exhibiting a wide age span.

> Alternate #1 — Ask the group to perform the above task non-verbally. Line up where you think you belong.

> Alternate #2 — Ask the group to line up as above non-verbally and blindfolded. Start as a blindfolded cluster. This seemingly improbable task can be accomplished rather quickly by some groups — other groups have been known to miss dinner.

Briefly — Line up by: Your sign (horoscope); the number of teeth you have missing (or left); hair shades (real or fabricated); shoe sizes, etc.

Looking for two approximately equally numbered groups, separate into half by:

1. Last name starts with A-M or N-Z.
2. Pants color (there are usually at least 1/2 blue pants in any large group).
3. Do you put left or right foot in your pants first?
4. Hands folded — is the right or left thumb on top?

5. Like or dislike — (any controversial, well-known personality)? Be prepared for some good-natured and incisive comments during this pairing up.

## People-to-People Surfing

The people-to-people, rolling-on-the-turf part of this activity is straight from the New Games folks. I've included it because it's fun (with the right group) and jives with the paper core gym surf ride (below).

Situate the group (as many as possible) lying face down on a grassy area so that bodies are parallel to one another and about 2' apart. If you have a grassy area on a slightly downward incline, use it; the surfer travels faster and usually farther.

Simply have a person (surfer) lie face down, in a perpendicular fashion, on the first 2 or 3 bodies on the turf. As the Malahini shouts, "Surf's up," the people in contact with the surfer roll over in a direction that everyone has agreed upon — slightly downhill is certainly easier. If the surf machine is well-controlled, the surfer will travel swiftly (albeit somewhat lumpily) to the "beach." Resituate the surf mechanism and repeat with another "Hot Curl" sequence.

This return-to-the-earth activity is a good follow-up to Tractor Tread (Human Caterpillar).

## Paper Core Surfing

This event is more in line with the pure stand-up-hang-ten surfing technique. It's as close to real surfing as can be accomplished on a gym floor; which isn't saying much, but...

To achieve Hodad status, you must acquire a number of paper cores (say 15). Paper cores are the inner cores of large paper rolls. Our free local source of these cores is the International Paper Company in Framingham, Massachusetts. They are apparently throw-away items, so check your local paper manufacturing companies for these essential playthings. The ones we use measure 24" long by 12" in diameter.

Place and arrange about 10-15 of these cores on the gym floor so that they are 18" apart (roller-to-roller, not end-to-end). Then place a 2' x 4' section of 1/2" plywood lengthwise on top of the first two rollers. This piece of plywood should have the corners and edges beveled and be well sanded to remove splinters.

The group should line up on both sides of the situated rollers to prevent wipeouts (basic spotting). The surfer jogs a few strides to gain momentum and jumps on the "surfboard" with a practiced double-footed leap, and rides the rollers — hopefully, to the end. There is obviously some risk associated with this activity, so spot carefully and prevent uncontrolled wild leaps onto the board.

## Surf Massage

If you're not into breakneck surfing, how about a surf massage? Place the rollers as before, but closer together (12") and ask someone to lie on their back so that their head is directed toward the destination. Remaining stiffly prone, the massagee is propelled forward by two pushers, each pushing on a foot. There is a unique bumpity-bump-bump sensation resulting from this propulsion that is quite unlike anything purchasable.

If you want to make this a group initiative problem, try moving a participant on top of the rollers (as above) the full length of a gym using only 15 rollers. An assembly line must be quickly and efficiently established so that as one is used up, it must be brought to the front and set down before the rider's head reaches that point. Be sure to have two spotters watching the rider's head and torso in case the group pushes faster than they "lay track."

## Balloon Blow-Up

If you are looking for a no-holds-barred histrionic way to demonstrate the teacher/actor role so often used in adventure presentations, try on one of these vivid mime roles.

Lie on the floor in a semi-fetal position with the tip of your thumb pressed against your lips. Begin blowing on your thumb, producing noticeable hissing sounds. (This is the sound of air entering the balloon — you.) Visualize your cramped body as a deflated balloon and try to think of air entering your arms and legs, and why type of movement your limbs would make as they begin expanding. Make the movements sequential and convulsively realistic. Also, be patient with the movements, remembering how long it takes to fill a large balloon.

Keep blowing and filling until your limbs begin to swell and force you into an eventual scarecrow-like standing position. Keep blowing until you are absolutely filled to your limit (cheeks puffed out, on your tiptoes, arms and legs rigid with air), and then BURST with a loud verbal POW or BANG or whatever you do best. You rapidly decrease in size, deflating toward the floor, all the while emitting loud, air-release, hissing sounds, until you end up in a heap on the floor.

*A variation* — Instead of bursting, simply let your air out, and like a balloon thus treated, jet yourself willy-nilly around the room until all the propulsive air is gone.

## Fried Egg Simulator

Watch for bruises on this one; i.e., don't get carried away during the hot frying pan time slot.

Begin again in the fetal position, but on your knees, face down on the floor. You are, in this position, an unbroken, fresh egg. To begin, ask someone to

Imagine an egg being broken onto a hot frying pan and try to duplicate, with body movements, the rapidly increasing formation of bubbles under the albumen; i.e., their constant formation and bursting. Can't picture it? Go fry an egg, and then, be one! Use your imagination (well-honed by this time) and finish off the sequence.

To make these silly mime sequences more meaningful to your audience, tell them what you are (to properly align their imaginations), but not what you are going to do — your actions should take care of that.

## Inch Worm

Sit on the turf facing your partner. Inch toward one another until you, and he or she, are close enough to sit on each other's feet. Grasp your partner's upper arm with each hand.

Now, decide which direction you two would like to travel. Lateral movement is out, so it's either north or south. After deciding, the partner (in whose direction you're headed) lifts her/his derriere off the ground and moves a foot or so toward whatever goal you have in mind: be reasonable. The second partner now lifts off the ground and in a cooperative, bug-like movement duplicates the step above and moves toward her/his partner.

Attempt to keep your bottom on your partner's feet and help the action by both pulling with the arms and slightly lifting the feet. Coordinate your movements and eventually speed up the process so that your pair is indistinguishable from a Loctan herodipus, inching comfortably along a branch.

## PDQ

During workshops and in various classes, I've discovered that a sit-down session facetiously dubbed, the "Play Determinant Quotient" (PDQ), acts as a fine deinhibitor, is good for more than a few group laughs, and clearly illustrates the instructor's role as actor and co-participant.

In your own presentation of this semi-skilled and mostly useful potpourri of shenanigans, the value extends from the participants' attempts, rather than the dialogue that comes so easily and vicariously.

Indicate to your seated listeners that you are going to introduce, by demonstration, a progression of "things to do," and that you would like each member of the group to approximately duplicate your manipulations, sounds, movements, etc. Explain that all these nostalgic doings are self-tests and are to be scored individually on a pass-fail basis. Further indicate that the "tests" will begin easily and become progressively harder.

All of this preliminary patter is to develop interest and psych the group for trying something new, mysterious, and with a bit of pizzaz. If your earlier presentations during the workshop (class) have been effectively spontaneous, your audience (you are an impromptu actor, after all) will eagerly anticipate the next bit of zaniness.

### The PDQ "Test"

1. Take your right index finger and insert it into your mouth and attempt to make an oral popping sound by levering the finger of choice against the inside of your cheek and rapidly out of your mouth (keeping the lips pursed in an approved manner).

*Author's Note* — Attempting to write about these facts of profitless dexterity is probably as tedious as reading about them. It's predictably more fun to digitally abuse your cheek than to read about it; so back to your finger and lever away. Have you ever seen someone try to "pop" their cheek and achieve only a fleshy "sploop"? It's funny, and entertainingly useful in a group setting as the expert poppers attempt to aid the hapless sploopers.

1. (a) Try the opposite finger in the other cheek: historically more difficult.

2. Snap your right finger and then the left finger, achieving a distinct snapping sound. Remember — all these performances are on a pass/fail basis. Goodnaturedly emphasize the failures and jokingly remark on outstanding efforts.

3. Snap all the fingers of one hand against the thumb in rapid succession, achieving three or four distinct sounds.

3 (a) And with the other hand and fingers.

4. Mention that the next test is entirely conceptual and that only YOU will know if you passed the test.

    Point your index fingers at one another so that the finger tips actually touch one another. Do this about 10-12 inches in front of your face. To "pass" the test, you must *see* a small link sausage visually form between your fingertips. This is definitely a pass/fail test; you either see it or you don't. Don't laugh — I'm being serious...kind of.

    If people (you) are having trouble making this visual connection, tell them to look beyond the fingers or to cross their eyes. If *you* still can't see the sausage, I don't know what to say: I'm sorry. Better drop this one from your test list.

    If you slightly separate your fingers, the link sausage (which has fingernails on each end — gross!) will float in mid-air. Keep trying.

5. I'm not going to try to depict this next one, at least not "by the numbers." It's an age-old, two-handed trick used to delight young children (and young minds) by opposing palms, juxtaposing and intertwining the middle fingers, twisting the palms against one another in opposite directions, as the fingers find their way, and finally causing the middle fingers to flip-flop in opposite directions.

It is amusing to watch and fun to help someone try to accomplish this fairly intricate, but well-known movement.

Another remember — You are trying to present a series of maneuvers that *will* result in occasional and obvious failure, in order to share the consequences of trying a new and possibly intimidating task.

6. Cup your hands and blow *across* (like across the top of a bottle or bullet shell) the small aperture formed between the second and third joint of the thumbs. This produces a hollow hooting sound that is the newfound delight of practicing youngsters and anathema to their parents and teachers..

    You can extend or supplement this "test" outdoors by placing a blade of grass (wide blades for deep sounds, narrow blades for higher notes), between the thumbs (as above) and blowing directly *on* the tightly held blade. The grass acts as a vibrating reed, producing a variety of animal and unearthly sounds.

7. You can finish this formal (?) part of the testing sequence by demonstrating something difficult that you can do. Try whistling loudly through your teeth. Or, touching your tongue to your nose. Or, playing a recognizable tune (I've always had good luck with "You Are My Sunshine") by cupping your hand in your armpit under your shirt and...you know!

The folks in your group (more group than audience by this time) are beginning to demonstrate with alacrity those ridiculous pranks that not so long ago amused their friends and aggravated their teachers and parents.

A couple of tested maneuvers that have proven humorous and acceptably bizarre are: (a) Put your finger in either ear and seemingly extend it into your oral cavity, resulting in an obvious and moveable bump in your cheek (use your tongue, please!) (b) Produce a nose-breaking sound by cupping your hands over your nose/mouth area and convincingly "pop" your nose by subtly snapping a thumbnail against your teeth.

I don't think there is any need to list more of these PDQ's, because each group knows more than enough tricks to further your purposes of relaxing overly serious seminar participants and demonstrating an engaging level of play. Even the participants who don't actively take part are taken by the spontaneous nature of the responses and the level of group enjoyment. The test, after all, is no test at all, but simply an invitation to play.

### Mrs. O'Grady — A genuine no-prop deinhibitizer that's more fun than embarrassing.

With about 6-8 people (including yourself) standing in a circle, ask the person to your left or right the following sequence of questions and also indicate to them what their reply should be. This is a very traditional game:

You: "Did you hear what happened to Mrs. O'Grady?"
Them: "No, what happened?"
You: "She died!"
Them: "How did she die?"
You : "With one cocked eye."

At this juncture, you close one eye tightly and hold it closed until the game is over. The person who was answering your questions then asks the identical series of questions to the person next to her, and this continues around the circle until all the participants have, "one cocked eye."

When the questioning role is yours again, continue to add embellishments to the way Mrs. O'Grady died. E.g., "With her mouth awry" (and twist your mouth grotesquely to one side); "...breathing a sigh," "...with her leg held high" (lifting one leg off the floor); and "...waving goodbye." By the time all of these movements, sounds and postures have been continued by all members of the circle (as the questioning creeps humorously and interminably around from person to person), physical fatigue and a certain hysterical monotony allows an unselfconscious abandonment to the game. Why else would a semi-sophisticated adolescent stand on one leg, waving a hand absently with one eye closed, his mouth twisted to one side, while emitting a series of metronome-like sighs?

If you have student leaders or another teacher that can initiate the questions, you can begin other O'Grady circles. Don't include more than 8 people in a circle for obvious reasons of physical fatigue and tedious repetition. If things are going too slowly the next time the questioning comes around to you, include two "things to do" in your obituary.

You do not debrief this "theater in the round," simply enjoy it.

## Leather Bubbles

I like this! And I really like the long bubble life. These four paragraphs are taken directly from the Adventure Counseling Curriculum Guide of the Hamilton-Wenham Regional School District, Hamilton, Massachusetts.

"From time immemorial, the blowing of soap bubbles has been a form of amusement for children, young and old. A formula is here given for a solution which will produce bubbles of surprising size and durability.

Half an ounce of soap — preferably castile — is cut into shavings, put into a pint of water and gently heated until the soap is dissolved. The solution should be allowed to cool and should then be filtered. Into three parts of this solution should be mixed two parts of glycerine, and the mixture thoroughly shaken in a bottle. It will at first be clear, but will soon become turbid. After a day or two, the solution will be found to be whitish or turbid at the top and clear underneath. Pour off the turbid portion and use the clearer part for the blowing of soap bubbles; or, better, siphon out the clear portion and keep it for use.

A bubble made from this glycerine liquid will *last for hours*, if not disturbed by draughts of air, and if allowed to rest on some soft woolen fabric. New clay pipes should be used in the blowing of the bubbles, and contests may be held in the blowing of the largest bubble or the most lasting one.

A pleasing game for all ages is played by arranging a cord, or some sort of screen, across the room, the bubble-blowers taking opposite sides. The object of the game is to blow the bubbles and force them over the dividing line into the enemies' territory, by using small, oriental-type hand fans. A piece of cardboard from a box or the back of a yellow pad works OK, too. The opposing side tries to fan them back again. Every bubble that bursts in the territory of either side counts as a point against that side. An umpire is necessary to decide on the points of the bubble warfare. The game is often indulged in by people who have passed their childhood days, but who seem to enjoy the pastime, nevertheless."

## Big Leather Bubbles

A fellow named David Stein manufactures a whimsical device called the "Bubble Thing," which makes bubbles in the 3'-12' category and sometimes "as long as a bus!" Dave's instant bubble mix is, "Mix one cup of Joy or Dawn dish detergent with 10 cups of water. For longer lasting bubbles, add 1/4 cup of glycerine or Wesson oil to the soapy mixture."

The bubble-making device looks like — it really doesn't look like anything I can think of. It's a plastic rod with a loose triangular arrangement of filigree cloth (like rick-rack, but different) draped below the rod...you better get one.

For use summer or winter. "Winter bubbles crystallize into rainbow-colored spheres, then shatter."

## Autograph Seekers

Here's a means of achieving some emotional adventure and sizeable amount of vis-a-vis stress.

The following list represents your autograph worksheet. The task is to select any ten of the following 25 items below by placing an X in front of each of your choices. A player will then seek the autograph of an interviewed person to fit each of the ten categories or conditions that you have X'd. The autograph signifies that you have actually talked with a person and have asked the necessary question(s) to determine if that person fulfills what the item indicates. You must have a different autograph for each of the ten items. No winners or losers in this game, just a good time and some personal growth.

1. Thinks the President is doing a good job —
2. Born under my astrological sign —
3. Prefers to work alone —
4. Likes liver —
5. Reads poetry —
6. Looks attractive to me —
7. Has a part-time job —
8. Likes break dancing —
9. Might be intimidating to me —
10. Believes in magic —
11. Owns an Alligator shirt —
12. Has a tattoo —
13. Appears to be friendly —
14. Likes mint chocolate chip ice cream —
15. Plays a musical instrument —
16. Advocates openness —
17. Drinks beer —
18. Enjoys competition —
19. Sleeps in a waterbed —
20. Drives a sports car —
21. Uses Nautilus —
22. Wears Jockeys —
23. Has had a root canal —
24. Likes the President —
25. Thinks UFO's are real —

This activity requires some moxie with a dash of chutzpah, and is subversively arranged by teacher-types to initiate conversations. The actual autograph-seeking can be accomplished within a school setting, but stalking real world folk is much more adventurous and satisfying. Be careful, though, you might initiate more conversation than anticipated and end up with a friend — and you know how friends are, they can be so demanding and personal...and tie up the phone, too.

## Chapter 8
# *Curriculum Tidbits*

**Pulse Line-Up**

Having people form a line because of height, age, etc., is useful as an ice-breaker and as a means of revealing something about yourself without bragging. Add this simple line-up to your collection. Ask people to line up as to their standing pulse rate. Let them determine what their pulse rate is right there, right now. Show them where the carotid pulse is located and say START. Measure thirty seconds (60 seconds is interminable) of beats and times 2 for a minute's total.

If people want to know if or why their pulse rate is high or low for their age level, be noncommittal; this low-key line-up is not meant to serve as a diagnostic clinic.

**Another 50/50 Group Split Ploy**

Always looking for another unobtrusive way to divide a group in half? This sit-down/stand-up ploy recently showed up at a workshop, and does exactly what it's supposed to.

Ask your group to pair-up. Indicate that one person of the pair must decide to stand the other sit. All standing players make up one group (team) and the sitting players represent the other. If there is an odd participant, quickly put them on the team that *you* think might need another person, or ask him/her to choose a standing or seated position.

I haven't used this technique often enough to know if the standing/sitting choice produces a different dynamic or skills discrepancy between groups. I'm sure if you make up a valid-sounding theory and couch it in pedagogic terms (cognitive, affective, psychomotor) that whatever you say will be well received. Sound familiar?

**Dial-a-Quote**

"The difference between my quotations and those of the next man is that I leave out the inverted commas." — George Moore

Need a quote, a word, or a phrase to fill a blank in your proposal? I think most of us at one time or another have searched about for the right words or phrase to express what we felt, but couldn't synaptically release. Sometimes a proposal will be accepted if the right text buttons are rhetorically pushed. Here are some "buttons" to read through and use to the best of your needs.

All of these words and phrases have been used and stated in a variety of ways before, so don't feel guilty about borrowing them, because they are part of what should be a shareable pool. I collected them from a series of books (including some stuff from *Cows' Tails & Cobras*, *High Profile*, and *Silver Bullets*, that I forgot I had written), introductions, letters, articles, and whatever I deemed was generic and useable enough for the dial-a-quote process. If you see something here that looks like your work, be flattered — I like what you said, and I'm sure someone else will, too. You have contributed to idea-sharing at its best. Note that I have left out the quotation marks, hopefully making it easier for you to borrow a phrase or two.

*Dial-a-Quotes*

Trust, within the framework of an adventure curriculum, is gained with patience, thoughtfulness, and care, over a period of time, and can be damaged or lost in a few seconds.

Unfortunately, many children grow up in such a protected environment that the chance to learn day-to-day survival skills never materializes.

Each task is designed so that a group must employ cooperation and some physical effort to gain a solution.

The problem-oriented approach to learning can be useful in developing each individual's awareness of decision-making, leadership, and the obligations and strengths of each member within a group.

They also serve to break down some of the stereotypes which exist so comfortably in our social network.

Initiative problems are a non-pareil for building morale and a sense of camaraderie — when a group need a morale boost or a means of gaining behavioral insights, a well-chosen game or initiative problem was a surefire and enjoyable way to accomplish that goal.

If what you are presenting is geared only to successful completion, and failure is non-existent, then boredom replaces challenge.

Reasonable risk-taking is part of living.

Games can provide the morale growth and sense of camaraderie that facilitates group cohesion and enthusiasm for the program.

It's hard to turn your back on obvious fun.

Trust is a powerful and essential education tool; it is the key to personal involvement.

An individual will seldom take a physical or emotional chance, if they perceive callousness and unreasonable risk as part of that risk-taking.

A group surrounded with positive experiences and successes will experience trust, growing apace with personal confidence.

...a chance to try potentially difficult and/or frightening activities in an atmosphere of support and caring.

...being able to "back off" when performance pressures or self-doubt become too strong, knowing that an opportunity for a future attempt will always be available.

...respect for individual ideas and choices.

...their eager wish to participate illustrates clearly that people will respond to challenging, enjoyable, and meaningful activity curricula.

Risk is normal in the daily lives of all human beings and is essential to their education.

Safety is an essential ingredient, but to deny or reduce the risk factor in educational units is to run counter to the educational process itself.

Adventure activities have been used effectively by a variety of teachers, counselors, therapists, camp directors, and church leaders.

...an effective, engaging way to bring people together to build trust and to break down the artificial barriers between individuals and groups of individuals.

These **PA** activities have been evaluated as having improved self-concept, improved the ability of members to take risks, and improved the ability of group members to cooperate and work well together.

...Thus the ropes course is not simply a series of cheap thrills and military oriented obstacles...

...there is a good feeling in knowing that there is something to be worked toward before success can be expected.

...lessens their normal sensitivity to failure because the activity is engrossing and fun.

...the group was laughingly supportive of any effort, no matter how inept.

...increased confidence in his/her physical and psychological ability to overcome problem situations.

...unafraid of failure, because of the supportive nature of the group and the knowledge that if I continue to try, I'll probably improve.

...keep the curriculum fresh, exciting, and non-repetitive.

...increased level of agility and physical coordination.

...the use of teams, points and competition has consciously been minimized.

...as a person matures, s/he needs to handle the anxiety that precedes any new venture.

Students are regularly out in weather which ranges from sunny and warm to cloudy and close to zero.

...sufficient for conditioning and remains within the realm of fear, fun and functionality.

...a willingness to appear inept in front of others.

**PA** is unprecedented in its success in providing students with activities which are focused on enhancing self-esteem and mutual support.

...solving problems that are designed so that group members must take advantage of their combined physical and mental capabilities in arriving at a solution.

...develop abilities that contribute to group decision-making and leadership.

...foster appreciation and respect for differences existing within the group.

...appreciation of the interdisciplinary nature of real problem solving.

**PA** would self-destruct in a few years if teachers used only a few successful activities over and over again.

Games emphasize fun, give and take, a non-competitive nature, and play for the joy involved.

Adding outdoor adventure to our curriculum allows us to address the needs of more students.

By emphasizing team sports, we offer those students who are not team-oriented another chance not to participate, to become a discipline problem, or to become disillusioned with physical education.

The benefits derived from outdoor adventure education fit well into the philosophy of physical education. Benefits:

- increased physical fitness
- motor abilities
- mental abilities

- social-emotional abilities
- self-esteem increase
- interpersonal relationships
- gaining new insights
- challenge
- fun
- personal effectiveness
- sense of well-being
- body image
- achievement

Adventure activities require complete concentration of all of one's faculties and energies.

These activities offer opportunities to learn and develop lifelong leisure and physical activity skills.

...a physically exciting and accepted philosophy toward education of the total person.

Teachers using adventure curriculum activities have reported that their adventure adaptations are successful beyond all expectations.

Positive educational change regularly occurs as the result of accepting and reshaping adventure activities.

Adventure training works because people need the stimulus, respond to the vehicle and like the results.

Adventure training allows most students to achieve beyond their initial expectations with a resultant growth of self-confidence.

Adventure training defines compassion, trust, and commitment through jointly experiencing a series of demanding and exciting activities.

Adventure-based activities are designed to supplement, add to and embellish traditional programs — not replace them.

The emphasis is not on how well you perform, but how well you try.

The obvious results, measured in personal satisfaction and growth of self-esteem, more than compensate for a winning score.

...activities which offer fine physical and mental challenges and a satisfying spectrum of accomplishment levels.

Because of the various stresses involved (fear of failure, physical harm, human fallibility), there are unparalleled opportunities for the establishment of trust

Adventure education activities provide physical and mental challenges with pizzaz.

- non-competitive mutual support
- positive self-image
- personal confidence
- dramatically new and exciting
- enhanced self-confidence
- improved agility, coordination and physical fitness
- psycho-social objectives (referring to mutual support and self-confidence)
- commitment
- trust
- group cooperation
- getting comfortable with the group
- flexibility and creativity
- joyful, fun-loving approach
- alternative approach
- recognition and unanimous acceptance
- spontaneous creativity
- cooperative, supportive atmosphere
- accomplishment and personal worth
- jois de vivre
- unpredictability
- stressful
- fear
- fatigue
- compassion
- laughter
- pain
- love
- anticipation
- coerce
- encouragement
- spotting
- support rope
- to "get the feel" for something
- debilitating
- confidence
- momentum
- motivation

- responsibility
- bizarre
- stereotype
- initiative
- peace of mind
- funding
- educational concepts
- assessment
- innovative
- effective
- validated
- transferable
- diffusion
- evaluation
- cajole
- cardiovascular
- coordination
- emotional
- supportive
- conscientiousness
- malinger
- opt out
- onus
- struggle
- wide range
- unpredictability
- demonstrate
- discomfort
- realistic
- frustrating
- limberness and flexibility
- imagination
- uninhibiting
- sequential movements
- attentive and concerned
- intimidating
- satisfaction
- related

- process (debrief)
- obstacle
- perceived risk
- attitude
- embellished - expanded - adopted
- inept
- volunteer
- conscientious attempt

## Setting a Tone

Charlie Harrington (former Pittsburgh Steeler rookie and all-time Adventure rookie) of Arlington, Massachusetts, uses an amusing and attention-getting way of indicating an infraction of the rules while a group is attempting an initiative problem (touching the "electric fence," landing in the "poison peanut butter," etc.). His flagging tool is a brightly colored bandana, stuffed casually but noticeably in a back pocket. Upon spying a blatant (or subtle; sometimes called sneaky) infraction, Charlie throws his marker to the ground (a la the NFL) and shouts "HEAVY LUMPS"; which exclamation has no significance, except to draw attention to the infraction and its perpetrator.

This delightfully superfluous action and announcement is a fine example of what an adventure instructor can do to add to the enjoyment of, and instill fantasy into, an obviously fabricated situation.

### *Adventure Education Tips and Plagiarizable Material*

(that may also apply to any responsible educational approach)

An individual will seldom take a physical or emotional risk if they perceive unreasonable risk as part of that risk-taking.

A group surrounded with positive experience and success will experience trust growing apace with personal confidence.

Trust is gained with patience and care over a comfortably long period of time and can be damaged or lost in a second by carelessness or inconsiderate behavior.

*Program activities must regularly display an element of fun.*

If an activity is enjoyable, don't continue doing it every day until it is no longer enjoyed. If what you are doing is so geared to successful completion that failure is non-existent, then boredom replaces challenge.

Be ready to personally attempt whatever you are asking your students to try — right there, right now. Involve yourself regularly in curriculum activities — let the students see you succeed, fail; laugh and live with them.

Operating with *calculated abandon* and being *reasonably unreasonable* sounds good, but be aware that programmed adventure differs from pure adventure in that the path and outcome of the programmed approach are known. Operate to your known level of safety.

## Splicing Made Hard

Learning to splice three-strand rope with an experienced teacher at your side is no great task. Learning to splice from an illustration is self-flagellation of the third kind (the fourth kind involves trying to follow instructions over the phone).

Here are a few illustrations of the three basic splices that are clearer than most: start flagellating.

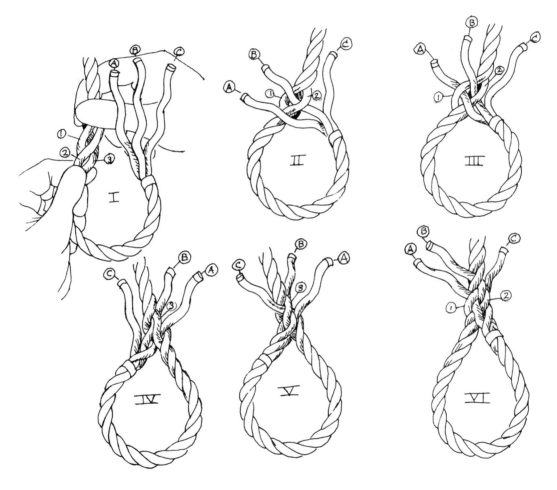

The eye splice is used most often, then the end (back) splice. The short splice is seldom used.

If you get stuck and can't figure out what you are doing wrong, don't call. My number isn't (508) 468-7685.

## Good Cents

How many pennies do you have hoarded?  I should ask, how many are reluctantly stored, because who really wants those omnipresent coppers that seem to reproduce themselves and appear everywhere they shouldn't — under dressers (where they get caught by the vacuum and make a clinkety-clank sound all the way up the tube), washing machines, bureau tops, etc.

It bothers me to buy things that cost $1.41, because I'm bound to get $.04 change and they end up in the rapidly filling fruit jar and then what do you do with them?  Put them in rolls and take them to the bank?  If you have functional age children, you can make the counting, stacking, and stuffing seem exciting for about 15 minutes — and then, they split for the video and the oceans of pennies on the rug remain for you to rake together and put away — 'till the next time.

Spend them.  For what, penny candy?...no such thing anymore.  Stores frequently ask (via cute cash register signs) for your pennies — until you try to pay for something.  Sure, at $1.41, they love your penny, but 141 of them?

It would make an interesting movie theme to offer someone a million dollars if they could spend (actually in-the-store spend), ten thousand dollars of pennies within a reasonable time span.  (Save your trip to the Casio — that's 1,000,000 pennies and considering that one hundred pennies weigh 10 ounces, a quick Nautilus membership might be in order as a prerequisite to the competition.)

### Birthday Penny Largesse

Grab handfuls of cents and liberally sow your back yard with these copper discs.  There's usually a bit of guilt associated with the first couple of sweeping tosses, but the solo feeling of tossing money indiscriminately to the winds is very satisfying.

*The objective benefit* — When the birthday party kiddos, surfeit and vibrating from a parentally planned sugar overdose, swarm onto the yard, they will soon discover the unburied treasure and manually gobble them up with gusto, to be taken home and stored in someone else's fruit jars.

### Take Them to the Mall

This plan, although effective and satisfying, hints at subversive or revolutionary action; have a good rap ready for the 17 year-old mall security guard.

Let your kids throw pennies by the fistful into those hokey mall fountains that have signs telling you to keep out of.  A worthy charity will probably (I wish I were sure, but...) benefit, children love the excess, and your copper coffers begin from zero again.

### Posterity Plan

Put the pennies in a bottle or jar and bury them, all of them, and make a treasure map — great fun — with the idea that some future generation of _____ (insert appropriate surname) can dig them up and cash in on their numismatic value as a downpayment on a Porsche (or whatever monumental extravagance you and I will never be able to afford).

### A Penny Stunt

Ever tried to see if you could pick up a penny from a table (bar) top by just placing your flat palm against the coin, lifting and closing your hand to a fist and somehow miraculously finding a penny nestled there?

Performing such feats of worthless dexterity is entertaining for awhile, but after the third or fourth time, it's a bit of ho-hum. The challenge can be extended by using more pennies and seeing how many can be lifted and grasped in one swipe — personal world records are a natural.

So, how do you do it? ...Sweaty palms help. Place the fleshy part of your palm (just below the root of the index finger for the first penny) on top of the coin. Press down hard, but as unobtrusively as possible (be cool, remember, this is part skill, speed and *trick*), for about 3 seconds and in one swift motion, lift and close your hand. Considering a series of optimistic if's, you should find a penny in your palm when you look — unless you used a dime on the table and if a penny shows up, let me know *that* trick.

A couple of practice grabs and you'll have it, I think. Beefy palms help. If the coin keeps falling from your hesitating grasp, moisten the side of the coin that contacts your hand (your choice — saliva, beer, Perrier).

After mastering the single coin move, attempt two coins, then three, etc. Continue to place the coins on the table so that they make contact with the fleshy part of your palm. Refer to the illustration for Alberto Gunizau's (1982 World's Penny-Lifting Champ — runner-up '83-84 largely because he lost the tip of his middle finger in a bowling accident), patented start, which is aptly referred to as "Gunizau's Gamble." Beyond the initial 8 coin arrangement, it's up to you. See you at the nationals.

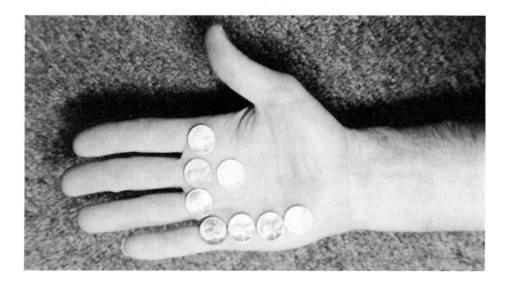

### *Got Some More Pennies?*

I'm still trying to get rid of all those collected coppers for you.

In front of a student group, ostentatiously pour out about 500 pennies onto a table top. Tell your class (4th to 6th grade, maybe 7th) that they can come to the table and take as many pennies as they want — to keep! (This idea is going to cost you 500 pennies, but what else were you going to do with them?)

Ask the students to line up and take turns pocketing the pennies. When all the coppers are gone, discuss what happened. Who took the most? How do they feel about getting $$ for nothing? Were they excited, doubtful, mad — what?

Let the comments flow. Suggest that the students write a story about what they experienced and discussed.

## Oral Adventure

I was involved in a workshop recently where truly prodigious amounts of *GORP* were consumed by the participants (the instructors helped). As a means of reducing the intake and expenditures, we purchased and mixed a concoction gustatorially referred to as generic or macro-GORP. The ingredients were:

1.   Foil-wrapped chocolate Hershey kisses
2.   Shelled (shells on) roasted peanuts
3.   Grapes (with seeds)

All of the above items were admittedly tasty and attractive to the palate, but required a pre-oral digital commitment that slowed consumption and increased attention to what was going over the lips (and onto the hips?). It was reported — after a brief period of initial dismay — that the generic GORP allowed more time for the tactile enjoyment of spontaneous mouth-stuffing.

There was some movement to substitute prunes (with pits, of course) for the grapes. The prune group liked the idea because a prune kind of looks like a big raisin. The idea was ultimately rejected because of the large colon movement that was inevitable, considering how much GORP was being munched.

After buying a quantity of the above items, mix them all in an opaque plastic bag — so that no one can see what they are grabbing.

This reporting is a bit whimsical, but generic GORP was actually a hit. Try it for a change of pace.

Thanks to the Nantahala Outdoor Center staff for participating in this oral experiment and to Gary Nussbaum (Radford University, Virginia) for buying the stuff.

**True Grit**

I'm not going to spend a lot of words on this, because it sounds weak — you know, like I'm just filling up space, but I know this simple activity works and for certain audiences, it's ideal therapy.

In the 60's, I worked as a "trail teacher" for an outdoor education center in California, taking sixth grade students on ecology hikes, leading campfires, teaching basic biology, etc. During this week of residential "camping," we regularly provided craft time so that students could use forest products (acorns, pine cones, bark, etc.) and their ingenuity to create a handmade object d'art. Usually, the slap-dash final product was a pencil or napkin holder or some such semi-useless, "Isn't-that-nice, dear?" circle-file type geegaw.

But, the significance of this hands-on activity was that students gained a tactile sense of what they could achieve with some elbow grease and time. Kind of like the occasional occupational rewards that we don't get enough of.

Many 4" x 4" pieces of 120 grit sandpaper were provided to "improve on nature." What really happened is that some students who had *never* done anything manually worthwhile (to them or anyone else, I suppose) got turned on to making things smooth, or "soft," as they used to say, with sandpaper.

You say, come on, Karl, what's the big deal with the sandpaper and what's the next game, anyway? I say, it *is* a big deal to provide a student with a low-cost activity that provides immediate and deserved satisfaction.

Try this yourself. Come on, if you're going to smile and shake your head, you can at least try this little experiment. Find a *small* piece of hardwood (oak, maple, teak) and, using a knife or whatever, give it round contours. Then, starting with 80 grit sandpaper, further smooth the edges and take out all the grooves and scratches. Then progress from 80 grit to 100 grit to 120 to 150 to 220 to 320 to 400 and finally, to the magic 600 grit sandpaper. When you start using the bigger numbers (finer grit paper), the tactile enjoyment of making your object "soft" is a sensory adventure not to be denied.

I have seen troublemakers, bored kids and non-achievers gain an inordinate amount of satisfaction from this coarse to super-fine grit progression toward achieving the luster and practically unbelievable smoothness that 600 grit paper allows.

Practical tip — buy garnet or aluminum oxide sandpaper: Don't waste your time with glued-on grit.

Touch the finished product to your cheek — your lip: Nice, huh?

### The Constrictor Knot

Having used and taught knots for years, it's a treat to discover a "new" knot that is easy to tie and uniquely useable; i.e., serves its own purpose.

The constrictor knot literally acts as a clamp for whatever objects you want held together. In conjunction with a half hitch, it is ideal for hauling boards up into a tree. Learn the knot and I guarantee you will find uses for it.

Geoffrey Budworth, author of *The Knot Book* (available through PA) offers this tip for tying the constrictor knot: "If the object you want to tie the knot around is soft, use hard cord for the tieing. If the object is hard, use soft material to tie the knot. The effect will be the same. In each case, it will grip like a boa constrictor."

# CONSTRICTOR KNOT

# *Elements of an Adventure Curriculum*

In developing your curriculum, the following components should be an integral part of the final product. It is, however, appropriate to stress some elements more than others, depending on the curriculum that you plan.

The qualities that make up the Project Adventure Approach to curriculum include:

1. A sense of adventure, unpredictability, drama and suspense. This tone may emerge from the situation (a cliff, slum or canoe trip) or from the teacher who builds drama, anticipation, suspense and mystique into the learning experience for students through stories, comments and even humor.

2. A consistently high (but accomplishable) level of expectation, demanded and created by both the intrinsic and external forces. Students need to be convinced that not just anyone could have done this, and that the teacher *cares* that the goal is reached.

3. A success orientation in which growth is supported and encouraged and in which the positive is emphasized. Encouragement is one crucial ingredient in resolving the conflict between high expectations and the need for a successful experience.

4. An atmosphere of mutual support in which cooperation, encouragement and interpersonal concerns are consistently present.

5. A sense of enjoyment, fun and the opportunity to laugh at a situation, each other, and one's self.

6. An approach to learning which makes use of group problem-solving, which allows for a variety of personal contributions and which presents problems that can't ordinarily be solved individually. The rewards are set up for group effort, rather than individual success or competition.

7. The use of a learning environment that is more complex, more engaging, less predictable and less familiar than a school classroom.

8. The merging of intellectual, social, physical, and emotional learning and development.

9. A significant amount of cognitive work, related directly to abstractions and questions previously developed in the classroom, or subsequently to be developed.

10. The combining of moments of active involvement with moments of personal and group reflection and evaluation. An awareness that teachable and learnable moments are unpredictable but necessary ingredients in a curriculum.

11.  A definite organization and structure which define the limits of the experience and states expectations but within which the participants have freedom to make decisions, choices, and mistakes.

12.  An economic and structural reasonableness which allows the curriculum to effectively compete for dollars and other resources within an educational economy which is limited in its resources.  Neither too long, too exotic, nor too expensive.

## A Quickie

Peter Richards, Atlanta, Georgia, suggests a twist of an old initiative problem (Blind Polygon) that makes it even more useable; no props necessary.

"Remember the one with a length of rope and blindfolds, and you try to make a perfect square with the rope?  Here's a new twist:  Have your group *join hands* and, blindfolded, try to make a perfect square or triangle, etc."

It works.

## How Old Do I Think I Am?  A Circuitous 50/50 Group-Split Ploy

If the game you intend to play doesn't have to start right now, try this revealing share-something-about-yourself method of halving a group.

Ask the oldest players to begin forming a line to your left and facing you, youngest to the right.  Most importantly, indicate that no one is to reveal their age; i.e., let the line form by where each person *thinks* they should fit in:  no declaring or digital displays allowed.  Allow a couple minutes for this to happen, as the banter and repartee is an important part of the communication and cooperation you are trying to facilitate.  (This ploy works best with a group displaying a wide chronological age span, but can also be used with a school class by requiring that their age position be to the nearest day.  It seems that someone's age is always of interest, no matter how wide or narrow the span.

After the line stabilizes (no one jostling for a new position), ask the people to declare (volunteer only) their ages, starting with the youngest.  Offer much applause for the oldest, no matter what the actual age, and call that person the most venerable (or experienced) — not the oldest.  There is occasionally someone who has grossly over or underestimated where they should be in line.  If their chosen position casts them in a good light, make note of it.  If a 40+ individual ends up in the 20's section, move right along to...asking the youngest end of the line to walk around toward the most venerable end until each person in the group represents half of a vis-a-vis pair.  Starting with the oldest/youngest couple, ask each *pair* to count off, 1-2, 1-2, etc.

All the 1's over here, and 2's over there, equals a well-divided group — by age, anyway.

## Pickup Prelims

Need two equally numbered teams? Are you about to choose the two best athletes and ask them to pick sides? Don't! The results are predictably devastating to the last chosen few (overweight, inept, unpopular, ethnic, blemishes, too tall, too short, too something).

Try a few of these low-key pickup techniques, and you might find that the students will look forward to the next set of zany comparisons.

The following is a list of comparisons that hopefully will give you close to a 50/50 split, and if parity isn't achieved, at least the students will experience the fun of personally comparing a non-threatening object, fear, action, etc., and also of becoming part of a group, albeit only briefly.

Say, "All blue colored pants to my left, and all others to my right." Continuing, "Levis left, others to the right." Use Nike shoes, Puma, New Balance, Etonic, etc. Use Chic, Jordache, Sassoon, etc. Who's conforming? This exercise might lead to some interesting comments and discussion by a mature group as to why certain makes of clothing and shoes are so popular.

Also use (1) color of eyes, (2) Inny or Outy (belly button)? (3) When your hands are folded, is your right thumb or left thumb naturally on top? Also, when you fold your arms, is your right or left arm comfortably on top? (Both the following have to do with heredity.) (4) January through June to the left, and July through December to the right. (5) Male and female (This smacks of skins and shirts — probably not a good idea.) (6) When putting on pants, left leg in first, or right leg in first? (7) Both socks on before putting on shoes, or one sock, then a shoe? (8) Likes beer, doesn't like beer. (9) Watches Dynasty or doesn't. (10) Split up into Horoscope sign groups and then choose two equal groups of six signs. What?

So, there's a start and there are obviously lots of things to compare. Try not to choose comparison themes that will prove to be embarrassing. Chubbies to the left, beanpoles to the right...

## Accessible Ropes Courses

Four sites currently involved with using ropes course elements with the handicapped are:

Vinland National Center
3675 Ihduhopi Road
Loretto, MN 55357

Mt. Hood/Kiwanis Camp
Portland State University
Box 751
Portland, Oregon 97207

Bradford Woods Outdoor Education Center
Indiana University
5040 State Road 67N
Martinsville, IN 46151

Camp Courageous of Iowa
P.O. Box 455
Monticello, Iowa  52310-0455

University of New Hampshire
New Hampshire Hall
Durham, NH 03824

## Government Surplus Wants You!

This article on Federal Surplus Property may prove to be the most valuable (monetarily) bit of information that I have made available over the past years in BOT's, and I don't know why I haven't mentioned this goldmine of gear previously.  Preoccupied with other games and goodies, I suppose.

There was an article written in 1979 about the stupendous amount of good, useable surplus gear available to certain qualified groups.  The article was written by Jack Shakeley and was distributed by the Grantsmanship Center, a non-profit educational institution.  I will be quoting from this article.  If what I quote and edit seems interesting and you think your center, school, etc., may qualify, I'd suggest writing for the entire article from:  The Grantsmanship Center, 1031 South Grand Avenue, Los Angeles, California 90015.  Cost is $1.10 per copy.  The name of the article is "Federal Surplus Property:  Need A Submarine Cheap?"

I have been going to the surplus property center in Taunton, Massachusetts, for years, picking up various gems for our program at ridiculously low prices.  Some of the items included:  Cross Country skis (10th Mountain Division, c. 1950); navy wool bib pants; poplin wind pants; desks; chairs; chalk boards; parachutes (sized from about 20' diameter to 50' — and that last number is not a typo).  I won't mention the prices, because you wouldn't believe me.

There are also items there in the warehouse that have questionable value, but are so attractive that you just have to have one.  I'm thinking particularly of a silver-coated fireman's suit that included the coat, pants, and a large-visored hood.  What a buy, and just the thing for riding the zip wire or playing *Foes & Questors*.  I also remember buying one hundred mailbag hooks for a *dollar*.  How can you pass up anything that costs a penny?...and if you are going to buy one, you might as well have a hundred.  Anyway, I would have been embarrassed to buy only one.

As an interesting aside — My father (Radm. O.C. Rohnke, U.S.C.G. Ret.) in 1955 was captain of the Coast Guard icebreaker Eastwind, operating as part of Operation Deepfreeze, then commanded by Admiral Byrd.  When I was nosing around the cold weather surplus material at the G.S.A. in Taunton, Massachusetts, I spied some particularly heavy looking bib-type pants. On closer inspection, I saw the stenciled words EASTWIND and the date - 1955. These same pants had been aboard my father's ship over 30 years ago.

My dad has been retired now for over 15 years, and lives with my mother in Bradenton, Florida. I asked him if he would like to have the pants. He smilingly turned them down, observing sagely that they didn't fit into his lifestyle in Florida. Too true — good thinking, Ace! So, I'm keeping them tucked away for that trip to the Arctic or Antarctic that I need to take in order to tick it off my "Have you ever?"...list.

So, who's eligible for all this federal largess? I quote directly from the above-mentioned article. "Basically, there are three eligible organizations. First and largest, is the public agency. This group includes all state, county, municipal, and local government units.

The second group is non-profit health and education agencies, with a few other non-profits thrown in. These include hospitals, medical clinics, health centers, schools, colleges, universities, child care centers, museums, etc. Every non-profit organization must show evidence of non-profit status by the IRS, which means a 501 (c) (3) letter of determination.

The third group of eligible organizations is a little unusual. These are the organizations that conduct activities called service educational activities of interest to the Department of Defense. Falling within these groups are the Red Cross, civil air patrols, Boy and Girl Scouts, Boys' Ranch, etc.

Every year the federal government declares more than 4 billion dollars' worth of goods as excess. Of this amount, about 3 billion worth is declared surplus. Perhaps as much as 400 million of this surplus finds its way to eligible non-profit organizations and local governments."

I'll include a few addresses to write to for specific state information. I'd include more, but these are the only ones I have left from the original article which lists addresses for all the states. Get yourself some mailbag hooks; they make great fetishes.

*New York*

NY Bureau of Federal
Property Assistance
Bldg. 18, Campus Site
Albany, NY 12226
(518) 457-3264

*Pennsylvania*

Dept. of General Services
Bureau of Surplus Properties
2221 Forster St., Box 3361
Harrisburg, PA 17125
(717)) 787-6996

### Rhode Island

RI Dept. of Administration
Div. of Purchases
State Warehouse, Box 8268
Cranston, RI 02920
(401) 464-2081

### Maine

Allocations Officer
Maine State Agency/Surplus Property
State Office Bldg.
Augusta, ME 04333
(207) 289-2933

### Massachusetts

Mass. State Agency for
Surplus Property
Park Sq. Bldg., Rm. 502
31 St. James Avenue
Boston, MA 02116
(617) 727-5774

### Missouri

Missouri State Agency for
Surplus Property
117 N. Riverside Drive
P.O. Drawer 1310
Jefferson City, MO 65101
(314) 751-3415

## Chapter 9
# *Ropes Course Construction*

### The Playpen

The following rejuvenated group initiative problem, called *The Playpen*, fell into disfavor many years ago because of an unfortunate accident (broken sternum), that was the result of an after-hours' slip. The Playpen is a useful group problem that indicates the value of efficiently working together and is functionally safe, if unauthorized use can be avoided.

Get out your PHD (posthole digger) and get set for a good physical workout. Dig a series of 2-1/2' deep holes arranged in a circle that measures about 30' in circumference. There should be 15 holes placed 2' apart and about 2-1/2" deep.

Cut a series of trunks and limbs of various lengths (from 4' to 6') and of a minimum 5" in diameter. Some of these stumps can be left bifurcated to provide a unique stance.

Pour some Cuprinol into the bottom of the holes before placing the stumps, to retard rot. Use black locust wood if available, and forget about rot. Set the posts as vertically as possible, and tamp the dirt fill with gusto. Pour some more Cuprinol onto the log/soil interface area.

Ask a group of students to stand in a circle behind the stumps of the Playpen. On a signal (GO works fairly well), they are to mount the stumps (one student per stump), and join hands. This simple group erection is timed from GO to hand joining. Ask the group to try again to see if they can better their time (probably a minute or so). With a bit of thought and cooperation, their recorded time should drop dramatically and continue to decrease for their third and fourth attempts. The emphasis, of course, is on group efficiency, in contrast to individual stumbling about — it works, and the rapid results are undeniable.

*Do not* allow anyone to step from stump top to stump top in an attempt to "walk" around the Playpen: sternums have been known to suffer.

## Wagon Wheel Traverse

A typical ropes course has its share of "bottlenecks"; i.e., those areas where interested students have to wait for some time to try a popular or slow-moving element. The high elements are usually the queue producers, because of the understandable deliberateness (white knuckle syndrome) that besets the temporary agoraphobic climber as the 30' - 40' mark is reached, but many of the low elements can become crowded, also.

For example, the tension traverse (including the triangular arrangement) is popular because of its demand for attention to balance and concentration, coupled with a programmatically welcome physical need for trust (spotting); however, only two students can be on the diverging cables at one time.

The Wagon Wheel Traverse arrangement provides balancing room for six students and twelve spotters to use the element simultaneously.

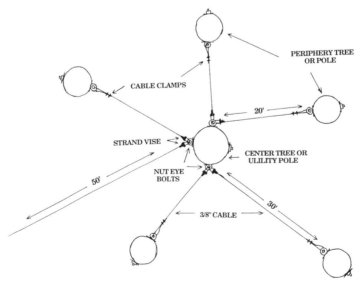

**WAGON WHEEL TRAVERSE** (TOP VIEW)

This event is best fabricated with telephone poles so that an open, grassy area can be used, eliminating the need for the extensive clearing that is necessary in a wooded plot. As you can see in the diagram, the event is basically a series of 4-6 cables (spokes) radiating from a central pole (hub) to peripheral support poles or trees.

Students are free to balance their way to and from on more than one set of cables. Also, look at the number of Wild Woosey's available. Is the plural of Woosey, Woosey's or Wooseys? I'll bet there's one of those i before s (or is it i before e, or e before i, or we before why) rules that applies here. It doesn't matter anyway, because woosey is an acronym, so the rules don't count. If you don't like the name (singular or plural), call it whatever you like. What an opportunity! To attach a significant, inventive and meaningful name to a popular event. Here's a catchy one — call it the Two-Diverging-Kinda-Loose-Cables. Intense, eh?

If telephone poles are used, a "dead man" (a dreadful term to use on a ropes course; rivaling "dead stop" as a terse explanation of how a person brakes on a zip wire ride), anchor must be used for each spoke cable or the cable will irritatingly loosen itself time and time again. This anchor arrangement is not necessary if live trees are utilized.

*A few construction hints and needs:*

1. The center pole should be sunk at least 4-1/2" feet in the ground. Use two 3/8" staples on either side of the pole's apex as clip-in points for the traverse ropes. Use two 5/8" x 10" nut eye bolts, placed at about knee height for the cable connection points.

2. The peripheral support stumps should be 4' in the ground and about 3' above ground. A single 5/8" nut eye bolt in a periphery pole connects the spoke and rim cables.

3. The 4' TP "dead man" should be buried 3 ft. deep in a horizontal position; i.e., perpendicular to the cable. Also dig a narrow temporary trench that extends about 5' of the 10' from dead man to pole, to allow the 1/4" guy cable to run straight. Drill a hole in the center of the dead man, then reeve and cable clamp or swage the wire rope to the log.

4. Strand vises can be used as cable connection devices at the center pole, but utilize cable clamps at the peripheral support poles to allow eventual re-tightening of the spokes.

## Delayed Pendulum

Here's a ropes course idea that, to my knowledge, has yet to be tried. I've been meaning to build one for over a year now, but the occasion ($) hasn't been right. Unfortunately and sadly, ropes course building has become just that — building, and not much innovation. There are about 25-30 elements that have proven to be effective and can be safely used, so there is little incentive to come up with new ideas. Folks choose from a catalog what they want in their woods.

If you try this idea, let me know how it works out. I don't get as much building time in as I used to, but I'll get around to this one eventually and let you know if it's safe, fun and functional.

The object, as in the platform-to-platform swing, is to move from one high platform to another. This event can be built low to the ground, but the height factor is intriguing and certainly more challenging.

Choose two high, stout trees for cable supports. Try to choose trees that do not require a lot of limb trimming and ones that have a clear path between (so that "selective pruning" isn't necessary).

Build a platform about 20' up on one of the trunks. Install a horizontal cable (3/8" diameter) about 25-30' above the platform. Back up this cable. The cable should slant *slightly* down toward the far support tree.

Attach a length of 5/8" multiline to the cable by means of a splice-thimble-rapid link-two wheel ROSA pulley, so that the rope can be easily grasped (knotted) while standing on the platform.

(Here's where some trial and error comes in, so use a belay while experimenting.)

Place a cable clamp on the non-belay cable about (depends on the distance between the trees) 10' out from the platform support tree. The multiline/pulley rope is attached on the cable beyond the cable clamp.

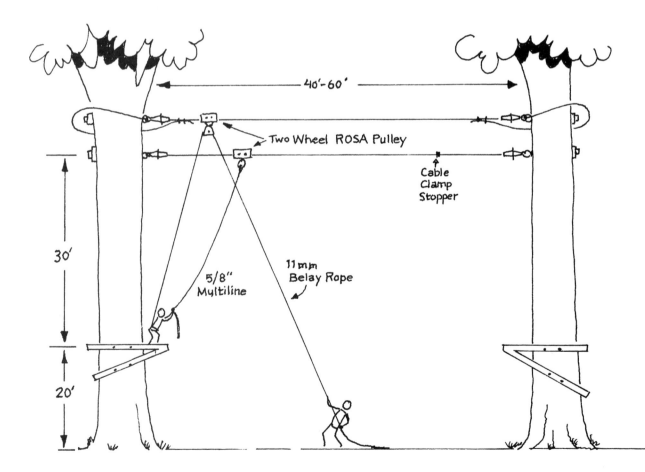

198

This set-up allows, via an initial pendulum motion, momentum to develop for a zip-like movement across the cable until another cable clamp stopper is encountered about 10' short of the far support tree. (See why you need a belay and why you haven't yet built the far platform?)

So, it's swing-zip-swing-PLOP (or whatever) onto the far platform.

After you have adjusted the cable clamp stoppers to positions that allow a smooth finish at an eyeballed point on the far tree — build a down-slanted platform there.

So that you won't damage your ROSA pulley, reeve a drilled section of hardwood or auto tire onto the cable before attachment. This buffer should be juxtaposed on the contact side of the cable clamp stopper.

Sounds like fun, eh? Well, sure it is!...I think.

A two-wheel ROSA pulley is affixed to the belay cable so that the belay moves with the participant.

During the planning stage, exercise some compassion for the poor belayer, and don't make the traverse distance so long that the belayer has to run to keep up. Realistically, a distance of 40-50' should be maximum for this event.

The belayer should stand about 15' out from the starting tree and have a smooth, level area to move laterally on for 20 or so feet.

## Jus-Rite Descender

Have you ever had a tickle in the back of your consciousness that whispers annoyingly, "There must be a better way to do that!" concerning a sequence or procedure that is obviously inefficient or klutzy. I try to utilize those peripheral and uncomfortable tickles to drag out a self-satisfied smile or two by experimenting with solutions on the ropes course.

Serendipity is a good word to stick in here somewhere, because many workable solutions have proven to be the serendipitous result of a sometimes unreasonable amount of trial and error, and because it's just a neat word. Anyhoo, here's a solution that works simply and well, but first the problem...

Situation — Anxious 135-pound belayer looking up at an equally anxious 200-pound climber who's looking down from a precarious perch that s/he is about to detach themselves from (FALLING!). The anxiety quotient can be uppped significantly by adjusting those people-poundage figures.

As the more experienced (I hope) of the two, the belayer *knows* when that chunk of beef falls, the weight differential twixt belayer and climber *will* result in an impromptu meeting (vis-a-vis) an undetermined but disconcerting number of feet off the ground. There is a small matter of hot hands and derriere, but at the moment of leaving the ground, that is of secondary concern.

You have probably seen this sequence enacted more than once and have experienced firsthand the anxiety referred to earlier. My feeling is that the more dynamic the belay, the less pressure the system (rope, cable, bolts, belayer, swages, climber) has to statically absorb. Programmatically, we have advocated over the years not having the belayer tie into an anchor point (ONLY on a ropes course, bottom belay situation) and not belaying someone more than 30-35 pounds heavier than the belayer; with some poundage leeway recognized for the skill and experience of the belayer.

So, where does the mental tickle come in?...The *Jus-Rite Descender*...

Cut an 8" x 10" x 12' hardwood log and skin it. Beech strips as easily as skinning a snake, and oak has comparative suction bark, but whatever hardwood you choose will do. Use a drawknife for the debarking procedure, keeping the bevel of the blade up, if you are skilled in woodcraft, or bevel down, if you are like me. Wear gloves to protect your knuckles.

After the stripping process, take your PHD (posthole digger) and dig about a 3-1/2' deep hole approximately where you would stand to belay a specific ropes course element. Now you and your buddy(ies) take that bare-bone log and "Iwo Jima" it upright into the hole. In this New England area, a log should last about five years, unless you are lucky enough to have used a locust log, in which case the wood will probably outlast you. Cheery thought! To increase the log's longevity, pour some wood preservative in the bottom of the hole and liberally soak the wood/soil interface. Pour some of this liquid over the log yearly and your descender will last longer than tenure.

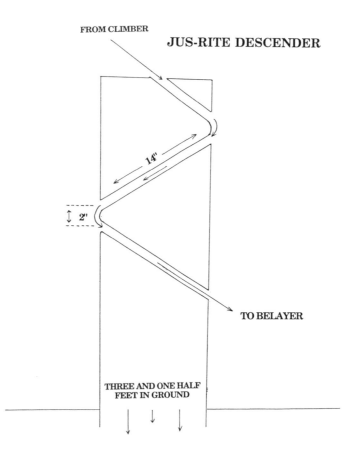

FROM CLIMBER

**JUS-RITE DESCENDER**

14'

2'

TO BELAYER

THREE AND ONE HALF
FEET IN GROUND

Now you have an impressive 6-7' of stripped trunk sticking out of the ground, and well tamped, I hope. Using a stepladder, climb to the top of the log and, starting dead center, drill a 5/8" angled hole to the length of a 16" auger drill bit. A power drill and alternator will make short work of this task, otherwise, plan on a grand arm workout. When augering by hand, drilling the holes before placing the log makes sense.

The drill bit should exit about 12-14" down from the top of the log. Measure down vertically about 2" from this hole and drill back into the log so that the angle of the drill is approximately the same as the top shaft. Repeat this procedure on the other side of the log so that you have a total of three 5/8" x 16" shafts descending from the top center in a zig-zag pattern down and through the log.

Reeve the belay rope through the top hole and on down, using as many shafts as necessary (Jus-Rite), depending upon the weight of the potential faller. The rope comes out the bottom hole at about three feet from the ground and goes directly to the belayer. A classic belay stance can be used, or simply hold onto the rope with two gloved hands. There is certainly more image in the Gor-Tex; Vibram; 60/40; leather-gloved stance, but two hands works just fine.

The angle of the shaft precludes a shearing effect on the rope. The two or three inches between holes on the side of the log provide friction over a longer path than a mechanical device permits. The system is adjustable for different weights of climbers by adding or subtracting shafts, or by having the belayer shift one way or another around the log.

*CAUTION:* If you let the rope "sing" through the holes by dropping someone too fast, the rope may become surface-scorched.

Use of the log allows a trained lightweight individual to belay *any* sized student. Knowing that you are not going to be pulled off your feet and/or get your butt blistered by a fall provides a contagious confidence that further nudges the hesitating student to try.

A teacher's comfortable confidence level is a predictable series of adventure teaching plateaus. The higher plateaus, reached by experience and confidence, result in a casually competent style that allows you to say with believable conviction, "You _will_ be safe!", "The rope _will_ hold!", "The knots _do_ work!", etc. If your presentation is halting, unsure and faulted with an occasional nervous "Oops," well — would you confidently tie in?

The one obvious drawback to this massive belay helper, aside from a certain lack of portability, is that use of the log is limited to only those ropes course elements that do not require the belayer to laterally follow the climber, but then, how many students have you seen accidentally fall from a Burma Bridge? You can count them on one finger, right?

## Heebie-Jeebie

The object, like attempting a Two Line Bridge, is to make it from one support tree to another, on belay. The crux of the event becomes most apparent as the student arrives (in a scrunched over position) at the crossing of the hand ropes — no hints, just directions.

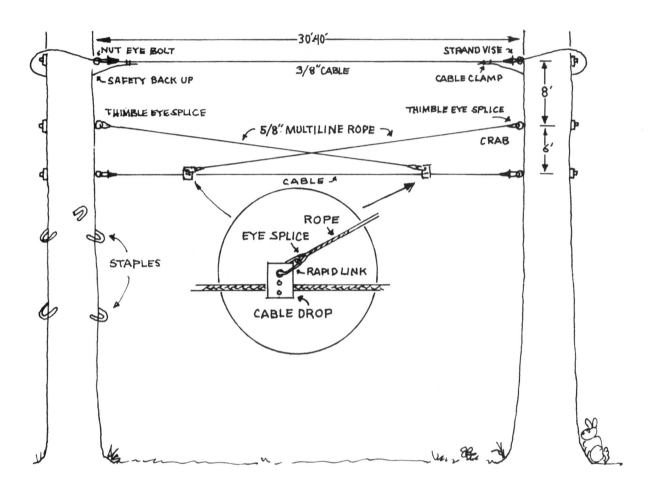

I have, since writing the above instructions for the Heebie-Jeebie, talked with Tom Quimby (one of **PA**'s National Certified Trainers), and he related this variation to me.

Build the event no higher than 10' and make all the lines, except the belay cable, from 3/4" rope. Splice where B intersects A. In this way, more people can try more often, since the completion percentage isn't very high.

## Centipede

In a past BOT's, I included a detailed illustration of a new ropes course element called *The Vertical Playpen*. The "playpen" is an excellent high event, but building it requires a time and materials commitment that most folks can't afford. So, here's another "newish" high event that is much easier to build and install — and, of course, fun to mess around on. The scenario suggests climbing — your psyche suggests discretion.

Picture 4-8 vertically connected 4 x 4's (end to end), swaying gently from a high eyebolted branch. Each 4 x 4 displays varied sequences of hammered-in 1/2" staples.

The Centipede is a simple climbing event that offers unique access to higher things. Take a look at my illustration attempt and the following text for instructions on how to make your own. Don't hesitate on this one — it's honestly easy to fabricate and suspend.

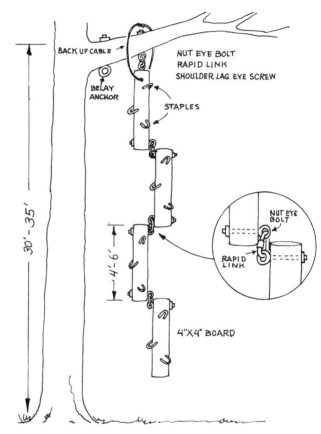

- Measure the height from whatever tree branch or cable that you want to hang this event.

- Considering that you will be using 6-8' sections of 4 x 4 boards to fill the vertical space, determine how many boards you will need.

- Using a 1/2" drill bit, drill each board end on-center to a depth of about 4". Insert and screw down a 5/8" SLES (shoulder lag eye screw) into each hole — 2 per board. Don't try to save a couple of bucks by using the bent-over type of not-so-strong eye screws that are commonly found in hardware stores.

- Hammer in 1/2" staples along the length of each board, using 14-16" as a vertical spacing guide and your imagination for spatial orientation (side-by-side, alternating, spiral, free form). You must pre-drill twice with a 7/16" drill bit for each staple, to prevent splitting the board. Tap the staple with a hammer to mark the board at the desired location, and drill at those two marks. Each 1/2" staple should be hammered horizontally into the holes to a depth of approximately 2".

- Connect the boards (SLES to SLES) with 1/2" rapid links.

- The branch (cable) that you wish to connect with should have an additional eye bolt (or juxtaposed cable clamps) for belay rope use.
- Haul this segmented contraption up using a single rope/pulley arrangement and clip the top SLES into the 5/8" nut eye bolt, using a wide-opening locking steel carabiner, or a 5/8" rapid link. Done!

Ideally, the end of an 8' bottom board should be about 8' off the ground so that a short (4-5') stapled bottom segment of 4 x 4 can be removed, to preclude unauthorized use.

If this event is not being utilized for access to other high ropes course elements, and is an end in itself to facilitate the lowering process, ask a student to pull the bottom 4 x 4 away from plumb (as you would on the Dangle Duo), so that you can lower the participant briskly without having to worry about body contact with the staples or boards.

Regularly check the security of each 5/8" SLES, and particularly the top one. If the entire Centipede arrangement is twisted counterclockwise on a regular basis, there is a chance that one or more of the SLES's may twist out. As extra insurance, set up a back-up belay for the top 4x4 as per the illustration.

### Staples

If you build ropes courses, or plan to string a few cables for your own program, this next time and $-saver will more than pay for your subscription.

Use 1/2" galvanized staples in place of PVC pegs — that's it. I could just stop there, because everything else I write is simply supportive, but...

The staples are placed in a pole or tree with the use of a hand sledge (a one-hander that weighs about 2-1/2 lbs.). It takes me about 12 good hits to place a staple in hardwood, and 6-8 whacks for softwood. Leave enough sticking out to provide a sufficient hand or foot hold. Here, I'll outline one on this page to give you an idea of size, and mark on it about how far I slam it in.

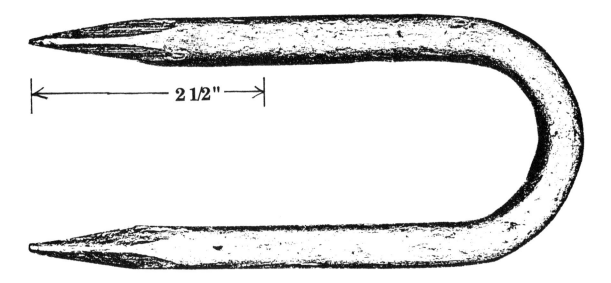

$\longleftarrow$ 2 1/2" $\longrightarrow$

Notice that the part sticking out of the tree provides an ideal foot hold, and also allows a firm hand grip without having to worry about losing your finger (like sticking your finger through the eyehole of a 1/2" or 5/8" SLES) — as the result of a fall.

Not having to drill a tree with a multispur bit, preliminary to placing a PVC peg, if for no other reason, makes the change worthwhile.

3/8" galvanized staples also have numerous uses on a course. The following list will give you an idea where I use the two sizes.

### 1/2" staple

1. To replace climbing and step-up pegs (PVC).
2. Clip-in points for a Fidget Ladder.
3. Connector point for Tension Traverse hand ropes.
4. Supports for Rebirth (Hole in One) Tire.
5. Self-belay points on a tree climb. (Must be oriented vertically.)

### 3/8" staple

1. Attachment points for the Spider's Web.
2. Attachment points for the Maze.
3. Lock-up point for a swing cable or haul system.

## Staples Again (later issue)

Project Adventure ropes course builders continue to use 3/8" and 1/2" diameter staples for various clip-in and connector situations. Because a **few** staples have cracked during sledge hammer installation, be aware of the following: some staples arrive from the manufacturer with the pointed ends somewhat splayed apart; i.e., more than parallel. Also, some staples have been received that have a "flattish" bottom to the U.

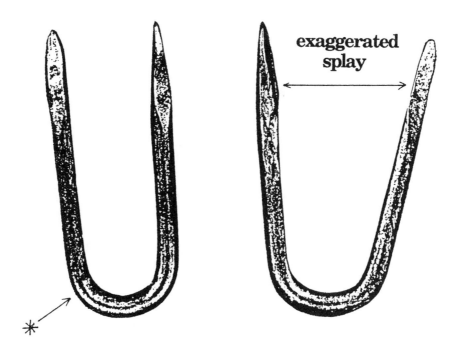

exaggerated splay

When a splayed staple is driven into wood, the diverging ends tend to continue separating, putting undo stress on the U portion, until (If the staple is pounded far enough in) a crack occurs at the juncture of the straight shank and the beginning of the curve — at the * on the illustration.

The obvious solution is not to use splayed staples, but since most are received with some splay evident, the most expedient and frugal action is to place the staple on its side on a hard surface (concrete, e.g.), and hit the staple ends with a hammer to reduce the splay; i.e., returning the shanks toward being parallel.

Some trees are obviously harder than others, so that the number of sledge blows required for satisfactory insertion is necessarily increased. If the U end of the staple begins to flatten because of increased and more powerful blows, it's a good bet that the sharpened ends are no longer penetrating. The solution is to remove the distorted staple and discard it, then pre-drill the tree or limb with a drill bit sized slightly smaller than the diameter of the staple; e.g., 1/2" staple — 7/16" drill bit. (Mark the tree surface with the staple points to locate the drill hole areas.)

I was told recently that a "flat" point on a nail allows the nail to hold better because the wider point breaks through wood fibers during the hammering process, rather than separating the woody tissue as a sharp-pointed object would. Use this physical fact to increase the holding power of staples in soft wood. Moderately grind off the sharp tips of a staple to achieve this capability. Be aware that no matter how powerful you are (or think you are), that blunted tips will not penetrate hardwood far enough to achieve sufficient holding strength.

Live oak (a warm weather quercus) has proved to be the toughest tree that I have come up against — even more so than hickory. Definitely a two-fisted slammer, and your shanks better be parallel. Another possible pre-drill tree is the southern Iron Wood (Causarina).

## Single Line Potpourri

Read this and pay attention, if your budget is limited and your sense of frugality likes multi-use ropes course elements.

Since you're still reading, I have obviously snared the interest (curiosity) of a skeptic or a ropes course aficionado...or maybe you're bored sitting on a New York to Boston commuter flight and the flight attendant just told you that there aren't any magazines, and reading the airbag sickness instructions just doesn't grab you like it used to — so, you down two or three cups of rank airline coffee, look out the double (scratched) plastic windows at nothing ('cause you're over the wing and at 12,000 feet, what's to see?), and out of desperation, reach between your legs into the bulging carry-on pack that doesn't fit under the seat in front of you, and attempt to find some "work," but by accident you grab December's BOT's. You figure, "What the heck," and begin to read — (before the coffee nails your nephrons and initiates not-to-be-ignored bladder synaptic signals, necessitating asking the two obese people snoring next to you to...

This is the stuff of imagination, because all the following events are based on a simple swing rope.

We'll imagine a gymnasium setting for these events (although with some searching outdoors, you can usually find the proper limbs or cables for swing line suspension).

1. *Swing for Distance* — There is some skill associated with attempting to swing distance on a rope; i.e., swinging and letting go of the rope. If the starting point is elevated (off a stump, pommel horse, Swedish box), more distance is gained by grasping the rope and jumping up and backward than can be accomplished by simply thrusting forward (length of pendulum principle).

    Adjust the landing area so that a jump mat or loose sand will meet the flying swinger. Judge the distance on this impromptu event as you would the running long jump. You will find that most participants will want to try this event over and over, notwithstanding their distance as compared to other swingers' efforts.

2. *Stump-to-Stump Swing* — Offer an elevated take-off and a similar landing area and you have an event that is given to many attempts, even if the first try is successful: point-to-point swinging just feels good.

    Try to arrange the take-off and landing points (adjustable) so that swinging to and from can be accomplished with varying degrees of difficulty. Do not make these areas so high that spotting becomes either impossible or of the please-don't-fall type.

3. *Sea Gull Swing* — This swing and pivot movement is a continuation and embellishment of the stump-to-stump movement described above. The swing itself is so constructed that the landing area (a 2" x 6" x 2' board supported on two vertically planted sections of 4" x 4" wolmanized lumber) appears to be misplaced or more accurately, badly placed. If the swing is attempted directly toward the 2" x 6" landing area, most people would whack their shins, so an alternate, wide-arc approach must be taken. This is a swing that (in deference to shins and ankles) should be demonstrated by an instructor.

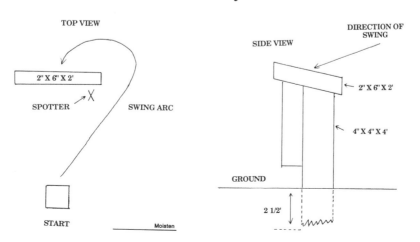

207

If the swing arc is either too great or too little, the participant will miss the landing area. A spotter should stand at X to prevent direct swings at the board. This event is also a let-me-have-one-more-try winner.

The drawing on the preceding page shows the proper swing path and orientation of the landing board.

4. *May Pole* — The indoor and outdoor variations of this circular swinging element differ somewhat, but a hard, thrusting start and holding on for a long ride are common to both.

*Indoor May Pole* — Hang a swing rope near the center of the gym (5/8" multiline is a good rope choice). Using four cone markers, set up a 12-3-6-9 o'clock arrangement on the gym floor with the rope hanging directly in the center of the developed circle. The distance from rope to cones varies as to the desired degree of swing difficulty — the farther the cones, the more difficult it is to achieve 360° swing circles.

The object is to try and complete as many 360° swinging circles around the cones as possible before making body contact with a cone.

Affix a section of tape to the floor (or use a convenient painted line) as a starting point. The swing must begin at that mark, but the swinger may use as long a running start as desired or possible. After the swing starts, the person on the rope may not touch the floor.

Upper body strength is a factor in this event at the maximum performance level, but almost everyone can achieve some success.

*Outdoor May Pole* — A swing rope is attached high on the trunk of a straight limbless (limbed) tree (or near the top of a well sunk 30' telephone pole). All obstructions near this pole or tree must be removed (other trees, shrubs, rocks).

The object is to see how many 360° turns the swinger can make around the tree/pole before either touching the ground or the support. The starting line is chosen by the swinger, but all turns are measured from that take-off point. Spotters are necessary around the support to buffer tree/pole contact by enthusiastic spinners.

A variation of this event, called *The Big Gulp*, involves setting up the swing on a tree that grows adjacent to a river so that 180 degrees of the swing's arc is over the water. Consequences of "letting go" during the water half of the swing are left to your imagination and contemplation of the swing's name.

The following events can also be accomplished with a single line swing rope. These events are included and explained in past issues of BOT's or the book, *Silver Bullets*.

1. Prouty's Landing
2. Nitro Crossing
3. Prusik
4. Scooter Swing
5. Disc Jockeys

**Ride the Wild Log**

This bouncing, jerking, log-ride activity injects some role-playing fantasy and surfer-like balance movements into a staid old ropes course element (which name is as predictable as its action — the Swinging Log).

Pretending briefly that you are Buck Hornbeam, acclaimed saddle-hardened bronco buster, or Duke Reefhound, the Hot Curl idol of the surf set, try swinging onto the swinging log (an arcing swing around one of the support trees), then, precariously balanced and *holding onto the rope with only one hand*, attempt to "ride the wild log" for 10 seconds. If you have a hat, it should be held in the free hand during your "ride": a hat is a necessary accoutrement in order to score more "rider-style points."

The swing onto the log need not be long, just enough to arrive there and impart some action to the log itself. Attach the swing rope to one of the support trees about 30' up the trunk. The start of the swing can be initiated from a placed section of log that provides a somewhat elevated takeoff point. Try the swing a few times to determine where to best place the stump.

Clear the area around the swinging log of all sharp or hard objects (rocks, limb sections) because spotting this event is difficult and potentially dangerous to the spotter resulting from the erratic action of the swinging log.

**High Profile Redux**

For you folks who have purchased the book, *High Profile*, here are a few exclusive additions direct from the author.

1. Place 3/8" washers behind softwood blocks (on the protruding lags) to keep the lead shields from pressing into the wood, resulting in an eventual loose block.

2. If the shield won't take (grip) in a thin-drilled section of cinder block, countersink the two 3/8" holes on the back of the block with a 5/8" spade bit, to a depth of about 1/2". This allows the sleeve to expand in the cinder part of the hole, rather than into the open space of the cinder block's interior.

3. Tie the haul rope for the platform from side to side on the platform, rather than front to back — the placement balances and holds the platform steadier against the wall.

4. Instead of inserting lag shields into the drilled wall holes, the procedure of putting a block firmly on the wall is speeded up by first turning the two lag screws about halfway through the block and then screwing the two lag shields onto the protruding lags. The shields, so attached, are lined up with the drilled holes and the block is tapped to cause insertion. Then, simply tighten the lags with a 9/16" socket wrench.

OK, sports fans, I hate to tear you away from such fascinating wall climb exotica, but it's time for that new, one-time-only, BOT's feature — *Custodian's Corner*: in which section we highlight the colorful and good-humored comments of your favorite dust-buster.

Frank adamantly indicates, "I ain't goin' up there to check nuthin."

And Herb, his Camel cigarette firmly pressed between determined lips, follows with a compassionate admonition, "You guys must be nuts!"

Nice going, fellas; keep that coffee hot, and if it doesn't move, paint it.


## *Tips on Preparing and Placing Polyvinyl Chloride (PVC) Rod*

The use of 3/8" and 1/2" diameter galvanized staples has almost entirely replaced the use of PVC pegs, but I've included the PVC write-up because some people still like the look and feel of pegs better than staples — you choose; both techniques work.

One and a quarter inch diameter PVC rod cut into six inch lengths and placed appropriately in a tree trunk (or telephone pole) are the best climbing substitute for limbs since God made trees; or somewhere around then...

Years ago, I tried using one inch hardwood dowels, but found that they rotted quickly and were obviously unsafe. Then I tried one inch diameter high-density polyethylene rod and this dazzlingly white substance seemed to be the answer until one day as I was lead climbing a tree to set up a belay, one of the pegs snapped underfoot; an unwelcome sound, considering my elevation at that moment. Escaping unscathed (Hooray for the three point climbing stance!), I checked the other pegs in that tree with a hammer and found them all to be brittle. Apparently, they were deleteriously affected by sunlight (ultraviolet rays), becoming, over a period of time, weakened and dangerous. So, for the second time, I replaced a set of pegs.

As an aside — The compartmentalizing capacity of trees due to trauma is impressive, considering that the scars of the original wooden pegs that were placed 5-6 years earlier are almost entirely covered by new growth. People ask if the drilling process, preliminary to placing the pegs, damages the trees. There is little permanent harm to the tree *if* the hole is quickly filled with something so that disease and/or insects specific to that plant are not allowed to enter. The PVC peg is placed within minutes after the hole is drilled.

My present choice for peg material is 1-1/4" PVC rod. I had heard so many good things about this "miracle" substance, notwithstanding its suggested carcinogenic properties (don't eat it), that it had to work. After three years of extensive use and hundreds of placements, there has not been one report of a broken peg or xylemic malignancy.

The PVC material is an unobtrusive gray color, is unaffected by temperature changes, cuts and shapes fairly easily, and can take a direct blow from a sledge hammer without breaking or bending. Admittedly, I have taken a few chips off the ends of some of the pegs as the result of repeated and badly aimed sledge blows (end of the day fatigue), but the sharp edges thus formed rasp off nicely, so there's no problem.

PVC rod can be purchased from Cadillac Plastics Company, a national business that is represented in most large cities. PVC rod comes in varying lengths and is not an inexpensive item, but the cheaper (less expensive) alternatives include wood dowels.

### PVC Construction Tips

1. Cut six inch peg lengths with a circular power saw. This rod can also be cut with any type of hand saw, including a hack saw, but why not cut a number of lengths in the shop and save time and hassle in the field?

2. Make sure at least one end of the six inch peg is cut flush so that hand sledge blows do not glance off.

3. Rough up the entire surface of the peg with a rasp to allow a firm grip for a climber and for the tree. I do this by putting the peg on a hard source and strike it repeatedly with the saw tooth edge of a rasp. A Four-in-Hand rasp is a handy purchase. There must a more efficient way to do this, but this Flintstone technique has served me well and it gives me a chance to sit down and pretend that I'm performing a skilled handcrafted task.

4. Chamfer both ends of the six inch peg. Chamfer is a fancy word that means, to bevel. I use it liberally to add to the artisan image. The chamfered end going into the tree allows the peg to enter without catching a sharp edge with your unprotected bod. If you have access to a milling machine, the ends of the peg can be chamfered easily and handsomely, otherwise a rasp does a tolerable and workmanlike job.

5. Drill the hole in the tree no deeper than the second joint of your index finger. How come? Because your finger is more convenient than a ruler and two joints' worth holds just fine.

6. Drill the hole (inch and a quarter diameter for hardwood; inch and three sixteenths for softwood), with a multi-spur bit or a speed bor (spade bit) if you are using a power drill. Use an expansion auger bit and bit brace, if you choose the lactic acid technique. Patience...it's a grand workout and you get to develop muscles that are useless for any other task that I can think of.

7. Try not to place the pegs more than two vertical feet apart, in order to create a reasonable climb. Consider how long your legs are compared to the typical student inseam measurement. Comments have been made in the past about my insensitivity concerning peg placement and I must admit to an occasional dispassionate tendency.

Additional uses for PVC rod — A two and a half foot length makes a dandy trapeze. Don't forget to rough up the surface of the rod with coarse sandpaper. A five or six foot section provides you with a fine and flexible tamper for packing dirt around a set pole or stump.

### Another PVC Trick

Using a taut cable for maneuvers that require body contact with the cable (hand-over-hand regain, commando crawl, etc.) is generally contraindicated because the small diameter of the cable, coupled with its unyielding nature, results in discomfort, and occasional injury (torn skin), and not much fun.

Placing a section of 1/2" PVC pipe over the cable allows expanded curriculum use of the cable. Don't confuse this PVC pipe covering with the molded plastic covering that is purchased as an integral part of the cable.

Such a tight covering enhances the look of the cable, but only slightly increases its usability — plus, it adds considerably to the cost per foot.

Reeve (thread) a section of 3/8" cable through a length of pipe to use as a hand traverse, swinging tire support, or whatever body contact cable activity you have in mind.

For example, if the cable is to be used as a hand-over-hand traverse, place one contact eye bolt about 8' up on a support tree or pole and connect one end of the cable to this eye bolt using a 3/8" strand vise. Reeve the free cable end through a measured length of pipe and after the tightening process (come along and haven's grips), secure the cable with another strand vise or cable clamps to an eye bolt at equal height, placed in a distance support tree or pole.

I apologize for the above installation directions if you don't know what I'm writing about, but the PVC pipe *idea* is my emphasis. Unfortunately, if I included all the building techniques needed for each idea, I'd use up half this periodical; which could then be called *Bag of Boredom*. Refer to the book, *Challenge By Choice* (available through Project Adventure) for frequently used low ropes course building techniques.

### Through Bolting Trees and Poles

A "better" method for attaching a cable to a support (tree, pole) is to drill through the support and place an eye bolt. Tree surgeons regularly do this to reinforce weak limbs or to protect valuable trunk sections from wind and ice. Here are a few drilling tips gleaned from many hours of "making holes."

*Au Naturel* (by hand) — If you can afford to rent an alternator (alternating current); terrific! Refer to section B; i.e., see below. If your budget won't allow the rental fee, hold a bake sale, plead with the parents, or ask your Mom, but try like the dickens to avoid hand drilling the **many** holes necessary to construct a ropes course. However, since I went through a Thoreauvian period (simplicity, simplicity, simplicity), here's a pat on the back (with liniment), and some ideas for you hard folks.

Buy or obtain a decent bit brace. It's hard enough to manually drill through a 14 inch hardwood trunk without having to combat excess friction. A bit brace with ball bearings pays for itself soon enough in time saved.

Keep the tip of the auger bit sharp by not throwing or storing it unsheathed in a tool box. Cover at least the tip of the bit with something (cork, foam, metal tube, etc.) to maintain its cutting edges.

Try to position yourself (on the ground, in a tree, or on a ladder) so that you can apply moderate pressure on the bit brace. It's impressive to the slack-jawed gawkers to drill through a hickory trunk 12 inches over your head, but so, so wasteful of your time, energy, and patience.

As you drill, remove the bit every two inches or so in order to clean the hole of shavings. Keep turning clockwise while pulling carefully backward on the bit brace to achieve this cleaning. Make sure the chuck is tight on the bit, or check your belay before pulling back too hard. You may have to turn counterclockwise a few turns to free the auger bit tip, before pulling backward.

Switch arms for turning the brace occasionally, if you anticipate drilling many holes. Although this may seem initially awkward, it postpones the 2 p.m. limp arm syndrome.

After drilling at height, don't just drop the bit brace or drill to the ground as a expedient. Trying to drill with even a slightly bent bit will convince you to respect the tools. A quick and efficient way to get almost any tool down is to improvise an impromptu zip arrangement. Attach one end of your haul rope to the tree that you are working in and have your "down" partner walk the other end of the rope away from the base of the tree. Attach the zipable tools to the rope with a carabiner and release, courteously indicating to your partner that you are doing this. A couple yards before the tools reach the end, your partner gives slack to the rope and the tools come satisfyingly to a stop. This technique not only saves time and the tools, but is obviously more fun than simply lowering the heavy things, and what's wrong with a diversion or two?...since you have been working so hard and all.

*Power Tools* — What a treat! These torquing demons eat right through the supports with little effort, leaving more time for planning, curriculum design, and other such excuses for obtaining an electric drill and power source. Checklist for a Good Drill: (1) Industrially rated with a minimum 1/2 inch chuck. (2) With a reverse — not absolutely necessary, but a tremendous time-saver. (3) The permanent ON button should be in a position that precludes accidental pushing. As an aside and a warning, if while drilling you lose control of the drill (it spins out of your hands), and the ON button has been depressed, lots of negative things can happen and rapidly. Unless the spinning drill cuts its own power source, your partner must pull the plug and *fast*. (4) High or low speed RPM is OK. It's easier to control a low RPM drill, but is obviously slower. A low RPM drill is best for metal drilling. Variable speed is a plus.

If you let the bit go all the way into the trunk, past the spirals, it will probably jam; i.e., continue spinning but not come out. If you have a reverse switch, use it. Otherwise, remove the drill by loosening the chuck and turn the bit out with a vise grip, or knock the bit through with a smaller diameter length of steel rod.

Use a 11/16" diameter drill bit. The slightly larger bit size (1/16" larger than the bolt shaft) allows easy bolt insertion. If you use a 5/8" drill bit, you will have to hand sledge the bolts into place.

When you plug the end of the drill wire into the extension cord(s), tie a knot (square knot) using both ends of the cords before plugging them together. This prevents unplugging at inconvenient times.

Pre-drilling for a SLES (shoulder lag eye screw) is best done with a spade or speed bore drill bit. Drill about one inch in at a time, pulling back frequently to clean the hole. Use a 5/8" drill bit for a 3/4" SLES.

## Ropes Course Longevity — Soil Compaction

It should concern you as to how long the trees on your ropes course are going to last, because without them, telephone poles become the creosoted answer for element supports. From an aesthetic and olfactory standpoint, I'll take trees any day.

It's amazing how fast a wooded area can be trampled down by participants' feet over the course of only a few months. The undergrowth will completely disappear (a benefit), and shortly thereafter, the soil will begin to compact. A manifestation of soil compaction is the appearance of roots that you didn't know were there. These exposed roots are damaged inadvertently by participant traffic, as students walk from event to event. Additionally, as the soil becomes more compact, less water can penetrate to the tree roots. The trees suffer in both instances.

To alleviate this heavy use problem, something must be put on the forest floor, particularly in the area of the highest foot traffic. Wood chips make a good covering. They are easily attainable, blend in well with the forest scene, are biodegradable and, most importantly, alleviate the environmental problems mentioned above. In the flush of building a new ropes course, don't forget the consequences of upsetting the delicate balances that occur in a forest ecosystem.

## *Through Bolts — NEB, TEB, OEB*

There is an on-going and general concern about the load placed on bolted-through-the-tree eye bolts by the force resulting from a missed trapeze jump attempt. (There are other belay situations on a high ropes course that occasionally result in a "catch," but none as frequently and predictably as a result of the trapeze attempt.)

I can understand the concern, and it's this "what if?" type of thinking that often results in safer rigging being developed. The concern is heightened after watching a ropes course participant plummet past the safety of that slim PVC trapeze (silver dollar eyes, churning legs, flailing arms — awesome!).

But the belay works: the belayer is well trained and confident, the "jus-rite descender" adds controlled friction, the "shear reduction block" maintains the rope's tensile strength, and the anchor bolts don't break. (I have never experienced or heard of a belay bolt that Project Adventure placed as ever having failed, but if it did, there is a back-up system on all belay cables, of equal or greater strength than the original set-up. This is an example of responding to the "what if?"... thinking that I referred to above.

A ropes course cable belay is dynamic in the following ways: (1) The nylon mountaineering rope, because of its elasticity, absorbs much of the fall's impact. (2) The two trees through which the anchor bolts are placed are flexible enough to be pulled inward as the result of a fall. (3) The belayer (if the jus-rite descender is *not* used) provides another dynamic (moving) factor.

### *Thimble Eye Bolt Placement*

Thimble eye bolts are obtained from electrical supply companies (Graybar, in Boston), or from local power companies. Their advantage is that they have a thimble arrangement forged into the head. PA also sells them.

After an 11/16" diameter hole is drilled through a tree or pole, the 5/8" diameter thimble eye bolt (TEB) is inserted into position. The thimble configuration should be aligned in a vertical position. If the thimble grooves are aligned obliquely or horizontally, the cable will slip off the grooves, cancelling the effectiveness of the built-in thimble. Use a washer at both ends of the bolt. The head end washer slows the tree's tendency to grow around the bolt head.

If the back of the trunk is craggy, it's wise to reeve the cable through the bolt eye before placing the bolt into the trunk. This is done simply to facilitate reeving the cable through the eye of the bolt.

Notice that the TEB nut has square and beveled edges. After you put a washer on the inserted bolt end, turn the nut on the threaded bolt so that the beveled side of the nut is toward the trunk. This bevel will allow the nut to turn against the washer even if it is not perfectly flush with the washer, which it rarely is, considering that the trunk has irregular contours.

The protruding threaded end of the bolt should be cut off if it's part of a low element because: (1) A threaded bolt end can cause injury (2) A cut and peened-over end of a bolt makes the fixture permanent and not the target for prankish theft.

On a high element, the protruding bolt can often be used as a hand or foot hold or as a back-up cable support. A vandal's interest seems to decline in proportion to increased height.

Use a hacksaw with a quality toothed blade, and cut flush with the end of the nut. It will take approximately 75 firm strokes to cut through a 5/8" bolt (that's a thinly veiled challenge), but don't bother cutting all the way through. When you're a bit past halfway (40 strokes), use a hammer to smack the end of the bolt at right angles and the shaft will snap off. A small work-saver, perhaps, unless you are cutting off many bolts.

When dealing with softwoods (pine, fir, etc.), it's a good idea to use a large washer called a "fish plate" to prevent the standard smaller "slug" washer from being pulled into the trunk while tightening on the nut or pulling the cable taut.

## Wood Preservatives

If you are using creosote, Penta, or Cuprinol for preserving wood on your ropes course — check out these paragraphs from *Harrowsmith* magazine.

"The three most common oil-based preservatives are creosote, pentachloropenol, and copper naphthenate. Creosote, the gooey, dark brown stuff used to preserve railroad ties and telephone poles, has some 200 major chemical constituents and several thousand minor ones. Many of these chemicals are toxic; some are carcinogenic; others, while not necessarily harmful to people, are damaging to plants."

"Pentachlorophenol, or "penta," was once readily available and is still occasionally sold, though its sale was restricted by the Environmental Protection Agency in 1984 because it contains dioxin, one of the worst toxic substances known to man."

"Copper naphthenate (best known by the brand name Cuprinol) — a sticky, dark green liquid — is less effective as a wood preservative than creosote or pentachlorophenol. It is also thought to be less harmful to plants and people."

"Water-based preservatives, such as those used in pressure-treated wood, are generally safer than the oil-based varieties. The green-tinted wood sold in lumberyards has been impregnated under pressure, or pressure-treated, with one of two water-based preservatives: chromated copper arsenate (CCA), or ammoniated copper arsenate (ACA). In their liquid states, CCA and ACA are toxic chemicals. But in the pressure-treating process, the arsenical compounds are chemically bonded with wood molecules so that they can neither leach into the soil nor be absorbed into the skin of people or animals coming into contact with the wood."

"Apparently, the only way to absorb the arsenical compounds into one's system is to ingest the wood itself. Short of taking a bite out of a green-tinted 2 x 4, the only way one might inadvertently take in small doses is by inhaling sawdust from pressure-treated lumber, or by breathing the fumes when burning it. Wearing a protective mask when sawing the wood seems like a wise precautionary measure."

## *Wood Rot*

To those ropes course builders who plan to be around for a few years, it is of some concern as to how long their masterpieces of ingenuity and perspiration are going to last; i.e., when will I have to replace the Beam, Swinging Log, Stump Jumps, etc. The following information is the result of some research, but mostly experience in the New England area.

First and last rule: If you anticipate your program lasting for at least three years, choose your cut trees wisely and buy pressure-treated lumber; variously called **wolmanized** or **outdoor wood**.

Some types of cut wood (felled trees) are more susceptible to rot (action of bacteria and fungus) than others. To wit, a brief comparison.

Wood susceptible to rot — ash, aspen, beech, birch, cottonwood, elm, oaks in the red oak group, poplar, fir, willow, spruce, maple.

Wood resistant to rot — cedar, black locust, oaks in the white oak group, sassafras, osage orange.

Sapwood (phloem) invariably rots faster than heartwood (xylem), so just because the surface of your Beam looks a bit time-worn doesn't mean that a break is imminent, but it's an indication that replacement should be on your mind. I had to replace a sugar maple Beam that measured 12" in diameter because it literally broke in half (with some help). This impressive section of wood came from a tree cut five years earlier. A piece of white oak might have given me 8-10 years, and a section of black locust would probably still be there when you and I are gone. So, the choice of wood does make a difference in element longevity.

A handy test for wood fiber soundness is to stick the log with the blade of a pocket knife (or with the Rockwell hardened C56-58, 7', hand-crafted, carbon steel blade of your staghorn, and nickel silver-handled, folding magnum deer slayer.) If the blade enters the log over an inch with just a moderate push, it's replacement time. As a further test, you can jump up and down on the log and listen for cracks, but this is obviously a poor image move, and not recommended without a belay.

It helps to remove the bark before placing the log. The bark, as the cambium quickly decays, provides an ideal protected habitat for various boring insects, bacteria, and fungi. The bark will slough off in less than two years anyway, so you might as well strip it initially.

Wood or lumber that is going to be placed in the ground must be chemically treated, or it will rot within 3-4 years, and in some cases, less than 2 years. Lumber that has been pressure-injected with Cuprinol (*Wolmanized* and *Outdoor Wood* are trademarks for this pressure-treated lumber), will last a minimum of 20 years in the ground (so the guarantee says). Treated lumber costs more than normal kiln-dried material, but if you consider your time valuable (three years from now), go with the expensive stuff. If you have the forethought to cut and cure a log, you can soak the end in preservative to achieve a long "in ground" life. Putting preservative on a fresh-cut log is next to worthless, but pouring a quantity of this aromatic liquid into the hole dug for the log will extend the life of the log. The most practical idea is to use a section of telephone pole that has already been pressure-injected with creosote.

Thompson's Water Seal is an effective liquid wood preservative that doesn't smell badly, and contains less toxic ingredients than most.

Tree platforms are best made from 2" x 6" sections of treated lumber. The section of a platform made from untreated lumber that rots most swiftly is the part juxtaposed to the tree; that part which remains moist. The vulnerable inside of that bolted section next to the tree is practically impossible to re-paint and, because of trapped moisture, is an ideal spot for decay-producing organisms to proliferate.

As a last $-saving suggestion: When buying lumber for a Wall, the four 4"x 4" sections should be treated lumber because of their bolted position on the support trees (potential rot area), but the 2" x 10" sections can be kiln-dried fir, spruce, etc. Look how long an unpainted New England barn can last. That's about a $75.00 suggestion!

## Telephone Pole Esoterica

Want to be conversant about telephone (utility) pole imprints at your next gathering? Are you embarrassed when someone asks, "How deep should I set a 35' pole?" You don't know a posthole from a pole hole? Here are some exotic facts that may or may not be pertinent to your knowledge bank.

| Length of Pole in Feet | Setting Depth in Feet |
|---|---|
| 25 | 5 |
| 30-35 | 5'6" |
| 40 | 6 |
| 45 | 6'6" |

"Continues in 5' lengths as to 6" depth increments up to an 80' pole, which is set at 10'."

## Backfilling

"Thoroughly tamp the fill material *by layers* until hole is completely filled around pole. Tamp any stones available against pole surface and finally form a dirt mound to give drainage away from the pole."

## Pole Breaking Strength

"The average transverse load applied 2 feet from the top, which will break the pole."

Class I (min. top circumference 27") - 4,500 lbs.

Class II (min. top circumference 25") - 3,700 lbs.

### Estimated Weight of Creosoted Poles

| | | |
|---|---|---|
| 30' Class I | — | 1,122 lbs. |
| 50' Class I | — | 2,563 lbs. |
| 35' Class II | — | 1,254 lbs. |
| 45' Class II | — | 1,876 lbs. |
| 75' Class I | — | 5,375 lbs. |

## Reading a Pole

The burned-on imprint at the base (about eye level) of a utility pole tells you where the pole is from geographically, what type of preservative treatment was applied, date of treatment, what the height is in feet, and what class pole it is. (Class pertains to diameter and/or circumference. A Class I pole is "thicker" than a Class II pole.)

The bottom set of numbers (sometimes hyphenated) is of most interest to you. It will appear, for example, as 3-35, or 2-40, etc. The first number is the pole class and the double digit number refers to the pole height in feet.

Just for fun, go out to the street by the front of your house and "read" a pole or two.

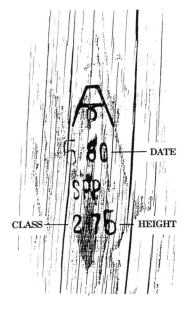

In order to collect telephone poles for your ropes course, why not have a pot luck pole party, where each guest must bring their own Class I 40-footer? Maybe just an imprint rubbing would be sufficient to qualify for dessert.

All of the preceding quoted information is from a training article by the New England Electric Company.

### Plastic-Coated Cable

The 7x19 galvanized aircraft cable that Project Adventure sometimes uses to build ropes courses can be purchased with a plastic coating. (The 7x19 designation mentioned above refers to the number of strands and fibers used in the cable's makeup. Generally speaking, the higher the second number, the more flex the cable will exhibit.)

The plastic coating doesn't make the cable any stronger, but it does protect skin, if a fall is taken against a bare cable on a low ropes course element.

If people are going to be walking on a taut, plastic-coated cable, they must wear sneakers. The plastic can be cut by Vibram soles or exposed boot nails.

The cost of the cable is about doubled by use of the plastic coating.

If you are having trouble picturing what a coated cable looks like, take a look at someone's bicycle lock cable.

If you want to use a strand vise at the end of a coated cable length, the plastic must be stripped off for the distance it takes for insertion into the strand vise; about 6 inches.

Use of cable clamps tightened directly on plastic-coated sections seems to work OK, but I wouldn't trust clamps on plastic for a belay set-up.

All in all, except for isolated instances, you are better off sticking to bare cable for your construction needs.

## How To Cut Cable

Let me get right to the crux of the cutting. Cable (wire rope) is either easily cut with the proper tool, or the cutting (?) becomes a time-consuming, exhausting exercise in frustration.

A triangular jaw cable cutter (not a bolt cutter; its parallel jaws will only squash the cable strands), when kept sharp, will efficiently slice through cable up to 1/2". The tool is advertised to be capable of cutting 5/8" cable and that's true, but it requires considerable strength of limb and a good leverage position. As an aside: A cable slicer of this type does a bang-up job of cutting rope, actually better than any knife I've ever used.

If you have access to a portable circular saw, buy a metal cutting blade and you have a combination that will zip through 3/8" cable in seconds; not bad at all for the price. Its only drawback, aside from an irritating screeching noise and an abundance of sparks, is that cutting at heights is a bit awkward (and ludicrous). Just be careful with your ground cable measurements and no trimming in the trees or beams will be necessary. Well...it sounds good, anyway.

A guillotine-like cable slicer is available that allows you to cut cable with a few well-placed hand sledge blows. Buy the expensive model (comparatively) made by Morse-Starette; others I have tried or heard of do a lousy job, dull quickly, or malfunction. This whacker/slicer is efficient and cuts the cable cleanly, but must be supported on a hard, unyielding surface — not a tree limb.

Let me make brief mention of using a hacksaw — **DON'T!**

## Tightening Cables

Please recognize that a taut cable can withstand less strain than a loose cable — actually, the looser the cable, the more weight (strain) it can withstand; measured within parameters of the cable's anchor points. But, it's often necessary to tighten the cables in order to make a ropes course event possible. For example, the cables of the Mohawk Walk. But, if it's a Pamper Pole/trapeze jump belay cable (and it's not also part of a Two Line Bridge), the cable can be left quite slack.

According to the title of this brief essay, I am supposed to be telling you about tightening cables, so on to the come-along and Haven's grip. Haven's grips, because I want to indicate how two of these handy grips are utilized for pulling a section of cable taut: the double Haven's grip technique.

Your efforts have resulted in one end of the cable being strand vised to an eye bolt (or cable clamped or swaged). The other end (working end) is reeved through another distant eye bolt and is received by the first Haven's grip. Let out 3-4 ft. of line on the come-along and attach the grip as far out on the standing part of the cable as possible. (If you are working at height, it's a real convenience to be able to lean out against a lineman's belt to secure the grip as far back on the standing part of the cable as possible.)

Then, start cranking in. The grips should be working against one another if you set them up correctly — (and after re-reading this somewhat murky bit of Haven's-grip-this and come-along-that, I'll understand if things don't just snap together) — and the cable will become satisfyingly taut.

*Extraneous Tidbit* — When you are tightening the cables on a Two Line Bridge (actually three cables), watch the first cable that you tightened as you pull in on the second. As soon as the first cable shows any slack developing, stop tightening the second cable — they are now as close to being equally taut as you can get them. Ditto for the third cable.

**Measuring Cable — "Measure 1,000 times and cut once."**

To keep cable waste to a minimum, think a bit ahead before cutting your desired lengths. With a measuring tape (50-100' fiberglass), measure from tree to tree (bolt to bolt). Utilizing this measurement, pay heed to the following if's.

- If you are using a strand vise at one or both ends, subtract about 6" for each one used.
- If you are using cable clamps, add 18" for each clamped end.
- If you are swaging, add 12" for each swaged end.
- If you are running the cable around the tree, use the tape to duplicate the cable needed and read the measurement right off the tape.
- If you are still in doubt, add a foot or two to your desired cable length — splicing short sections of wire rope is an esoteric art and beyond the scope of your needs or bandaid supply.

**Trapeze Construction**

Diving for a trapeze from the top of a subtly swaying Pamper Pole, a field house balcony, or from a block-supported platform is the **sine qua non** of commitment activities. I have heard combat veterans, pilots, skydivers, and rock climbers — all express the same general gut feelings about the trust, fear, support, commitment, etc., that are so often involved with the attempt (and the dry mouth, sewing machine knees, accelerated speech, etc.).

Here's how to make a safe, long-lasting trapeze. Fashion your trapeze from some unbreakable material. I recommend using 1-1/4" PVC U/V resistant (polyvinylchloride) rod, which can be drilled and shaped like wood, but which is stronger, as flexible, and is impervious to decay. Do not use wood dowels; they will eventually break if left outdoors.

Make a mark 1-1/4" in from each end of the 30" long PVC rod and drill through the rod at these marks with a 7/16" spade bit. Do your best to drill these holes in the center of the rod and parallel to one another.

It's much easier to get a hole started with a pointed spade bit than attempting to start drilling with a drifting high-speed spiral bit. If you have access to a drill press, use it. The holes you make will be predictably straighter than the ones attempted by hand.

Place a drop-forged 3/8" x 1-1/2" nut eye bolt into each of the two holes and secure them using an SAE 3/8" washer and single nut. The top portion of the eye should run parallel to the trapeze. Cut off the protruding threaded end of the bolt (just beyond the nut) with a hacksaw and peen over the ragged cut ends to secure a tamper-proof fixture.

To achieve a peened-over (buggered up) bolt end, further tighten the nut 1/2 turn or so, to expose about 1/16" of the cut end of the bolt. Grasping the trapeze, place the eye portion of the eye bolt on top of an anvil, vise, or substantial mass of metal. Strike the vertically placed cut end of the bolt with controlled, slightly angled blows of a hammer, until the edges of the bolt are beveled over and contoured to the nut.

Use a medium rasp or hacksaw blade to roughen up the smooth surface of the PVC rod, offering a secure grip for the sweaty palms to come.

The strongest, most permanent way to hang the trapeze is to use cable and strand vises, but first plan where you are going to suspend this aerial target.

## Trapeze Suspension

I had promised in a past BOT's to pass on this information about how and where to hang a trapeze...I almost forgot!

Fortunately, most gymnasium ceilings have exposed beams. Use these beams to hang the trapeze so that the swinging bar is about 7-1/2' from the end of the platform (for a high school student) and at about chest height for a 5'6" person. You should get about a 70% completion rate using the above measurements; i.e., actually grabbing the bar. It may be that the beams are serendipitously arranged, allowing you to place a series of adjacent eye bolts in the beams perpendicular to the platform, offering adjustable (comparatively easy or difficult) dives for the bar.

Do not adjust the height of the trapeze so that it hangs below the waist level of a student standing on the platform. A downhill dive will result, and most people cannot handle the G forces generated by catching the bar in this low position. Possible shoulder injuries may result. Helmets should be worn for this spectacular dive.

If there are no exposed beams in your gym. you may have to forego rigging this event. Drop ceilings often hide useable beams, but utilizing the area above a drop ceiling usually involves a cosmetic hassle with the building super or custodians.

Another potential ceiling structure, suitable for anchoring belays, trapezes, etc., is a poured concrete beam; tremendously strong, but laced with lengths of reinforcing steel rod. When you start drilling a hole, you "takes your chances," because even a carbide-tipped drill isn't going to make it through steel. Another negative tidbit about concrete — it is super-duper hard drilling stuff. I don't want to discourage you, but considering the hidden steel rods and the solidity of the concrete, it's like playing Russian Roulette with a jackhammer.

As a result of whatever drilling arrangement you succeed with, attach the two 5/16" trapeze strand vises into each one of the two beam support bolts; i.e., those 1/2" x 1-1/2" eye bolts placed in drilled holes and measured slightly wider apart than the 2-1/2' trapeze length. With someone standing on the platform, it becomes an easy task to adjust the height of the trapeze by having that person tell the worker on the ladder (or among the beams) to push more cable through the paired strand vises until the trapeze is centered, parallel to the floor, and at a functional height. Push cable through the strand vises with care and in small measure, remembering that the cable only moves through the strand vise in one direction.

It is somewhat more difficult to hang the trapeze using rope. Measure what you think is the right length of rope (5/8" multiline) needed by dropping a tape measure from the support eye bolts and having someone standing on the platform "eyeball" what appears to be the right length. Add 12" to each length to compensate for the eye splice at each end of the rope. The splices will take up more than 12", but don't forget the added length resulting from the use of a rapid link on one end of the rope.

Put a 1/2" thimble into each trapeze bolt and perform an eye splice around these thimbles with the ends of separate and equal lengths of rope. At the other ends of these ropes, perform another eye splice around a 1/2" thimble. Using a steel locking carabiner, clip these latter eye splices into the ceiling support eye bolts. If you measured the ropes accurately and performed the splices well, the trapeze should hang evenly and just where you want it. To be truthful, most of the time a rope-supported trapeze is slightly askew and a few inches away from an ideal height. Tying knots in the ropes and using different length rapid links allows easy adjusting.

## Bosun's Chairs — Made to Last

Suspended Bosun's Chairs (BC) make an OK low ropes course event that has fallen in some disfavor recently because the "chairs" are (1) difficult to spot efficiently and (2) hang enticingly as a target for knife-toting vandals.

I don't have an easy answer for the spotting problem, except to make the impact area less injurious (dig up the soil or add a six-inch layer of "chips"), but here's a new solution for #2.

In the past, we (Project Adventure builders) have suspended a section of cable from the top horizontal support cable and clipped an appropriate length of 5/8" diameter multiline (with a BC attached) to the vertical cable. At the end of the program day, the instructor was to unclip the rope section of the BC from the cable and store it inside. This procedure usually required a stepladder, so it was seldom done.

Here's a way to extend the vertical cable to within easy grasp, which reduces the amount of rope needed and, more significantly, "pad" the cable so it is not difficult or painful to grab with bare hands.

Cut a section of 5/16" cable 24" short of where you would like to position the chair; i.e., from top horizontal cable to 24" above where you want the BC to hang. Place a 5/16" strand vise at the top end of this eventual vertical piece (which will attach directly to a cable drop, or alternately, hang between two spaced 5/16" cable clamps attached to the horizontal 3/8" support cable). Reeve the bottom end of the cable (remember, it's not suspended yet — if it is, take it down; you're going too fast), through a section of 1/2" I.D. diameter PVC pipe. The pipe should measure a few inches shorter than the cable length. After reeving, swage a 5/16" thimble into the bottom end.

How's that look? — Not bad, just hanging there waiting to be grabbed. Can't beat that with a stick — or cut it with a knife, either.

Now, the chair. Cut a 3' length of 5/8" multiline and whip, seize or splice an eye into the middle of the rope around a 1/2" thimble. Reeve the two rope ends (both working ends in this case) through the two pre-drilled 3/4" holes in the BC's. Tie an overhand knot in each rope end after reeving through the holes, and pull the knots tight. This is your ultra-portable BC, and it clips functionally into the swaged eye in the end of the cable.

As you (whoever) swing from BC to BC, hands will grab cable covered by smooth PVC pipe. No more twisted ropes, having to horse around with a clumsy stepladder, draping long BC ropes over your shoulder and having the wooden chairs smack your shins, or having to replace slashed ropes.

I'm sure you can appreciate how using PVC pipe can be transferred to the fabrication of a swinging tire series — again, cable replaces rope. Inventing is fun when it works.

*Gentle reminder* — control your frustration amidst all this construction esoterica as we return anon to the mundane shores of hysterical functionalism..."he chortled in his joy."

## Climbing Poles

Having available a series of securely placed stumps of varying height is a sure grabber as a balance/flexibility exercise. The object is to climb to the top of the 4' - 8' stump and balance there for a minimum of 5 seconds. The balance problem becomes more acute on the stumps of smaller diameter.

These stumps, with small changes to the log's exterior, can be adapted for excellent bouldering practice attempts. With a chain saw, cut two or three shallow (1/2" to 1") notches in the log in areas that complement the natural irregularities of its surface. These small notches and holes or bumps are the "holds" for reaching the top.

Assign each climber a perfect score or 10 as s/he begins the climb (no belay), and subtract a point for each infraction of the strict climbing rules (1) Once a hand or foot has been placed in or on a hold, *any* slip or move that is not essential to the climb results in a point loss. The value of the exercise is in its difficulty and opportunity for improvement. Be strict — one point per slip or non-essential move. (2) A Climber is not allowed to use a hold above his own eye level. (3) The final move (usually a mantle of some sort) must be made cleanly and a balanced posture must be maintained for 5 seconds to keep a perfect score.

## Ding-a-Ling

If you already have a ropes course, this high commitment activity is a natural, and can be added at small expense.

Erect a 20-25' ladder in a vertical position directly underneath a high (30-40') belay cable. Ask 6-8 people to steady the ladder. The student of choice (his/her own choice, of course) ties into a belay rope, which is attached (via carabiners, rapid links, S/S pulley, etc.) to the belay cable above. A separate rope is also tied to the top of the ladder and anchored to a solid object (e.g., a tree) to prevent the ladder from falling to the ground.

The student begins to climb and continues to the top of the ladder, diligently eyeballing the overhead goal; a bell hanging from the cable and positioned about six feet above the top ladder rung. The object is to ring that bell. The chief ingredient of this ladder-to-nowhere event: fear.

Verbiage aside, this ropes course element is functional, useable, and fun.

Try making your own ladder, using 2" x 3" sections for the rails, and 1" hardwood dowels for the rungs. Commercial extension ladders are expensive.

Most of the time, I encourage people to name their own event, or change the name to suit the situation. I encourage you to keep this one — it's near perfect.

## Firecracker Ladder Construction

A firecracker ladder, hanging in its typically atypical fashion, appears to be a ludicrous joke. Your sense of fantasy will love it! Here's the way to be the first on your block to build a genuine firecracker ladder.

Cut a section of 5/8" diameter multiline or manila rope 18" longer than you want the ladder. Eye splice a 1/2" or 5/8" thimble into one end of the rope; pick either end — you can't go wrong.

The rungs should be 12" long with a narrow/wide groove arrangement as in the 9" rungs of the rope ladder, but with the two grooves cut right in the center of the rung. Bevel the rung ends to remove the sharp edge. Dip all finished rungs in Thompson's Water Seal.

Place the first rung into the rope about 16" down from the thimble, aligning the grooves to the proper strands; i.e., one strand-narrow; two strands-wide. Continue inserting rungs at 14" intervals, disregarding whether they are parallel to one another. Leave about 18" of rope below the last rung.

Tie off the rungs with waxed nylon cord, as explained in *Rope Ladder Construction*. If you use multiline rope, it will be necessary to add a waxed nylon cord whipping directly beneath each rung to prevent the rung from pushing the rope strands apart under the weight of a climber, and inching downward. Because manila rope is usually such a tight (hard) lay rope, this extra whipping is not as necessary when this natural fiber, unless you're really into whipping, or you're bored.

Some mention should be made about attempting to climb this unique ladder. It's pretty obvious that the alternating hand/foot technique is not going to work. After some humorous and vigorous experimentation, you will find the alternating two-hand/two-foot technique is THE way, and it probably is, but let the students figure that out.

An ascent up this semi-sadistic ladder is a demanding upper body workout and a first-class continuing commitment activity. A continuing commitment differs from a single commitment (zip wire ride, trapeze jump) in that a series of positive and often demanding decisions (overcoming pain, fatigue, fear) must be made to reach a goal.

The belay anchor points for both ladder types should be far enough away (2-3 ft.) from the ladder anchor point to help keep the belay rope from tangling or wrapping around the climber.

Having someone hold onto the bottom of the ladder makes the ascent much easier for the climber, and prevents sea sickness. If the ladder and belay rope begin to intertwine and spiral around one another, ask the person holding the bottom of the ladder to rotate her/his body (while firmly holding the ladder) in the direction opposite the spiral. A vigorous body spin will unspiral the belay rope and ladder.

## Flying Squirrel

I assume you know, but the name above and all the other fanciful and whimsical names that have been applied and adopted by the Project Adventure staff are chosen and used primarily so that everyone knows which activity or ropes course event is being referred to in a conversation, discussion, etc. "Did you notice the poor spotting on event #17?" See what I mean?

The Flying Squirrel event (explanation to follow) has little to do with a flying squirrel, but one day...I was installing a high limb belay anchor and noticed a lower dead limb that needed trimming. After making a few reciprocal passes with a bow saw at the base of the limb, I noticed what seemed to be a large dead leaf detach from mid-limb and begin floating to the ground. The "leaf" radically changed direction two or three times on the trip down. Only as the amorphous, darting object approached the ground (from about 50'), and flared its airbrakes did I realize that I had witnessed a rare daytime event — the flight of a nocturnal flying squirrel. This squirrely scenario was worth remembering, and so it is, via the name designation of this high ropes course experience.

The purpose of this basically passive element is to allow a physically and/or emotionally handicapped student to (a) experience the sensation of height on a ropes course and (b) to experience the trust of being on belay.

Sounds intriguingly complex. Nope — very simple, actually — here's the M.O.

Install a cable at height (40+ feet), or choose a stout hardwood limb. On this cable or organic support, affix a S/S pulley arranged in the non-belay pulley mode; i.e., the sheave wheel turns. Reeve a length of KMIII static rescue rope through the S/S pulley set-up so that the rope is long enough to measure from the ground to the pulley and back down, plus 15 feet. Tie a bowline-on-a-bight in one end of the rope and clip (locking carabiner) the two formed loops into a student's Swiss seat/Studebaker wrap pelvic tie-in. The group (minimum 8) grabs the other end of the rope and *walks* away from their position under the S/S pulley, at which juncture the clipped-in student begins to "fly."

From a student decision-making standpoint, it is important to establish communication between the person being lifted and the others...otherwise, this event is simply hauling a "sack of potatoes" up in the air.

Encourage the student to control his/her ascent/descent by verbal control of the lifters. This command status should be as the result of some pre-flight conversation by both parties.

*Considerations:*

- Tie a few overhand knots in the lifting end of the KMIII rope to aid gripping the rope.

- Do not use the S/S pulley in the static mode. It makes the lifting process too difficult because of increased friction.

- If you are concerned about your group's lifting ability or commitment level, clip two pelvic wrapped students to the end of the rope via a bowline-on-a-bight (Ref. Australian back-up belay).

- Control the speed of ascent (and descent, obviously), because 8-15 people pulling on a rope can raise a 150 lb. person with surprising ease.

- Make sure the footing is good where the lifters will be consistently walking.

- Do not use climbing rope in place of KMIII. Climbing rope stretches too much, and has 2,000 lbs. less tensile strength.

- If you are not familiar with placement of eye bolt anchors or cable lengths, call Project Adventure (508-468-7981), ask for me; I'll try to explain, or suggest alternatives.

## The Hickory Jump — Construction and Use

The stimulus for developing the *Hickory Jump* as a low ropes course event resulted from a nostalgic recollection of time I had spent during pre-adolescence, pretending I was Batman and wishing that I could heroically dive to a temptingly close tree limb which extended near to the top of my family's suburban roof garage. I did not attempt the jump (my survival instincts prevailed), but that long-ago challenge was powerful enough to stimulate the creation of today's Hickory Jump. Now, I jump with impunity, knowing that the consequence of missing the "limb" is a welcome landing in the arms of willing spotters.

This dive-to-your-limit ropes course element allows any latter-day Batman or Wonder Woman to jump for their imagined tree limb, comforted by knowing that if the goal isn't reached, a chain-link fence or cartop will not have to provide the landing area. Willing hands and arms "catch" the ersatz avenger if the trapeze bar is missed. The sequentially-placed take-off stumps of the Hickory Jump event are so arranged that almost everyone eventually finds their distance limit. The event is not so much a nostalgic "super friends" indulgence, but a combination self-challenge/trust exercise, that requires a significant personal commitment, and confidence in the spotters.

The Hickory Jump involves little purchased material for construction, but requires moderate-to-hard labor, depending upon the ease of digging at your chosen site. The dive to the trapeze is given to repetition by participants — "Let me have another try; I'm sure I can make it this time." — and is well worth the installation time and labor.

### *Planning and Construction*

Spend some time looking for two appropriately-sized and spaced-apart trees. A support tree for this element should measure a minimum of five inches in diameter at a height from the ground of eight feet, and be six to ten feet from the other support tree.

Take into consideration what the digging will be like at the potential site; otherwise, you may spend an inordinate amount of time placing the jump stumps. There is often no choice, and in such a case, just literally dig in, consoling yourself with a mental image of how dramatically useful this event will be for the students' developing sense of group trust and her/his self-image.

If two telephone pole sections (about 12') are available, and you don't mind digging a couple more holes, use them as trapeze supports. The benefits of utilizing telephone pole supports are that wood decay is practically eliminated, and you have the luxury of locating the poles wherever you like. Or, combine one tree and a pole or a pole and a bleacher support, or a pole and a goal post, or...

This low ropes course element was named the *Hickory Jump* because the first few jump bars were fashioned from hickory saplings. (As an historical aside: The first Hickory Jump was built at Hamilton-Wenham Regional High School in Massachusetts in 1975.) Tough stuff, that hickory — tensile strength akin to iron, I've read, but alas, being a "natural" product, the wood does eventually deteriorate, leading to replacement hassles every few years. However, if you take the trapeze indoors after each use, there's no reason not to use wood, particularly if you have a source of straight-grain hardwood.

For years, a permanently bolted bar (wood or metal) was used for the Hickory Jump. The disadvantages were:

1. Liability (not being able to secure the event).
2. Replacement problems (constant exposure to the elements).
3. Vandalism (availability at all times).
4. Breakage or bending (poor construction geometry).

The advantages, besides aesthetic, were nil, and so the logical change was made to a synthetic trapeze jump bar.

Here's the synthetic alternative (BOO-HISS). Inch and a quarter PVC (poly vinyl chloride) rod is now generally used as a trapeze bar. PVC's battleship gray color fits into most woodsy scenes; it has as much or more resilience (spring) than hickory; its plastic substance can be drilled and shaped like wood; heat and cold have relatively no effect on its strength, and it will last longer than you will. Apparently, its only drawbacks are:

1. Fairly high priced.
2. PVC is a proven carcinogen (don't eat it).
3. There is some evidence that PVC is affected by U/V exposure.
4. It's just not hickory! (You should know how to pronounce hickory, since you will be using and talking about this event. It is said, Hick-ry (accent on the HICK), not Hick-or-ry. Now you know.)

Remember to rough up the smooth surface of whatever trapeze material you choose, to help sweaty palms adhere.

PVC can be purchased in five or ten foot sections from a local plastic distributor or from Project Adventure, Inc. (PA will either sell you the stock rod or a finished product. Cut the length you want (2'-2-1/2') using just about any type of saw you have around; even a hacksaw.

Drill a 7/16" diameter hole at each end of the trapeze rod, and 1-1/2" from the ends. Try to make the two holes as parallel to one another as your eyeball drilling technique allows. If you have a drill press — use it.

Use a spade bit (Speed Bor is the commercial name) if the drilled holes are to be made hand-held — such a pointed drill bit won't dance around the surface to be drilled. Insert a 3/8" x 1-1/2" shoulder nut eye bolt (drop forged) in each hole so that the eyes of the bolt are on the same side of the trapeze and parallel to the trapeze bar. Put on a 3/8" SAE washer and an anti-vibration nut, tighten down and cut off the remainder of the bolt with a hacksaw. Done. If you can't find an anti-vibration nut, put on a regular hex nut. After you have cut off the excess bolt end, peen over the remainder with a hammer to prevent the nut from working itself free; and to preclude vandalism attempts.

Now, hang the trapeze. Place a 1/2" staple into each support tree at a height of about 10 feet, so that the staples face one another. Using either cable or rope, fashion two lengths that will support the trapeze from these two staples and so the trapeze hangs level at a height of eight feet. Use carabiners to connect the trapeze to the support rope/cable, so that disconnecting the bar can be accomplished easily. If you do nothing else from this point, at least you now have a swinging pull-up bar.

OK, the technical stuff is over. It's time for the type of work that slams the door on romantic notions about ropes course construction — digging a ditch.

The five or six sequentially placed take-off stumps need to be set in place. Considering that you will want the jump from the first stump to be challenging for shorter people, but not impossible, place the first stump five feet back from a line perpendicular with the trapeze's plumb. This first stump should protrude two feet, nine inches above the ground.

After having established where to place the first stump, use that mark to begin a ditch that will be approximately one and a half feet wide by three feet deep by five feet long, and dug along a continuation of the perpendicular line mentioned above.

If possible, use sections of telephone poles for the stumps. Telephone poles are pressure-injected with creosote (a caustic wood preservative that doesn't get along well with skin), which precludes rot and the need for stump replacement. Otherwise, use any type of logs available, except those which are particularly susceptible to decay; e.g., birch, hickory, poplar, which rot faster than oak, maple, locust and cedar. Decay in any kind of wood can be slowed by pouring Cuprinol into the bottom of the hole or ditch and, after setting the stumps, also around the direct/pole interface. Cut and cured logs will absorb the Cuprinol and last longer than freshly cut, wet logs.

Measure and saw each section of log or pole in relation to the first, shortest stump. Each stump subsequent to the first one should be two to three inches higher than the next, and juxtaposed immediately behind one another; i.e., actually in contact. The fifth or sixth stump will be so far away from the bar that not many people will be able to make the jump and that's intentional. Each individual should be allowed to find their physical limit and eventually be required to really trust their spotters — programmed trust.

After the log sections are cut and placed in the ditch — vertically, and in sequence — alternately shovel in dirt and tamp vigorously until the ditch is filled. Use a cut limb or pick handle as a tamper. Tamping the loose dirt vigorously is important, in order to set the stumps solidly. Without firmly set take-off stumps, this event becomes a dangerous joke. An instructor should give each stump a lateral kick before each day's use to ensure a solid take-off.

After the stumps are in and set, their height relative to one another can be easily adjusted with a chainsaw, so don't be dismayed if your initial measurements are incorrect; mine usually are, too.

### WARNING — Read this...or Else

This spotting recommendation *must* be followed, or someone will eventually be injured. The intention of the jumper is to grasp the bar, and if that is accomplished, it becomes the spotters' job *not* to let the jumper swing through (complete the arc of the swing). The swing-through causes an increased pull on the jumper's grip and can result in a spontaneous release, resulting in a quick trip to the turf — usually on the participant's back or neck. Frightened? Good — don't let it happen.

*Suggestions*

1. At a preliminary get-together, offer each student the chance to try a trust dive; i.e., simply diving off a stump into the spotters' arms.

2. Use a minimum of six spotters; two immediately behind the support trees and four in front. Use more spotters if the jumper is large, but do not place spotters so close to the first stump that their arms impede the jumper's dive.

3. Have spotters remove their wristwatches, otherwise the forward momentum of the diver may break the strap, band, etc.

4. Ask jumpers to remove large buckles, belt knives, or any sharp objects from their pockets.

5. Occasionally remind the jumpers, as they approach their distance limit, that it is much easier to catch a laid-out body than an I'm-not-going-to-make-it, folded pike position.

6. Suggest to the jumpers that they aim above the bar with their eyes, in order to get more distance from their dive — the old 45° and-up trick.

7. After everyone has made an attempt or two, suggest an additional challenge. Ask a volunteer if s/he would commit to dive for the trapeze,blindfolded, from the stump in front of the one from which they made their final successful attempt. This challenge is offered as a "step beyond the expected," so don't expect 100% participation (or 50%, for that matter). Allow more than one attempt per person, because the first dive is usually short.

   These blindfolded jumps should not be viewed as simply a daredevil stunt. Don't hesitate to ask more from your students than they are initially prepared to give; after all, the name of the game is Project *Adventure*. The commitment is real, the trust level is high; group support and enthusiasm is generally 100%, and the satisfaction from an attempt is apparent.

   Do not let the blindfolded participant jump until s/he is facing directly toward the center of the trapeze. Ask the potential jumper to extend their his/her hands, held together, toward the trapeze, and then, if necessary, rearrange their direction as per **your** instructions (this is a time for everyone else to stop talking). Watch each jumper carefully so that they maintain a correct orientation to the bar.

If a student plans to dive blindfolded from the Pamper Pole, this low-level attempt is a tremendous confidence-booster.

Go get 'em, Batman!  POW!  WHAM!  ZAP!

## The Mohawk Walk

This very popular low ropes course group initiative problem is simply a zig-zag extension of the Tension Traverse, with no rope to add support.

The object is to move the entire group from the initial support tree to the last support tree, using only the taut cables in between one another for balance. There are usually some adept (well-balanced?) students who can walk on the cables without support, like a tightrope performer, but since the emphasis in this case is on problem-solving and group completion, it's everyone on the cables (one at a time from the start), and go for it.

Let the person with the best balance lead.  It is this person (and the last person) who find themselves in the least-balanced position.  Falls (steps to the ground) will vary from occasional to frequent.  If you ask the group to begin from the start after each fall, you better bring bivouac gear, because you're in for a long stay.  The falls are going to happen, so have some fun and encourage laughter (the improbable "failure is fun" concept).  Set a goal of trying to make the entire traverse without incurring more than 10, maybe 20 falls (after a few tries, a workable number will present itself).  If the number is bettered or equaled, offer much fuss over world records, etc.; and if the goal is doubled, respond with good-humored jibes and encouragement to try again.  The beauty of this activity is the total group involvement toward achieving a goal and the unrestrained physical fun in attempting to reach it.

Hey, if it's that great, let's get one built.  OK, here's how.

Choose a location that has a level, uncluttered ground area and enough well-spaced four inch to sixteen inch diameter trees, at the base, to provide anchor points for the taut cables.

If where you're standing is good enough, pick the support trees so that five to ten cable lengths provide the best challenge for the students and the easiest drilling for you.

The cable lengths (distance between trees) should vary, with only the last cable being more than fifteen feet long.  The final cable can be up to thirty feet in length, only because there will be a tension rope attached to the second-to-last support tree.  This rope is attached and used exactly like a regular tension traverse rope (spliced and clipped to an eye bolt or tied to a limb at about fifteen feet), except that in this case, the rope is measured about eight to ten feet short of the final support tree.  You ask why?  I deign to answer as the challenge fairly announces itself.

Let's begin with the first tree and by-the-numbers, so that I can better record (remember) the sequence.

1. Drill through the trunk diameter on center so that the drill bit (brief clarification: the *drill bit* is that piece of fluted steel that rotates through the wood, while the *drill* is that mechanical device that holds the *drill bit* while drilling. Clear? You don't care? OK, that's it — no more clarifications; you'll just have to stumble along with my initial and often obscure syntax. Just kidding, folks...I wanted you to relax a bit before getting hit with the low tech rhetoric of ropes course building) is pointing through the tree toward the next support tree. The Mohawk Walk is not a high event; not even average height — it's a short event. The cable heights shouldn't exceed 18-20 inches (about knee high) to ensure an intact crotch if a participant's legs accidentally, and almost always suddenly, straddle the cable.

   Use a 11/16" x 16" auger bit for the hole making. If you plan to use a bit brace ...no more clarifications — bit brace identification is up to you) instead of an electric drill, more power to you. That was a small joke, folks, and if you aren't smiling, from this point on, I'll be technically serious, directly to-the-point, and boring. You're smiling? — Good, me too!

2. Place a 5/8" diameter thimbled eye bolt of appropriate length in this newly bored hole (thimbled end toward the next support tree), and turn a nut down on the threaded end over a fish plate washer. The thimbled groove in the head of the bolt should be perpendicular to the ground.

   Tighten the nut with an adjustable wrench and cut off any protruding threads with a hacksaw. Peen over the cut end with a hammer. This cut and peening procedure reduces vandalism and removes a shin-battering obstruction.

3. Drill a hole in the second support tree similar to the hole in tree #1, and point directly toward hole #1. Try looking through the completed hole, thinking of it as a sighting mechanism, and see how accurate your estimating abilities proved to be. If the hole doesn't sight directly at the other hole, that's OK — What the heck, we're not building furniture here!

4. Measure a length of 3/8" diameter cable (we use 7x19 galvanized aircraft cable) that is one a half feet longer than the measurement from tree @1 to tree #2; i.e., bolt-to-bolt.

   Using cable clamps, attach one end of the cable (either end: this is one of those unlikely times when you can't make the wrong choice) to the thimble eye bolt in tree #1. Attach the three 3/8" cable clamps (also called wire rope clips and, sometimes erroneously, U-bolts), so that the U portion of the clamps go over the working end of the cable — refer to the illustration.

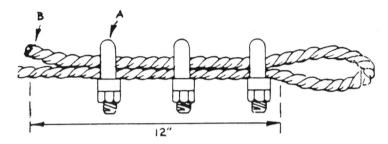

The first clip (A) is put on the cable one clip-base width from the working end of the cable (B) U-bolt portion over the working end. The working end should be a minimum of 12 inches from the loop.

To hold down the last short section of the working end, you can either (1) copiously wrap electrician's tape around and around the cables, or (2) squeeze on a serving sleeve. If you don't know what a serving sleeve is, use tape or call (508) 468-7981, ask for me, and I'll tell you. Notice, that's (508), not (800).

5. Reeve (that's kind of an *in* word meaning to insert a rope or cable through something, like reeving a rope through the cheeks of a pulley and I can't get into a further discussion of cheeks here, because this is a family publication), the other end of the cable through the thimble eye bolt (TEB) in tree #2. Thread the cable end up through the TEB opening so that the working end lies on top of the standing part of the cable. That sounds confusing, but it's simply done and allows you to put the U portion of the clamps on the cable so that the threaded ends point down. This orientation reduces the chance of getting scraped or gouged by the threads if they were sticking up.

Use the double Haven's grip technique (508-468-7981) to pull the cable taut. Then, attach the cable clamps and tighten them down.

6. Attach a 1/2" nut eye bolt or 1/2" shoulder lag eye screw to the second to last tree so that the eye points toward the final support tree and is approximately fifteen feet above the ground. This eye bolt is the anchor point for a tension rope. Cut the rope (5/8" multiline is a good choice) to a length that is about eight to ten feet short of the final tree. Eye splice one end of the rope in order to facilitate attachment to the eye bolt by use of a carabiner or rapid link. If you can't splice, tie a bowline knot in the rope end. You can learn to splice next week or so...

There are more exotic techniques for attaching cables that I have not mentioned (thank goodness, eh?) that are fine to use, but necessitate the use of more expensive and hard to find gear (strand vises, swaging, and nut eye bolts).

The popularity of this event stems from the infectious nature of a non-intimidating challenge and the group cooperation needed to finish the "walk" successfully.

Remember, it helps to get things started if the first person out on the cable has better than average balance: You, for example. No? Come on, embarrass yourself — it's fun.

## High Tension Traverse

I recently build a high (25') Tension Traverse with an overhead belay. It's a good event and every bit as challenging as the low event.

- Make sure the overhead belay cable is at least nine feet above the tension cable, and slanted slightly down in the direction that the participant moves.
- Use a ROSA pulley on the belay cable, with a double rapid link set-up between the ROSA pulley and the S/S pulley.
- Employ a permanently placed 5/8" x 12" turnbuckle on the bottom cable in order to adjust cable tension (relative difficulty).
- Remember that the higher you place the tension rope, the easier the event becomes.
- Belay loosely for a maximum challenge; even slight tension on the belay cable reduces the balance problem.
- As a belayer, walk ahead of the participant so that if s/he falls and holds onto the tension rope, this rope will not pull him/her back toward and into the tension rope support tree.

## Multi-Vine Traverse

From the tropic and torpid depths of the Ohio jungles comes this delightfully challenging ropes course element, via Gary Moore of Ohio State University.

The object is to cross a low or high taut cable (about 30-40' long) with balance help only intermittently available from dangling short spliced ropes. These interestingly sequenced ropes hang from an overhead cable that parallels the bottom one (the one you walk on). The two parallel cables should be at least 10' apart. The distance between vertical ropes depends upon how challenging you want the crossing to be. Having constructed a few of these Multi-Vine elements (low and high), I'd suggest hanging the first rope about 10-11' from the support tree or pole. The cable is more taut near the tree, resulting in greater confidence and commitment to make a longer lunge and grab. Mid-cable ropes should be closer together (say 8-9') because of bottom cable movement.

The dangling vertical ropes (5/8" multiline) should be spliced short enough so that a participant cannot hold onto one rope to reach another.

As a participant launches her/himself (the fine art of wire-walking is abandoned for the immediacy of survival leaps) toward a rope, be aware that you can offer substantial and largely unnoticed belay help by simply tightening up on the belay rope. Most successful traverses are in the hands of the belayer — success is where you find it.

As a safety consideration when this event is used as a low element, construct the bottom cable low enough to compassionately consider all crotch levels. Try including the Multi-Vine Traverse as part of a Mohawk Walk. Completing this Tarzan-like crossing as a group is a cooperative and confidence-building gem.

## Tension Traverse Set-Up Variation

As explained in some detail on page 132 of *Cows' Tails & Cobras*, we use 5/16" cable almost exclusively for the upper part of a swinging "rope" element on the ropes course.

New uses of the "swing cable" are to provide an easy clip-in/clip-out procedure for the one or two Tension Traverse support ropes, and to eliminate having to peg or staple the tree that anchors the support ropes.

If your Tension Traverse is set up as a single line or in the shape of a triangle, a single tree or telephone pole anchors the support rope(s). To prevent theft or vandalism, these ropes should be removed at the end of the day and set up the following day. In the past, either a ladder or permanent pegs in the tree were the only way to get the support ropes up to the clip-in point.

Measure a length of 5/16" cable (single rope traverse), and attach strand vises to either end (or use a combination strand vise and swaged end), so that if one end of the cable were attached to the clip-in staple, you could comfortably reach the lower end of the cable by standing on the Tension Traverse cable itself. Cut a length of rope that will extend from the end of the hanging cable to the end of the Tension Traverse cable.

Eye splice one end of this 5/8" rope around an appropriately-sized thimble and, using a 1/2" rapid link (or carabiner), clip the rope into the lower strand vise, making it ready for use. A 3/8" staple can be placed in the tree at the level of the lower swaged eye so that the cable can be locked to the tree.

If you are setting up a Triangular Tension Traverse, run a section of cable through the high staple so that both ends of the cable hang at the above-mentioned reachable height. Using a 5/16" cable clamp, seize the cable to itself just below the 1/2" staple it is running through. This seizing will save the use of two strand vises; i.e., $.

## Tired Two Line

If you have been looking for another high ropes course element to connect two support trees, this simple, but challenging event might serve your purpose.

The diameter of the two trees at the height chosen for this event must be at least 15".

Drill two holes through the tree trunk so that they are on the same level and 10-14" apart. Do not drill too near the edge of the trunk.

Drill another hole directly through the center of the same tree (same direction) so that the hole is at least 9' above the other two holes.

Change your position to the other support tree and repeat the drilling instructions above, so that the second set of three holes points toward the first set.

Insert and tighten thimble eye bolts of proper length. Attach the top cable with a strand vise at either end and affix a back-up.

Attach the two lower cables and tighten them using a Haven's grip/come-along combination. These two parallel cables must be fairly tight to allow a reasonable success ratio. Or, use H&H turnbuckles (one on each cable) to allow easy tension adjustment.

The object (obviously, I hope by this time), is to *walk* on the parallel cables from one tree to another. Cable lengths of 25-40' provide a doable and enticing challenge.

Use a ROSA pulley on the top belay cable to alleviate tugging the belay rope. You can apply a little tension to the belay rope without the participant's being aware of the help. The belay rope should be affixed behind the participant (Peter Pan position), unless you plan to allow holding the rope for support; it all has to do with whatever challenge/success level you are trying to develop.

As on cable/balance events, jogging shoes with knobs on the soles do not work well — the knobs catch on the cable. Tennis shoes work best. Bare feet is contraindicated — too painful.


## Rope Ladders

A wooden-runged rope ladder provides access and egress with style from any ropes course element. In addition, a hand-crafted ladder is aesthetically pleasing, and its construction is surprisingly easy. Include your students in the construction of the ladder. It's genuinely fun (in contrast to digging post holes), and the good-looking result of a handmade rope ladder generates many satisfied smiles and predictable nods of approval.

### Rope Ladder Construction

To build a 20' rope ladder, you will need the following materials:

1. 43' of 5/8" multiline rope. The extra three feet of rope is necessary in order to include an optional short splice in the bottom of the ladder. Manila rope of the same diameter can also be used, but it's harder to work with and will not last as long outdoors because of its comparative susceptibility to rot.

2. Four 3' sections of 1" hardwood dowel (birch is serviceable, but ash is better) to be cut into sixteen 9" sections.

3. One 1/2" or 5/8" galvanized thimble.

4. Approximately 100' of waxed nylon cord.

Tape the ends of the cut multiline with plastic electrician's tape so that they don't unravel while you are working on the ladder.

Find the center of the 43' section of rope and seize in the thimble at that juncture. Seizing is the wrapping/whipping process of securing the thimble in the bight of the rope that designates, in this case, the measured center of the rope.

Using a dato blade on a table saw or a circular saw, cut two grooves 1" in from the ends of the 9" dowel sections (rungs) so that the grooves oppose one another; i.e., so they occur on opposite sides of the dowel. Cut the grooves to measure 3/16" in depth by 1/2" and 5/8" wide respectively. Be consistent with each dowel so that the narrow grooves are on one side and the wide grooves are on the other. These grooves are made to receive the three strands of rope; one strand in the narrow groove, and two strands in the wider groove. Refer to the illustration.

If you don't have access to a power saw, use a round rasp to make the grooves — more time-consuming certainly, but in some ways more satisfying.

Using a power sander (or hand sanding), slightly bevel the edges of the rungs to remove the sharp circumference edge.

Dip each birch rung into a container of Cuprinol to stain (mahogany, redwood, teak) the blond wood and appropriately match the decor of your gymnasium and, of course, to preserve the wood.

After performing a secure seizing, reeve a rope (cord) through the thimble and tie the ladder onto the base of a tree, pole, etc. Grab the two loose rope ends at the bottom of the ladder and pull equally hard to help remove any kinks or turns in the ropes. Pull on the ropes frequently while inserting the rungs to make sure that the rungs are parallel to one another.

Measure 18" down the ropes from the base of the thimble and insert a rung in both ropes so that the rung forms the base of an isosceles triangle with the thimble as the apex. Twist the three strands of the rope in such a way as to provide an opening for the insertion of the run or use a fid to separate the strands. Make sure the single rope strand goes in the narrow groove of the run and the double strand fits in the wider groove.

Measure 14" down the two ropes and insert another dowel. Eyeball this rung with the first one to make sure that they are parallel to one another. Pull on the rope ends each time a rung is inserted to facilitate this visual placement. Continue to insert rungs at 14" intervals until there is approximately 2' of rope left on each side.

Cut the waxed nylon cord into 4' sections and using this cord, make an X lashing at each juncture of rope and rung. This very basic lashing doesn't involve fancy knots or intricate tying procedures, just tightly wrap the cord back and forth across the rope/rung juncture until you have used up about half the cord, then change direction and criss-cross the remaining cord on the unwrapped part of the juncture. Finish off with a square knot or two. Leave enough cord, while tying this knot, to get sufficient leverage in order to make the knot tight. This lashing will work loose if each wrap isn't taken tightly and if the final knot isn't secured well.

Perform a short splice in the two loose bottom ends of the rope in order to finish off the ladder. This splice also provides a bottom rung to the ladder. If you haven't learned to splice and don't want to bother, leave the two ends taped and dangling: splicing is an ego trip, anyway.

### Vertical Playpen

A *new* ropes course element! These don't come along every day, so you better check this one out. I've found over the years as a ropes course builder, that we (builders) get into a routine of what we build. Although ropes course construction is viewed as an innovative undertaking, it's actually like any other construction work — satisfying upon completion, but otherwise physically demanding and fairly repetitive. "You want a Two

Line Bridge?"  Bang, bang, bang...there's your Two Line Bridge — hey, it's a business.

But occasionally, a new element forces itself onto your consciousness; sometimes as a serendipitous mistake, often as the result of on-the-job conversations with other builders, and rarely as a pure gem of inspiration. The Vertical Playpen is the result of some "light bulb" innovation and a generous dollop of sharing, particularly with Bob Ryan, PA builder, and newly designated full-time spouse.

The Vertical Playpen (VPP) resembles the Dangle Duo event, in that a series of obstacles must be overcome to reach the top of the event; however, the VPP offers a series of varied challenges rather than the predictable ladder-like ascent on the Dangle Duo.  As each level (5-7) is reached, the climber must evaluate her/his position, look ahead, and decide on the next plan of ascent — the cognitive and physical approach that so well defines the adventure education ideal.

The following illustration depicts the event.  If you would like to have a VPP built as part of your collection of impossible-things-to-do, contact Project Adventure.  If you are planning on doing the work yourself, and this excellent illustration by Plynn Williams (you *knew* I didn't draw it), doesn't suffice, give me a call and I'll help out on the phone as best I can.  If you call collect, I'm out of the office.

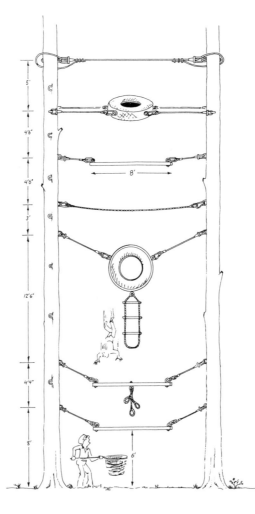

### The TP Shuffle

Can't drive a nail without whacking a digit or two? Get the hives when you look at a blueprint? Develop a headache when you read, "...and then put Tab A into Slot B, when B has been folded under Slot C"? Here's balm for your shattered ego, a genuinely easy to build initiative event called, "The TP Shuffle."

*Materials List*

>       One 20-25' telephone pole

*Tools Needed*

>       None, Zero, Not any

*Building Instructions*

With a class or a few friends, place the chosen telephone pole (TP) horizontally on a flat grassy or ungrassy area. Done! Hoo Ha — was that great? I could build ropes courses all day!

If you are also interested in what to do with that pole lying out there, here's the low-down, and it's even more fun than building it.

Ask a group of about twenty students to halve themselves and with their newly formed group to stand (balance) on opposite ends of the TP so that the two groups are facing one another in single file. Establishing this face-to-face queue is not the problem. The difficulty lies in having the two groups exchange ends of the pole without touching the ground. Time the entire procedure and assign a 15 second time penalty for *every* touch with the turf (man and woman eating alfalfa sprouts). After an attempt, ask the group to talk things over and give it another try; the sprouts are still hungry.

As the individuals exchange ends, they do not have to assume any particular sequence at the beginning or the end of the task, just so that the groups have switched ends from N to S, or E to W, or NE to SW, or SSE to NNW...

If you have just purchased a new set of tools and feel chagrined that you are not going to get a chance to "...let Stanley help you do things right," here're two variations that require some building.

1.  Dig two holes with a posthole digger (PHD) about 18 feet apart and 2 feet deep. Cut two 3 foot sections of pole, place them in the holes and tamp in dirt firmly around them. Do not cut these 3 foot sections from your 20 footer.

    Lift the long pole and rest it horizontally on top of the two short poles; the longer pole then being parallel to and twelve inches off the ground. Drill the top pole at each end with a 5/8" extension auger bit so that the holes extend well into the two vertical short poles. With a sledge hammer, drive 5/8" machine bolts through these holes and into the lower support poles so that the bolt heads are flush with the pole. These bolts might be obtained, with a bit of luck and cajoling, from an electric or telephone company. If you can't scrounge or buy bolts, perhaps a sheet metal strap placed over the top pole and nailed to the vertical poles beneath might do the trick.

2. An even easier method of elevating and situating the pole (if you have access to a chain saw) is the following:

   Cut two 3 foot sections of telephone pole (not off the end of your TP pole, please!). Now, cut a V notch in each 3' piece. Shape each V so that the TP pole will fit solidly. Locate each notched 3' section at each end of the TP pole (about 2' in from the ends), and lift the pole (lots of people) into the notches: so simple.

   The people problem is the same, but the approximately twelve inch elevation of the log allows a bit more maneuverability for the participants and facilitates penalty spotting by the instructor. The elevated pole also proves easier to move on because there is no roll to the pole, but take your pick of techniques and have some fun.

## TP Shuffle Revisited

In a previous BOT's, I detailed the presentation and construction of an initiative problem that has become a standard ropes course offering. How come? (1) The completion objective is b & w; you make it as a team or you don't. (2) It's easy and inexpensive to build. (3) There's lots of unselfconscious touching going on. (4) Progress from the first attempt to the second is easy to measure. (5) People like it.

Here's a variation I though of recently called the *Aussie Switch*. Set three logs or telephone poles on the ground in the following configuration.

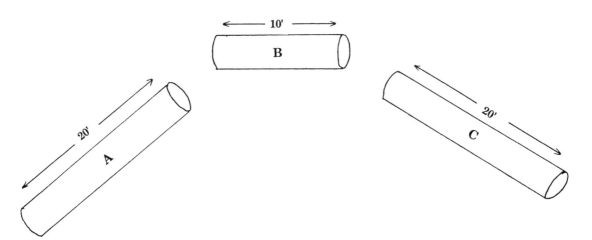

Ask three people to stand on log B and to remain on that log for the duration of the initiative problem.

The object is for Team A on Log A to change places with Team C on Log C without touching the ground. The three people on Log B act as designated helpers (DH) to aid the transfer as it pertains to Log B.

If you are timing the exercise, add a 15 second penalty whenever someone touches the ground.

Remember that groups A, B and C are all part of the same team and are not competing against one another; otherwise this could become a very physical problem.

## Trolley Construction & Use

Trolley 4" x 4"'s can be as short or long as your group needs dictate. A trolley two feet long with only room for two people is useful for a special needs population or for younger students that have trouble cooperating beyond a one-on-one situation. Trolleys up to 16' long have been built for large groups to offer an additional challenge.

Buy the least expensive 4" x 4" stock available. Even rough cut green wood is OK for this event. Don't try fabricating the trolleys from 2" x 4" stock, because the 2" wood depth isn't enough to countersink the knots. If you leave the knots on the surface of the boards, it makes the "walking" attempts frustratingly difficult and not as much fun.

Using a try-square, draw a line across the board every 12", and on this line, find the center of the board. Using a 1-1/2" drill bit, drill each one of these center marks to a depth of 2". A spade bit (speed-bor) does a good job of making these holes (set up a drill powerful enough to handle such a large-headed bit). These holes can also be drilled using a bit brace and an Irwin adjustable bit. I mention this only because I have done a few this way (years ago) and know that it can be accomplished. If your boards measure 12', that means you have 20 holes to drill; a substantial physical commitment for one person. If you have students helping, maybe a bit brace is more functional from an I-helped-build-it standpoint.

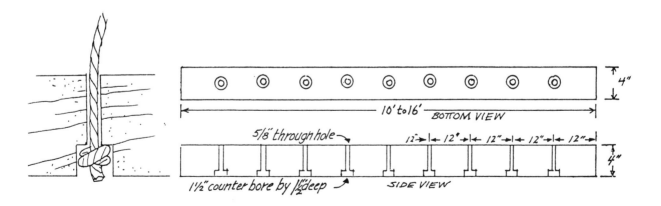

5/8" through hole

10' to 16'

BOTTOM VIEW

12" 12" 12" 12" 12"

1½" counter bore by 1½" deep

SIDE VIEW

4"

4"

Using a 5/8" bit, drill through each large hole on center. (To keep the drill bit from splintering through the far side, watch for the tip of the spade bit to just break the surface and then turn the 4" x 4" over and, using this pin-hole as a guide, drill in the reverse direction.)

Cut 20 five foot long pieces of 1/2" polypropylene or 1/2" multiline rope. Reeve a cut section of rope through each hole. (It may be necessary to tape an end of the rope to make it fit through the 5/8" hole without cowstailing.) Tie an overhand knot in the rope end exiting from the large countersunk hole. Tighten the knot as close to the end of the rope as possible without dissolving the knot. Pull the knot into the countersunk hole with a jerk on the other end of the rope. Any part of the knot which sticks above the plane of the board must be tapped into the hole with a hammer. Using a propane torch, burn each inserted knot sufficiently so that it partially melts in the hole and cannot become untied accidentally.

Either tie another overhand knot in the opposite end of the rope, or if you have the time and patience, perform a back splice in each rope end. This end knot or splice provides the students with a handle.

Using a medium rasp, remove all sharp corners and splinters from the board.

## Implementation

If you want to make the event a bit more difficult, drill the first and last hole only an inch in from the ends of the 4" x 4". This provides rope for two additional people, but 2 less board feet to stand on.

When you ask the group to use these props to move from point A to point B, don't set the 4" x 4"'s on the ground parallel to the destination. Throw them down or cross them so that their position doesn't indicate possible usage.

Tie another overhand knot about 1/3 of the way down each rope. After the group has mastered the 1-2-3 right; 1-2-3 left technique, suggest that they try making forward progress by all holding onto the lower knots. This bent-over "spoon" position makes the group more vulnerable to the domino phenomena.

If you have a hot-shot, I-can-do-anything leader type that needs a bit of humbling, suggest that he/she take the first position on the boards and call signals from there.

A section of undrilled 4" x 4" can be included on the field as an obstacle which must be crossed as part of the problem. The results of this attempted crossing are usually humorous. Don't point out the efficient side step technique of crossing the 4" x 4" until the problem is being debriefed.

A video tape of the whole problem-solving process, particularly with this problem, is a valuable and entertaining teaching tool.

## Trolley Variations

If you need a trolley for 16 people and don't have room in your Chevette to transport two 16' lengths of 4" x 4" boards, and...

If you want the group to move the trolley over an obstacle, but you're afraid that the boards will crack, and...

If you want to add a distinctly bizarre touch to the regular Trolley approach, do this.

Cut the 4" x 4" boards into 6 or 8 foot lengths, then add the holding ropes in regular one foot increments. Place 1/2" SLES's (shoulder lag eye screw) into one end of each board, and clip the two eyes together with a 1/2" rapid link. If you want to make the trolley problem even more of a problem, use boards only 4' long and attach four of the boards together. This approach may cause a disjointed group to become even more so.

As you and your group try to make it from point A to B on top of the rope festooned trolleys, and someone happens to step off the trolley into the poisoned peanut butter, et. al.; rather than assigning a time penalty, simply ask the faller to get back on the trolley backward from his/her starting orientation; i.e., a 180 degree switch. The faller is then vis-a-vis the person who was formerly viewing their backside. This penalty adds to the confusion and makes forward progress even more difficult and giggle-prone.

## Big Business

I *like* this problem! It has all the right ingredients for an engrossing, useful, and enjoyable initiative task. There is one substantial drawback: the necessary building blocks (an integral part of the problem), are either fairly expensive or very expensive. But take a look at the makings of this entrepreneurial delight, before making budget decisions.

Your group (keep the numbers small: 4-5) is charged with construction of a free-standing tower of any shape or size, using only the provided building materials.

The company you own won an invitation to build a small scale tower to prove that your architects and builders can do it for the least cost and the highest profit. Obviously, other invited contractors will be clawing at the same mercenary gains.

There are two stages to this problem. These two stages are structured to allow enough time to complete the problem in a class period (45-50 minutes).

### *Stage One    (20 Minutes)*

Plan your tower (architects) and practice building a prototype or two (builders). You may take the blocks from the container and build as many practice towers as you like (lots of trial and error), but at the end of this stage, all the blocks must be disengaged and placed back in the box.

## Stage Two    (16 Minutes)

From the START, your group must construct a free-standing tower (balanced long enough to be measured by the judge). This building period is timed. After recording the final time, number of blocks, and the height of the tower, the three BIG BUSINESS GRAPHS are used to determine your result: the profit.

## Clarifications  And  Real  Life  $  Hints

Allow 200 LEGO blocks (or a facsimile) per team. Include more small blocks than large ones. Also include a base plate to provide stability. If you don't know what LEGO is, ask any married friend with young children. There are other building implements on the market that are useable for this problem and which don't cost as much as LEGO.

## $ BIG BUSINESS GRAPHS $

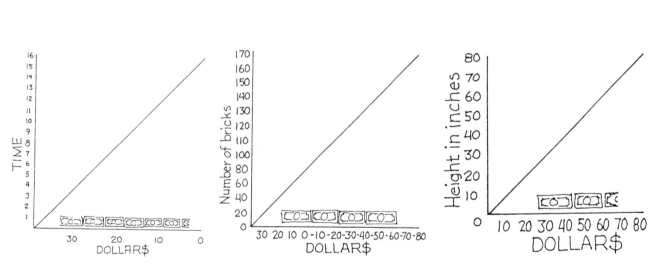

## Zig Zag

Object: To transport a group across a designated area without touching the ground with either the available boards or any part of a participant's body.

*Rules:*

1. For the boards to be used, they must fit into the slotted posts; i.e., they may not be turned flat and placed on top of a post.

2. If a participant's body or a board touches the ground, a time penalty may be assigned or the gropu may be required to start over.

3. 2" 6" should be used as traversing boards.

4. Board BC should be equal to the space DE.

5. Board AB and CD should be less than the distance between DE so that only board BC will fit space DE.

6. Posts are placed so that approximately 14 inches of the post is above ground and 3 feet is in the ground. The top of the posts are notched appropriately for the boads with a chain saw.

7. Distances AB and CD measure 7 feet 6 inches, and distance BC measures 7 feet nine inches.

8. Refer to the illustration below.

START

FINISH

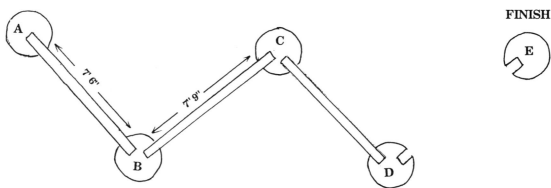

## A-Frame

Here's a six-person problem that requires a unique solution. The idea for this interesting initiative problem was received from Tom Steele of SUNY Cortland, who originally hear of the details from a group of German exchange students.

The object is to move the A-frame apparatus with one person aboard, from point A to point B (30 ft.), using the five available 18' sling ropes. This problem works well on grass or asphalt.

*Rules:*

1. The A-frame must maintain at least one point of contact with the ground at all times and never more than two points of contact.

2. Only one person can made body contact with the A-frame apparatus and he/she must avoid contact with the ground. The remainder of the people must stay at least 10 ft. from the A-frame when it is in use. This 10 ft. minimum is obviously necessary because of the radiation hazard involved in A-frames of this sort.

3. The ropes may not touch the ground at any time during the passage over the restricted area.

*A Solution*

Tie the five sling ropes to the apex of the A-frame using a series of bowlines, clove hitches or whatever knot(s) you feel comfortable with. Stand the frame vertically (2 points of contact at the base) and ask one of the six participants to stand on the horizontal cross bar. As this individual rocks from side to side (each left/right rocking motion is coupled with a thrust forward), the other five participants support the A-frame with the previously attached sling ropes. There is scant chance of the frame and rider falling over if the rope holders remain alert.

The A-frame itself can be built from lashed saplings or more uniformly from sections of 2" x 3" lumber bolted together with three 3/8" x 3-1/2 carriage bolts.

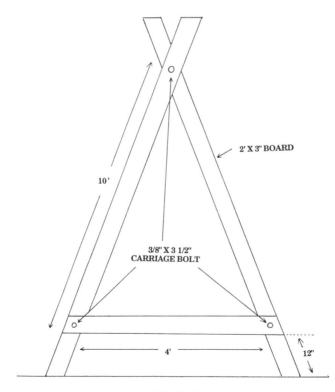

**A - FRAME**

## Chicken Wire Crossing

I have not participated in or introduced the following initiative problem for over twenty years, but it keeps coming back to mind...so, I'm going to tell you about it.

It was a stark and dormy night at the North Carolina Outward Bound School in the fall of 1968, as, amidst darkness and bluster, I contemplated the downed and precariously balanced log that provided the only way across the precipitous canyon that yawned absymally before my trembling size 12's. (Ref. Bulwer-Lytton Contest book, *It Was a Dark and Stormy Night...*)

The OB program had been started at the North Carolina site, I think, in 1966, so that by the time I began instructing there in '68, a ropes course had already been built and various initiative problems (called initiative *tests* at that time) had also been installed at the various woodsy sites. One of the "tests" was the *Chicken Wire Crossing*, located in a deeply cut stream bed near the old zip wire site. After twenty years, I'll bet the event (and even the memory of the event) is long gone locally, so maybe this expository revisitation will rejuvenate what I remember as an engrossing physical and mental group problem.

Take a look at the illustration. The object is to move your entire group across the log (for whatever fanciful reason you want to make up), without touching either the ground or the chicken wire (which is, of course, galvanically sensitive to human touch). Contact with the ground under the log results in a trip back to the start for the offender, but the merest touch of the chicken wire causes a galvanic polarity reversal of the creosoted log's hydrochlorine gas — the whole group (everyone who has safely made it across the log) must return to the start and begin again.

Note that the construction of the chicken wire barrier is such that a person cannot crawl across on top of the log *and* under the barrier. The only prop allowed is a 15 ft. section of 9mm sling rope.

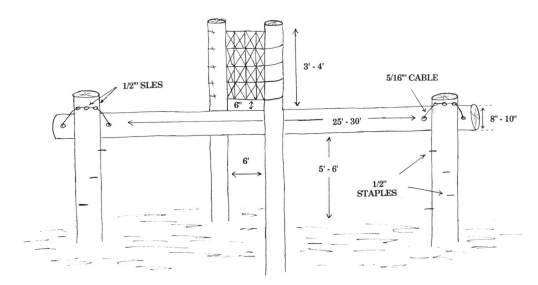

**CHICKEN WIRE TRAVERSE**

*Considerations:*

- Do not suspend the horizontal log more than 6' above the ground for safety reasons; any higher and spotting becomes unreasonable.

- Conceptually, the chicken wire and adjacent support poles extend indefinitely upward; i.e., no one may climb the poles. Wrap chicken wire around the poles as part of the installation process, and no on will even think about climbing the poles, considering the potential for chlorine gas being produced.

- More than one person is allowed on the log at a time, but no more than four. Assign at least one spotter per person on the log.

- After a participant has made it under the chicken wire without touching, they must regain to the top of the pole (log) before getting credit for making a successful passage. It may be useful to paint a white stripe on the underside of the log about five feet from where it is suspended from the vertical support. This stripe would act as a NO TRESPASS sign to the upside-down log rider.

## Swing Aboard, or Prouty's Landing

This activity is a simple and enjoyable combination of the *All Aboard* and the *Nitro Crossing* initiative problems.

Set up a portable 3' x 3' All Aboard-type portable platform a few feet away from your nitroglycerine initiative problem rope. Exactly how far to set the platform can be easily determined with a bit of trial and error swinging. Think: challenging, but not frustrating. Perform the T&E swings before the students show up.

The object is to get an entire group (12-16) onto the platform and maintain a balanced group position for 5 seconds. Since you have already set the platform into toxic PCB (peanut colored butter), any transgressions into this highly corrosive material results in a trip back to the starting point for detoxification (you want to end up sterile?...you do?) and another try. You may want to outline the toxic area with a rope, or just scratch a circle in the dirt.

## Disc Jockeys

The object is to choose one of the two available swing ropes and move the entire group from a designated safe area out and into the situated hoops, discs or tires (refer to the illustration). The first attempt is not timed; succeeding attempts are performed under the clock. The same rope used for the *Nitro Crossing* can also be used for this event.

- Make available wooden discs, hula hoops, or bicycle tires equal to the number of participants.

- These discs, hoops, or tires are arranged in a pyramidal fashion with the pyramid base located 8 feet from the two swing ropes. Discs are somewhat symmetrically set about 14" apart.

- Any two feet on a disc is the limit. If three feet end up on a disc, both participants must return to the start.

- A participant can step to only one more disc or hoop beyond the one they initially land in, IF only one foot makes contact with the first disc or hoop. As soon as both feet are located on a disc, that is where you stay.

- If you can't swing or step to a disc, a participant must be physically passed to a disc further on in the pyramid. A passed player must accept the first disc they touch; i.e., no steps after being put down.

This initiative problem has all the right elements for classic status, except for the large number of props necessary, but in a ropes course setting, that should pose no problem.

Go out of your way to try this one — it's better than most. And don't forget to try twice so that the students get to appreciate how efficient they have become.

## Gymnasium Jungle Cruise or a Rolling Raft Adventure

This dynamic initiative problem has all the right ingredients for fun and challenge. The only limiting factor that I can anticipate is the need for Rabid Nuggets (used tennis balls); you're going to need lots of them.

The challenge is to move your entire group from one side of the gym to the other side, using only the following props:

1. A 4' x 8' section of 3/4" plywood.
2. 100 to 500 Rabid Nuggets (depending on the dimensions of the gym floor being used).
3. 4 broom handles with a rubber cane tip affixed to the end of each.

As always, the gym floor is covered with a horrendously corrosive substance that can't be touched without dire consequences; i.e., starting over. The available props are resistant to all noxious substances.

Has your imagination conjured up a solution yet? Rowing/paddling over, on top of all those nuggets sounds like it could be interesting. To be honest, I have not tried this problem yet, but I did pass along the idea to John Hichwa, at the John Read Middle School in West Redding, CT.

John gave it a try and here are the results taken directly from the newspaper article forwarded to me. There's no moss growing on you, John.

"The teacher randomly divided the class in half, gave each group a plywood sheet, 125 tennis balls and four dowels. Instructions were limited — get to the other side by propulsion of only the people on the raft. He also told them not to race. The only thing we want you to do is see if the groups can be successful."

"There are many ways to propel a rolling raft, and not all the plans were good ones. A member of a successful team described their strategy at the debriefing held after the first crossing."

And the article continues in great detail about how the groups made or didn't make their trips across, but I'm not going to include any answers and spoil the discovery for you and your "teams." Make sure you bevel the corners of the plywood section and sand all edges. As soon as my source of Rabid Nuggets fills the ole nugget bin to overflowing, I'll try out my rubber-tipped J-stroke.

## Poker Chip Initiative Relay

The program objective of these sequential initiative problems and incentive chip awards is to provide a continuing interest in low ropes course elements beyond the initial group participation that involves the here-it-is-give-it-a-try level.

As you attempt to follow the time setting and point subtraction system, remember that time parity between two systems will depend on the group's ability to function as a team in contrast to individual adeptness. Vary the elements and times as fits your situation and group size.

The immediate objective is, after establishing a total time (three or four initiative problems in sequence), to bring the time back to zero or into the minus category. The group is essentially competing against themselves. The less time it takes to complete the initiative problems, then the less time needs to be subtracted from the total. The total time, for consecutive completion of all three elements, is the time block from which the remainder of events will be subtracted. The emphasis is on both team efficiency (initiative problem participation) and personal ability (individual attempts at challenging events).

Different colored poker chips are awarded for seconds achieved by individual effort. White - 5 seconds  Red - 10 seconds  Blue - 15 seconds

As these chips are pooled at the end of the relay, a final time is established.

### Time Setting Events

•*Nitro Crossing or Electric Fence*

•*Wall*

•*Beam*

These three elements are to be attempted in sequence with no timeout allowed between events.

•*Time Chip Events*

•*Tension Traverse* - 2 seconds for each 12" that the participant passes beyond the 15 ft. mark (round off to nearest five digit) and a 15 second bonus for making the entire cable.

•*Fidget Ladder* - 15 seconds for each run made with the feet (both) beyond the starting rung. Hand and foot contact only. There is a 60 second bonus for touching the tree with the forehead.

•*Track Walk* (including end swing) - 60 seconds for completion without falling. 45 seconds - one fall, 30 seconds - 2 falls, 15 seconds - 3 falls.

A typical Initiative Relay attempt by a group of 12 participants might look like this:

> The Nitro Crossing takes the group 8 minutes. The wall - 5:30.
> The Beam - 6:30. Total time for the three consecutive events -
> 20 minutes. This is the time base to subtract subsequent
> "Poker Chip" events from.

Average group times for the "chip" events are:

| | |
|---|---|
| Tension Traverse | 5:15 |
| Fidget Ladder | 5:45 |
| Track Walk | <u>4:30</u> |
| | 15:30 |

Subtract 15:30 from the initial 20:00 established time to get a final time, which acts as a goal for future attempts.

## Bridge It

I'm sure you have been to conferences or clinics where they "teach" communication procedures, team-building, pyramidal management, organizational and developmental skills — need I impress you (bore you) any further? What it comes down to is, are you learning anything about the jargon-loaded skills mentioned above, or are you being burdened with a series of valid but often inappropriate techniques for whatever "people" skills are being touted?

I was recently introduced to a "people" skills teaching game that sparked total enthusiasm, resulted in an engrossing task and was (hallelujah) fun.

Split your group (15-20) in half. The method employed for this halving is worth repeating, also. Rip two full page pictures out of a magazine and cut them up into jigsaw-like pieces to equal the number of people in the group (so that the pieces from both pictures equal the total number of people). Toss all the pieces willy-nilly into a container and ask each participant to draw out one piece. After all the pieces have been drawn, ask the players to pool their pieces to make a picture — two defined pictures, two random groups. Try to choose either appropriate or humorous pictures — cigarette or Kotex ads are probably not appropriate. You get the picture.

You will need the following props x 2; i.e., one set for each group.

    4 - styrofoam cups

    8 - 8" small diameter sticks (to be gathered previously by the

        participants

    1 - roll of masking tape

    1 - small box of LEGO or Tinker Toys or the like

    1 - paper & pencil (or pen)

    1 - set of terminology

You will also need the following items to be used by both groups.

2 - card tables

1 - sheet or blanket

1 - chair for each person

2 - rooms

*Set-Up Procedure:*

Place the card tables next to one another. Hang the sheet or blanket vertically over the separation point of the tables. (How you suspend the sheet is your pre-initiative problem). Divide the chairs equally on each side of the sheet.

Place all the props for each group on separate tables.

The terminology mix-up could read like this: Side A - The word *top* means *bottom*; *side* means *under*; and a laugh means *high*.

Side B - The word *tape* means *wide*; sticking out your tongue means *how many*; and criss cross means *parallel*.

Add or subtract words to increase or decrease the confusion.

*Procedure*

Explain to both groups that the tangible purpose of this exercise is for each separate group to build a bridge toward the other group (sheet) so that the bridges meet and look as much alike as possible. Do not offer any guidelines except to say that only the offered props may be used. Try fabricating a story about two countries that are separated by a body of water, but want to establish a trade and cultural relationship. The river is plagued by bad weather and almost constant fog. The countries have a common language, but the dialects differ considerably.

In order to establish a necessary dialogue between groups, three five minute meetings have been arranged (be very strict on the timing) at a common meeting site (another room). As the members adjourn to the meeting room, remind them that they must not look on the other side of the sheet; offer blindfolds if necessary.

Only one member from each group may talk at each meeting, and the pair must sit facing one another, separate from the other people in the room. No comments from the group are allowed during this time (only laughter!).

The timing of the planning and building sessions should look like this:

Separate groups are shown their building area and props and are given seven minutes to talk over the problems of building the bridge (amongst themselves, *not* with the other group), and to begin construction if they choose to.

*1st*   5 minute meeting of the chosen group representatives in a separate room.  A new representative should be chosen each time.

7 minute discussion and building time back at the site

*2nd*   5 minute representative meeting

5 minute discussion and building time

*3rd*   (final)  5 minute representative meeting

10 minute race to get the work accomplished.  Be strict as to the deadline.

Then comes the unveiling (and groans or dismay or shouts of glee), and a period of time set aside for debriefing the process, levels of accomplishment, and comparison of approach.

The physical result is apt to surprise you as to the architectural accuracy achieved.

The problem and process is engrossing, revealing, and fun.

## The Chasm

The Chasm is a fairly sophisticated group initiative problem that provides a series of thinking and physical challenges toward successfully achieving a solution — besting the ubiquitous poison peanut butter.

The group begins in front of a suspended log (c) and must transport each member past the end line (i) without touching the ground en route.  A ground touch necessitates that contaminated individual returning to the start.  That's where the cleaning solution is, of course.

Three 12' sling ropes (9mm kernmantle or the like) are included as props to be used wherever necessary to facilitate the passage, or more realistically, to make the passage possible.  If you find the distance from the swing rope to the end line to be unreasonable, it may be the result of a longer or shorter swing pendulum arc.  Adjust as seems necessary to maintain the challenge, but precludes frustration.

*Chasm Key*

   a. Support trees or telephone poles.  These may have to be guyed.
   b. Saplings of about 2" in diameter that are lashed together by the participants.
   c. A 6" beam (bark removed) supported about 3' off the ground either by lashing or cable supports.
   d. A square lashing (with nylon rope) or cable support.

e. 5/8" diameter multiline rope passed around and secured approximately 5' off the ground to two support trees or poles. A transport knot or truckies' hitch arrangement will tighten the rope nicely. PVC pegs or staples keep the rope from sliding down the supports.

f. 3/8" diameter cable strung between two supports, to act as rope swing anchor point. If telephone poles are used, guy wires will be necessary.

g. 5/8" diameter multiline rope used as a swing rope. The thimble spliced end of the rope is attached to the wire by means of a 1/2" rapid link. The top of the swing rope should be at least 20' off the ground.

h. 3/8" cable clamps

i. A length of any diameter utility rope staked to the ground to act as a finish line.

j. 3/8" cable clamps attached to the wire cable to prevent the swing rope from sliding side-to-side.

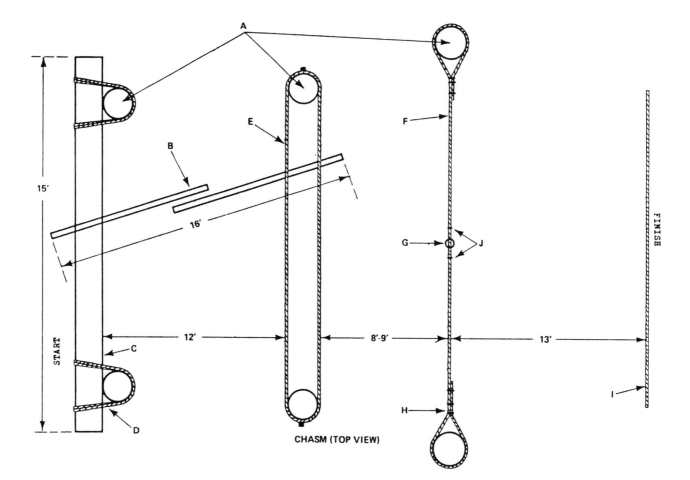

CHASM (TOP VIEW)

## Paul's Balls - Stack 'em Up

In a previous BOT's, I detailed two activities using old tennis balls: *Frantic* and *Balls Galore*. Here are two more tennis ball games to further justify retiring more of those dead fuzzies that aren't responding to your devastating top spin shot.

But first, a preliminary bit of excitement using paper cores. (Hold onto those balls over there, or I'll have to collect them!) Paper cores are the discarded center sections of industrial rolls of paper. These substantial cardboard cylinders measure about 3 feet long and have a diameter of approximately 16". The best part about them is that they are free — usually. Try to find an industrial paper producer in a city near you and ask for the core discards; they are usually glad to get rid of them. Take a station wagon or pick-up truck and load up, as there are all kinds of adventure uses for these multi-purpose cylinders. The reason I've written all this core material information (while you're standing there fiddling with your tennis balls), is that the cores are integral parts of the following activities.

1. *Stack 'em Up* - On a flat uniform surface, see how many cores can be stacked on top of one another to form a column; no props allowed, just people. The record number of cores is more than you would initially believe.

   *Caution:* If the column begins to fall (watch the top) during the stacking process, let it go! Trying to catch the tumbling cores is unnecessary and dangerous. I'd suggest not allowing a stack more than 8 cores high.

   You will need your completed column for *Paul's Balls*, but if you feel like knocking the stack down (How can you resist?), give each person a tennis ball or two and see if they can knock off one core at a time by throwing the balls. You can also try a group blow. Ask everyone to blow on the stack in unison. It won't work, but it looks funny seeing thirty people trying to blow over a huge paper column.

2. *Paul's Balls* - This active, minimum skill activity was named after its originator, Paul Somebody-or-Other. If his name had been Fred, we would have had to think up another name — Fred's Balls isn't very catchy.

   Each person has one tennis ball. The object is to see how long it takes the group to put all the balls into the core column by lofting them up and in. The column should obviously be as tall as the group can make it, giving credence to the "in" game name of *Ultimate Paul's Balls*.

   It's interesting to witness and hard to explain how engrossing this simple group task can be. After timing an attempt, ask the group to see if they can better their time by developing strategies, being more efficient, etc. How do you get the balls out? I'm sure you and your students will find a way.

If you have your hula hoops available, an alternate game is to see how long it takes the group to toss all the hoops up and over the column. If one of the girls in your class happens to be named Hilda, you might come up with a game name that fits the situation...or Harriet or Helga.

### Evolution of the Spider Web

"We replaced our soccer nets this fall and, as I hate to throw anything away, I was contemplating uses for what was left hanging on the goal frame, when one of my fifth graders carefully climbed through a tear in the net.

"Well, you don't have to drop a carabiner on me to see what the next logical step should be...a pair of scissors...and a few more holes. As each new class came to play soccer and saw what I was doing to the soccer nets (principal included), the natural challenge of 'can you?' or 'who can?' and 'which team can get all?' — and you know where it goes from there.

"By the end of the day, word was out and my last class brought out a large cardboard spider which we hung on the edge of our once-upon-a-time soccer goal — and in their best soccer attire, we finished the day doing spider web.

"As I was taking my new spider web off the goal frame, I carefully cut away excess net (side angles), leaving a large flat surface with a neat, heavy-duty seam along the top. I use 1/2" multiline which is zig-zagged in and out of the net and secured by wound, waxed nylon cord. There is an eye splice at each end of the multiline, and Bungee cord to the eye splice to two trees (outside), volleyball standards (inside). More Bungee cord for bottom corners.

"Using an old soccer net can give you an easy to set up, portable web. You can cut the net in the same pattern as if you were using nylon line and get a better visual effect for your web. It's a great way to recycle some old gear."

— Walter Moore, Ann Antolini School, New Hartford, Connecticut

### The Dessert Desert

Nicki Hall forwarded this **different** initiative problem, saying that she particularly liked not having to take her group, "from A to B over some noxious substance" in order to achieve a goal. The goal in this case is materially gastronomic and subjectively cooperative.

Here's the whole problem as received.

### Food Adventure Group Problem

"You and your classmates are on a school-sponsored hiking, canoeing and camping trip in New Hampshire's White Mountains. This afternoon, after having taken a particularly long and arduous trek on Mt. Washington, you returned to base camp to relax and to feast on an eagerly-awaited dinner. Much to your dismay and horror, bandit raccoons had raided your pantry supplies during your absence and had scattered food, utensils, and cooking information everywhere. Your leader, in an attempt to create some order, has assembled a bagful of supplies and another of cooking implements and has given them to your group. Your job is to make dessert for the class from these available materials. You realize that her request is a serious one, as a welcome treat at this moment could really help to boost the spirits of your demoralized friends.

*The Task*

1. Using only the given ingredients and utensils, you are to *create* and *prepare* for baking a good dessert. (Note: As no cookbook is available, you must decide what supplies should be used and what amounts would be appropriate. Utilize past experience and the knowledge of the whole group as a guide.)

2. You must keep a record of all procedures. We want to recreate a cookbook. Appoint one member to do the record-keeping.

3. You will have *exactly* one-half hour to finish this task. Complete clean-up of the work space must be included in the allotted time. Baking time is extra, but please indicate the oven temperature and cooking time for instructors who will finish your product.

4. A video tape will be made of your group's processing of this problem."

## Object Retrieval or Chuck-A-Hunk

This splendid initiative problem involves all the good stuff — thinking, imagination, action, fantasy, risk and an attractive solution.

The object is for a group to retrieve a fairly heavy (10 lbs.) object that is located near the center of an outlined diameter of approximately 30'.

You will need the following props and geographical set-up:

1 - 2' section of 2"-2-1/2" diameter hardwood log

1 - length of retired belay rope that is longer than 50'

1 - length of 9mm sling rope or 1" webbing that measures 18-26' long

1 - locking carabiner

1 - ammo can or bucket with bail

1 - substantial hardwood tree to locate near the center of your 30' diameter outlined area. This tree must stand alone within this circle and display a trunk/limb bifurcation (crotch) at a height of 12'-15'.

*Rules:*

- Only the props listed above can be used to retrieve the object.
- If *anyone* touches the ground inside the circle, the person *closest to the object* must start again from outside the circle.
- Set a time limit: 20-30 minutes is reasonable.

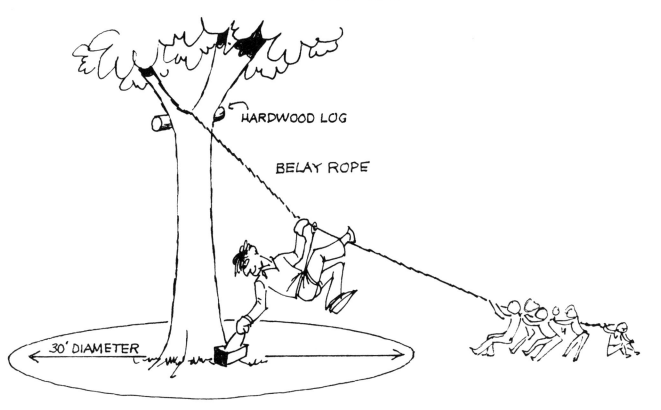

**The Meuse**

If you own a copy of the old *Cows' Tails and Cobras* book (early issue, black cover), look under "Board Stretcher" (pg. 75) for a primitive presentation of this event. Paul Radcliffe has revived this old initiative problem by writing up a nifty full-o-fantasy introduction and physically extending the problem by adding more "islands." Here's Paul's write-up — you can blame the illustrations on me.

*Goal:*

"In search of rare pink porpoise eggs, your expedition team must safely cross the bogs of Lost Swamp. Surprisinly, you have discovered that the boggish water of the swamp is still inhabited by saber-toothed beavers, sneaker-snapping turtles, and the leather-liking Great White Bog-Water Shark. Careful study by your team seems to indicate that their continued existence is directly dependent upon eating whatever "fast-food" is available in the swamp, with amazing regularity. Your precise calculations suggest that you have only _____ minutes to safely cross the swamp before the feeding frenzy will begin again. Time allowed is a function of group size and perceived prowess. Twenty minutes for a group of 10 is about average."

*Rules:*

1. Your team must start from the same departure point only using 4 boards and rope available.
2. Passage can only be made by staying on high ground and avoiding all contact with the swamp's water; high phosporic acid content.
3. Should team members or props come in any contact with the water, you must return to the departure point and start over.
4. Subtract one board to make the eventual solution more difficult.

*Prop Tips*

- Use 4" x 4" x 8" boards for the planks. 2" x 4" x 8" boards nailed together will also serve this function.
- Use cinder blocks for the "islands."
- Allow use of a 12'± section of 9mm rope.

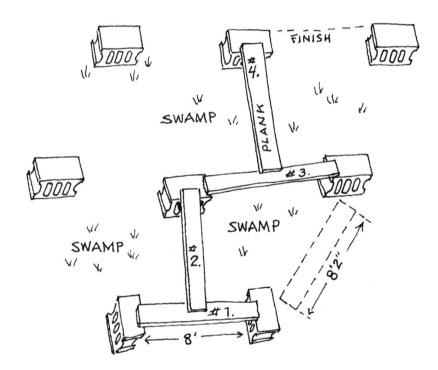

Remember, placement of the cinder blocks is key to making this initiative problem work. Spend some time before the students show up, making sure that the "islands" are in a functional position.

## Chapter 10
# Ropes  Course  Implementation

### Zip Wire Endings — How to Stop a Zipper

*Enthusiastic Instructor*  — "Just look at the initial drop on that cable. What a ride!"

*Concerned Administrator*  — "How do they (*they* means anybody but her/him) slow down?"  "How do they stop?"

And that's as it should be — concerned enthusiasm.  As there is a beginning, there will be an ending and hopefully a gradual one, in this case.

Here's another zip wire innovation to ease the concerns of riders and worriers, called the Bunji Brake.

There are basically two types of zip braking systems, the gravity and trust brakes.  The gravity brake uses the force of gravity to slow and stop the rider — accelerates down and decelerates up.

The 2-3 auto tires located at the end of the ride act as buffers in case you engineered the ride too swiftly: a safety fudge factor.  These tires are reeved onto the cable before the cable is attached.  Use a 5/8" diameter drill bit to drill the tires — through the tread, with holes drilled 180° from each other.

The trust brake necessitates some kind of apparatus to slow the rider down; something that the rider must "trust" to keep her/him from hitting the lower support tree or pole.  The trust brake is usually longer and incrementally swifter than the gravity brake ride, with the bottom attachment point of the cable, in this case, being considerably lower than the starting point.

A somewhat primitive and eventually expensive braking device was initially tried by clipping a carabiner onto the cable with a 75' section of slash (retired) climbing rope attached to the carabiner.  The descending pulley (rider attached) would hit the carabiner and a belayer holding the rope would try to provide a dynamic belay and gradually slow the rider to a stop.

*Problems*

1. The carabiner had to be changed frequently because of excessive and rapid wear on the carabiner.

2. Unless the belayer was experienced s/he could be pulled off their feet as the result of providing too static a belay.

3. The pulley became a cosmetic mess due to the metal-on-metal contact with the carabiner.

We needed a detachable "soft" device to take the place of the carabiners and a solid belay mechanism to take the place of the "soft" belayer. Project Adventure now uses (and sells) a rubber-ended block of mahogany that bolts onto a zip cable to take the place of a carabiner. This block, which measures 4" x 4" x 10", has an integral through eyebolt for shock cord (bunji cord) attachment.

The human belay factor has been replaced with a length of bunji cord. The zip-stop scenario goes like this. The rider takes off from a platform and after gradually picking up speed to maximum (the trust brake ride is not as initially fast as the gravity brake zip), the pulley strikes the zip wood block approximately 3/4 of the way down the cable length. The block is pushed by the pulley (negligible resistance) until the attached length of 1/2" bunji cord (length varies as to the speed of the ride; i.e., maximum speed), gradually brings the rider to a compassionate stop. Some trial and error is necessary on each new ride to determine the best place for the bunji holder(s) to stand, and how long a length of bunji cord is necessary.

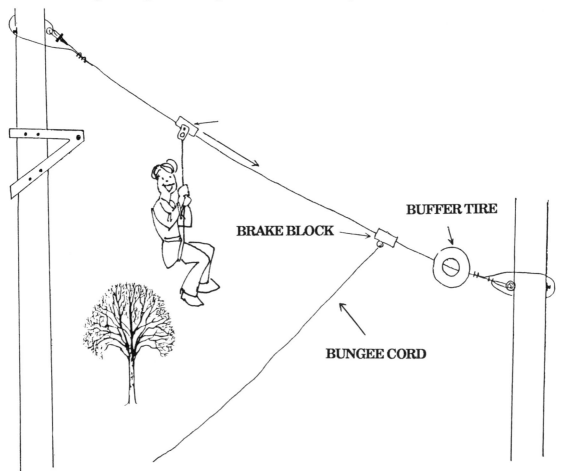

BUFFER TIRE

BRAKE BLOCK

BUNGEE CORD

If you have read this section just to be polite, thank you and continue on to the next engrossing tidbit. If you are interested in installing a bunji brake system, and my explanation hasn't been explicit enough, give me a call at (508) 468-7981, and I'll try to verbally fill in the gaps. The information is free, but the call is your nickel.

### Sizzle Seat

Getting tired of fried buns as the result of extended belay stints? Here are a couple ways to combat the heat without using mechanical shearing devices.

Put on a pair of oversized *cotton* cut-offs (levis, etc.) over your regular attire. This double padding takes the sting out of belaying, but can be uncomfortably warm on a hot day.

Do not wear nylon shorts or pants for belaying. The synthetic fiber of the material transfers the friction produced heat of rapid rope movement. A long dynamic belay can literally melt your pants, and put permanent stripes on your buns.

Sylvia Shirley of William and Mary College in Virginia sent me the plans for a belay apron some time ago. The canvas aprons work quite well and fit loosely enough to provide good air circulation. You can embellish an apron in many ways, but basically the canvas simply puts another layer between your sensitive seat and the rapidly running rope.

Be advised that just because you are using a belay apron you still need leather-palmed gloves to prevent rope-burned hands.

Note that the nylon webbing on the belay seat can be secured by either using velcro or buckles. I personally like the buckle around the waist and velcro on the leg closures. Use a substantial weight canvas for the seat.

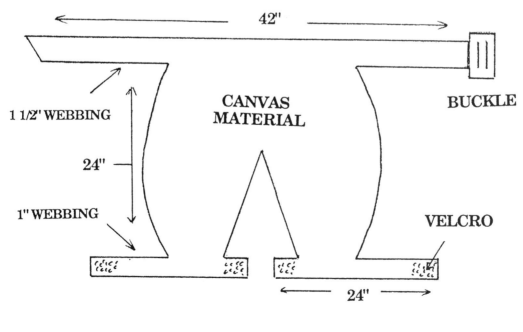

## SIZZLE SEAT

## High Belay Set-Up Solution

This "solution" has been used for years as a workable and sometimes frustrating way to set up belay ropes at the beginning of a school day, without having to lead climb (lobster claw or carabiner clip-in techniques) or climb without a belay.

The technique involves stringing a length of nylon cord (or whatever cord you have) from the ground up and through paired rapid links that have been previously placed on the cable and back to the ground; a vertical trolley clothesline, if you tilt your head and imagination. The object is to attach your belay rope to this cord and pull it up and through the two rapid links or spin/static pulley, and then back down. The frustration mentioned above results from the rope getting stuck as an attempt is made to pull the cord/string through the belay device, causing a no-go situation or breaking the cord (depending on the frustration level), or dissolving of the knot (usually a clove hitch) tied onto the end of the rope.

Here's an embellishment that reduces the above problems and even lets you pull the rope through an SR block *or* an SS pulley with 99% success.

Purchase a few 3/4" eye screws. Hold an eye screw with a pair of pliers so that the eye portion is held firm by the jaws. Heat the screw length with a propane torch until it glows and then push the entire threaded shaft (right up to and including the bottom of the eye) directly on center into the end of a belay rope. The hot screw will literally melt its way into the nylon end of the rope (amidst smoke and acrid smell), resulting in a heat-sealed bond when cooled.

The eye size of the screw head is less than the diameter of the rope so that tying a cord to the eye will allow a direct pull through a comparatively small orifice (SS pulley cheeks). Such a direct pull cannot be achieved by tying the cord around the end of the rope using a clove hitch, timber hitch, etc.

Don't bother tying a bowline — simply reeve the end of the #4 nylon cord through the eye and tie an overhand knot in the end of the cord.

### Considerations

If you are going to leave a rapid link on the cable for a period of time, you must liberally grease the threads of the link, or they will rust in a permanently sealed position.

If you leave an SR block out in the elements, the steel portions will rust unless painted. The rust will not reduce the strength of the block, but it's unsightly and might result in a diminished trust situation.

Shear reduction devices are expensive to replace if stolen.

Use unattractive cord (to mitigate rip-off temptations) and tie it to a placed cleat or staple at least 10' up on the trunk of the support tree to reduce the chance of theft or curious tampering.

## Belays

There are lots of reasons to tie on a belay of some sort while building high elements in trees. A couple of reasons deal with responsibility to self and family, and it's obviously going to slow down the day's work if you slam into the turf from 30-40'. But the real reason for a belay is to preclude PAIN. Never a truer phrase was offered than by the battered sage who uttered (gasped, moaned, etc.), "The fall wasn't bad, but the ending...!"

Avoid the inevitable, and use some type of belay set-up to protect yourself at height. And for you folks interested in the quality and length of life — a belay produces dramatically better results than massive doses of vitamin C.

It's fairly obvious that a bottom belay set-up provides constant protection, but it necessitates involving a belayer who could be doing other work. So, consider the following static and dynamic self-belay techniques. The static tie-in is deceptively simple, and effective. The moving (prusik) belay is a time-honored tree workers' belay system.

### Static Tie-In

I just realized that this technique has no name and there's not much to recommend *Static Tie-In* as being worthy of remembering. How about *Rollo's Wrap*? Rollo was (probably still is) an inept climber I knew a few years back. It seems an appropriate name, considering Rollo's propensity for *falling* — an exclamation I heard with some frequency whenever he got more than few feet off the ground.

There you are, 30 feet up amidst the branches of a _____ (fill in your favorite) tree, and ready to do some work, but you don't want to take up any more of your belayer's time, so you situate yourself solidly amidst the limbs and ask for some slack. Take a large bight in your belay rope and pass the formed bight over and around the *base* of a convenient and substantial limb. The base of this branch should be slightly above you. After the bight comes around the limb, clip a *locking* carabiner through the bight and then also include the standing part (rope leading to belayer) and working end (rope leading to you) in the carabiner. Lock the gate and pull the bight snugly to the limb. Yell "Off Belay" to your belayer and relax, because you have established a self-belay. Rollo's Wrap is secure and can be easily adjusted if you need more rope for working. Don't give yourself more rope than absolutely necessary; even a short fall on a static rope can be _____ (fill in your favorite pejorative phrase from "Accidents in North American Mountaineering").

### Dynamic Prusik Self-Belay

Tie a length of 5/8" diameter multiline around your waist or clip a formed loop (figure 8, bowline-on-a-bight) in the multiline to harness or Swiss seat. As the result of the bowline tie-in or loop clip-in, there should be a tail (working end) left over of about 6'. The standing part of the rope that stretches away from you should measure at least two times the height that you plan to climb. If you are going to clear a tree trunk of limbs to 50', you will need 100+ feet of rope.

Ascend the tree to the height that's needed and climb over or through a substantial living limb or crotch that will serve as a belay point, and descend a few feet. Take the 6' tail mentioned earlier and tie a prusik knot with the tail's free end around the descending standing length of rope. There should be no more distance between you and the prusik knot than 1/2 the length of your arm.

This self-belay prusik system allows you to work with both hands free at whatever height you choose by simply moving the prusik knot up or down the vertical standing length.

You can use rope other than the multiline mentioned above, but be certain of its safe working load and its ability to hold a prusik knot tied onto itself.

Practice this technique near the ground and with a bottom belay until you have confidence in the system and yourself.

## Belay Techniques — The Munter Hitch

Over the years, Project Adventure workshop leaders have been emphasizing and teaching the body belay (standing hip belay) as the best way to develop a one-on-one trust situation between belayer and climber. I still personally believe this to be true, but there are so many useful and effective ways to belay that we are now demonstrating a number of proven belay methods and letting the workshop participants choose which technique will work best for them in *their* work situation. Here's one that functions well, but is not well known in this country.

I feel justified in suggesting that you give this method a try, as outlined in the following description written by Andreas Kubin. I was surprised to hear that a special threaded carabiner was necessary for maximum safety, so be aware, but use any ole "crab" just to see how it works. It's interesting to see the hitch reverse itself when the pull is alternated from working end to standing part. Go get a rope right now and try it. You *know* you'll forget it if you put this down.

Please don't send me irate letters about the use of pitons in the diagrams. I am just as appalled and shocked as you are about the blatant representation of such a destructive device. This is exactly the way I received the drawings. I can only hope that you understand why I used the illustrations as is. (I can't draw worth a stitch.) Make sure you keep this copy of BOT's away from your kids (second drawer, under the socks, works pretty well).

"There is a belay method that has gained almost universal acceptance in the last ten years among the climbers of Europe. It is called the half-mast release (Munter hitch) and was introduced by Werner Munter of Switzerland. The technique gained prominence through publications of the German Alpine Club's Safety committee after an impressive demonstration by Italian Climbers during a U.I.A.A. teaching convention.

Of sole importance to the half-mast system is a particularly complicated locking carabiner with a wide opening and a screw gate, because in performing the Munter, the rope can be laid over the spring-loaded catch and conceivably be pushed open under stress! Since most screw carabiners close against the catch, it repeatedly occurs that through the letting out or taking in of the rope, the screw gate opens. The new Chouinard reverse locking carabiner whose screw closes on the joint of the catch, removes this source of danger.

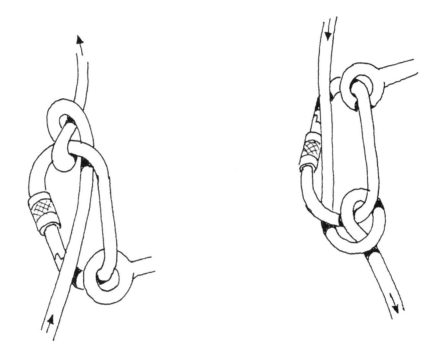

The enthusiasm Americans have for the bare-handed hip belay lies in the fact that most have never caught a sudden leader fall of any length. Like a mediocre insurance policy, it's great until you need it. More than 90% of all European climbers protect themselves with the half-mast release, a belay method which because of its simple application and small source for error, has gained wide acceptance over all other methods — why not by the Americans?"

Because we like gear — that's how come.

### What Rope Is This?

Having trouble identifying or differentiating between various ropes course swing ropes? I've tried tags, color coding, and tape sequencing — all with limited success. The other day, while doing some ropes course work at Duxbury High School (Duxbury, Massachusetts), I noticed that their multiline swing ropes were identified by pieces of affixed adhesive tape.

Each length of tape had the name of the event spelled out with an indelible felt-tipped pen. What a simple, functional idea. Yeah, Duxbury!!

## Superfluously Redundant Award

The winner of this bi-decade award will remain anonymous due to the predictable deluge of laudatory cards and letters that result from this much-awaited announcement.

The nice-going, slap-on-the-back and camaraderie-filled hug this time goes to the originator of the *Sticht Plate Gang Belay*. Believe it or not, folks, here's how it works.

*Person one* handles the rope coming from the climber; largely a two-handed "Old Man of the Sea" hauling technique.

*Person two* provides the well-known "speedshift" (2nd-gear-to-3rd) motion that exemplifies the braking action of the Sticht plate.

*Person three* ties a simple overhand loop for every 3' of rope that comes through the Sticht plate. The knot closest to the plate provides the failsafe element of this gang belay, because it is said in *the book of rocks and ropes* that a "camel can't pass through the eye of a needle."

*Person four* unties the knots as they come from person three, making sure to always leave one knot in the rope.

*Person five* neatly coils the unknotted rope.

This technique, although presented tongue-in-cheek, is workable and has been used successfully by instructors interested in maximum student participation and a failsafe belay system.

Nice going, anonymous belayer, wherever you aren't.

## A Peter Pan Belay

As the student clips a locking carabiner into his/her Studebaker wrap as preliminary to a climb, the question is, should the rope remain in front of the body or be switched around to the back?

Some feel that if the rope remains in front that the novice climber has more of a tendency to reach for the rope in a tight spot than relying on his/her climbing ability. Also, while climbing a tree on a ropes course, there is more chance for the rope to get tangled or hooked onto a peg or limb if the rope remains in front. However, if a fall occurs, the faller's position (flight attitude) becomes almost horizontal to the ground (Peter Pan style), lining up the individual's head as a potential battering ram. Fortunately, there are few obstacles underneath high ropes course elements to ram into; except the ground.

If the climber is attempting to climb up a wooden blocked wall, the presence of the wall itself indicates that the rope should be left in front. A wall is a fairly large target to miss as the result of a fall, particularly if your belay rope is attached to an eyebolt in that wall. The climber's proximity to such a large mass of uniformly hard material is also a good reason for having the students wear helmets.

But, standing on a high wire with the rope behind the individual lends itself to increased commitment. (You know the rope is there, but you can't see it or touch it. Surely you have seen students reaching behind for the rope for no other reason than to check and see if it's still there.) And, the occasional belayed face-first trip to the ground is an unavoidable visual experience, unless it's an eyes-closed descent.

It's not strictly a case of one way is bad and the other good, but rather where and how the belay is being used, that makes the difference.

### A Belay Problem

The Balance Beam, more commonly called the "Cat Walk" in ropes course parlance, is a high log walk element and is the subject of the following belay poser.

If a student falls off the left side of the log and the rope to the belayer is on the right side, is it necessary to climb up the tree and pass the climber's end of the rope back to the right side of the log before the next climber ties in? No fair reading on until you at least try to think of an answer.

If you are using a bowline-on-a-bight/carabiner in the rope end and clipping into a Swiss seat, tie a bowline-on-a-bight in both ends of the belay rope and use whichever end facilitates the belay.

I apologize if this explanation seems superfluous to you experts, but the problem is real and often an embarrassing one. I also apologize to you folks who have no idea what I'm writing about.


## *Down Under*

I had the opportunity in March of this year to lead a workshop in Australia. The weather was fabulous (although any place is better than New England in March), the participants enthusiastic and friendly, and the hospitality superb.

I never used to take the expressed affliction "jet lag" seriously, having only travelled to the west coast and back a few times. After having experienced, en route to Brisbane, a "coach" seat for 28 hours, losing an entire day from my life (international dateline) and having been fed an interminable number of plastic meals, I became acutely aware of something that kept tugging at my eyelids and causing my head to seek the horizontal. The "lag" was worth it — Australia isn't a place, it's an experience. Ripper Mate!

During the workshop, I learned a new (new to me) method of belaying on a ropes course that is worth passing along.

## Australian Back-Up Belay

A problem situation concerned with belaying that has plagued adventure teachers struggling with 30 or 40-to-one student-to-teacher ratios, is how to handle the need for more trained and responsible belayers on high elements. One solution is to use more static belays. Another means is to utilize student belayers, a somewhat risky but often workable solution.

The following belay technique provides another answer that is surprisingly reliable and disarmingly simple, in fact so much so that if I hadn't tried it myself (as faller and belayer), I would have summarily dismissed the idea as laughable, and potentially dangerous.

Acting as the belayer, tie on a Swiss seat arrangement, Studebaker wrap, or put on a commercial harness. Using a figure 8 loop or bowline-on-a-bight in the end of the belayer's end of a rope (imagine a bottom belay situation on a Burma Bridge), clip the formed loop(s) into the harness (ventrally) with a locking carabiner. Here comes the simple part. As the climber climbs, the belayer backs up and continues backing up until the climber reaches his/her goal, in this case, the cables of the Bridge. If the climber falls, the belayer literally does nothing, except eventually walk forward to let the climber smoothly down. There is nothing to let go of and no rope movement to burn exposed skin.

So, where's the mystique? Sorry, it's all gone — in this case, replaced by bare bone functionality.

*Problems? Contraindications? A couple.*

1. If the climber is much heavier (over 50 lbs.) than the belayer, clip the two loops of the bowline-on-a-bight, at the end of the belay line, into two side-by-side "back-up" belayers.

2. The belayer must have an obstacle-free back-up path to follow for the length of the belay. This technique does not work if the climber plans to move laterally on an element; e.g., across a Two Line Bridge; well...maybe on a telephone pole course in the middle of a field, but not amidst a stand of trees. Beware the clear-cut mentality. "Woodsman, spare those 432 trees."

3. After the belay "catch" is made and lowering begins, there is a natural tendency to be pulled forward at faster than a walk. Simply be aware of this and control your forward speed by leaning back.

4. If the belay is a long one (over 200'), supply the belayer with an ice axe on frosty days. That's a joke — I say, *that's a joke, son!*

So, if your problem is how to safely train enough belayers for use with additional students on high ropes course elements, try the back-up belay. It works "down under."

## Sky Walk — a Portable Mohawk Walk

*Object* — To move a group (15 folks) from a safe area, over a series of tautly strung rope sections (that traverse a putrid mass of rotting asparagus tips and artichoke hearts) to another safe area.

Tie (bowline) one end of a 100' rope (1/2" KM III is best because of its characteristic static quality) to a tree about three feet off the ground. Choose trees of a sturdy appearance and workable diameter. Run the rope to another tree about 10-20' away, pull the rope to make it taut, and take a round turn about the trunk at about the same height as above. Continue this routine until you run out of rope and finish off with a round turn and a couple of half hitches around the final tree.

With the natural give of the rope and the resultant slack under weight, passage on the rope by a single person is very difficult. Let a few try, to underline the difficulty.

But, if two or three persons, holding hands, make their way out on the rope, the passage becomes considerably easier, although still a challenge. This cooperative move resembles a human tension traverse.

The group moves in sections of 2-4, until the rotted delicacies are overcome. The ropes may need retightening from time to time.

## Prusik Knot Ascent

This vertical, monkey-on-a-string activity is a rainy day must.

Climbing ropes, those traditional vertical fixtures which all too frequently dangle unused in a gymnasium, can be utilized for this technical and satisfying technique of ascending a rope.

The actual climbing procedure (seek experienced help to actually learn the knots and procedures) is a mountaineer's rope ascending technique used primarily in rescue situations.

From a practical standpoint in a school setting, the use of the ropes and technique allow almost any student to reach the top of the rope (usually 20') under their own power; a considerable accomplishment for a student that has trouble with one pull-up.

Ordinarily, three 8' sections of 9mm kernmantle rope are tied individually end-to-end forming three 3' or 4' diameter rope circles (slings). The knot of choice for joining the rope ends is the double fisherman's knot, also called a barrel knot.

Each of these three slings is tied onto the vertical climbing rope by means of a prusik knot (refer to the illustration), a knot closely resembling a taut line hitch. This knot, properly tied, maintains a grip on the climbing rope when the sling arrangement is pulled downward, but can be slid up or down the rope after the pressure is released.

One sling goes under the arms, leaving the two remaining slings, one for each foot. As each sling is moved (no pressure exerted), the other two slings hold the weight of the climber. Develop a repeated 1-2-3 sequence for a smooth, relaxed ascent.

For a bit more comfort and efficiency while jockeying up the rope, tie on a Swiss seat/Studebaker arrangement, and tie a short sling onto the vertical rope using a prusik knot and clip the other end of the sling into the harness via a bowline/carabiner combination. Only one foot sling is necessary, also tied to the vertical rope with a prusik knot, so that a 1-2, 1-2 movement system develops. Reverse your sequence of moves for the climb down.

Considering that the ascent, particularly the first time it's tried, will be physically taxing, indicate to the students that some energy should be reserved for the climb down. Coming down requires as many physical moves as ascending. The descent is not a gravity-fed slide to the floor.

*Caution:* If you have any questions as to whether a student, because of ineptness, corpulence, hives, etc., will poop out, require that they use a belay so that there is a means of getting them down without having to call the fire department.

There are mechanical rope ascenders (two or three popular types) available at rock climbing specialty stores that allow much greater ease in moving up and down the ropes (1/2' KM III kernmantle rescue rope, in this case). These ascenders come in sets of two and are rather expensive, but offer the advantages of being easy to use, attach and detach to and from the rope quickly and allow more students to participate per rope in use. A belay is still a prudent choice with the use of these mechanical ascenders.

Set up a number of these vertical sections of KM III rope in the gym to involve as many students as possible, but consider how many belayers will be necessary or available, before you festoon your rafters with rope.

To add variety, fix a bulb horn or bicycle bell at the top of each rope to provide an audio reward for having reached the top. HONK! DING DING! Relax, coach. A little stress, a little fun — it's all part of the experiential game.

### Rope Vault or Tarzan's Triumph

Continuing the precept that "the simplest are the funnest," Jerry Clapp's addition to an earlier BOT's, *Single Line Potpourri* segment, provides further proof that you don't need extensive props or materials to produce popular multi-use events.

A single swing rope is the essential prop in this physical/fun stunt. You will also need portable high jump standards, in addition to some landing pads. (Landing pad sounds better than crash mat, but you know what I mean.)

"The object is for 'Tarzan' to stand back as far as possible (from the bar) and let the rope swing toward the high jump standard. When the rope returns, the young swinger runs alongside, reaches up and grasps a tight hand hold, jumping as s/he nears the bar. His/her momentum, if timed properly, will carry the jumper/vaulter over the bar. Coupled with a quick hand release, the vaulter will end up clearing the bar and landing on the mats — where s/he can beat on her/his breast/chest to signify their triumph.

### Safety Hints

1. Caution the students that if they do not have enough momentum to clear the bar — just hang on and enjoy the return ride.

2. Make sure the landing area is smooth enough to preclude ankle injuries.

3. Caution the students to make a feet-first landing — headstands smart from 6 ft. up.

4. Set the high jump standards in opposite directions so a cross bar hit does not upset the standards.

5. To give the rope its initial momentum, do not swing the rope, simply let it go from a pulled-back position.

The secret to this event is timing. Start low and let the gang develop their skill in small height increments. It is possible to clear 10 feet or more if you have some real swingers in the crowd.

This is a good one! Instructors will have to beat the kids with sticks (ed. note: use foam swords) in order to close down the activity."

I'll attest to the popularity of this kind of swinging event, having set up a similar situation in a workshop that involved vaulting over stacked paper cores. I don't know if it's the swinging movement, the inherent challenge in clearing an obstacle, the self-competition, or what — but it does stimulate and hold the interest of an active group.

### Swing to Safety

This simple swinging element is included in *Cows' Tails & Cobras* (pg. 84), but I would like to emphasize and expand on the event because of its usefulness in: (1) Teaching a student how to achieve a long pendulum swing on a rope. (2) Building upper body strength or the determination to achieve more strength. (3) Capturing the intrinsic joy of movement that a rope swing engenders.

Hang the swing rope from a limb **at least** 20' high, remembering that the higher the anchor point, the longer the pendulum of the swing. Grasp the dangling rope in your hands at about eye level (mark where you grasp it with tape), and walk away from the plumb line to a point that allows you to still grasp the rope at that tape mark, while standing on the 2nd rung of a step ladder. Dig a 2' deep hole directly below where you are standing and firmly place a section of telephone pole or a section of hardwood log (locust, if you can find it), so that the pole measures to the 2nd run of the step ladder. The diameter of the pole should measure at least 8" and a bit more, if attainable.

Swing from this pole (over a cleared area that includes no rocks, punji sticks, or poison ivy), a number of times to determine where a logical maximum swing arc would end; i.e., where you would land after letting go of the rope at the end of the pendulum. Ask two or three other people to perform the same swing and release to determine where an average landing point should be located. Using this "scientifically" determined landing point, measure about 6" back toward the take-off stump and erect a hurdle 12" high and perpendicular to the line of the swing. The hurdle itself is simply a small cut and trimmed sapling balanced on top of two 12" vertical sections of cord wood placed 6-8 feet apart. The pieces of cord wood are not placed permanently in the ground, so that they can be moved forward or backward to vary the swing's difficulty. The object, then, is to develop enough momentum on the swing to clear the hurdle after releasing the rope.

The novice Tarzan (A) will attempt to throw himself/herself forward toward the hurdle to gain the necessary speed and momentum. This convulsive attempt at propulsion usually results in a quick trip to the turf or a foreshortened swing.

The thinking-man's Tarzan will jump backward away from the stump (while holding onto the rope, right?), thus increasing the length of the pendulum and therefore the arc of the swing, resulting in more distance and the desired result of easily clearing the hurdle.

This event is infectious — an initial failure often leads to repeated tries to clear the hurdle, either ending in a successful landing or self-promises to build additional arm strength.

## Rosin Bag

Ever watch a big league pitcher reach down off the mound, grab a small whitish bag, perform a quick hand-rubbing ritual, and toss the sack unceremoniously aside? Do you know what's in that dusty bag? Rosin is what. This powdery substance serves the dual purpose of drying sweaty palms and acting as an object of inspiration.

A rosin bag doesn't cost much, but the amount of use and inspiration available on a ropes course is worth the couple bucks.

Offer a rosin bag to a participant who is about to dive for the Hickory bar. It's amazing how much confidence a simple pat-pat-pat to the palms can offer a hesitating student. There is, of course, the advantage of having dry palms when diving for a trapeze (or swinging on a rope), but the real advantage results from offering an "edge" to a doubtful or hesitating performer. The edge is mental, as most marginally helpful substances or talismans offer, but mental is the name of the game on a ropes course.

Try a bag, but don't get hooked; high grade rosin is surprisingly addictive.

## The Green Box

Storage of ropes course material on-site has always been a temptation because of what-to-bring-with-you worries and transportation hassles — (Here, you carry it!). Various schemes have been used; some more successful than others. For example, if you have a pre-existing storage shed nearby, use it if security of the structure is lightweight, vandalproof — lightweight in contrast to heavy-duty vandals; i.e., serious, tool-toting lock smashers.

If a shed is not available and hundreds of dollars worth of gear are the snatchables at risk, try storing the valuables (and not-so valuables) in a "green box."

Project Adventure began using a Greenlee 2' x 2' x 4' sheet metal box (green, of course) two years ago, with continuing satisfaction and success. The interior volume of the box is large enough to hold **everything** you need to run the ropes course, including all of the high and low elements. Contents of the box normal include: belay ropes, swing ropes, fidget ladder, foldable stretcher, blanket, helmets, carabiners, and assorted slings and webbing — all stored without having to fold, tuck, or compartmentalize each item.

The lock (ordinary master lock type) is recessed into the box, protecting it from moisture and attempts at cutting or sawing the hasp. There are two large folding handles on the ends of the box through which a cable or chain can be reeved, to allow locking to a tree. Making off with this hefty, gear-filled box would be no small task for wimpy vandals on foot.

If your "ropes" area is subjected to only minor vandalism, try the #665 Greenlee storage box as a welcomed convenience factor for heavily-used ropes courses (and similarly used instructors).

## A Reagle Net

Project Adventure usually has one or more interns in attendance at our Wenham site during the year. Charles Reagle, from Radford University in Virginia, was with us during this last summer and as the result of a what-should-I-do-now? day, he painstakingly and laboriously handcrafted a small (4' x 8') cargo net. I forget how long he said it took to make, but you don't want to know from a $/time standpoint. But, Charles did a bang-up job, so we *had* to find a function for this mini-net; I mean a real program function. Surprisingly (and typically serendipitous), the two classic ropes course activities we used for incorporating the net were arguably changed for the better; the net actually worked and worked well. Here's how and a brief report.

## Trust Fall Net

If you don't know what a trust fall is, look in *Silver Bullets*, pages 80-82; I can't bring myself to explain it again. Anyhow, one of the potential dangers of falling backward into a spotting line has been the tendency for some fallers to fling their arms akimbo and smack their erstwhile protectors in the chops — largely painful; not much serious damage. But, the trust that is slowly building is significantly reduced: Enter the Reagle Net. If the net is held by the spotters (about 16 people, 8 on each side), in a position that takes the place of their arms, the problem of getting whacked by flailing appendages is almost eliminated.

After having set up the trust fall for years by having people catching people (flesh on flesh, so to speak), I was a bit reluctant to give the net high grades on trust building (there was no question of functionality), because the net was doing the catching (...producing a comfortable landing, by the by). As I questioned the group, however, I found that trust was in the eyes (and emotions) of the beholder and that these beholders cared not a wit what did the catching, as long as they were sufficiently caught. The net won a few points that day and grudging acceptance from a middle-ager who thought he had seen it all.

## Fidget Ladder Net

Unless you have considerable padding or an airbag under the Fidget Ladder, you know that eventually someone is going to hit the ground fairly hard. And, it's also well known that this dervish of a ladder is difficult to spot without risking injury to the spotters from the whirling ladder rungs. Re-enter the Reagle Net!

This time, hold the net on the ends only, as it is placed under that part of the Fidget Ladder which receives the most falls; i.e., the first move the participant makes. With about 6 people (3 on a side) holding the net and moving with the participant, the chances of hitting the ground or getting hit by the rungs is greatly reduced. AND (big and), there are more people involved in a meaningful way.

For you folks who don't want to spend your hours splicing and reeving, I don't have many solid recommendations for substitute nets, but try these ideas:

- Use sections of old tennis nets.
- Deep sea fishing nets (heavier rope).
- Nylon semi-trailer net covers are strong and about the right net opening size.
- Contact me and I'll give you Charles' address.

So, Charles, as you read this in December, comfortably situated in the semi-south, know that you have made the big time — a feature section in BOT's. It's worth a smile and a Coke, eh?

## Knot Terminology

When teaching knots to a group, learning is facilitated if the students know a few simple vocabulary words and terminology phrases associated with ropes and knots. The following is a *very* basic primer.

*Knot* — a tie made in the rope itself. Example: Overhand.

*Hitch* — a "knot" used for attaching a rope to an object. Example: Clove Hitch.

*Bend* — the "knot" used for tying two ropes together. Example: Sheet Bend.

All three of the above terms seem to be related by the knot designation, and indeed they are. Differentiation of terms facilitates explaining the different uses of knotting.

*Working End* — that end of the rope used to tie with.

*Standing End (Part)* — that end of the rope opposite the working end and often attached to an object.

*Hawser Layed* — refers to rope construction that is twisted to provide strength and flexibility.

*Kernmantle* — parallel synthetic rope fibers surrounded by a woven sheath of similar synthetic material.

*Bight* — that curved, uncrossed portion of the rope that forms between the working end and standing part.

*Loop* — when the working end crosses over the standing part, or vice-versa.

## Studebaker Wrap

I wish I had the skill to illustrate the following Swiss seat type of body tie-in, but after a few blank page attempts, I think you're better off with this verbal description and a blank page.

Folks in workshops over the years have asked for a tie-in method that would combine the relative comfort and support of a regular Swiss seat and the security of a waist wrap. While fooling around with a length of rope, I came up with this attempt at a combination compromise called the *Studebaker Wrap*. The name, for those of you not familiar with the 1950's Studebaker automobile, refers to that model made famous by its designers for its Push-Me, Pull-You appearance; i.e., looking the same fore and aft.

The wrap is tied so that the classic Swiss seat is combined from a functional and visual ventral/dorsal standpoint.

I'm writing the following description for those of you who know how to tie a Swiss seat. Using a 26' long section of 9mm kernmantle rope or l" tubular webbing, tie on the well-known front Swiss seat and, as you finish, rather than tying off, continue the sequence by duplicating your initial maneuvers to include your posterior. This finished torso wrap is simply a double Swiss seat and allows clipping in to the front or back with improved support.

Give it a try and let me know what you think. If you don't know the Swiss seat tie-in, don't attempt two of them.

Finish off the rope or webbing wraps with a square knot and adjacent safety knots (half a double fisherman's knot).

**Say What?**

Everything that goes up, must come down, but when?

What do you say to a nervous student who has been in the "position of potential" long enough and sometimes too long? Are there effective words of wisdom that can be confidently offered to cause the knee-shaking, gulping, misty-eyed student to boldly "go for it"? Sometimes yes, sometimes no — how's that for concise ambivalence?

The first right words or word offered at the right time often makes a difference, and will on occasion cause a hesitating participant (trapeze jump, rappelling, flea jump, etc.) to make the move that completes an activity. Such well-intentioned words of encouragement are often unequivocally rejected by a student ("Keep quiet!"; "Leave me alone!"; "I don't need that!"), and that's a pretty good indication that further attempts at ground-level, profound rationale should be terminated by *all* good-intentioned spotters, spectators, and instructors, at least until another plateau of commitment has been reached.

*Situation* — Student has been crouching on a wall platform for about five minutes, anticipating the jump (dive) to a trapeze. Close contact has been kept with the wall (tree), as the obviously nervous participant attempts to convince his/her body to make a move that the mind is still questioning. It should be apparent, at this juncture, whether the student really wants to complete the activity.

As an aside — I believe that a student who has come this far has more than completed his/her class requirement: a conscientious try at the offered obstacle. Remember, instructors — constant cajoling borders on coercion and if a student attempt is eventually made because of your impelling personality, the choice to perform becomes more your decision than the student's.

If it seems obvious that no attempt will be forthcoming within a reasonable length of time, offer a compassionate escape; to descend and try again at another time. There's nothing wrong with manana, and success manifests itself in diverse ways.

If the student "wants it," but is having trouble making the right move, try the following lines that have and have not proven effective for the author in the past. "Wanting it" is demonstrated by repeated movements to and from the point of no return. Each of these, often spasmodic attempts are punctuated by exclamations of self-deprecation, usually associated with several deep rapid breaths. Other manifestations of the syndrome (for the clinically interested reader) are: rolling of the eyes skyward, re-establishing contact with the closest solid object, repeating approximately the line, "I can't do it; I really want to, but I can't," looking out toward the horizon, or in the case of a first rappel, looking directly and agonizingly into the eyes of the belayer (or a trusted person), almost committing to the task, and then drawing back at the last possible instant.

Don't say, "I know you can do it." You *don't* know that. I have never experienced a positive response from this often used cliche. I think instructors say it to make themselves feel better when the situation becomes tense.

1. After a student has made a few unsuccessful attempts, suggest that the next try be *the* one, and make it coincide with a counting sequence. Let the student decide which number is the GO signal. Try this technique only twice. If the counting doesn't work, repeating the 1-2-3 GO sequence simply reinforces the negative element of not trying.

2. Ask the student to turn around and face away from the intimidation aspect of the event. When a level of composure is re-gained and the participant seems calmer and re-committed, a turn and try often results in a successful attempt.

3. "I've been standing here belaying and attempting to help you for over 15 minutes. This is no longer just your thing, it's mine, too — you owe me a good attempt."

4. "Trust me — I am not going to let you fall."

5. "Do you want to do this?" (Answer is a tremulous "yes.") "Then let me help you." "Follow my directions exactly." Then proceed to talk them through the event. Don't verbally stumble — know what you are going to say and voice it confidently. If the answer to your first question is "no," then initiate a sequence for letting the student retreat. Sometimes the knowledge that there is an escape will compel them to completion.

   Occasionally, words don't work and are obviously inappropriate. Be confident and understanding enough to be quiet at times.

6. I'm giving away a professional secret on this one, because I've had more success with the following few words than with any others, but timing is important.

   The action must occur toward the end of a class or session. The student should have made more than one abortive attempt. Other students should be in attendance and obviously (not verbally) waiting for a try.

   "Janice, you know the choice to do this or not do it is up to you, but I'm going to have to ask you to make a decision now; we just don't have any more time today. Now step up there and GO, or let me help you come down." This is at least a 50% ploy.

## Mental & Emotional Quickie Special

Dr. Lee Gillis (Georgia College) reports that he is having good luck with his counseling sessions by asking people to perform initiative tasks as pairs. For example, trying to make it through the Spider's Web as a group of couples. Doing it as diads puts more on-going emphasis on how the pair functions together. It's something to talk about.

## The KB Syndrome

"I can't do anything at heights, except hug the beams." An expedient way to combat the Koala Bear syndrome and become functionally at ease with height is to spend time at height (comfortably) in a belayed position.

When you look down from 20-30', things take on a different perspective in comparison to ground level viewing; smaller, often upside-down — frightening. It takes a while to become accustomed to that disconcerting difference in perspective and the time spent acclimatizing should not require precarious positions or exaggerated expectations ("Come on Esther, I know you can do it!").

Try sitting for a couple hours on a platform at about 30' (don't forget to use a belay and keep your eyes open) on more than one occasion. This time spent at height, coupled with a developing trust in the belay system and your own inner cool (Ooomm) should reduce the what-am-I-doing-here? horrors. I'm not putting you on about this, as I have seen it work numerous times with individuals who professed chronic (but sometimes convenient) vertigo.

## How Long Is Too Long?

Situation — Student standing anxiously on the Flea Jump platform, Pamper Pole, Cat Walk, etc.

"I really want to do it, but my feet won't move." "Oh, wow — I can't believe I'm so scared." "Can I come back and try this later?" "Do I *have* to do this?"

Dissolve to tears, self-recrimination, embarrassment, and perhaps a convulsive, inept attempt that occurs more as a result of emotion than determination.

The above scenario is not an uncommon predicament on high ropes course events. Unfortunately, because of misunderstanding or instructive oversight, the hesitating student begins to perceive the event as a win/lose situation, rather than recognizing the intended challenge; a sentient, conscientious attempt.

The answer seems to be in effectively outlining what the curriculum expectations are, and what you (the instructor) physically and mentally expect from the students.

There seems little value in leaving a student on a platform or cable to agonize for 15 minutes about whether to "take that step," etc. Being in a position of potential is enough to qualify for the TRY, that stepping stone to the next level of commitment or completion.  The longer a student dwells on the attempt, the more it can become the instructor's personality or peer pressure or fear of failure that provokes the completion move.  Any resulting decision is most likely not the individual's, but the result of various good-intentioned anxiety ploys.  There is no doubt that an individual can be prodded (coerced) into extraordinary efforts by the pressures mentioned above.  The military uses such stress techniques effectively ("No one eats tonight, Mr., until you make that jump...") and with justifiable cause:  discipline above all.  But to emulate the DI's methods and means within a school setting is negative, unproductive, and unacceptable.

Go for it!

Bob Nelson

# Chapter 11
# *Disclaimers/Opinions*

Every now and then (much more "then" than "now"), an insistent sense of responsibility urges me to make sure that you all are using BOT's material in the safest possible way. This convulsive caring has resulted in the following collection of "posterior protectors," more decorously referred to as disclaimers. These you-better-be-careful platitudes satisfy an author's need to feel responsible, but serve practically no legal function. Make up a few of your own; it's kind of fun, and may impress someone.

## *Disclaimer — of Sorts*

*Bag of Tricks* is not meant to be an instructional tome, rather a lighthearted presentation and sharing of current ideas and procedures in the field of adventure education. If an included area requires technical knowledge and you feel unsure of your skill level, put that idea aside until your training is commensurate to the activity. There's enough silly stuff here to take its place until your technical bag of tricks is plumb with confidence.

Do I sound like your mother? Sorry, just doin' my job.

### Ye Olde Blanket Disclaimer

I would like to formally exonerate myself and everyone I have either talked to or looked at, from everything that has anything to do with whatever you're upset about — also to include weekends.

### *Other Disclaimers*

*Bag of Tricks* is written and edited by Karl Rohnke. He enjoys writing and editing this periodical and thanks you for perusing its contents, but beware the Jabberwocke and other unseen hazards of adventure programming. Proceed carefully with abandon and try out your schemes personally before allowing your students to taste the "thrill of victory" — you aren't allowed many official "agonies."

Please use good sense in attempting to utilize the games, climbing techniques, initiative problems, etc., that are included in *BOT's*. Some of the activities require specialized training or esoteric know-how. Be overt about being baffled by the covert — seek experienced help when necessary.

*      *      *      *      *

If you've got it, flaunt it. If you haven't got it, don't fake it — somebody will get hurt. So much for this quarter's disclaimer — a study in sledgehammer subtlety.

*      *      *      *      *

*Bag of Tricks* is an educational quarterly written and edited by Karl Rohnke. Since I have not tried all the ideas and schemes sent in by readers, I trust you will approach any trial and error situation with caution. Everyone needs some adventure — no one needs injury.

*      *      *      *      *

*Bag of Tricks* is written and edited by Karl Rohnke, but he isn't taking the blame for misuse of any of this disparate material — so be careful; use common sense and all those other pay-no-heed platitudes that make up your basic disclaimer.

*      *      *      *      *

## Hey, listen!

The author has almost achieved maladroit immortality on a couple badly chosen occasions by not following his own survival instincts. In other words, I can't take responsibility for the misuse of any information offered in *Bag of Tricks* . Use the ideas as you best interpret them and seek experienced (not well-intentioned, but experienced) help with technical problems when necessary.

### Self-Serving Justification

"Men resemble one another in that they do best those things which please them most." — Juan Manuel

If you keep reading and looking long enough, you can find someone who agrees with you about anything. To wit, the following quotation from *Success Magazine* :

**FOR, AS THE EDITORS OF *DECORATING YOUR OFFICE FOR SUCCESS* OBSERVE, "THE SUITABILITY OF YOUR OFFICE DOES NOT DEPEND ON IT BEING NEAT, MODERN, ELEGANT, OR STYLISH. IT DEPENDS UPON HOW IT SUPPORTS YOUR MORALE AND SELF-DETERMINATION. THE IDEAL OFFICE IS ESSENTIALLY ONE THAT WILL ELEVATE YOUR SPIRITS WHENEVER YOU ENTER AND STICK IN YOUR MEMORY AS A PLACE YOU WANT TO GO BACK TO. IT SHOULD SUGGEST INTERESTING AND EXCITING THINGS ABOUT TO HAPPEN."**

Photo of my office withheld so as not to offend your cosmic sense of order and sequence.

### A Rational Rationale

...climbing then, is not simply a matter of several thrill-seekers thrashing about on an impossibly difficult rock face. It is rather a sport of fine challenges, demonstrating a satisfying spectrum of accomplishment levels. A something for everyone sport.

The availability of a challenging and climbable set of rocks or rock faces is a matter of geographical location: no rocks, no climb. However, a practice climbing wall build of sized hardwood blocks, bolted at various angles and positions onto the bricks or concrete of a gymnasium wall provides an innovative approach to a variety of needs.

1. The further and aesthetic utilization of school facilities.
2. Provides an indoor (all weather) physical education station.
3. Allows beginning climbers to develop strength, expertise, and confidence toward facilitating their performance at an actual rock climbing site.
4. Allows students (whether or not they want to continue their efforts in actual rock climbing) to participate in something new without a pre-sensitivity to failure, remembering that student success is simply a genuine **try**.
5. Because of the various stresses involved (fear: of failure, of physical harm, or human fallibility, etc.), there is the unparalleled opportunity for the establishment of trust.
6. Provides a physical and mental challenge with pizzaz. Participation is genuinely fun.

### Tegwar

Tegwar is an acronym for, That-Exciting-Game-Without-Any-Rules, and as a game it presents a classic mental/physical exercise in logical confusion. Any obvious lack of rules within or surrounding a game requires a fairly complex set of non-rules or acceptable confusers to make play possible.

For example, if you are going to plan a Tegwar variation of soccer (and you can't really, because Tegwar is Tegwar and only alludes to soccer in order to explain Tegwar), you must ignore all the rules — better yet, recognize that there are no rules, and then establish touchstones of play; i.e., those gems of illogic that suggest sequence, scoring, win, lose, etc., but which are only pivotal focal points of concentration. To score or make a good play is an illusion that lasts only long enough to feel good and then melds into the next acceptable sequence of physical action. Recognizing that there are no established guidelines, then operating meaningfully within a game context without consistent regulations is the key to understanding how a decently unorganized, semi-serious potpourri of play can be exciting and fun without any rules.

I've burdened you with all this twaddle to simply indicate that Tegwar is child's play, which is probably the best kind. Think of the above as a roundabout introduction to an initiative problem. Take any game and reduce or change the rules to that point where the structure of the game remains intact, **all** participants feel good about being part of the action, and the joy remains or has increased. A formidable task, but it's worth a try or two, and who knows what might emerge? It's better than running laps.

## How Safe Is Too Safe?

Can an individual or a program be too safe? ...What did he say? I must have read that first sentence incorrectly. Safety is the cornerstone of adventure programs, on a par with concepts like, "home," "trust," and "belay": a bastion of unassailable acceptance and truth in concept.

But, the answer is yes, you can not only be too safe, you can suffocate a program with it. Blasphemy! Heretic! Anti-American! But you can go too far toward each end of the **SAFE-HAZARDOUS** spectrum, and it's not difficult to spot the extremists.

Solo climbing (unbelayed) is an example of genuine hazard; going overboard in the pursuit of a greater adrenaline boost. Or more programmatically, canoe tripping through white water without flotation devices: an obvious breech of common safety practices. But these examples are easily found, pin-pointed and eliminated by folks who want their programs to continue. A consistently unsafe approach will eventually lead to a physical disaster and a weakening or dissolution of procedures and program.

The commitment thief is a much more difficult curriculum offender to recognize, because everything s/he does is safe...stultifyingly safe. Recognizing that there must be a hint of hazard to make the **GO** commitment meaningful, a zip line that begins at a height of 10 feet is not only ho-hum, it's impractical. A double-belayed student on a Two Line Bridge (2 belay ropes, 2 sets of crabs, 2 belayers) involves so much rope, the perceived danger becomes less of falling and more of getting tangled in the excess belay line. A trapeze that is practically at arm's length doesn't make the event safer, it just eliminates the challenge. Etc., etc., etc.

A program, to remain viable, must be safe (low accident record). To quote a program truism I've used many times at conference presentations and workshops, "We (Project Adventure) wouldn't remain in business very long if we were dropping kids out of the trees." The parameters of safety become more recognized as a concerned approach continues and matures.

The danger of weakening the student's potential commitment is the lack of perceived danger (hazard, risk), and it's difficult to generate that perception when it's obviously not there. The students know...

After a period of time, many of the students will recognize that the events are not really as hazardous or difficult as they first appeared: experience, insight, perception — growth. Score one for the teacher's team!

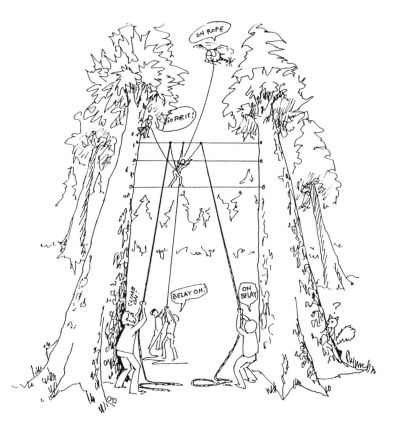

### Personal Opinion

I receive a lot of junk mail here at work; i.e., mail I have not solicited nor have any interest in. And, being listed as President (CEO) of Project Adventure, Inc., the circle file mail leans heavily toward business matters (generally, how to get on top and stay there by being a jerk).

Just before leaving work the other day, I scanned this following piece of "junk mail" data from a leading copier firm. What it says is so much the antithesis of what I feel constitutes a successful, satisfying working day that I want to share it so other experiential educators can, in good faith (if big business says it's good, it's bound to be suspect), avoid this time-killing by-product of climbing the corporate ladder. And, I quote...

And, I quote,

*"Dear Mr. Rohnke*, (I love the personal touch)

There is a key question concerning your future as an executive.

**What will my typical work day be like?**

From now on, an executive typically will devote nearly five hours of **every** working day to leading and attending meetings. This is a conservative evaluation. Right **now**, the typical highly-placed executive spends more than 5 hours each day on the job in meetings. In fact, the higher you rise, the more time you will have to allocate each day strictly for meetings. Right now, the typical CEO logs 6 hours plus in the meeting venue every life-long working day.

You'll spend much of the 3 hours you have left in your day reading to catch up on vital information and you'll be expected to know more than ever. You'll write. You'll think. You'll do some doodling. That will leave you with no time for lunch and a cold dinner, unless you think fast and doodle a lot less. And I'm not kidding." No time for lunch? You gotta be kidding.

**Creativity — "If you know exactly what you are doing, you are not being creative."**

Some people seem to be inherently more creative than others, but perhaps it's just a matter of interest rather than proclivity. I have a feeling that most folks are, or can become, creative, but unconsciously choose not to, in favor of the "bible" approach; i.e., referring to a compilation of facts and techniques that apply to their area of interest or need. And that's OK; it's certainly not copping out, just saving time and energy for other scholastic or recreational endeavors.

The capability to be creative is there if given half a chance. Here's what I do to encourage the flow and if it works for you — great! If it flops, look to other suggestions or continue to use prepared texts and lesson plans as guides for your ongoing curriculum. Some create, some implement, some administrate.

*By the numbers:*

1. Refer to other texts on your preferred subject to gain leverage on the inertia of where-do-I-start. Use other peoples' ideas to act as a stepping stone for embellishments that make an idea work within other environments or contexts. Changing the rules, vocabulary or setting of a game or puzzler can produce a strikingly fresh and new situation. Examples: The Clock (formerly "Ring Around the Rosie"); Aerobic Tag (a variation known in the vernacular as "Smear the Queer"), 2 x 4 (gleaned from a book on coin and match stick problems).

2. If you are a coffee drinker, drink two cups while making a long, solo interstate drive somewhere and then orient your

thinking toward creating in some specific area of program need (a new initiative problem, ropes course event, belay device, working tool, etc.). Let your thoughts drift, but keep them on the subject area, even if the same lousy idea keeps cropping up. If an idea seems like a good one, write down a word or two only (remember, you're driving) to remind yourself of where this fragile and fleeting inspiration came from and where it's going. This brief notation is important. If you mistakenly think the idea is so good and significant that forgetting it is impossible, by the time you attempt to think it again (what?) it may well be gone and not retrievable. (Comparisons of the mind to a computer are interesting and apt, but the automorphic button for idea retrieval hasn't been located yet; it must be near the thymus.)

If you are not a coffee drinker, drink only one cup or try a no-doze type of pill. I know it seems facetious, somehow unhealthy and smacks of cheating, but the brief caffeine boost works for me. It must be an increase of blood flow to the brain due to the vasodialator characteristics of caffeine. It's only temporary, but all you need is a start.

3. When you wake up early some morning and aren't still tired, hung over, emotionally distant, cold, full bladder, etc. (it's hard to be creative when other signals are getting in the way), direct your thoughts as in #2 above. This relaxed, mentally floating position is one of my favorites and has resulted in a couple of curriculum elements of note — the Pamper Pole and Hickory Jump.

4. Go to the geographical area that needs your cerebral time and with no one else around, lie on your back and let the area and artifacts flood your thinking (ideally, but sometimes not possible because you're not supposed to lie down on the job — I know, it's a corny aphorism, but in application it's too true). I saw a cartoon recently that showed a fellow sitting at a desk staring dreamily out the window. Two co-workers were watching and one remarked, "The boss lets him do that because his last idea saved the company $1,000,000." Creative thinking is a tremendous asset to any business, but its perpetration does appear sometimes too relaxed; i.e., too relaxed for a "no pain, no gain" corporate mentality.

5. This next suggestion is an adjunct and aid toward creating the setting for uninterrupted thought. Buy a pair of shooter's "ears," those earphone-like appendages that shut out sound, rather than enhancing it. They are sold to reduce the risk of injury to your inner ear because of loud sounds (gunfire, machinery, engines, etc.), but their efficiency also cuts out almost all other distracting sounds.

If you can get used to people mouthing their words (every office comedian thinks this is an original and hilarious joke), and the reputation of being a recluse, the "ears" often make a hectic, noisy day more tolerable. You **can** hear the phone ring.

Being creative is fun when it works, but the stage must be set; otherwise, a good idea is pure chance or more often, the result of necessity (good ole serendipity).

"The truth is that each one of us is creative. It was more evident when we were children and playing, because creativity is play-oriented and depends on a faith in ourselves and what we are doing. It is associated, therefore, with those adjectives we use to describe children's play — spontaneous, effortless, innocent and easy."

"Creativity is a different way of looking at things, a different way of looking at ourselves. When we are creative, when we are at play, we open ourselves to our own experiences. We discard preconceptions. We become aware. We begin to live." — Dr. George Sheehan

I have undoubtedly popularized and embellished more peoples' ideas than I've had original ones of my own, but that's part of the creative game. Every now and then, a sparkling new idea will surface and you will feel justified for all the daydreaming and creative plagiarizing.

Cooperative plagiarism is a productive mind game that I constantly pursue during creative down time. When there's just nothing there (in the windmills of your mind), that's the time to grab a book on the subject you have loggerheaded with and begin designating new thought directions by assaulting what you have (muddled mass of non-functioning ideas) with other folks' notions and inclinations. It's amazing how a simple written comment by another person can stimulate an idea or cause the branching out from a weak idea toward a web of fascinating alternatives. Change size, direction, kinesthetic orientation, rules — make it different, really different, and you make it yours.

## An Insight

So often in adventure clinics and classes student responses are immediate, boisterously positive and largely superficial — there's not much time for introspection in a fast-paced workshop. Occasionally, someone will write a letter, after a few days (usually weeks), and pass along a time-mellowed insight concerning people, a moment, or an emotion. Sometimes a response is beautifully sensitive, even artistic. I hesitate to lay that on you, Monique, but anyone who can so clearly see through the smokescreen of *Fire in the Hole*, and so accurately (subtly) pinpoint the real rationale of "just popping balloons" deserves to be quoted.

"'Fire in the hole,' he yelled

with smiling enthusiasm.

We reached out to our partners,

laughing and squirming, and hanging on

tightly.

A delicate balance

between struggle and embrace

weaved through the pairs,

as the discomforts of hugging a stranger,

vanished with each bursting balloon.

It was the gentle transition into familiarity,

(filled with nervous laughter),

as the stubborn balloon resisted the force

of two clutching friends (resulting in a shattering 'pop'),

that made falling into each other,

more than just a game."

— Monique Gil-Rogers


## Debriefing, Processing, Values Clarification, or Whatever Cognitive Jargon Seems Currently Appropriate

Ropes course activities and initiative problems are great fun and variously stimulating, but a large part of their educational value can be diminished if an instructor rushes from one physical/emotional high to the next without pausing and offering the group an opportunity to reflect upon and talk about the experience. Watching an otherwise bored class turn on to an adventurous curriculum element can be a tempting stimulus for a teacher to move quickly to another activity before the "magic" is lost.

I think a time for talking about "what went on" during an activity can often be captured by an alert/experienced teacher, without having to formally sit the group down and program the debriefing. "Hey, chicken, whatsamatta with your knees? They get the shakes?" Such demeaning comments provide the opportunity for a discussion of program rationale and how come we're here. Pick your spots at emotional high and low points, when morale is at ebb or flood, not just when the clock says it's time.

To completely eliminate discussion wastes a valuable teaching tool and probably indicates an instructor's (1) lack of caring or confidence (2) ignorance of the value of such an experience (3) boredom level.

Debriefing can also be overdone with many groups. Stopping after each activity for an in-depth "meaningful" discussion is probably too much for a normal group. Interest will wane if the group knows a "heavy" time awaits them after each action experience. However, some groups (adjudicated youths, emotionally disturbed students, etc.) need more scheduled discussion time.

To help you develop your own patter and line of questions, here are a few debriefing topics that you can bring up to stimulate discussion, or change the direction of a deadend dialogue.

| | |
|---|---|
| Leadership & Followership | Spotting |
| Group Support | Sexism |
| Peer Pressure | Carryover |
| Negativism - Hostility | Fear (Physical - Psychological) |
| Efficiency | Joy - Pleasure |
| Competition | |

Read *Islands of Healing*, Project Adventure's new Adventure Based Counseling book, for a detailed presentation of how to facilitate a functional debrief session.

## A Cloudy Day Lament

Most adults pay lip service to the need for and the fun involved in play.

It's hard to combat society's interpretation of play and frivolity as being synonymous; and more difficult to maintain a playful attitude concomitant with the overwhelming seriousness of adulthood.

Even the vocabulary reeks of intent and purpose.

## General Reading for Extra Credit

Everyone knows that insurance coverage, liability concerns, and premium payments provide prime topics of discussion and debate whenever adventure educators get together. Amidst this seemingly endless round of issues is an uninformed attitude that really bugs me; i.e., the cavalier acceptance (mostly inadvertent) of accident-prone activities because they are traditional, followed by the mass non sequitur that insinuates any activity is dangerous (risky) if it appears to be. (This is a letter-to-the-editor written by the editor: noblesse oblige.)

I'm not going to quote a bunch of supportive statistics or try to write around the issues, so here's the tell-it-like-it-seems story!

We'll visit the traditional school gymnasium first and consider the ubiquitous 20' climbing rope (4 on the male side and 4 on the female side of the gym; c. 1949). What are these ropes for, swinging? I wish that were true, as more fun and upper body development would result than from their intended purpose — to climb. That's right, straight up 20', no belay. A 3/4" pad on the floor is situated beneath the rope to prevent scuffing the basketball court surface.

How many pull-ups can the typical American student do? I think the answer is 0.75! Climb a 20' rope? Maybe that's why the activity has a fairly good safety record — no one can get off the floor. But, is the climb potentially dangerous? Of course. So, why is it continued? As the *Fiddler on the Roof* would exclaim — **Tradition!**

A newspaper report recently quoted the following unbelievable statistic. (I'm paraphrasing this because I don't have the article in hand.) "Over the past five years, 44,000 (that's 3 zeros) individuals in the United States suffered a paralyzing type of injury as the result of participating in football." How many "paralyzing type of injuries" would result in cessation of all adventure programming? 5,000? 1,000? 200? How many fingers do you need to answer this one. Why the ridiculous discrepancy? **Tradition!**

I recently observed a school-sponsored activity that has been performed yearly for decades — the building and burning of a substantial pile of wood as part of a team sports pep rally. "Yeah, team — burn them Tigers!"

As I watched the students building and climbing the potential pyre (eventually 40-45' high), I kept my camera ready to record what I suspected would be the A.P. tragedy shot of the year. The building, torching and dancing (all quite impressive and entertaining) went off without a hitch — no falls, burns, or beer busts (they drank it all). But, the potential for disaster was undeniably near the surface (any closer than passing an oncoming car at 55 m.p.h.?). The fact that nothing happened provides an undisputed reason for a bigger and better fire next year — **Tradition!**

Here we are on the playground. **Whack!** There go a few teeth, or add a line of facial stitches from getting bopped by a hard seat swing.

**Scrunch!** Billy just jumped off the teeter-totter and let his sister drop, posterior first from six feet — broken ankle, compressed vertebrae, concussion.

Hey, let's centrifuge the new kid off the merry-go-round and see how far he goes. How about playing tag on that geodesic monkey bar dome? Or, let's run backward up the slide and...OK, I'm obviously (I think) making fun of traditional activities that have entertained children for years, including you and me, but you have to admit that the general feeling (cuz-that's-the-way-it-is) has a lot do do with what's accepted without question and what is suspiciously and tentatively attempted, or disregarded as a fad; i.e., Project Adventure and its genre.

It just bugs me, that's all. Thanks for listening. Editor's note: Letters to the editor that disagree with the editor are generally disregarded.

**Conservative Reveries**

When and where should I consider using helmets on my climbing wall? How long should I continue using the same rope? What kind of rope is best? Should students be allowed to belay?

I could add considerably to the above question list, because people are concerned about safety and safety systems — and rightly so, as accidents tend to produce a reluctance toward continued programming. Considering all this, I thought you would be interested in some pertinent quotes from an overseas publication on climbing walls.

"A suitable indoor climbing wall site is one that allows virtually unrestricted access."

"Put simply, there is no need for any rules or regulations to protect individual climbers on climbing walls."

"Nobody is more aware than the climber of the risks involved and to interfere by insisting on the use of ropes or helmets is to distort the normal process of training and inhibits the climber from developing the judgement on which his safety depends."

"How climbers climb is a matter of personal choice and nobody should interfere. Put simply, climbers can be left to conduct their own affairs without interference."

These quotes were under a chapter entitled, "Professional Management for Climbing Walls." These comments are not tongue-in-cheek, but were written by knowledgeable individuals well-schooled in climbing techniques and ethics.

The obvious discrepancy in safety concepts points out how different ideas concerning safety can develop among groups that have little contact and less communication. It might also indicate how the U.S. suit-conscious mentality has affected our conservative decision-making about risk activities.

In this case, I'm just reporting, not judging.

**Where Did "Guns" Go? or Pop Gun Paradise Lost**

At my tenth birthday party, I received (from the six party-goers) six cap pistols and a couple holsters. No fake lasers, flashing lights, recorded ricochets or popping corks — just plain **click-click** (occasional **bang**) cap guns that detonated their onomatopoeia projectiles with a full-mouthed explosion that was punctuated by a combination of facial, throat and salivary gymnastics that far surpassed any miniscule **snap** produced by the black-dotted red rolls of caps.

The smell of used caps was great ("rockets' red glare, and bombs bursting in air..."), and it almost made the tedious loading procedure worthwhile. But who wanted to mess with caps when your life was on the line?  I needed at least 200 rapid-fire shots for my imaginary combat exploits and being limited to 50 unreliable caps was an unthinkable handicap.  Caps were fine for setting off with a rock on the sidewalk (3 & 4 deep — not much louder, but more smoke) or for some laid-back target practice, but when the action started, there was no better incendiary than that produced vocally by the oral imagination of the warriors.  I had some of my best exploits with a homemade plywood machine gun.  How can I possibly write what the staccato oral bursts from that treasured bit of wood sounded like?  I can still do it — I just tried out my air-cooled .30 caliber Browning Automatic Rifle imitation (BAR for you aficionados), and it sounded pretty good — but at over 40 years old, you just don't go around orally imitating a machine gun without checking out the immediate area:  I'm in the bathroom, so it's OK!

Why don't kids play "guns" anymore?  Vietnam horrors?  Handgun tragedies?  Vicarious fascination with electronic games?  Whatever — it's too bad in some ways, because games involving imagination (currently like D&D) are the most vivid and require the best role-playing situations.  As violent as society has become (domestic crime and mayhem), it's lamentable that "guns" (I'm referring to any game of the genre, like Cops & Robbers or Cowboys), can be a vehemently resisted substitute for Little League and other organized small folks' sports, or TV, or transistor radios, etc.  I liked "guns," I don't like guns.

If I have inadvertently tripped anyone's letter-to-the-editor switch by my flippant referral to your favorite cause — I apologize.  Relax...put the pen down...it's OK.


### Sound Familiar?...

This discourse on risk, etc., is part of a letter I wrote in 1980.  It's mildly interesting to see how much things don't change.

"...as a result, everyone thinks they know how to tie a bowline the right way, and, of course, their method of rappelling is the only safe technique.  I think this, I'm-right-because-I've-been-doing-it-for-10-years mentality is beginning to permeate the ropes course field.

When not many people were 'ropes courseing' it, the techniques of building and use were pretty much ignored by everyone except the people who were using the facility.  Now the programmed adventure niche has been educationally established and the prophets of doom (protectors of the kiddies) are suggesting that this is high risk stuff.  So, predictably you have the oldtimers who resent having limitations put on their efforts and innovations and a newly concerned set of individuals (concerned about environment, safety, liability, their own regularity, etc.), that are in conflict, so you don't know what to think.

To be more specific...A ropes course is as risky as the people who build it, the material they use, and the techniques they employ. Driving a car with bald tires is a genuinely high risk activity. Walking across a high (30-50') Two Line Bridge that is made of aircraft cable with a back-up system, and with a capable person belaying with approved rope is a **low** risk activity, **but** it's **perceived** as high risk: therein lies the value, and the dilemma.

**PERCEPTION** - difficult, dangerous, risky, exciting

**ACTUAL** - fairly demanding, not dangerous, risky from a personal failure standpoint. Contains the common factor **excitement**, without which there is little to sustain the activity.

Perceived risk is a valuable teaching tool — actual high risk (drunken driving, drugs, solo climbing, rush-hour traffic) has nothing to do with programmatic adventure.

### A Developed Philosophy Toward Adventure Through Quotes - or the Mellowing of an Ex-Outward Bound Instructor

"Anything that doesn't kill you makes you stronger."
> — Paraphrase of a Nietzsche quote

"If the only choice is between pain and nothing, I would choose pain."

> — Unknown

"Pain levels come and go, but a recorded effort is here to stay."

"If you take care of your ass, your ass will take care of you."

> — Old Muledriver's saying

"If I'm going to be challenged, I'd rather it be on my own time."

"Be fit or be embarrassed."

"A little adventure is better than no adventure at all."

All non-credited quotes are the author's fault.

*Opinion* — A less than regular feature where the editor lays some heavy mind rap on you — 'cause who else is going to listen?

I have written, and often repeat, the following loaded statement, because I believe it and regularly experience it, not because I'm trying to sell anything, or proselytize a belief.

"It's not that Project Adventure (approach and curriculum) is so great, but rather that the alternatives aren't so great."

Is **PA** the answer, then? Is velcro better than the zipper? It's all relative and depends upon so many variables that it would be wasted words even attempting the maze of philosophical intent and definition. But the fact remains that knowledgeable people have become more accepting of the **PA** *Challenge By Choice* approach, or are just plain bored with the repetitious alternatives. Old line teachers (young ones, too) are changing their teaching style from dogmatic, dog-eared lesson plans, to a more free-wheeling and spontaneous style.

I'm not so naive as to presume that folks more cognitive than I could poke holes in such simplistic attempts at getting to the root of it all. The daily and crushingly sad facts of poverty, prejudice, poor health, mental illness, and the myriad ills of the world won't be much affected by an adventure approach to education. But the potential for an improved lifestyle (we're not just talking pedagogic stuff here) is undeniably available and will be predictably ignored by the majority of the population, while we struggle with the various obstacles that we build for ourselves. Defining problems is fairly easy, while forming the amalgam of nitty-gritty solutions within the context of our day-to-day lives is so complex and uncomfortable that it (good stuff) rarely happens and we continue to believe that everything is OK because it's currently not bad enough to say it isn't.

Project Adventure is no longer a Project, and has certainly become more than a well accepted variation on an Outward Bound theme. **PA** designates an appealing approach to life and in 25 words or less, here's what I mean. Life should be approached with the knowledge that an individual (self) is capable of doing more than that person initially perceives can be accomplished. Indeed, Project Adventure has become a generic designation for an approach to life that involves the practiced ability to move beyond **self**-expectation.

Then why doesn't everyone perform and eventually achieve to a higher level? Because part of going beyond self-expectation involves temporary stretching of the psyche, including various levels of physical pain (sports-related, losing weight, etc.), emotional discomfort (personal relationships — particularly those involved with marriage and children), self-doubt and fear of failure, and many negative what ifs... (...I don't' make it?...appear the fool?...get hurt?).

Perhaps the greatest block to personal progress in most desired growth areas is regularly accepting obvious discomfort, because it's a known entity, rather than risking possibly greater unknown pain in order to gain greater rewards. A life of quiet desperation is an existence of drop-forged fear — strongly built and impressively long-lasting.

Do you know how I can get away with espousing such sweeping and fragmented philosophical statements of personal opinion?

- Because the editor has the final say as to what goes in BOT's, and I'm the editor.
- I don't have a Ph.D.
- I just turned 50, and genuinely middle-aged people are supposed to be opinionated.
- I try not to take myself too seriously, and you shouldn't either.
- And, more pertinently, what I've indicated above is basically true.

## Chapter 12
# *Safety*

### Flying Squirrel Rescue

No, you won't need a rescue scenario for the Flying Squirrel event, but since I just detailed how the rope-haul system works, I'd like to pass along how this pulley system can be used in a ropes course situation.

Imagine someone stuck on a zip wire about 25' away from the take-off platform and maybe 35' off the ground. One current student retrieval method involves sending a suspended rescuer down the cable from the platform to the stuck student (hanging less-than-merrily from his/her Swiss seat); then attaching harness to harness, using a locking carabiner, cutting the stuck person's static suspension rope with a knife (scissors) and subsequently lowering both individuals to the ground.

In order to preclude the rescuer having to descend the cable, try this following up and down technique and notice the *Flying Squirrel* similarities.

This indicated gear arrangement should be available on site. ROSA gold pulley (steel sheave) attached with a locking carabiner to a ROSA red pulley (aluminum sheave). The staff person on the zip platform attaches (snatch block capability) the ROSA gold pulley to the zip cable and reeves a length of KM III rope through the ROSA red pulley, so that both ends of the rope reach the ground. Allow the pulley/rope arrangement to "zip" down to the stuck student, then pull on the doubled ropes in the direction of the cable slope to see if this simple action will cause the double wheel zip pulley to become unstuck. If the zip pulley remains lodged, tie a bowline-on-a-bight in one end of the KM III rope and clip both loops into a rescuer's harness. The following action practically duplicates the Flying Squirrel haul system. Using 8-10 people, haul the rescuer up to the person to be rescued, clip in to one another face-to-face (use 2-3 interlocked carabiners to facilitate this attachment), complete the cut-away, and lower both individuals to the ground.

If you have been to a Project Adventure Advanced Skills & Standards Workshop, the previous explanation should make sense, and provide you with an alternate rescue technique.

If you are trained in ropes course use, but have never tried a high rescue, proceed with caution and with a back-up belay, in case...

If you are a reader who just wants to try something new — don't.

## Staples Testing

There was some initial doubt as to a staple's potential to withstand a leader fall, if used as a belay anchor point. So, a test was arranged that would duplicate a lead climbing fall on the ropes course. Two anchor points were tested: a 5/8" shoulder lag eye screw (SLES) and a 1/2" galvanized staple.

A 16" diameter red oak was chosen for the first test series. A 5/8" SLES was placed by pre-drilling the tree with a 1/2" spade bit to the entire depth of the screw portion and then turned in with a cheater rod. The 1/2" staple was hammered in with a hand sledge (a claw hammer won't work), so that there was approximately one inch remaining within the interior space between end of staple and the trunk.

Both anchor points were located in the tree about 12' above the ground, and about 10" apart.

The object, as per the U.I.A.A. drop test, was to apply a considerable falling force to the anchors individually. The falling object chosen was a 150 lb. spool of cable. The attachment between spool and anchor was a 7' length of 1/2" diameter static kernmantle rescue rope.

Using an overhead pulley, the spool was hauled seven feet above each tree anchor and dropped, insuring a free-fall of approximately 14 ft. Each anchor was tested three separate times.

*Results* — The 5/8" SLES exhibited the slightest downward bend (which may well have been separation of wood fibers) and the 1/2" staple showed no movement at all.

The second phase of this test was performed identically, except a large diameter white pine tree was used.

The 5/8" SLES was started with a few blows from a hand sledge and then turned in the remainder of the way using a cheater rod. Two 1/2" staples were also placed with the hand sledge; one oriented vertically to the trunk and the other horizontally.

*Results* — The 5/8" SLES broke on the first fall. Apparently, the softer wood of the pine allowed a bending of the outer portion of the SLES shank, while the deeper fluted portion remained stationary. The break occurred at the first turn of the screw.

The vertically driven 1/2" staple showed no movement after three falls. The horizontally placed 1/2" staple bent noticeably on the first fall and even more so on the second. The third fall caused it to pull out.

It had been our initial thinking that a horizontal placement of a staple was stronger than a vertical orientation (due to an earlier pull-test using a come-along), but the results of this more realistic dynamic fall test were undeniable.

As an aside to all these wham-bam tests, the bowline knots used on each end of the attachment lines were easily undone after the testing; another indication why not to use a figure 8 loop in a situation where you know the knot will be severely stressed.

Many thanks to the unselfish efforts of this year's PATT (Project Adventure Testing Team) who gave up valuable (?) office time to brave the rigors of a spring afternoon (sun, bugs, sore muscles).

## Helmets — Who Needs 'Em?

You want to know what I think about helmets?...I'm going to tell you anyway!

Helmets cause my head to sweat and my ears to get cold. They are troublesome to adjust and often still don't fit right. Shared by lots of heads, helmets are at the least a hassle, and at the worst, a health and safety concern. However, helmets are necessary safety apparel for selected ropes course elements.

Helmets are necessary to: lessen potential liability concerns; reduce the severity or chance of head injury from things being dropped or knocked loose (wrenches, rocks, bolts, canned fruit), and more pertinently, to prevent a bare moving head from making contact with hard stationary objects.

Project Adventure requires wearing helmets on the following high ropes course elements.

*Cat Walk — Dangle Duo — Pamper Pole and Pamper Plank — Wooden Block Climbing Wall* (indoor and outdoor).

Purchase quality rock climbing helmets that adjust easily, fit well, and are certified to protect heads. Wear head protection when the situation demands prudence (your judgment). Try not to let your judgment be guided (manipulated) by fear or intimidation.

If an individual feels more comfortable wearing a helmet on all the elements, and if that sometimes symbolic head protection allows the student to feel more comfortable trying a difficult ropes course event, let 'em wear it.

End of helmet diatribe.

## OPB's (Occupational Protective Belts)

People who are newly involved with adventure programming and particularly with ropes courses predictably develop a tactile and functional fascination with harnesses and protective belts. This may be a survival reaction to the superintendent's edict that "You have been chosen to implement the Project Adventure curriculum." Fade to poignant images and pictures of people flying through the air while disengaging from cables and trapezes...Aargh!

Having used a variety of these save-your-life devices over the years, here's a personal recommendation and a couple caveats.

If you are going to be working in trees or positioning yourself on a pole for an extended time (over 15 minutes), I think the Klein tree climber's belt is a best buy. You will have to add a section of 1/2" diameter multiline rope as a tree wrap-around, but that's no big deal, and if you can't figure out the rope/harness arrangement, give me a call and I'll provide some verbal assistance (508-468-7981).

There are many OPB's on the market, but don't buy one for ropes course work. These narrow belts are not made for leaning against (freeing your hands for work) and, more significantly, they are not manufactured to sustain a substantial static fall. A static ending to a 4' fall would probably rupture the buckle arrangement and if it didn't, the single no-stretch belt around your mid-section might cause internal problems, resulting in more than a tummy ache.

If you're climbing on a ropes course, either wear a commercial rock climbing harness or tie on a Studebaker wrap using 1" tubular webbing. Wearing one of these pelvic protectors is still not going to make a static fall feel good, but at least you'll be around for another one.

Write to the following company for the address of a local distributor of their products. Klein sells telephone pole hardware including high quality safety gear. Ask for a catalog and the location of a local distributor.

>Klein Company
>7200 McCormick Boulevard
>Chicago, IL 60645

To purchase or look at a rock climbing harness, check your yellow pages for a climbing retail store near you, or write to the following company for their catalog.

>R.E.I. (Recreational Equipment, Inc.)
>Seattle, WA 98188

Project Adventure, Inc., sells the Troll rock climbing harness. Write for a free Ropes Course Source catalog. Box 100, Hamilton, MA 01936.

### Climbing Rope Replacement, Etc.

Of all the technical questions that I'm asked, "When should I replace my climbing ropes?" is the one for which I have become most reluctant to offer a definitive answer. There are so many variables and unknowns in the "life" of a climbing rope that a definitive answer is at best presumptuous and at the least, dangerous. Here are some cordage facts to ponder.

- New England Ropes, Inc. (the rope company in New Bedford, Massachusetts, that provides Project Adventure, Inc., with most of their cordage) has the following to say about checking rope for wear. "*No type of visual inspection* can be guaranteed to accurately and precisely determine actual residual rope strength. When the fibers show wear in any given area, the rope should be respliced, downgraded, or replaced."

- Estimating rope usage or wear by measuring rope elongation is not a valid technique. A well used rope length will actually measure shorter than the same rope length when new.

- Use of shear reduction devices dramatically increases the load-bearing capacity of a rope.

- Climbing ropes display an impressively large ultimate tensile strength, but this same rope can be easily cut by sharp edges and as easily burned by cigarettes.

### *Threaded Rod*

Do not use threaded rod for critical connectors on a ropes course. If there is any flex movement of the rod under pressure, the rod has a greater chance of breaking because of its threaded nature.

Another inherent danger is that a threaded eye may rotate off the rod unless a cotter pin is installed.

The only advantage to using threaded rod is its length (usually up to 72"), and the capability of using an eye on either end of the rod.

If the rod head is loose or placed under alternating pressures (walking on a cable?), the chance of eventually snapping the rod is greater than your program can afford.

### Cable Strength

People who are thinking about building a ropes course often ask, "How long does a section of cable last?", or "Just how strong is that stuff?" As the result of a winter storm, I now have a firsthand answer, rather than having to quote destructive testing tensile strength figures.

The folks at the Hamilton-Wenham Regional High School (the site of Project Adventure's original ropes course) called our office recently, and said that suggested that we bring the chainsaws. That was no joke, because two large beech trees had come down as the result of high winds (and old age). One of the trees had fallen directly onto the 280 ft. zip wire cable. They had mentioned this, so when I arrived, I expected to see broken cable and snapped bolts. What I did observe was a surprise. The falling tree had pushed the zip cable all the way to the ground, but the cable had not broken and although the connector bolts had bent, they were also still intact. The near support tree (18" diameter trunk with the platform attached) had been pulled over to about a 45° angle. There was still a considerable amount of tension on the cable. The significant fact remains that the entire length of a 12-year old non-galvanized fiber core cable and the connectors were intact.

It's pertinent to also report that the falling tree (diameter at the base was 27") was not simply uprooted, but snapped off about two feet above the ground, so that the force of the falling tree was considerable. The zip wire was actually hit by the ill-fated tree about 30 feet up the trunk.

The denouement of this action-packed adventure vignette is that: There's a lot of beech in 2 ft. stove sections curing for next winter's use, and a mess of cable has been retired to that ole junk yard in the sky. Now, on to a bigger and better zip.

## Tested for Safety

"The U.I.A.A. (International Union of Alpine Associations) has established several standards regarding the strength of rope when subjected to a fall (fall test), its ability to reduce the shock to a falling climber (impact force), and its elongation (static and at impact).

"The U.I.A.A. Fall Test duplicates, in the laboratory, the effects of a severe fall. 'Severe' designates large forces on rope as well as climber. The test is performed thus:

"An 80-kg weight is dropped from a height of five meters. It is held by a 2.8 meter length of rope passed over a 10 mm carabiner edge. Two measurements are taken: the number of falls held (five is the minimum for U.I.A.A. approval), and the impact force on the weight (1200 kg maximum). These figures provide a useful starting point in the comparison of different climbing ropes."

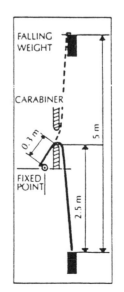

## A Safe Stack

If the idea of stacking paper cores (see *Paul's Balls)* to a height of 8 or more is distressing from a safety standpoint, or if obtaining the paper cores has proved difficult, try stacking firmly-inflated automobile inner tubes. If the stack falls over in mid-attempt, there is minimized danger of injury — falling inner tubes don't dent heads.

You may experience a couple problems using inner tubes and one is finding them, as most auto tires are now tubeless. Another hassle is storage (you will need about 25-35 tubes for a world class effort), unless you plan to deflate the tubes each time. If this deflation action makes sense, your time priorities are our of sync with the world.

## Not a Knot

This is what happens when a square (reef) knot collapses as the result of not being protected by overhand safety knots tied on either side of the square knot.

This simple but dramatic demonstration is quite effective toward convincing students that safety knots are more than just "window dressing."

## Hickory Jump Trapeze Bar

A young girl broke both of her wrists as the result of an unfortunate accident on a ropes course, because she was swinging on the Hickory Jump bar without spotters' support and she lost her grip. Such unsupervised use can be alleviated by substituting a trapeze arrangement for the bar. In this way, the trapeze can be removed after the supervised activity is over by simply unclipping the carabiners or rapid links that connect the trapeze bar to the support cables.

## Warning — Unsafe

*Wow!  Heavy rubric.*  But, worthwhile knowing.

One of the original Project Adventure publications that preceded *Cows' Tails & Cobras* recommended an initiative problem called, The Four Poster.  The problem involved supporting a number of students off the ground using only 4 substantial posts (cut limbs) and a sling rope.  The solution involves piling people on top of a hastily fabricated tee-pee arrangement utilizing the poles and rope.

The solution (the only solution that makes sense) is unsafe.  There is almost no way of insuring an individual's safety because of the variables of body position on the tee-pee, knot unreliability and ground condition (mud is a sure-fire ankle breaker).  Cut up those well-cured poles into 2 ft. lengths for the ole wood stove and pile your students with confidence onto the All Aboard.

## Destructive Testing, or "You Make It, — I'll Break It"

Here's good news for those of you trying to prove a safety point.  The following load figures represent the breaking or disfiguring points for a number of commonly used ropes course fixtures.

*The tests were performed by the Arnold Greene Testing Laboratories in Natick, Massachusetts, as a contract fulfillment for Project Adventure, Inc.*

*Happily, all items broke at above their maximum advertised levels.*

> 5/16" strand vise - cable broken inside the strand vise at 8,520 lbs.
>
> 3/8" pear-shaped link - connecting 5/16" cable broke at 9,660 lbs. Link did not disfigure.
>
> SARA Rescue Pulley - *One* eye broke at 6,220 lbs.
>
> 5/16" swage - slipped at 8,400 lbs.  No breakage.
>
> "Spring Thing" - 600 lbs. for complete compression.  3,660 lbs. for disfigurement.
>
> Open 1/2" rapid link - 1,650 lbs.        } compare — this strength;
>
> Closed 1/2" rapid link - 22,000 lbs.     } discrepancy is significant
>
> ROSA Gold Pulley - 11,400 lbs.
>
> Spin/Static Pulley - 11,650 lbs.

**Running Self-Belay**

Based on personal experience, other teachers' war stories, and an article I recently read in the *Climbing Magazine*, "Off Belay" #46, I want to re-emphasize some negative feelings about static self-belays on ropes courses.

If you are not familiar with this type of belay — good; you're better off. But for the sake of being knowledgeable in the field, here's a quick run-down.

Picture a high Two Line Bridge set-up. The climber ties or arranges something around his/her body (Swiss seat, sit harness, Studebaker wrap), and from this tie-in, a short length of rope extends to the belay cable, and via a carabiner/bowline, is clipped to this cable. If a fall takes place, the static rope obviously prevents the climber from falling to the ground, but the hapless hanger usually ends up somewhere below the bottom cable, suspended.

It is this suspended position that presents a serious health problem. It is an unusually adept student that is physically capable of climbing her/his own static belay rope to get back up onto the Two Line Bridge, or Burma Bridge, or whatever. The suspended student is temporarily "safe," but stuck and becoming rapidly and increasingly uncomfortable. If the tie-in is a bowline around the waist, unconsciousness can result *in less than a minute*, and depending upon the position of the suspended body (horizontal or vertical), brain damage can result unless there is a *quick* (less than two to three minutes) means of getting the student safely down.

If the student is in a harness arrangement, there is more "hang" time available, but according to results that have been gleaned from carefully controlled tests, even the most expensive harnesses can cause "loss of blood pressure, respiratory distress, intense pain, and a loss of consciousness" within 15 minutes.

Think it through, could you get a suspended student safely down in less than 15 minutes? Do you have an extra coil of rope at the ropes course site? Extra carabiners? A knife? Do you or your working partners have the knowledge or expertise necessary? (Read how to perform the *Flying Squirrel* rescue in the Safety section of this book.)

Obviously, what I'm saying is DO NOT use a running self-belay. A bottom belay (belayer-to-upper cable-to student) is the safest method, and is applicable under almost all circumstances where a belay is necessary.

## *Where the Accidents Occur*

There is a generally held misconception that adventure programming leads to a higher rate of accidents (per time of participation) than in more traditional physical education classes. Not true, as quite the opposite is actually the case. This erroneous thinking stems from observing or contemplating the commitment necessary to attempt a high ropes course event. On most of the high events, there is a built-in "perceived danger" that is further cultivated by the programmer to make the event more challenging; hopefully resulting in a greater sense of accomplishment when the "impossible" has been attempted.

There are some ropes course elements that, because of their nature (safety depends on spotting), result in a higher chance of an injury occurring. I'm not in any way trying to blacklist these following events, only trying to make you aware of things that have happened in the past, so that being forewarned, you can take steps to make the events safer in the future.

Unfortunately, I don't have the space to explain the rules for each event. Refer to *Silver Bullets* and *Challenge By Choice* for a write-up on most of these stunts, initiative problems, and events.

1. *Electric Fence* — injury areas: ankles, wrists, and neck.
   *Do not allow...*
   
   (a)...indiscriminate (but well-intentioned) tossing of people over the rope.

   (b)...diving over the rope and attempting a shoulder roll.

   *Encourage...*

   (a)...constant spotting — instructors should spot the first couple of students over the rope.

   (b)...a compassionate attitude.

   (c)...a concern for efficiency rather than time.

2. *Stump Jump* — injury areas: sternum, ribs, ankle.
   *Do not allow...*

   (a)...rapid sequence jumps; the spotters can't keep up.

   (b)...attempts that are the result of peer pressure and emotion, rather than a personal desire to "make the jump." This is a hard one to judge — be conservative.

   *Encourage...*

   (a)...surrounding the landing platform with spotters (at least 8).

   (b)...making a trial jump from the landing platform to an outlined area on the ground.

   (c)...read #2 (b) above.

3. *Hickory Jump* — injury areas: back, neck, sternum, ribs.

   *Do not allow...*

   (a)...swinging through after a jump. The spotters must stop this action to prevent a dorsal trip to the turf.

   *Encourage...*

   (a)...a minimum of 6 spotters.

   (b)...removing spotters' wrist watches.

   (c)...checking the stumps for soundness before allowing a jump (give the stump a good, lateral kick).

   (d)...pre-jump stretching exercises of the shoulder muscles

4. *Reach for the Sky* — injury areas: wrist and arm.

   *Do not allow...*

   (a)...stacking people 4 high, unless a belay is used.

   *Encourage...*

   (a)...lateral spotting (right next to the wall on both sides of the people pile).

   (b)...removing pencils, pens, combs from pockets.

5. *Wall* — injury areas: wrist, arm, ankle.

   *Do not allow...*

   (a)...more than 4 on top of the wall at one time.

   (b)...anyone to hang over the wall, unless they are supported by two people.

   (c)...jumping off the back of the wall.

   *Encourage...*

   (a)...lateral spotting as in #4.

6. *Balance Broom* — (Witches' Broom) — injury areas: fingers, shoulder.

   *Encourage...*

   (a)...spotting by at least 3 people (let the participant achieve a disoriented state, but prevent a "crash").

7. *Cargo Nets* — injury areas: wrist, arm, neck.

   *Do not allow...*

   (a)...rolling head-first over the top of the net.

   (b)...climbing up and over a net that is 10-15' high, without an overhead belay.

*Encourage...*

>(a)...spotting by 2 people at the bottom of the net if
someone is swinging into the net.

I have observed or heard of injuries having occurred on all of the elements mentioned; these are not empty concerns. Take note of how many of these elements involve a belay.

Those of you who have taken a chance or two in life (getting out of bed or driving to work), realize that living is chronic chance-taking. A number of people were killed a few years ago while eating ice cream at a soda fountain by a badly aimed airplane — how would that look on your epitaph? Kinda' makes you want to go out and do something crazy...like taking cholesterol pills.

If we can share an awareness of the hazards that are combined with our work, we're better able to anticipate and reduce the consequences.

# Chapter 13
# *Humor*

Nilson cartoons that for some reason or another have not seen print. They deserve a few chuckles by those of you who have proctored or participated in these initiatives.

***Barometer Machinations — or, Three Ways a Barometer Can Be Used to Determine the Height of a Building***

Think for at least 17 seconds before peeking at the technical answers below.

1. Lower the barometer by string from the roof and measure the string.

2. Drop the barometer off the roof and note the time it takes to fall — Re: formula for falling bodies.
3. Find the building superintendent and offer to give him the barometer if he will tell you the height.

## Rent-a-Friend

The title of this blurb refers to an advertisement that I chanced on recently (also called Plugged-in-Pals). For $19.95, you get a tape of a gregarious former cab driver who tells you all about himself and asks about **you**. Pauses are built-in, so you can talk back — a provided workbook suggests humorous responses. I've not included the address — this is too much!

Also available to cat lovers "who would prefer to avoid kitty litter," an ersatz cat (Petster) can fulfill all your petting needs without the hassle of hairballs and torn screens. This furry, fake-out (complete with pink ears and black whiskers) plays on its own (depending on its diet of Duracell), and purrs when stroked (I'm not sure where). And, if you leave *it* alone, it goes to sleep only to "stir at any sound, touch, or shadow." I wonder if this mechanical marvel lands on its feet if dropped upside-down?

## Zen and the Abattoir of Time

This is a verbatim copy of a note left on my desk recently by a frequenter of my office and sometimes contributor to BOT's (inadvertently, this time).

"Talk to you tomorrow (or today, as you read this on Friday; or is it still Thursday, in which case tomorrow still applies). Whenever..."

Name withheld to protect the identity and whereabouts of the author, who is currently struggling somewhere between Thursday and Saturday.

## Letters From Willie Welfare

These excerpts from actual letters received by the Welfare Department, are for real.

Both hilariously funny and sad — for your enjoyment and appreciation of education.

"I am forwarding my marriage certificate and my six children. I had seven, but one died which was baptized on a half of sheet of paper."

"I cannot get sick pay. I have six children. Can you tell me why?"

"I am glad to report that my husband who was reported missing is now dead."

"This is my eighth child. What are you going to do about it?"

"Please find for certain if my husband is dead. The man I live with now won't eat or sleep or do nothing till he knows."

"I am forwarding my marriage certificate and my three children one of which was a mistake, as you will see."

"My husband got his project cut off two weeks ago and I haven't had any relief since."

"I have no children as yet, as my husband is a bus driver and works night and day."

"In accordance with instructions, I have given birth to twins in the enclosed envelope."

"I want money as quick as I can get it. I have been in bed with the doctor for two weeks and he doesn't do me no good. If things don't improve, I will have to send for another doctor."

## Procreation — The Generic Game

This extremely popular, one-on-one activity has been around for years, and is played enthusiastically by literally billions of dedicated athletes and non-athletes alike.

As assumed of any traditional activity, procreation has undergone numerous rule changes and strategy ploys over the years, but the basic game has endured to produce its current and largely unchanged (c. Austrolopiticus) form. *Object* — varies demographically, but the basic game has primarily to do with the viability of species.

*Rules and Procedures* — Have your group diad-up, and as a pair, attempt to fulfill the biological destiny assigned to your species. To begin play, the male member

## Censored

This cartoon, drawn some years ago by Bob Nilson (cartoonist who illustrated *Cows' Tails & Cobras* and *Silver Bullets)* was put (years ago) in the holding file because the hapless individual about to receive the hook was/is a stereotype.

It is, however, a fine, political-type cartoon, and is closer to the truth than many of us would like to admit.

*Bag of Tricks* is, after all, an unexpurgated quarterly...kind of...

*The following excerpts are from essays and themes written by COLLEGE students. Ungabaleegable!*

"On the night of April 14, 1865, Lincoln went to the theatre and got shot in the seat by one of the actors in a moving picture show. The believed assinator was John Wilkes Booth, a suspended insane actor. This ruined Booth's career."

"France was a very serious state. The French Revolution was accomplished before it happened..."

"Queen Eliz. was the virgin queen. As a queen she was a success. When Eliz. exposed herself before her troops they all shouted 'Hurrah.' Then her Navy went out and defeated the Spanish Armadillo."

"Franklin invented electricity by rubbing two cats backwards and declared 'a horse divided against itself cannot stand.' Franklin died in 1790 and is still dead."

"Bach was the most famous composer in the world, and so was Handel. Handel was half German, half Italian, and half English. Beethoven wrote loud music because he was so deaf."

"Christopher Columbus circumcised the world with a 100-foot clipper, later landing the Pilgrims on Plymouth Rock. The winter of 1620 was a hard one for these settlers. Many people died and many babies were born. Captain John Smith was responsible for this."

You have to accept the above with a sense of humor and with a declaration of great sympathy for the English professor that had to red pencil the papers. "...defeated the Spanish Armadillo," is that great, or what?

\*     \*     \*     \*     \*     \*

Project Adventure has been offering workshops in various educational areas for years. Recently, the staff did some brainstorming in response to the expressed need for clinic diversification; the results are as follows.

Any reader response? Additions? How about a workshop on "Adventure and Your Horoscope?"

**Future Facetious Workshops**

*Self-Improvement Workshops*

— Creative Suffering

— You and Your Birthmark

— Ego Gratification Through Violence

— Dealing with Post-Self-Realization Depression

— Whine Your Way to Alienation

— How to Overcome Self-Doubt Through Pretense and Ostentation

— Overcoming Peace of Mind

— Guilt Without Sex

*Business Career Workshops*

— Money Can Make You Rich

— Talking Good So You Can Improve Speech and Get a Better Job

— I Made $100 in Real Estate

— Under-Achiever's Guide to Very Small Business Opportunities

— Filler Phrases for Thesis Writers

*Home Economics Workshops*

— How You Can Convert Your Family Room Into a Garage

— Basic Kitchen Taxidermy

— Sinus Drainage at Home

— 101 Other Uses for Your Vacuum Cleaner

*Health and Fitness Workshops*

— Exorcism and Acne

— High Fiber Sex

— Bio-Feedback and How to Stop It

— Skate Your Way to Regularity

— Optional Body Functions

— Tap Dance Your Way to Social Ridicule

## Annotated Ropes Course & Adventure Curriculum Black-Listed Word & Phrase List

There are a few words and terms that, although frequently used in the abstract and often out of context, denote such pejorative bodily and emotional consequences, vis a vis adventure, that their use must be assiduously avoided...and occasionally abetted if things get too serious.

1. Almost all those gems of graffiti which have been clandestinely inked, cut, burned, and otherwise emblazoned on THE WALL. A 12' wall, that fabricated bastion to the attainment of the impossible, is the quintessential "blank page" for unknown authors to anonymously vent anger, joy, frustration, and, of course, to vividly describe in the vernacular, the vice-principal's sexual preferences, generic quirks, and other idiosyncratic exotica.

2. "Oops!" Not well received as a belay or spotting exclamation.

3. As a means of explaining the braking system (not breaking) on a zip wire, describing the terminus as coming to a *dead stop*, seems a bit final.

4. Carabiners are called many things, and some of the abbreviated terms are both descriptive and useful. However, with a group of interested onlookers in attendance (parents), calling to your belayer, "Do you have any crabs?" might result in some understandable confusion.

5. A shoulder lag eye screw, a useful ropes course hardware item, produces a colorful acronym: SLES, pronounced, of course, sleaze. It makes obvious sense then, that the leather pouch which attaches to a worker's safety harness is called a SLES-bag. Again, be sure of your audience before calling for carabiners and shoulder lag eye screws in the workmen's vernacular.

6. The buried anchor point that secures a guy line is called a "dead man." It would be occupationally unthinkable to call it anything else. Notwithstanding the other worldly aspect of the term, could *dead woman* be substituted 50% of the time?

7. If a ropes course builder uses 5/8" diameter cable to build a Burma Bridge, s/he has used cable that is obviously overly strong for its intended use. In this context, the phrase "overkill" has been inappropriately and frequently used. Try "over-engineered" — much more acceptable and technically accurate.

## Not-So-Brave New World

Recognize anything from this delightful and devastating scenario?
Excerpted from the Yurt Foundation, 1987 calendar.

"Once upon a time, the animals decided that they must do something heroic to meet the problems of a 'new world.' So, they organized a school.

They adopted an activity curriculum consisting of running, climbing, swimming, and flying. To make it easier to administer the curriculum, all the students took *all* the subjects.

The duck was excellent in swimming — in fact, better than his instructor, but he made only passing grades in flying and was very poor in running. Since he was slow in running, he had to stay after school and also drop swimming in order to practice running. This kept up until his web feet were badly worn and he was only average in swimming. But average was acceptable in the school, so nobody worried about that except the duck.

The rabbit started at the top of the class in running, but had a nervous breakdown because of so much make-up in swimming.

The squirrel was excellent in climbing until he developed a frustration in the flying class, where his teacher made him start from the ground up, instead of from the treetop down. He also developed 'Charlie horses' from over-exertion, and then got a C in climbing and a D in running.

The eagle was a problem child and was disciplined severely. In the climbing class, he beat all the others to the top of a tree, but insisted on using his own way to get there.

At the end of the year, an abnormal eel that could swim exceedingly well and also run, climb, and fly a little, had the highest average and was valedictorian.

The prairie dogs stayed out of school and fought the tax levy because the administration would not add digging and burrowing to the curriculum. They apprenticed their child to a badger, and later joined the groundhogs and the gophers to start a successful private school."

## Chapter 14
# *Miscellaneous*

**Tic Tac Tedium**

I've never liked Tic Tac Toe because when I was a kid, someone always seemed to be using up or messing up my clean sheets of paper by scribbling

on an empty sheet and *then* saying, "You wanna play?" or "Come on, you first." People artlessly criss-crossing my untouched 3 hole lined notebook paper with a messy #1 pencil (crayon was the worst), and the fact that I usually lost did not increase my tic-tac-toe training time. But some people like the game, so here's a variation to extend your playing time — uck!

Create the minimum grid cypher on someone else's clean white sheet of paper. Give one player 4 pennies and the other player 4 nickels. Play the game in a regular fashion. If the metronome-like moves end up in a "cats" game (about every time, if the players are paying any attention at all), continue playing by alternating turns and sliding a coin until someone eventually ends up with THREE IN A ROW. Great fun, eh? No? Forget it.

**Word Association Adventure Potential Test** — More universally recognized as the **Rohnke/WAAPT**

Here's a test that measures practically nothing (sound familiar?), but it's fun to take and administer. The list can obviously be added to or subtracted from, depending on your audience. The real beauty of this non-evaluative gem (as compared to those super-serious tests steeped in validity), is that you can feel justified in completely ignoring the results — because Karl made up the questions and format, and what does he know?

Offer the following words printed on a photocopied sheet with a space left next to each word. Record the sport, activity, or item associated with the word. If you don't want to go to the trouble of recording answers, give the words verbally and ask for a response — self-grading for fragile egos.

Try the test yourself! How can you refuse? I'm not offering any answers because you are the resident expert, and anyway...we might disagree.

There are some words included in this list that are practically generic and can be associated with more than one activity. Grade liberally; remember, everyone gets a ribbon.

| | | |
|---|---|---|
| **Ensolite** | **Beal** | **Ambient Pressure** |
| **Bent Shaft** | **Hang Ten** | **5.10** |
| **Counter Force** | **Self-Arrest** | **Schraeder** |
| **Pintle & Gudgeon** | **UIAA** | **EB's or RD's** |
| **Fish Scale** | **Herringbone** | **J Stroke** |
| **Wedeln** | **Bong** | **Kabar** |
| **Shimano** | **Klister** | **Side Pull** |
| **Embolism** | **Kevlar** | **Draw** |
| **Loft** | **Sticht** | **Jam** |
| **Telemark** | **REI** | **Jibe-O-Duck** |
| **Zipper the Pins** | **Friends** | **Ferry** |
| **Eddy Turn** | **Optimus III** | **Arch-Thousand** |
| **33 PSI** | **Glissading** | **Cordura** |
| **Belay** | **Svea** | **Wanigan** |
| **Brace** | **Gaiters** | **Etrier** |
| **Sheets** | **BCD** | **Presta** |
| **Cadence** | **Nikonos V** | **ANSI** |
| **Gaff Rig** | **Munter Hitch** | **60/40** |
| **Mantle** | **Loran** | **End Shifter** |
| **Chock** | **Piolet** | **Jumar** |
| **Blue Wax** | **Bergschrund** | **Victorinox** |
| **Vibram** | **Catching a Crab** | **J Valve** |

| | | |
|---|---|---|
| Rolling Resistance | May Day | Hot Curl |
| Skirt | Sun Cups | PFD |
| Standing Waves | Feathering | Skeg |
| MSR | Slalom | Prusik |
| PLF | Dia-Compe | Declination |
| Blue Hole | Silva | Randall |
| XXX Beaver | Lignostone | RURP |
| Spenco | Twist Lock | Bat Hook |
| Tumblehome or Rocker | Bonk | Para-Pente |
| Third Hand | Grundwalla | DIN or ASA |
| Smearability | Long Horn | Hot Pogies |
| Drafting | Keeper Hole | Shark Skin |

**Pipe Line**

### A Tip from Terry

Refer to *Big Word*. "Print each word in a different colored felt marker or highlighter and run that marker over the top edge of the letter cards for that word. If (i.e., when) the letter cards get mixed together, they are then easy to sort out quickly." From Terry Knight, Kitchener, Ontario, Canada.

An additional quote from Terry's letter. "Games that I like from BOT's I write up on index cards so that they are handy. I keep them at school so that when I (or someone else on the staff) needs a certain game or initiative problem, they are easy to find and refer to. Kids love them. We now have a GAMES unit in each grade, and you guessed it, we never do things like basketball, volleyball, etc., *in that unit*."

Yes, I did guess it, and I agree. I underlined *in that unit* above because I think traditional, competitive games are great fun to play at times — not all the time.

### Sand Sliding

When I was a teenager, growing up in Hawaii (c. 1954), I learned how to sand slide. I continued beach skimming while living in California and have even pursued some summer gliding here in Massachusetts at Crane's Beach. If you live near the shore or vacation there, this little-known, fast-moving activity is worth trying to learn.

Of the 275 or so people that BOT's goes out to each quarter, I'll bet there are less than 5 that will actually try sand sliding, but writing about skimming is nostalgic therapy (it's December — HELP!) if only for me, and if just one person becomes proficient, it will be worth the space and time. Even if you are a sand board cognoscente, I'll bet my board design dimensions will provide you with a longer and more stable ride. Is the hook set? Better read this, or you may miss out on the next national fad.

The object of sand sliding is to stand-up ride a shaped plywood board on the beach for as long a distance as possible over the thin layer of water that results from a breaking and receding wave.

Rides of 100 feet on a gentle beach slope are not uncommon on a good day (smooth flat sand at near low tide), and even longer rides (100-200 yards) can be accomplished when working as a team. But first you need a board.

If you have ever seen someone sand skimming, they were probably using a round board. After having tried many shapes and sizes over the years, I think the following board dimensions will give you the best ride, and it's not round.

Buy a 4' x 8' section of 1/2" marine plywood (it's the smallest section that most lumber yards will sell). From this piece, you can fashion two boards — one for you and one for the little boy who lives down the lane. Cut the 4' x 8' in half so that you have two 2' x 4' pieces. Measure down 9" and across 9" from one of the corners down the edges, and draw a line connecting these two marks. Scribe the same measurement lines on the opposite short corner. Using a circular saw, or whatever kind you have, cut along these two dotted lines, producing a board shape as illustrated.

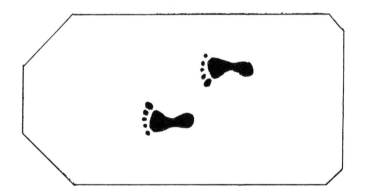

At the opposite end of the board, measure 2" up and 2" across on both sides. Cut along the connecting dotted line as above. Refer to the illustration.

Using a medium rasp and then sandpaper, smooth off these cut corners to produce a contoured rounded shape that is less apt to do harm to your body if the board hits you; i.e., if you hit the board.

Using a power sander (or by hand if you're on an island with nothing else to do), contour the front end (9" cuts) so that at the board tip at least 1/4" has been removed from the depth (thickness). Begin sanding 18" back from the front of the board. Also, contour the two rear corners, but not nearly as much.

After you have sanded and fine-sanded (120 grit sandpaper is good) the entire board, put on at least three coats of polyurethane varnish or whatever color(s) of paint you choose (use marine paint). We used to decoupage Playboy centerfolds onto our boards, but this requires considerably more work, time and inclination. Being 16 years old helps.

Round skim boards are ok, but you can't get the distance obtainable with the "bitchin'" board that you are now holding.

Sand sliding can be practiced at any time of year in New England if you don't mind (I do) wearing wet socks and suit in winter. Check the tide tables so that you arrive at around low tide. Also, check the calendar so that you arrive around July.

Stand holding your board (we're at the beach, ok?) with both hands at waist level so that the big bevel is forward and the flat of the board is parallel to the beach. As a wave comes in and begins to recede, step and throw the board as above; forward in a sliding movement. Watch the board skim over the 1/8" of water film. Do this a few times until the board skims predictably — avoid throwing the nose down first.

First ride (attempt) coming up. Again, watch for a good wave, begin running forward and throw the board. If you are right-handed (and throw the board well), you should now be running slightly behind and on the left side of the skimming board. As you move to step on the board, put your left foot on first and then almost immediately afterwards, the right, so that your feet are set approximately as illustrated. This step-hop onto the center of the board is the key to a good start — now, ride! You won't have any trouble recognizing when the ride is over because (1) The board will hit a dry patch of sand and stop immediately (you won't), (2) The board will glide down toward the ocean and stop (gradually) in deeper water, (3) Your feet inadvertently change position; an edge digs into the sand, and...

I'll mention a couple of other things and then stop because I find that I'm really enjoying myself and the words are piling up rapidly.

After you become a proficient rider, ask a sand-riding partner to run along next to you and offer the end of a knotted rope (5'), or more indigineously, a knotted towel. Grab the rope and let your partner haul you down the beach for as long as you can guide the board to thin water, or until your hauler begins to experience serious oxygen debt. Be empathetic and change positions after a couple rides. You can even change pullers in mid-ride (tag team technique) for a long, long ride — my P.B. is close to 1/4 mile.

If you throw the board down consistently well, try a belly-flop ride. With your head closer to the beach, the sensation of speed is dramatically increased. Remember to take your fingers out from under the board before flopping on top.

There's more, but...I appreciate your forbearance; back to 30° and slush. Merry Christmas and if you're going to Nassau for the holidays, I hate you.

## Para-Pente

I'm still not sure how to pronounce this new sport's name (new to me and apparently to most of the population of this country). Find someone who can "talk" French to help your tongue, or just make a phonetic attempt. I'm sure after it infiltrates California (i.e., OUT WEST), that a properly catchy commercial name will be applied. Wild Wings is the name used by the company, Wild Things, in North Conway, New Hampshire, that manufactures this flight device.

After recently completing a "Silver Bullets Day" (a contractual day of games, initiative problems and trust activities) at Dartmouth, the outdoor education consultant there, Brian Kunz, asked if I would like to join him and an associate for a day of Para-Pente. I responded enthusiastically. because I had just read an article in *Outside* magazine about this burgeoning sport and was duly fascinated: as all people who dream of flying are wont to be. It's the issue with Rheinhold Messner on the cover.

The sport itself consists of hiking to a high spot with a 6-7 lb. para-wing stuffed into a pack — the degree of slope and take-off depends on the participant's expertise level — then deploying the chute in such a way that it becomes fully inflated overhead ("hop and pop,"), and finally taking a couple steps toward the incline (cliff) and hopefully into the air.

The stuff of dreams, I'd say — but it works, and to the extent that thousands of Europeans are hiking/climbing to the top of very high mountains and "flying" back down. Purists are mumbling about cheating...and...poor show..., but as a mountain sage pointed out, "Great notoriety and acclaim are awarded for the ascent, but no one cheers for the descent."

The rectangular chute resembles the maneuverable parachute being currently used for sky diving, with a big difference. The "Wild Wings" chute material is lighter in weight and stiffer — kind of like crinoline — so that it can be easily carried and easily deployed from a laid-out position on the ground, behind the flyer.

I don't want to offer any instructional details because I have only tried this exciting sport once and my skill level hovers at sub-novice — but I flew, and I'm writing only to encourage you to find out more about Para-Pente. Maybe not something for your teaching Bag of Tricks, but certainly a grand inclusion for your list of "Have you evers..." The first step is worth a couple gulps and the rediscovery that there's more to life than Diet Coke.

## The Ultimate Game

This is from the book of Old Games...

You have been sent on a journey. You had no choice about when or where it started. You have no indication when, where, or how your trip will end. All you know for sure is that there is an eventual end.

There are numerous rules that apply to this journey (more than Foes & Questors), and you have to learn them as you go.

All you know is that once the trip starts, you must continue, whether you feel like it or not. You begin play with no possessions and when you finish, you must turn in all that you have accumulated.

The name of the game is life, and I hope you're enjoying it — in some respects, it's the only game in town.

## Don't Just Stand There

Watching a group stumble, giggle, and bludgeon their way through the "Nitro Crossing" initiative problem for the umpteenth time is bound to have a stultifying effect on your enthusiasm and humor and flexibility and what all. Remember the key to enthusiasm for your students? Variety! Treat yourself to some variations on life when you have the opportunity, or try to make that opportunity happen. Go white water rafting, hot air ballooning, parachuting, something, so that you can renew that dry mouth, what-am-I-doing-here sensation that so poignantly slams the door on vicariousness.

Experience for a change that unique position of being a student and trusting what someone else is telling you. "You'll be OK, just keep your..." "I'll be right here if you need..." "Keep your hand on that line and try to..."

*Compassion. Fear. Empathy. Joy. Exhilaration. Pumped-Up. Glow. Commitment. Dry Mouth. Worthwhile. Satisfied. Self. Together. Anticipation.*

Go on a weekend scavenger hunt and see how many of the above words you can check off as the result of participation in some activity.

## A Portable Depilatory Tool

On a recent flight to Chicago, one of our interns (Dave Klim from Lyndon State College, Vermont), was absent-mindedly picking at fiber tufts on his heavily "pilled" Patagonia fleece jacket. If you own such a jacket, I'm sure you have done the same thing during a boring moment or two (sitting in O'Hare Airport for three hours *is* boring; i.e., picking off small tufts of fleece material that invariably pill up on that type of jacket. Dave had collected a small pile of "pills" next to his seat, but looking at the jacket, there seemed to be no difference in its appearance. Just a few minutes later, I observed a large pile of knotty fleece material where the small collection had been, and a smiling intern, actively **combing** a noticeably improved jacket. Using a small pocket comb (the black plastic kind that you see on the ground everywhere that always looks brand new, but you don't dare pick up and use because your mom said not to; and you might get COOTIES), for a heavily pilled jacket can be made to look used, rather than discardable, with a few minutes of self-combing. In keeping with atavistic urges, you can submit to the grooming tendencies of simian cousins and comb a friend's coat while you are being similarly groomed. Can you handle it?

## Australian Survival Information

As the result of a recent one-month sojourn to the land "down under," I have recorded a number of facts and situations that might be of interest to travelers, or just fun to read for the typical *YANK*.

*Writer's note* — The following comparisons are the result of cultural and distance differences between countries and are not meant as demographic situations to be intellectually dissected or held up to the light of pure nationalistic truth. Read for fun, mate!

1. Hot and cold faucets are reversed; i.e., hot is on the right and cold to the left. With soap in your eyes, this information may save your skin.

2. When writing the day and month, reverse them; i.e., 5/28/86 becomes 28/5/86. Why? Because that's the way it is.

3. All driving is on the left side of the road; not the wrong side, mate, the left side. Interestingly enough, the steering wheel *and* shift column are also reversed.

4. The toilet is *not* in the bathroom, therefore if in extremis, don't ask to go to the bathroom. The WC (water closet) is the toilet, which flushes (by pushing a button) in a most explosive way. Toilets down under do not swirl clockwise or counterclockwise — they implode.

5. Most orange juice is only one star quality. Drink beer — *Aussie* brew is best!

6. Vegemite is an Australian breakfast institution and has a taste and consistency that is distinctly acquired. Use sparingly and smile. I like it, but in excess, it's deadly.

7. Barramundi fish is excellent (****) eating. It's the fresh water fish that Crocodile Dundee spears in the movie.

8. The coins used as currency pretty much duplicate ours in the U.S., but since the switch from British currency was only about a decade ago, vernacular names have not developed for the individual coins. Nickel, dime, penny, etc., are non-existent. It's one cent, ten cents, etc.

9. Napkins are seldom offered or used. Eat neat!

10. Men — There are no individual urinals in public toilets. An entire section of wall, with a convenient trough beneath, has been set aside for your aiming pleasure (or lack of). I particularly liked the painted tile motif.

The following word comparisons are interesting. Aussies reading this —
pity a poor Yank who took incomplete notes.

| Australian | American |
|---|---|
| crooked (not crook-ed) | sick |
| take away | take out (food) |
| give away | yield (road sign) |
| wind cheater | sweater |
| doona | quilt |
| bloke | fellow |
| overtake | passing (driving) |
| to tick | to check (list) |
| spanner | wrench |
| torch | flashlight |
| prawn | shrimp |
| tinnie-stubby | beer can - bottle |
| Rice Bubbles | Rice Krispies |
| aeroplane | airplane |
| the Monday, the Tuesday | Monday, Tuesday |
| caravan | trailer |
| holiday | vacation |

There are many more comparative similarities than differences between
our cultures. The differences make up the spice that makes the travel and
interaction stimulating. Bonzer mates — it was a fine journey. S'truth.

## Brief Report on Adventure Brewing

It works! Zymurgy is not just a good scrabble word. Combining the simple
elements contained in a brew kit, plus sugar, water, and yeast, makes beer
— and not a bad brew, at that. John Rittermeister and I whipped up the
first batch with some trepidation, but the immutable laws of science and a
robust gang of yeasties worked their cosmic magic to produce a highly
palatable beverage with, as they say, "a lovely head"; and at about $.08 a
pint, the price is right.

Definitely a low-risk adventure with considerable potential rewards. The
next batch has currently been turned over to that androgynous and prolific
group of biological workers (yeast) with the heady results tantalizingly
unknown but suspected of consummate consumable quality.

## The Big Bang Theory in Zymurgy

If you will remember awhile back in BOT's, I made mention of home brewing some beer...well, I've continued doing it on a small scale because I kind of like beer, and brewing your own reduces the cost considerably.

I found out something about following directions that I would like to pass along — follow them, particularly those pertinent to the formation of dissolved gasses in a sealed container.

After actually brewing the ingredients, and if you want a "head" to the beer, it's necessary to add a tad more sugar to the bottled brew to act as supplemental food for the various yeasts and, in so doing, some gas is produced as a by-product of this additional fermentation. Most of the gas is held in solution, because the brew is now bottled and *sealed*.

I have said all this leading up to a zymurgical caveat — don't add more than 1/2 teaspoon of sugar to each bottle before capping, or the bottle may burst. If it doesn't blow while sitting there "curing," chances are it may when you start jostling the bottle around before opening — and, if it's still unblown at the point of removing the cap, all that potential will shoot itself straight up and out the bottle neck, manifesting Bernnouli's principle right up your olfactory orifice.

## Weather Balloon

This suggestion may well be inappropriate or unusable for most programs or situations, nonetheless you should know of the potential for glee (I can't think of a more descriptive word in this case), that an inflated 12' (that's foot) diameter balloon produces within a group.

I'm sure there are a number of games that can be (or have been) developed for use with large balloons; i.e., Earth Ball types, but just the Gargantuan presence of this bubble-like plaything is enough to produce smiles, and exclamations of disbelief.

As this Godzilla of balloons descends toward your group, hands and feet press toward the undulating rubber surface expecting a substantial resistance, but encounter only a fleeting, bubble-like wobble as IT blobs slowly...so slowly away from your push toward the next ambivalent receiver. Things this big should be inertial, but this big thing isn't — overwhelming in some ways, but kindly persuasive in its enveloping rubberness.

When it breaks, you may experience that poignant sorrow, so long set aside and lately unappreciated, of a child that pops or releases a favorite or only balloon.

Such a humongo balloon is not sold at local five and dimes, but searching around surplus stores may turn one up. Remember, each state has a government surplus properties center that has goods available to non-profit organizations, including schools. See *BOT's* article, *Government Surplus Wants You!*

You will need a power inflator to blow up a balloon of this size...there just aren't enough alveoli around to do the job by mouth. Sounds like some great oral adventure, eh? Don't bother; this is supposed to be fun, not a residential experience. A commercial vacuum cleaner will do the job.

Don't use helium. It's expensive (compared to vacuum cleaner exhaust) and some of your smaller students may disappear.

## Seasons

Some folks in Fairbanks, Alaska, called the Project today (November 17th) and mentioned that the temperature was 8°F. A teacher from Ontario was also on the phone and said there was over 12" of fresh snow on the ground. Now, I know that Hamilton's 48°F today isn't balmy, but Massachusetts sure looks good right now. This ectomorph is already looking forward to spring. Any of you folks down south (I mean *way* down south) need any heavy adventure consulting...say in mid-February?

## Rubber Band Man

Portable fitness, that's what I'm telling you about.

As the result of undefinable mid-back pain a couple years ago (resulting from things I probably shouldn't have been attempting — but it was fun, etc.), I found myself casting about looking for symptomatic relief and hopefully a "cure." After visiting a number of chiropractors (a story in itself), one particularly knowledgeable fellow, who was sympathetic to an ex-jock's laments and age-eroded self-expectations, made a suggestion that not only helped my personal joint/muscle/nerve situation, but has since provided me with a lightweight, functional and inexpensive means of maintaining upper body (arms and torso) conditioning. This is a male/female thing, so don't stop reading 'cause of gender.

Surgical tubing it is! Buy a 5/16" (O.D.) x 6' length (about $2.50) and tie an overhand knot in one end and a bowline loop in the other end (or any-kind-of-do-it loop, if your bowline resides in the circle file of your mind). The loop should be big enough to slip in three or four fingers. Various tubing diameters and whatever length you want can be purchased at a surgical supply store — one of those I-don't-want-to-go-in-there places that sells wheelchairs, bed pans, emesis basins, and such.

Find a door that closes inward; i.e., toward you (best to go home and do this, or the tubing salesperson will steal the idea or think you're nuts). Close the knot into the door jam at a height that seems convenient to each exercise sequence. Pass your hand (fingers) into the loop and step back until some tension is put on the tubing and your muscles. The difficulty of each exercise is varied by the distance you stand from the door and the number of repetitions that you choose to attempt.

I had specific arm movements and number of repetitions that I was assigned to do as physical therapy. I found that the exercises were so easy to accomplish (notice I did not say "easy to do"), that after the affliction pain was relieved, I continued and expanded on the various movements as part of my personal fitness plan.

The type of exercises are pretty much up to you. With your hand in the loop, there are many movements and planes to use and operate within — swimming motion, lateral and back draws, cross-chest pulls, etc. Experiment and set up your own program — that's what I did and I'm always changing it as per boredom level and where I happen to be; i.e., geographically.

The tubing travels well in a suitcase, so there's no reason to leave it home.

If you can't find a convenient door to use (or can't figure out my spatial door closing instructions), tie the knotted rubber end onto something fairly substantial.

If one strand doesn't provide enough of a workout for your finely-tuned upper bod, double the rubber strand — but I'll bet 50-70 reps will tax most muscles.

*  *  *  *  *

When workshop people get together in the evenings, it's not uncommon for a few "pops" to be shared and such socializing often produces a sense of euphoria and camaraderie that results in an on-the-spot song. Most of these ditties have a life span that is commensurate with their content and melodic quality. This song is an exception and I think you will agree if you take the time to juxtapose verse and tune.

### *That PA State of Mind*

To the tune of The Gambler , by Kenny Rogers<br>Words by Edward E. Gamble June 10-14, 1987

On a cool summer's evening, in a mansion south of Ipswich,

I met up with a bunch of folks — outdoor freaks by trade;

And the thing that makes them different

Is the way they make their living,

swinging through the treetops making sure they're all belayed.

 (Refrain)

You've got to know when to hold 'em.

Know how to mold 'em.

Know when to take up slack and when to let out line.

You never give them the answers while they're working on the problems,

'Cause they've come here to develop — that **PA** State of Mind.

When the day starts a-dawning, there ain't no time for yawning.

We just grab a bite and hit the field to dry the morning dew.

Soon my clothes are just a sopping, as I learn the Cobra flopping,

playing Toe Tag, smelling dirt, and learning games these folks call "*NEW!*"

>    (Refrain)

Now the Dangle Duo's beckoning, as I cross the Burma's reckoning,

just how much nerve it's gonna take to climb the Pamper Pole.

But I find the task exciting, once I flush the fear I'm fighting,

and they vanish in a flash, right down that high up toilet bowl.

>    (Refrain)

As I finish up my training, I don't notice that it's raining,

I can't feel the soreness, bug or rope 'neath my behind.

'Cause they challenged me by choice, so that now I can rejoice,

knowing as I do that I've attained that **PA** STATE OF MIND!

>    (Refrain)

## Aerobies

From California, of course. The only innovative thing that I know for a fact started in the northeast and moved west is ***Project Adventure.*** Nonetheless, this streamlined, long-distance toy is a gem, particularly if you are disappointed with how far you can't throw a frisbee. This rubberized anorexic donut goes farther than any thrown object should go, producing rapturous feelings of Olympic capability. I have always liked throwing things for distance: the javelin, discus, flat rocks, 45 r.p.m. records, so the Aerobie device was made to order for fantasy fulfillment. The world's record for throwing an Aerobie is over 1,000'; try to imagine throwing something that far. I love world records!

There are games to play with an Aerobie, but the pure joy is in the throwing. Beware! Aerobies like to get stuck in trees — that big center hole is made for limb insertion. They also get lost faster than you can say eight dollars, so limit long distance throws to wide open areas.

An idea — which I'm sure has already been tried in California — is to form a foursome and play a regular round of golf using the Aerobie as the object of play. A good golf drive goes 200+ yards, which is also true of the distance to be expected from a well-thrown disc. What a treat to be able to walk the links carrying only three or four Aerobies. Sand traps? No problem.

***(Ed. Note:*** Written about six weeks after the above.)

I was recently in Washington, D.C., doing the tourist bit with my family. While visiting the Air/Space Museum, I saw a prototype of the Aerobie made of paper and dated 1967. So, if you have a good idea and are dismayed that no one is paying attention, just think of how long it took the Aerobie to become commercially acceptable.

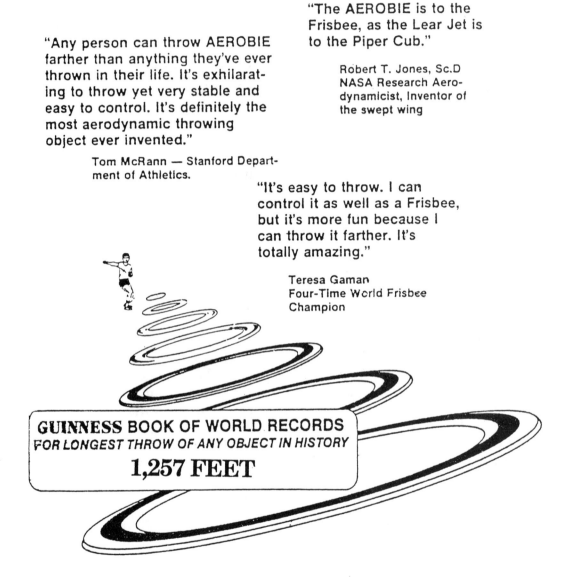

"The AEROBIE is to the Frisbee, as the Lear Jet is to the Piper Cub."

Robert T. Jones, Sc.D
NASA Research Aero-
dynamicist, Inventor of
the swept wing

"Any person can throw AEROBIE farther than anything they've ever thrown in their life. It's exhilarating to throw yet very stable and easy to control. It's definitely the most aerodynamic throwing object ever invented."

Tom McRann — Stanford Department of Athletics.

"It's easy to throw. I can control it as well as a Frisbee, but it's more fun because I can throw it farther. It's totally amazing."

Teresa Gaman
Four-Time World Frisbee
Champion

GUINNESS BOOK OF WORLD RECORDS
FOR LONGEST THROW OF ANY OBJECT IN HISTORY
1,257 FEET

I like these charts that threaten you via statistics; subtly indicating that you are going to die if you don't...

So, insert your non-biased participation level of activity (choice of 8 — how can you go wrong?), and personally estimate whether you have 40 or 50 years left of "shuffling about this mortal coil."

## The Minimums for Health

### Minimums for cardiovascular fitness per week*

| | |
|---|---|
| Walking | 12 mi. |
| Swimming | 900 yd. |
| Skiing (downhill) | 6 hr. |
| Running | 9 mi. |
| Rope skipping | 75 min. |
| Racketball | 4 hr. |
| Cycling | 24 mi. |
| Aerobic dance | 3 hr. |

*Spread over 4 days per week.

### Insurance against heart attack

| Calories expended per week:* | Annual death risk drops by: | Miles Walked** |
|---|---|---|
| Less than 500 | 4% | 6 or less |
| 500 to 999 | 22% | 6 to 12.5 |
| 1,000 to 1,499 | 27% | 12.5 to 19 |
| 1,500 to 1,999 | 36% | 19 to 25 |
| 2,000 to 2,499 | 38% | 25 to 31 |
| 2,500 to 2,999 | 48% | 31 to 37.5 |
| 3,000 to 3,500 | 54% | 37.5 to 44 |
| Over 3,500 | 38% | 44 or more |

*The average person burns 80 calories per mile. A 175-lb. man burns 100 calories.

**Includes background exercise such as walking to the bus stop and climbing stairs.

The following Haiku was offered as an answer to a question on an exam. The question was, "What is adventure?"  The author is Lawrence (Muncie) McLeod.

Brink wish,

    Not death wish.

        Security at the end of its tether.

          Stretched thin,

            Taut,

              Tense,

                Straining,

                  But not quite,

                    Letting go.

                      To fall,

                    Caught,

                  By back-up lifted

                Or lowered

              Securely

            To a stable area,

          Thankful,

        Wondering,

     Next time?

I think it's also appropriate and useful to include Muncie's insightful and well-stated answer to a corresponding question, "What is the difference between Adventure and Programmatic Adventure?"

"Both adventure and adventure education stimulate the feelings of uncertainty and risk in the participant.  However, with adventure education, the activities have been planned and are overseen so as to reduce the potential for harm to the student.  Because of the control over the physical situation, the student's experience of adventure becomes a highly personal one in which s/he confronts her/his own feelings and limitations.  Further, because of the group context in adventure education and the personal context, the student is able to relate her/his personal experience to the experience of others, promoting an atmosphere of camaraderie and trust."

## Rockwell Enigma

I've carried a folding knife for years, ever since my first professional involvement in the outdoors. I wore a few holes in my pockets from the constant presence of the knife until I discovered a small belt holster at L.L. Bean and copied it — except I left off the snap-top for easy access, but that's another story.

A knife has become my vademecum (for your lexicon buffs, there's even a toothpaste carrying that odd name), and I find it indispensable as a tool. As a weapon, my 2-1/2" manually-operated switchblade isn't very useful, and in these days of the ubiquitous handgun — what's the use?

I'm running off a bit here — back to the reason I started to write this section: to unlock the secrets of the Rockwell scale of hardness.

For years, I have seen the numerical symbol (C55-60 or C58-60 or C "something" referring to the hardness of a particular knife blade, but I had no idea what the numbers meant and no one I asked seemed to know (or care).

Maybe it had something to do with the number of quenchings, firings, or incantations necessary to produce, as they say, a fine blade. I really wanted a blade with a C57-60 rating measured on the Rockwell scale of hardness, just because it sounded like you needed a C57-60 blade: I'm an easy sell. Well, blade fans, I recently read an article that destroyed the mystique Rockwell had established over the years, but replaced it with some great trivial knowledge that I'll pass on to you.

This hardness scale, established by the Rockwell Tool Company, measures the hardness of steel in a scale measuring from C3 to C68. The letter C refers to the test of a hard metal and the higher the number, the harder the steel. "Hardness is tested by measuring the penetration of a diamond cone into the steel under a force of 150 kilograms — C3 to C68. The lower the number, the faster the steel will lose its edge, the easier it will be to resharpen: the higher the number, the harder and more brittle the steel."

So now you know, and being awash in metallurgic knowledge, the choice of your next nickel silver bolstered Rosewood-handled magnum trophy-hunter will be simplified. If it's not between C3 and C68, don't buy it.!

## Climbing Grades

I have, in past BOT's, blithely referred to or inaccurately compared some physical action to a decimal configuration that began with the digit 5, such as 5.3 or 5.9, etc. For example, "getting out of his poorly parked car involved a 5.6 move."

These numerals refer to a difficulty grading system in rock climbing called the YDS (Yosemite Decimal System), or internationally called the American system.

This system (and many others that use numbers and letters) allows rock climbers to grade or rate various climbs to either inflate their egos (sour grapes on my part), or advise other climbers of that particular route's difficulty.

Using the YDS, a 5.0 is a **very** easy climb.  Currently (with some disagreement among climbers — controversy is part of the sport — the highest grade is an unbelievable 5.14a (imagine climbing an overhanging sand dune).

If this grading folderol interests you at all, the following comparison chart is worth perusing.

| French | Amer. | Aust. | German | English | English | 5.11c | Aust. | 8- | 6a |
|--------|-------|-------|--------|---------|---------|-------|-------|------|------|
|  | 5.9 |  |  |  | 7a |  | 24 |  |  |
| 5+ |  | 17 | 6 | 5a |  | 11d | 25 | 8 |  |
|  | 10 |  |  |  | 7a+ |  |  |  | 6b |
| 6a |  | 18 | 6+ |  |  | 12a | 26 | 8+ |  |
|  | 10b |  |  |  | 7b |  |  |  |  |
| 6a+ |  | 19 |  | 5b |  | 12b | 27 | 9- | 6c |
|  | 10c |  | 6- |  | 7b+ |  |  |  |  |
| 6b |  | 20 |  |  |  | 12c | 28 |  |  |
|  | 10d |  | 7 |  | 7c |  |  | 9 |  |
| 6b+ |  | 21 |  | 5c |  | 12d | 29 |  |  |
|  | 11a |  |  |  | 7c+ |  |  | 9+ | 7a |
| 6c |  | 22 | 7+ |  |  | 13a | 30 |  |  |
|  | 11b |  |  |  | 8a |  |  |  |  |
| 6c+ |  | 23 |  |  |  | 13b |  |  |  |

Under the American (YDS) column, note that the numbers start at 9 — that's actually 5.9.  So, this chart is a bit elitist in that it begins at about the highest level I've ever climbed.  Do I mind this type of journalistic humbling?  Nah..., but I do want to quote something Chouinard (if you don't know who *he is,* stop reading now and begin the next item) said recently in an interview.  "In the greater scope of things, how important is it that Americans climb 5.14?  The grading system has to be flawed anyway when an out-of-shape 48 year-old (himself) can now do a 5.11 when in 1960 at his prime, he could barely do a 5.10."

So, since Chouinard and I are both over 45, logic has it that it's the system that's skewed, rather than an eroding of the spring steel and dynamite body I used twenty years ago.

Removing yourself from a blocked auto at  a 5.5 level of difficulty adds to the color and variety of your speech and doesn't hurt the image much, either.

**P.S.**    The Brits, in a masterpiece of rhetorical succinctness, rate climbs as either "Bloody hard or bloody easy."


## Rolling Out the Ropes

While leading an adventure curriculum workshop in Georgia a while back, one of the participants facetiously (I hope) said that he was an advocate of the 3 R's in his "fizz ed" program; i.e., "Readin' the Role, Rollin' out the balls, and Relaxin'."

Ignoring or forgetting that an adventure curriculum has more components than just a high ropes course can result in a lot of "rope rollin'," resulting in unsafe attitudes and practices — specifically, letting students participate on elements of the ropes course without supervision, and rationalizing that since the class is so big, it's the only way the kids will get anything done.

If it's necessary to revert to "rollin'" anything, let it be balls — at least it's safer.

## Social Concern Forum

Considering the large subscribership of BOT's, I believe it to be the moral responsibility of those involved in production of such a socially-aware periodical to attempt on occasion to address various concerns of the world's population. The quarter, the editor has chosen a broad spectrum concern to fit a demographic cross-section of the readers.

September's topic (to rival June's fascinating presentation of how to build and use a Mohawk Walk) is World Contentedness, and is aptly titled, "Happiness Through Responsible Hedonism."

The following checklist represents an excerpt from that timeless tome, "60 Minutes or 60 Years to Possible Happiness." Simply seek and achieve each item on the list (the time line is up to you), and a certain sense of fulfillment will infuse your heretofore jaded psyche.

**HAPPINESS**
(contentedness)

**WISDOM**
(a mature understanding of life)

**MATURE LOVE**
(sexual & spiritual intimacy)

**TRUE FRIENDSHIP**
(close companionship)

**SENSE OF ACCOMPLISHMENT**
(lasting contribution)

**SELF RESPECT**
(self-esteem)

**AN EXCITING LIFE**
(stimulating existence)

**FAMILY SECURITY**
(taking care of family)

**PLEASURE**
(an enjoyable life)

**A WORLD OF BEAUTY**
(beauty of nature and the arts)

**SALVATION**
(eternal life)

**A WORLD AT PEACE**
(free of war and conflict)

**EQUALITY**
(equal opportunity for all)

**A COMFORTABLE LIFE**
(a prosperous life)

**SOCIAL RECOGNITION**
(respect, admiration)

**FREEDOM**
(independence, free choice)

Not a bad checklist, all in all. Keep it around; it's worth referring to every now and again when your priorities get screwed up. The rhetoric is tongue-in-cheek; the list is pure gold.

## A Peachy Trick

This "trick" doesn't have much to do with adventure, but having used it and being impressed by its functional simplicity, here is BOT's first sally into the world of gastronomics.

As the result of a fruitful decision about five years ago, I purchased and planted a peach tree. This year, it produced over 60 lbs. of fruit. As part of processing beaucoup peaches, all that fuzzy cover stuff had to come off. A dreaded task, until my wife said (here's the trick), just dip them into boiling H2O for 30 seconds. Wow! The skins literally slip right off in your hands.

## Values Clarification via Murky Discussion

Need something intense and meaningful to talk about? Here's a useful list of randomly arranged topics that are crying for prioritization. Give a copy of these topics to each student and ask him/her to list each item as to its importance, as they define their own values.

There are, of course, no right or wrong answers, however. Fine tune your noncommittal responses and be prepared for some insightful discussion.

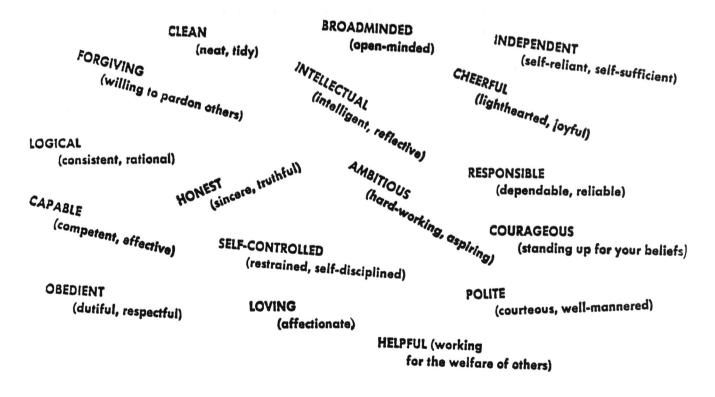

# Chapter 15
# *Quarterly Quotes*

While reading, driving, listening, playing, working, I always keep an eye and ear out for quotes that appeal to me, for no other reason than I like to re-read them at a later time. ***Bag of Tricks*** is advertised as idea-sharing, reporting of what's new in adventure education, and all that good pedagogic stuff to help you implement and/or build your own program, but Quarterly Quotes is something that I include for myself. I hope you have enjoyed these occasional quotes over the years: here's a bunch of my favorites.

Robert Heinlein —*The Notebooks of Lazarus Long:*

"Always listen to experts. They'll tell you what can't be done and why. Then, do it."

"$100 placed at 7% interest compounded quarterly for 200 years will increase to more than $100,000,000 — by which time it will be worth nothing."

"Climate is what we expect; weather is what we get."

"A committee is a life form with six or more legs and no brain."

"To enjoy the flavor of life, take big bites. Moderation is for Monks."

"Courage is the complement of fear. A person who is fearless cannot be courageous."

"Do not handicap your children by making their lives easy."

"Don't try to have the last word. You might get it."

"A child is a person who can't understand why someone would give away a perfectly good kitten."　　　　— Doug Larson

"When I was younger, I could remember anything, whether it happened or not."　　　　— Mark Twain

"...you have to understand that in dealing with these kids, the **Challenge By Choice** philosophy doesn't start until they are off the ground.

　　　　— summer camp ropes course leader

"...a regular beer stays on the tongue like ice cream; a light beer slides off like a sherbet."　　　　— William Least Heat Moon

"If growing up means it would be beneath my dignity to climb a tree...I'll never grow up...not me!"　　　　— Peter Pan

"...we play for the sake of the game, for play itself.  In this manner, we participate in the essence of existence."

　　　　— George Leonard

"Conscience is the inner voice that warns us that someone may be looking."

　　　　— H.L. Mencken

"Everything is a subject on which there is not much to be said."

　　　　— C.S. Lewis

"Possum settin' up on a branch of a tree,

Can't jump down cause he got a trick knee!

Got a trick knee by walkin' after dark,

Stepped in a hole dug by an Aardvark!"

　　　　— newspaper cartoon

"I refuse to arrange a world war in every generation to rescue the young from a depressing peace."　　　　— Kurt Hahn

"I thought the window was down, but I found out it was up when I put my hand through it."　　　　— from an insurance form

"Imagination is more important than knowledge."

　　　　— Einstein

"Nothing succeeds like excess."— Oscar Wilde

"...there is no literature which proves that competition is inevitable.  It seems instead that competition is learned."

　　　　— AAHPERD book reviews

"One thorn of experience is worth a wilderness of warning."

— James R. Lovell

"Balloonists have an unsurpassed view of the scenery, but there is always the possibility that it may collide with them."

— H.L. Mencken

"It may be that wet wool is warm, but dry cotton is warmer."

— Rufus Little

"Better to wear out than rust out."

— Anonymous

"Lack of vigor is often mistaken for patience."

— Kim Hubbard

"Egotism is the anesthetic which nature gives us to deaden the pain of being a fool."                    — Herbert Shofield

The essence of education:  "Realizing that you didn't know that you didn't know."                    — Anonymous

"As a city bicyclist, you're part of a team sport.  The only problem is that the other players often don't realize you're on the court."

— Josh Lehman

"Experience is like a light on a caboose, illuminating only where we aren't going."                    — George F. Will

"To find order in anything, it is most important to know the limits imposed from outside the game, to know what the game is **not**."

— George Leonard

"If youth be a defect, it is one that we outgrow only too soon."

— H. Prochnow

"Truth is obvious, after its discovery."

— Anonymous

"...I want you to face each other, back to back."

— S. Webster

"I was only joking when I told you I didn't mean what I said about reconsidering my decision not to change my mind."

— Anonymous

"Ulcers are hereditary...we get them from our kids."

— bumper sticker

"If you don't know where you are going, you will probably end up someplace else."                                    — Anonymous

"Winter is Nature with Her pockets turned inside out."

— Anonymous

"If practice makes perfect, then failures —    even lots of them —    might just be part of success?"          — Anonymous

"Most great discoveries are made by mistake and the bigger the funding, the longer it takes to make the mistake."

— Ann Landers

"What we don't know is much more interesting than what we know."

— NOVA — WGBH TV

"It now costs more to amuse a child than it once did to educate his father."

— Herbert Prochnow

"The only people who mind getting wet are the ones that are dry."

— KER

"I have found that the best way to give advice to your children is to find out what they want and then advise them to do it."

— Harry Truman

"We lived for days on nothing but food and water."

— W.C. Fields

"Happiness makes up in height for what it lacks in length."

— Robert Frost

"The vitality of thought is in adventure.  Ideas won't keep.  Something must be done with them."          — Alfred North Whitehead

"...you don't understand, because you're taking what I say in context."

— S. Webster

"When large numbers of men are unable to find work, unemployment results."          — Calvin Coolidge

"Originality is undetected plagiarism."

— Dean Inge

"My memory is the thing I forget with."

— a child's definition

"The white man's real burden is a lot of other white men."

— Anonymous

"Watch out w'en yu er gittin all you want.  Fattenin' hogs ain't in luck."

— Joel Chandler Harris

"She has a nice sense of rumor."

— John H. Cutler

"Those who live in stone houses should not throw glass."

— Anonymous

"You can't fool all of the people all of the time — but it isn't necessary."

— Anonymous

"Many would say, 'I'm afraid,' if they had enough courage."

— Anonymous

"Bore:  A person who talks when you wish him to listen."

— Ambrose Pierce

"No matter where you go —    there you are!"

— A.E. Newman

"Sure, you're as tough as when you were thirty, you're just falling apart
faster."
— Gloree Rohnke

"Logic is the art of going the wrong way with confidence."

— Peter's Quotations

"If you don't say anything, you won't be called on to repeat it."

— Calvin Coolidge

"One final paragraph of advice:  Do not burn yourselves out.  Be as I am —
a reluctant enthusiast...a part-time crusader, a half-hearted fanatic.  Save
the other half of yourselves and your lives for pleasure and adventure.  It is
not enough to fight for the land; it is even more important to enjoy it.  While
you can.  While it's still here.  So get out there and hunt and fish and mess
around with your friends, ramble out yonder and explore the forests,
encounter the grizz, climb the mountains, bag the peaks, run the rivers,
breathe deep of that yet sweet and lucid air, sit quietly for a while and
contemplate the precious stillness, that lovely, mysterious and awesome
space.  Enjoy yourselves, keep your brain in your head and your head firmly
attached to the body, the body active and alive, and I promise you this much:

I promise you this one sweet victory over our enemies, over those desk-bound people with their hearts in a safe deposit box and their eyes hypnotized by desk calculators. I promise you this: you will outlive the bastards." — Edward Abbey

"Play so that you may be serious."

— Anacharsis (C. 600 B.C.)

"Play is the exultation of the possible."

— Martin Buber

"In every real man a child is hidden that wants to play."

— Nietzsche

"Play is vital to all humanity. It is the finest system of education known to man." — Neville Scarge

"The right to play is the child's first claim on the community. Play is nature's training for life." — Frederick Froebel

"...we take chances, risk great odds, love, laugh, dance...in short, we play. The people who play are the creators."

— Holbrook Jackson

"In the early formative years, play is almost synonymous with life. It is second only to being nourished, protected and loved. It is a basic ingredient of physical, intellectual, social, and emotional growth."

— Ashley Montague

"A rut is a grave with the ends knocked out."

— Frank Hubbard

"Teamwork is essential —    it allows you to blame someone else."

— Anonymous

"...yeah, but!"                    — often heard in a ropes course context

"No member of a crew is praised for the rugged individuality of his rowing." — R.W. Emerson

"A good idea doesn't care who has it."

— passed on by Plynn Williams

"The secret of effective leadership is sincerity; once you can fake that, you have it made." — Anonymous

"A lot of parents pack up their troubles and send them to summer camp."

— Raymond Duncan

"Fools rush in — and get the best seats."

"All probabilities are 50%, either a thing will happen, or it won't."

— Murphy's Law — Book 2

"...personal and substantive growth is both predictable and measurable when one's reach slightly exceeds one's grasp."
— Nancy McLaughlin, Adventure<br>workshop participant

"The quickest way to a man's heart is through his stomach."

— Harry Sphincter (the first proctologist to<br>attempt heart surgery)

"I've always longed for adventure, to do the things I've never dared — now here I'm facing adventure — then why am I so scared?"

— Rogers & Hammerstein

"The experience is over for now

    but I have learned...

        I know it can happen...

I reach out for tomorrow,

    ready,

    excited,

        open...

Today has changed my life.

        I have grown..."   — George Betts

"I looked up and saw a squirrel jump from one high tree to another. He appeared to be aiming for a limb so far out of reach that the leap looked like suicide. He missed — but landed, safe and unconcerned, on the branch several feet lower. Then he climbed to his goal, and all was well.

Since then, whenever I have to choose between risking a new venture or hanging back, I remember those crazy, air-borne squirrels and think, 'They've got to risk it if they don't want to spend their lives in one tree.'

So, I've jumped again and again. And in jumping, I've learned why the squirrels so often do it: it's fun."

— Oscar Schisgall

"If you're waitin' on me, you're backin' up."

— forgettable country & western song

"I'd like to go by climbing a birch tree,

And climb black branches

up a snow-white trunk

Toward heaven, till the tree

could bear no more,

But dipped its top and set me down again.

That would be good both going

and coming back.

One could do worse than be a swinger of birches."

— Robert Frost

"You get what you get, when you go for it."

— Barry Manilow

"Writing was meant to be a hobby.  An act of willful play..."

— J. Updike

"If it's clean, it isn't laundry." — Murphy's Law — Book 2

"A blue light danced before her eyes, painting phosphorescent figure-eights on the velvet dark.  She turned her head aside, blinking away the retinal afterimage, which lingered like a fading stain of color."

— Edward Abbey

"A good scare is worth more than good advice."

— Ed Howe

"But wait a bit, the Oyster cried,

Before we have our chat;

For some of us are out of breath,

And all of us are fat!"        — Lewis Carroll

"In 30 years, a man can remember a good many things that ought to have happened."        — Farley Mowat

"Do not fall into the error of the artesian (teacher) who boasts of 20 years' experience, while in fact he has had only 1 year's experience —    20 times."

— Trevanian

"It never occurs to an adolescent that he will someday be as dumb as his father."        — Mark Twain

"I would have to say our best buy was the IBM 4331, which gives the whole company a means of communicating electronically and neatly. But it also gives everyone the ability to screw up at the speed of light."

> — Purchasing Manager, Lexidata
> Corporation

"Some things have to be believed to be seen."

> — Ralph Hodgson

"This is either a forgery or a damn clever original."

> — Frank Sullivan

"When choosing between two evils, I always like to try the one I've never tried before."
> — Mae West

"The object is not to completely avoid butterflies in the stomach, but to attempt to get them to fly temporarily in formation."

> — Tom Del Prete

"It takes a big zipper to make an elephant fly."

> — Disney World Jungle Cruise Guide

"In two words: im possible."   — Samuel Goldwyn

"Most of the time I don't have much fun. The rest of the time I don't have any fun at all."
> — Woody Allen

"A hyperactive child is a kid who can't sit still for long periods of time and listen to Colonial History."   — Richard Baudler

"...we may be in the brink of an actual seller's market for wild and free-wheeling creativity for the clever, the goofy, the whimsical and playful. If ever there were a time to cultivate one's own audacity, foolishness, and wit, this is it.   — *Success Magazine*

Tombstone inscription: "Died at 30. Buried at 60."

"Many epitaphs signify a grave error."

> — Anonymous

"It is useless for the sheep to pass resolutions in favor of vegetarianism, while the wolf remains of a different opinion."

> — Dean Inge

"I have never been hurt by anything I didn't say."

> — Calvin Coolidge

"It may be that the race is not always to the swift, nor the battle to the strong — but that's the way to bet."

— Damon Runyon

"Woman was God's second mistake."

— Nietzsche

"If basketball had never been invented, where would they hold high school dances?"                                    — Anonymous

"Scream when you want to scream.  Roll on the floor.  Surprise everybody!"

— Leo Buscaglia

"What do you mean, she fell into an open personhole?"

— *Ladies Home Journal*

"If you cross a fly with an elephant, you'll get a zipper that doesn't forget."

— Who Cares

"In humor, there is truth.  We need to take humor more seriously."

— Ralph Nader

"Eschew obfuscation"

— Bumper sticker on VW diesel Rabbit observed recently on the Massachusetts Turnpike.  Back window decals read MIT and Harvard.  Driver (so lively and quick):  smoking a pipe;  moustache, turtleneck, sports coat — perfect!

"Craftsmanship affords the antithesis of instant results."

—NCOBS

I was recently offering a student the opportunity of trying a lower rappel than the more intimidating one that was initially presented.  Her reply is a study of resigned confidence:  "If I'm going to drown, I'd just as soon it be in the deep end of the pool."

— Name withheld due to my Swiss cheese memory

Edward Abbey, a lover of landscapes, about littering roadsides with beer cans —

"Beer cans are beautiful — it's the highway that's ugly."

"Sometimes I've believed as many as six impossible things before breakfast."

— Lewis Carroll

"...genuine, pure play is one of the main bases of civilization."

— Homo Ludens: A study of the play
element in culture.

"To be first and be correct is the most important. To be first and wrong is not so good."                    — Samuel Ting

"Beware of our lawyer."          — warning sign on a residence

"A rolling stone gathers momentum."

— Anonymous

"Young men are fitter to invent than to judge, fitter for execution than for counsel —    men of age object too much, consult too long, adventure too little."                    — Francis Bacon

"Tell me, Oldtimer, where did you get your good judgment?"

"Experience."

"And how did you get your experience?"

"Bad judgment!"          — Anonymous

"We find ourselves striving for the all-American dream; good job, house, family, color TV and new car. When we obtain these goals, we will be happy. We go to school or work each day and then come home to read, watch TV, have dinner and go to bed. On weekends, we clean house and the yard and maybe go out for dinner or a movie or a ball game. We look forward to retirement. Our life is routine. We are comfortable. We know what to expect from each day. We are bored."

— Penny Bolio

"All an education does is open an empty mind; it doesn't fill an empty one."

— Malcolm Forbes

"Bad weather always looks worse through a window or sounds worse on a tent fly."                    — KER

"Self-centered people are the ones who spend so much time talking about themselves that we never get a chance to talk about ourselves."

— *Bits & Pieces*

"We are so ruled by what people tell us we must be that we have forgotten who we are."                    — Leo Buscaglia

"For he knew, as all students did, that the basic purpose of instruction was not so much to teach young people good things as to fill up all their time unpleasantly. Adults had the notion that juveniles needed to suffer. Only when they had suffered enough to wipe out most of their naturally joyous spirits and innocence were they staid enough to be considered mature. An adult was essentially a broken-down child."

— Piers Anthony, *Centaur Aisle*

"I took the other road, but only because it was the lazy road for me, the way I wanted to go. If I've encountered some resistance, that's because most of the traffic is going the other way."

— Edward Abbey

"Forget your opponents; always play against par."

— Sam Snead

"SUCCESS IS DOING WHAT YOU LIKE TO DO AND MAKING A LIVING AT IT."           — KER

"A nose conjures more than it reveals —     it is a luxury in the economy of the senses."           — KER

"Life is what is happening to you while you are making other plans."

"Some people will believe anything if it is whispered to them."

"Fate is blamed for many accidents, but we feel personally responsible when we make a hole in one."

A workable and refreshingly brief philosophy of life..."...love, trust, dare — and keep on doing it."

"Not one person in a thousand can keep his/her hands in their pockets while giving directions."           — *Bits & Pieces*

"Your first line of defense should be the thoughtful use of your head, not the covering of it."           — Magazine article, *Learning to Rock Climb*

"The meek shall inherit the earth, but not the mineral rights."

— *Success Magazine*

"Humor bridges the gap between the perfection we seek and the imperfections we're stuck with."

— Robert Wieder

"The weather is here, wish you were beautiful."

— bumper sticker

"John Cogi's 4:3 is a piano composition that calls for four minutes and thirty-three seconds of total silence as the player sits frozen on the piano stool. I have not heard 4:3 performed, but friends tell me it's Cogi's finest composition."

"Don't just do something, stand there."

— Robert Hutchins

"Give me gradual improvement rather than postponed perfection."

— John Murray

"I don't want to achieve immortality through my work. I want to achieve immortality through not dying."

— Woody Allen

"Definition of a genius: a person who aims at something no one else can see...and hits it."

"One of the great mysteries of life is how the idiot that your daughter married can be the father of the smartest grandchildren in the whole wide world."
— *Bits & Pieces*

"There are three kinds of lies: lies, damned lies, and statistics."

— Mark Twain

"The only thing keeping us from our fondest dreams is our fondest fears."

— Patricia Sun via Animal Town Game Company

"A keychain is a gadget that allows us to lose several keys at the same time."
— *Bits & Pieces*

"**LIFE** — the one race you lose by finishing first."

— Lung Cancer poster

"...a ropes course is the Swiss Army Knife of experiential education."

— Mike Stratton

"Campers roughing it in a county park in Iowa plugged in so many coffeemakers, TV sets, electric blankets, and refrigerators that the park transformer exploded from the overload."

— news item

"If a person is standing with one foot in a bucket of ice and another foot in a fire, you could say — statistically — that on the average, the person is very comfortable."
— Unknown

"Take some more coffee! I've had nothing yet, so I can't take more. You mean you can't take less. It's very easy to take more than nothing."

— a liberal paraphrase from Lewis Carroll

"To laugh is to risk appearing the fool.

To weep is to risk appearing sentimental.

To reach out for another is to risk involvement.

To expose feeling is to risk exposing your true self.

To place your ideas, your dreams, before the crowd is to risk their loss.

To love is to risk not being loved in return.

To live is to risk dying.

To hope is to risk despair.

To try is to risk failure.

But the risk must be taken, because the greatest hazard in life is to risk nothing.

The person who risks nothing, does nothing, has nothing, and is nothing.

S/he may avoid suffering and sorrow, but they simply cannot learn, feel, change, grow, love, live.

Chained by certitudes, they are slaves, they have forfeited freedom.

**Only a person who risks — is free.**"

"It's fun to do things you're not made to do.  I was playing when I invented the aqualung.  I'm still playing.  I think play is the most important thing in the world."                    — Jacques Costeau

"All other species play to play.  We're the only species that plays to win. Maybe that's why there are so many losers."

— Lily Tomlin

"Every child has inside him an aching void for excitement and if we don't fill it with something which is exciting and interesting and good for him, he will fill it with something which is exciting and interesting and which isn't good for him."                    — T. Roosevelt

"Don't be so humble, you're not that great."

— Golda Meir

Response to a famous quote and recent discoveries about how various chemicals are naturally released in situ.

"...It's apparent that 'because it's there' has at least become a valid explanation for the climbing urge —    but only when the 'it' is understood to be chemicals within, not mountains without."

— Glen Randall

Chemicals considered (norepinephrine, phenylethylamine, endorphins).

"A desire to have all the fun is 9/10's of the law of chivalry."

— Dale Sayers

"Three o'clock is always too late or too early for anything you want to do."

— Sartre

"Show me a nation who's national beverage is beer, and I'll show you an advanced toilet technology."     — Mark Hawkins

"You can discover more about a person in an hour of play than in a year of conversation."          — Plato

"In spite of the cost of living, it's still popular."

— Kathleen Norris

Overheard in a summer camp situation:  "Who cares who wins; it's only a game."          — Anonymous

"It's better to have loved and lost than to do 40 lbs. of laundry a week."

— Lawrence Peter

"...the facts are wrong!"          — Einstein

"An ounce of image is worth a pound of performance."

— Anonymous

# THE BOTTOMLESS BAG
## INDEX

*Refer to page 2115 in *Webster's Unabridged Dictionary* — Just so you have an interesting X-word to look up.  Now make up a game and call it Xyster.

## Why THIS ONE?

Down in the *Bottomless Bag* shipping room (my basement), the unlikely book stacks proclaiming THIS ONE hint of a surreal Lewis Carroll adventure. THIS ONE?? Certainly. Taking more of this and less of that (it's more or less the same), we'll have us finish in a tie, despite the driving rain.

Pure whimsy, you might guess, and I suppose that's 97% true, but the blatantly commercial 3% is how to get your book noticed when it's shelved amidst the millions. Ever notice when book browsing how your shifting gaze is drawn to an interesting or contrasting book spine? When the first printing of *The Bottomless Bag* became available, it was open-mouth obvious that I had neglected to put anything on the spine: inadvertent omission — I just forgot. I was moderately upset for about 3-4 seconds, then quickly recognized how uniquely different and starkly noticeable the unblemished spine appeared. That pure white 1-1/4" x 11" spacing, sandwiched amongst the typically dark spines of the world's serious books (there's lots of them) stood out like a snowball on a black rug. "Why look, the poor fellow forgot to spinate his book. Or did he? Here, I'll take a look." Gotcha!

The blank spines resulting from the first printing were truly serendipitous. THIS ONE (still lots of white space) resulted from an in-brain conversation I initiated with a fictional librarian. In this reverie, after unsuccessfully looking for a specific book at a local library, I approach the main desk and inquire, "Do you have any books that specialize in adventure education?" The attractive librarian, turning slowly and pointing to a starkly contrasted book on the shelf just behind her, replies with a knowing smile, "Have you tried THIS ONE?"

That's it; that's all — 97% whimsy. Is that nuts, or what?